ELGAR STUDIES IN HUMAN RIGHTS

Discourse on human rights has grown ever more visible and essential, with human rights principles being discussed and scrutinized on both the international and national stage. This series brings together high-quality works of scholarship in the field of human rights, primarily in law, but particularly those with a critical or analytical edge, or those taking innovative and interdisciplinary approaches. Books in the series also address concerns at the intersection of human rights and other fields such as trade, the environment, international investment and religion, thus contributing to the depth and breadth of scholarship so vital to understanding the complicated matters at stake.

Titles in the series include:

Refugees, Regionalism and Responsibility
Penelope Mathew and Tristan Harley

Expanding Human Rights
21st Century Norms and Governance
Edited by Alison Brysk and Michael Stohl

The Legal Protection of Refugees with Disabilities
Forgotten and Invisible?
Mary Crock, Laura Smith-Khan, Ron McCallum and Ben Saul

Contracting Human Rights
Crisis, Accountability, and Opportunity
Edited by Alison Brysk and Michael Stohl

Using Human Rights to Counter Terrorism
Edited by Manfred Nowak and Anne Charbord

Using Human Rights to Counter Terrorism

Using Human Rights to Counter Terrorism

Edited by

Manfred Nowak

Professor of International Human Rights, Vienna University, Austria; Secretary General, European Inter-University Centre for Human Rights and Democratisation, Venice, Italy

Anne Charbord

Expert Consultant in International Human Rights Law, specializing in counter-terrorism, Paris, France

ELGAR STUDIES IN HUMAN RIGHTS

EE Edward Elgar PUBLISHING

Cheltenham, UK • Northampton, MA, USA

Published by
Edward Elgar Publishing Limited
The Lypiatts
15 Lansdown Road
Cheltenham
Glos GL50 2JA
UK

Edward Elgar Publishing, Inc.
William Pratt House
9 Dewey Court
Northampton
Massachusetts 01060
USA

A catalogue record for this book
is available from the British Library

Library of Congress Control Number: 2017955163

This book is available electronically in the **Elgar**online
Law subject collection
DOI 10.4337/9781784715274

Printed on elemental chlorine free (ECF)
recycled paper containing 30% Post-Consumer Waste

ISBN 978 1 78471 526 7 (cased)
ISBN 978 1 78471 527 4 (eBook)

Typeset by Columns Design XML Ltd, Reading
Printed and bound in the USA

Contents

List of contributors vi

Introduction 1
Manfred Nowak and Anne Charbord

1. Key trends in the fight against terrorism and key aspects of international human rights law 12
   Manfred Nowak and Anne Charbord
2. Impact of post-9/11 counter-terrorism measures on all human rights 92
   Martin Scheinin
3. New counter-terrorism measures: Continuing challenges for human rights 125
   Ben Emmerson QC
4. The complexity and challenges of addressing the conditions conducive to terrorism 166
   Fionnuala Ní Aoláin
5. One step forward, two steps back: The Security Council, 'foreign terrorist fighters', and human rights 195
   Lisa Ginsborg
6. Acting ethically in the shadows: Intelligence gathering and human rights 236
   Richard Barrett and Tom Parker
7. The preventive criminal justice strategy against terrorism and its human rights implications 265
   Ulrich Garms
8. Questions of accountability in countering terrorism 300
   Lisa N. Oldring

Bibliography 338
Index 351

Contributors

Richard Barrett has worked for the British government in the Security Service (MI5), the Foreign Office and the Secret Intelligence Service (MI6). He was Director of Global Counter Terrorism Operations both before and after the 9/11 2001 attacks in the United States. From March 2004 to January 2013, he headed the UN Monitoring Team concerning Al-Qaida and the Taliban. He also helped found the UN Counter Terrorism Implementation Task Force (CTITF), a coordinating body that aims to ensure effective counter-terrorism cooperation within the UN system. Within the CTITF, he led Working Groups on terrorist use of the Internet and on countering the appeal of terrorism. He was also known for his work on countering the financing of terrorism and is an adjunct Professor of Law and Financial Integrity at Case Western Reserve University in Cleveland, Ohio. He advises governments and international organizations on violent extremism and conflict resolution.

Anne Charbord is a human rights lawyer who specializes in human rights and security. Since 2006, she has worked in various capacities for the United Nations (UN), including with the Office of the UN High Commissioner for Human Rights (OHCHR) and the UN Office on Drugs and Crime. She has served as an advisor to the first two UN Special Rapporteurs on the protection and promotion of human rights while countering terrorism, Martin Scheinin and Ben Emmerson, and led the OHCHR's initial work in the CTITF. She also provides advice to non-governmental organizations (NGOs) on human rights and counter-terrorism issues. She is a guest lecturer at Vienna University and has lectured at the Institut de Sciences Politiques in Paris. In previous roles, she has served in Organization for Security and Co-operation in Europe (OSCE) field operations, working in Bosnia and Herzegovina and Kosovo. She is a graduate of the Université Robert Schuman and the European Inter-University Centre for Human Rights and Democratization (EIUC), and holds a doctorate in international law from the University of Vienna.

Ben Emmerson QC is an international lawyer, specializing in national security and counter-terrorism, international humanitarian law and international criminal law. He was UN Special Rapporteur on counter-terrorism and human rights from 2011 to 2017, and currently sits as a judge on the Appeals Chamber of the International Criminal Tribunal for the former Yugoslavia (ICTY) and the International Criminal Tribunal for Rwanda (ICTR), appointed under the Mechanism for International Criminal Tribunals (MICT). He practices from Matrix Chambers in London.

Ulrich Garms works for the Terrorism Prevention Branch of the UN Office on Drugs and Crime (UNODC). He provides advice to requesting States on their counter-terrorism legislation, and designs and delivers training on the investigation and prosecution of terrorism cases to investigators, prosecutors and judges, primarily in countries in Sub-Saharan Africa. He has led the development of several UNODC publications on human rights aspects of criminal justice in terrorism cases. Prior to joining UNODC, Ulrich Garms worked for the OHCHR, the UN peace-keeping mission in Sudan, the Special Tribunal for Lebanon (the first international tribunal adjudicating terrorism cases) and the ICTY. He also served as the Registrar of the Human Rights Chamber for Bosnia and Herzegovina. Ulrich Garms holds law degrees from Italy and the United States.

Lisa Ginsborg works at the European University Institute (EUI) Centre for Media Pluralism and Media Freedom in the Robert Schuman Centre for Advanced Studies. She has worked as a Post-Doctoral Researcher at University College Dublin (UCD), as a Teaching Fellow at the European Inter-University Centre for Human Rights and Democratisation (EIUC), and was a visiting researcher at New York University School of Law and at the Sydney Centre for International Law at the University of Sydney. Previously she worked in the legal department of the International Secretariat of Amnesty International (2006–2009) and in the NGO Liaison Office of the Office of the UN High Commissioner for Human Rights (OHCHR) (2005–2006). She has also worked as a consultant for a number of human rights organizations and as a lecturer on human rights undergraduate and postgraduate courses. She holds a PhD in Public International Law from the EUI in Florence, Italy.

Fionnuala Ní Aoláin holds the Robina Chair in Law, Public Policy and Society at the University of Minnesota Law School and is concurrently Professor of Law & Associate Director at Ulster University's Transitional

Justice Institute (Belfast). Her book *Law in Times of Crisis* with Prof. Oren Gross (Cambridge University Press, 2006) was awarded an American Society of International Law (ASIL) Certificate of Merit for creative scholarship (2007). She is co-author of *On the Frontlines: Gender, War and the Post Conflict Process* (Oxford University Press, 2011). Ní Aoláin was appointed by the UN Secretary-General as Special Expert on promoting gender equality in times of conflict and peace-making (2003). She has served as Expert to the International Criminal Court (ICC) Trust Fund for Victims (2015), and Consultant to UN Women and OHCHR on a Study on Reparations for Conflict Related Sexual Violence (2013). She was nominated twice by the Irish government as judge to the European Court of Human Rights (2004 and 2007). She is Board Chair of the Open Society's Women' Program, and serves on the Board of the Center for Victims of Torture and the Georgetown Institute for Women, Peace and Security. In 2017, she was appointed third UN Special Rapporteur on the promotion and protection of human rights while countering terrorism.

Manfred Nowak is Professor of International Law and Human Rights at Vienna University, where he also heads the Vienna Master of Arts in Human Rights, an inter-disciplinary Human Rights Centre at the University and the Ludwig Boltzmann Institute of Human Rights (BIM). In 2016, he was appointed Secretary General of the EIUC in Venice, which is responsible for the organization of seven Masters programmes in all world regions, together called the Global Campus of Human Rights. He served as independent expert for the UN and other organizations in various capacities, including as international judge in the Human Rights Chamber for Bosnia and Herzegovina in Sarajevo (1996–2003), as Vice-Chair of the EU Fundamental Rights Agency (2013–2017), as UN expert on enforced disappearances with different mandates (1993–2006) and as UN Special Rapporteur on torture (2004–2010). In 2016, he was appointed by the UN as Independent Expert leading the Global Study on Children Deprived of Liberty. He is author of many books and articles on international human rights law and practice, including well-known commentaries on the International Covenant on Civil and Political Rights and the UN Convention against Torture as well as a recent book on *Human Rights or Global Capitalism* (University of Pennsylvania Press, 2016).

Lisa N. Oldring is Advisor on Human Rights and Security Policies with the OHCHR in Geneva. She has been the principal author of UN reports on human rights and counter-terrorism legislation and policy; global surveillance practices and the right to privacy; the use of force; targeted sanctions; foreign fighters, and other issues. She has served as legal advisor to international commissions of inquiry on Darfur, and on Lebanon, as well as Special Advisor to Mary Robinson, former President of Ireland, in her position as Chair of the GAVI Board. Previously she was an attaché to the International Committee of the Red Cross and human rights field officer with the first UN human rights mission in Rwanda. She holds a post-graduate degree in international law (Graduate Institute of International Studies, Geneva), a bachelor of laws and an undergraduate degree in criminology (University of Alberta).

Tom Parker has served as an adviser on human rights and counter-terrorism to CTITF, as the Policy Director for Terrorism, Counter-terrorism and Human Rights for Amnesty International USA, as a war crimes investigator with the ICTY, and as an Intelligence Officer in the British Security Service (MI5). He has taught undergraduate and post-graduate courses on international terrorism in Yale University's Residential College Seminar Program, Bard College's Globalization and International Affairs Program, and the National Defense University at Fort Bragg. He is a graduate of the London School of Economics, the University of Leiden and Brown, and has held research fellowships at Yale and Duke universities.

Martin Scheinin is Professor of International Law and Human Rights at the EUI in Florence, Italy. In 2016–2018, he also served as the EUI Dean of Graduate Studies. In 2005, he was appointed as the first UN Special Rapporteur on the promotion and protection of human rights and fundamental freedoms while countering terrorism, a position of trust he held until July 2011. During this time he conducted a number of country visits to Turkey, Tunisia, Peru, Egypt, Spain, South Africa, the United States and Israel, and engaged with States, regional international organizations, victims of terrorism and of human rights violations, civil society, national human rights institutions and other stakeholders. During his six-year term he identified many conceptual issues of concern for the mandate, which have remained challenges for his successor and the rest of the international community, notably those posed by overly broad and vague definitions of terrorism. He also contributed to the joint study prepared by UN Special Procedures on the global phenomenon of secret detention in the fight against terrorism, and identified ten areas of best practice in countering terrorism, which remain a staple reference today. Prior to that, in 1997–2004 he was a member of the UN Human Rights Committee, the treaty body acting under the Covenant on Civil and Political Rights. Before arriving at the EUI in 2008, he worked for 15 years as professor in Finland. In 1993–1998 he was Professor of

Constitutional Law at the University of Helsinki where he also got his doctorate in 1991. In 1998–2008, he was Professor of Constitutional and International Law and Director of the Institute for Human Rights at Åbo Akademi University in Turku, Finland.

Introduction

Manfred Nowak and Anne Charbord

In 2000, terrorism claimed 3329 fatalities; in 2015, 29 376 individuals died at the hands of terrorists.[1] Far from subsiding, terrorism has become an enduring threat to international peace and security, and a permanent feature of people's lives. By indiscriminately affecting large cities, smaller towns, religious leaders, passers-by, men, women, children, war-torn countries, large economies, North, South, East and West, most individuals are now acutely conscious that they, or a loved one, could be the next victim. Al-Qaida – the epitome of terrorism in 2001 – has become a franchise, while new terrorist groups have emerged, together with a novel modus operandi. Some of these groups control large swathes of territory, are financially independent, and are involved in full-fledged armed conflicts. Beyond causing immense suffering to the populations that live in territories under their control and beyond, through the commission of atrocities involving serious human rights violations and war crimes, these new terrorist groups are accused of the most appalling international crimes, including genocide, crimes against humanity, and trafficking.

In turn, some of the conflicts in which these groups are involved are national, regional, international, and transnational, due to the ever-larger numbers of foreign terrorist fighters who join them and now pose an acute and growing threat to international security,[2] but also to the growing numbers of States involved in the conflicts, with varying degrees of involvement. Their consequences are felt the world over, particularly as they have led to the massive displacement of people escaping violence, leading to a 'migration crisis' for countries around the Mediterranean and

---

[1] Institute for Economics and Peace (IEP) (2015), *Global Terrorism Index 2015* (New York: IEP); IEP (2016), *Global Terrorism Index 2016* (New York: IEP).

[2] UN Security Council Counter-Terrorism Committee (2015), 'Analysis and recommendations with regard to the global threat from foreign terrorist fighters' (Report prepared by the 1267 Committee), UN Doc. S/2015/358.

beyond. The close links between armed conflict and terrorism also mean that where there was once unity in the Security Council in adopting measures to counter terrorism, the Council has been paralysed over measures to address the situation in Syria, while the civilian population is bearing the brunt of the violence committed by several parties to the conflict in the name of terrorism, or of countering terrorism. These terrorist groups are also involved in transnational acts of terrorism, either directly or by proxy, having called on individuals wherever they are, and with whatever means at their disposal, to carry them out. The phenomenon of radicalization, while far from understood, appears to lead a wide range of individuals to plan and commit acts of terrorism, sometimes without any direct contact with terrorist groups. Acts of terrorism are no longer defined by large-scale planning, or the use of bombs or suicide bombers; they can be small-scale, and include machine guns, knives, or vehicles.

At the same time, since 2001, counter-terrorism measures have been adopted in all corners of the world. With every attack, new measures are considered, to the point that they now permeate nearly every aspect of life, from browsing the web to donating to a good cause, entering a shop or buying a plane ticket. Nearly every area of States' regulations now includes some element of countering terrorism, from immigration and banking to civil society, communications, education and the provision of medical care. Some States have declared a state of emergency to deal with the threat, others have engaged in torture, extraordinary rendition and secret detention, secret mass surveillance activities or targeted killings; and others yet have adopted legislation that gives sweeping powers to the executive through rights-limiting administrative measures, which increases the powers of their intelligence agencies, does away with judicial control when charges are linked to terrorism, or aims to counter violent extremism while seriously impacting on individual rights, often in a discriminatory fashion. More and more human rights are impacted, and all human rights have the potential to be impacted by these measures.

This broad-brush assessment begs the following question: why is it that since the horrific attacks in 2001 on the territory of the US, and despite the number of counter-terrorism measures that have been adopted, the threat of terrorism is greater than it was? There are many ways in which to approach this question. From a legal perspective, however, the role of respect for human rights in any effective counter-terrorism strategy is central.

When asked why it is important to respect human rights while countering terrorism, the answer of the human rights community is often confined to a simple argument of basic principle: namely, that States must uphold their international law obligations. But dogmatic arguments rooted in international law weigh little with State authorities responsible for protecting their populations from the threat of terrorism. This is particularly true when they are set alongside arguments made by the security community (broadly speaking, the intelligence agencies, the military and the police), which often considers that protecting citizens' security and human rights pull in opposite directions, and force States to choose the former at the expense of the latter. This deep-rooted view has obstructed the full application of the human rights framework in countering terrorism.

But what if the human rights arguments actually addressed the concerns of governments? What if the human rights answers helped governments to reduce the threat of terrorism more effectively? What if human rights law was seen as a powerful tool in governments' struggle against terrorism, instead of an inconvenient obstacle? This book aims to show how some of the excesses of post-September 2001 counter-terrorism legal and policy choices have been counter-productive, and offer another perspective to States on how respect for human rights can lead to more effective counter-terrorism action.

It is increasingly clear that the strict security approaches that had been adopted in the immediate aftermath of 9/11 have not only been ineffective, but they have also been counter-productive. As stated by the United Nations (UN) High Commissioner in his opening statement to the 35th session of the Human Rights Council:

> Counter-terrorism must be prosecuted intelligently: that is, while preserving the human rights of all. Please remember this: for every citizen wrongfully detained under a vague anti-terrorism law, and humiliated, abused, or tortured, it is not simply one individual who then nurses a grievance against the authorities, but most of their family too. Send one innocent person to prison, and you may deliver six or seven family members into the hands of those who oppose the government, with a few who may even go further than that. The cost of a wrongful detention dramatically outweighs whatever benefit it is perceived to accrue. To counter violent extremism, we must stand firm and insist on its opposite: peaceful inclusion.[3]

Too often, governments have forgotten that the fight against terrorism is in fact a fight for the values of human rights. Where terrorism is fought through means that violate human rights, or that undermine fundamental

---

[3] Opening Statement by Zeid Ra'ad Al Hussein, UN High Commissioner for Human Rights, http://www.ohchr.org/EN/NewsEvents/Pages/DisplayNews.aspx?NewsID=21687, accessed 22 June 2017.

freedoms, the result is that more individuals are ready and willing to resort to the unacceptable use of terrorist violence. This is unfortunately what the figures given at the beginning of this introduction show. And the price future generations will have to pay if nothing changes will be even greater than the cost that is borne by the present generation.

While providing a substantive legal analysis of the links between human rights and counter-terrorism, this book focuses on the importance of respecting human rights as an essential component of an effective counter-terrorism strategy. The main argument that the book develops is the fact that beyond the perceived dichotomy between human rights and security or, as often put, liberty and security, a State's lack of respect for human rights not only hinders its current fight against terrorism but in fact perpetuates the problem. It will show that, contrary to the conventional wisdom, respect for human rights does not hinder the fight against terrorism; it actually assists it from a moral, legal, judicial and operational perspective. The objective is to go beyond taking stock of what has happened, through an analysis of the legislative changes and the human rights violations that have occurred since 2001. The book aims to contribute to finding an explanation of why what has happened has sometimes not worked and will continue not to do so, and how to 'get it right', through a more paused, principled and longer term vision of the great many challenges of defeating terrorism. Thus, following an overview of the various developments at institutional level, and an analysis of developments since 2001, the book examines how a human rights compliant response to countering terrorism can assist from an operational, legal, judicial and moral standpoint.

Each chapter is written by an expert who has worked on these issues at the international and regional levels in great depth. The experts all have a wide breadth of practical experience of dealing with these challenges first hand: some have had an international or regional mandate given to them by an international body to examine these questions, others have worked on these issues at the international level and have therefore a unique mix of practical and theoretical approach to them. In all cases, it is their work at the international, regional and national level, with governments, non-governmental organizations (NGOs), the judiciary, the police and the victims, which adds value to this publication. Each chapter focuses on a cross-cutting theme, and significant examples from various countries or regions are drawn upon to illustrate the arguments made.

The co-editors have both worked on these issues at the international level. **Manfred Nowak** was the UN Special Rapporteur on torture from 2004 to 2010. Throughout this time, working with governments, intergovernmental and NGOs, victims and witnesses, and through various means, including fact-finding missions in Georgia (including Abkhazia and South Ossetia), Mongolia, China (including the autonomous regions of Tibet and Qinjang), Nepal, Jordan, Paraguay, Togo, Nigeria, Sri Lanka, Indonesia, Denmark (including Greenland), the Republic of Moldova (including Transnistria), Equatorial Guinea, Uruguay, Kazakhstan, Jamaica, Papua New Guinea and Greece), he has gained an invaluable insight into the use of torture in the global fight against terrorism. Together with other Special Procedures mandate holders, he prepared studies on the situation of detainees in the US detention centre at Guantánamo Bay (Cuba) and on the global phenomenon of secret detention in the fight against terrorism. **Anne Charbord** has been working on human rights and counter-terrorism issues mainly for the Office of the UN High Commissioner for Human Rights (OHCHR) since 2006. She has provided assistance to the first two UN Special Rapporteurs on the protection and promotion of human rights while countering terrorism, Martin Scheinin and Ben Emmerson, and she has also worked on these issues for the High Commissioner and within the UN Counter-Terrorism Implementation Task Force, in New York, where she was the first to represent OHCHR within that body, and to lead its Working Group on Human Rights. Together, they wrote **Chapter 1**, entitled **Key trends in the fight against terrorism and key aspects of international human rights law**. The chapter provides a general overview by highlighting key developments and assesses what 9/11 has changed in terms of answers to terrorism at the international and at the national level. Following a short historical approach to the way terrorism has been dealt with by the UN, the chapter identifies some of the key conceptual and legal fractures between pre- and post-2011 responses to terrorism by identifying main trends in the fight against terrorism while contrasting them with international law, such as the use of the war paradigm, the externalization of measures to limit the applicability of human rights law, attempts at circumventing the prohibition of torture, reliance on intelligence and national security doctrines, and the instrumentalization of various branches of law to counter-terrorism. The chapter then recalls critical aspects of international human rights law, notably its ability to respond to the serious threat of terrorism faced by many governments.

Martin Scheinin was appointed as the first UN Special Rapporteur on the promotion and protection of human rights and fundamental freedoms while countering terrorism, a position of trust he held until July 2011. During this time, through a number of country visits to Turkey, Tunisia, Peru, Egypt, Spain, South Africa, the United States of America and Israel, as well as through research and engagement with States, victims, civil society, national human rights institutions and other stakeholders, he identified the main conceptual issues of concern for the mandate, which have remained as challenges for his successors and the rest of the international community, most notably those posed by overly broad and vague definitions of terrorism. He also contributed to the joint studies prepared by UN Special Procedures on the situation of detainees in the US detention centre at Guantánamo Bay (Cuba) and on the global phenomenon of secret detention in the fight against terrorism, and identified ten areas of best practice in countering terrorism, which remain a staple reference today. Martin Scheinin wrote the second chapter, entitled **Impact of post-9/11 counter-terrorism measures on all human rights**. The chapter highlights how measures that have been adopted in the post-2001 context have undermined the whole gamut of human rights – civil, political, economic, social and cultural. In particular, it explains the key role played by the UN counter-terrorism regime, particularly Security Council resolutions 1373 (2001) and 2178 (2014) and the Al-Qaeda sanctions regime, before looking at key human rights concerns posed by this regime, notably the absence of a definition of terrorism, which has enabled States to adopt wide-ranging measures which have impacted on the rights of many individuals, including women, children, civil society, minorities, human rights defenders, political opponents and individuals in detention and led to increased powers given to the executive, increased surveillance and increased criminalization of preparatory offences.

Ben Emmerson was appointed second UN Special Rapporteur on the promotion and protection of human rights while countering terrorism in 2011. Throughout his six-year tenure, and through country visits in Burkina Faso, Chile, Tunisia, Saudi Arabia and Sri Lanka, he examined the human rights consequences of the change in nature of international terrorism, including the human rights challenges posed by the fight against Islamic State in Iraq and the Levant, and of the new tools States have developed to counter the threat, some of which are highly controversial from a human rights perspective. He focused on the use of drones in counter-terrorism operations, the use of mass digital surveillance for terrorism purposes, the negative impact of measures to counter terrorism on civil society and the rights of migrants. He developed framework principles for securing the accountability of public officials for gross or systematic human rights violations in the course of countering terrorism, and a set of framework principles for securing the human rights of victims of terrorism. He also addressed the human rights impact of measures to prevent and counter violent extremism. In **Chapter 3**, entitled **New counter-terrorism measures: Continuing challenges for human rights**, Ben Emmerson explores the counter-terrorism measures that have been adopted by States in response to new and emerging terrorist threats and continuing terrorist attacks in the years that followed the immediate post-2001 context. The chapter examines how a number of recent developments in countering terrorism pose particular threats to human rights, including the increased use of remotely piloted aircrafts ('drones') in counter-terrorism operations; mass digital surveillance for counter-terrorism purposes; measures to address the phenomenon of 'foreign terrorist fighters'; measures to counter the financing of terrorism which seriously impact on civil society; measures to counter-terrorism which impact on the human rights of migrants; and measures to address 'violent extremism' which can also adversely impact on a range of human rights. It persuasively concludes that these new measures adopted with little regard for human rights and for which there is little accountability will likely be, like those adopted in the aftermath of 2001, not only ineffective, but also counter-productive, by fuelling the violent actions they are meant to be curtailing.

Fionnuala Ní Aoláin was appointed third UN Special Rapporteur on the promotion and protection of human rights while countering terrorism in 2017. She is a leading expert in the field of human rights, national security and feminist legal theory, having extensively focused her work on emergency powers, conflict regulation, conflict and post-conflict societies, transitional justice and gender issues. She has examined at length counter-terrorism issues, with her initial work on the use of force by State agents during the conflict in Northern Ireland through to a later publication on the use of exceptional courts across numerous jurisdictions, with particular emphasis on post-9/11 developments. She has also focused on the specific issues surrounding the role of women and gender in terrorism and countering-terrorism. In **Chapter 4**, entitled **The complexity and challenges of addressing the conditions conducive to terrorism**, Fionnuala Ní Aoláin seeks to advance a better understanding of the causes of terrorism as defined and understood by States, inter-State agreement, and international institutional definitions. The chapter addresses some of the challenges in defining terrorism, which underscore how difficult it may be to hone in on the core phenomenon without engagement with the wider context of politically motivated individual and collective violence. The chapter sets out in broad scope some of the sketchily agreed-upon conditions conducive to the production of terrorism. The analysis cautions against linear over-reaching on defining what constitutes the causes of terrorism. Ní Aoláin argues that we should not circumvent the inevitable realization that causalities overlap, and that there are intersectional explanations clarifying the phenomena of terrorism. Ní Aoláin thus convincingly notes that identifying broad causes are a necessary but not sufficient means to explain the resort to terrorist violence in particular cases and geographies. The chapter also addresses individual mobilization to terrorism through the lens of empirical analysis combined with the theoretical lens of masculinities. The chapter brings a welcome focus on gender, which has been largely missing from the discussions of terrorism causes and is a major oversight, and affirms the importance of a gender lens as a means to advance greater empirical sophistication and theoretical attention to understanding the contexts and conditions that produce terrorism.

After working in the International Secretariat of Amnesty International and for the OHCHR, **Lisa Ginsborg** wrote her doctoral thesis on the UN Security Council, counter-terrorism and human rights after 9/11, looking specifically at the implications of the work of the UN Counter-Terrorism Committee and the 1267 Sanctions Committee on international human rights standards. In **Chapter 5**, entitled **One step forward, two steps back: The Security Council, 'foreign terrorist fighters' and human rights**, Lisa Ginsborg analyses how, through resolution 2178 (2014) the Security Council imposed a number of binding measures to be taken by all UN Member States to counter the threat of 'foreign terrorist fighters'; and terrorism more generally. She notes how the resolution is reflective of both the problems and the 'progress' made in the last decade in the field of counter-terrorism. In its failure to define terrorism while imposing broad counter-terrorist measures, and in its introduction of a legally problematic definition of 'foreign terrorist fighters', it repeats some familiar mistakes of the post 9/11 Security Council action, while also introducing some new human rights risks by entering more forcefully into the regulation of border crossing. However, the resolution also shows some signs that the Security Council may have learnt, at least in part, that the complete disregard of human rights is not always helpful from a security perspective. Further, the resolution is significantly new in its focus on countering violent extremism (CVE) in order to prevent terrorism under the guises of Security Council Chapter VII action. While significant risks remain in its implementation, related to the abuse of the notion of extremism, discriminatory practices in community engagement, civil society repression through CVE engagement, the right to privacy and freedom of expression online, Ginsborg concludes that resolution 2178 reflects the hope that a more preventive long-term approach may also be entering the Security Council agenda, in which human rights promotion and protection are seen as a vehicle to prevent and counter terrorism.

Richard Barrett is a leading expert in security and counter-terrorism. After spending 25 years with the British government working in the

Security Service, the Foreign Office, and the Secret Intelligence Service, including as Director of Global Counter Terrorism Operations both before and after the 9/11 2001 attacks in the US, he led the Monitoring Team that supports the UN Security Council Committee pursuant to resolution 1267 (1999) from 2004 to 2013. He was also a founding member of the UN Counter-Terrorism Implementation Task Force, and chaired its Working Group on terrorist use of the internet and countering the appeal of terrorism. He has since been designated as one of the Global Experts of the Alliance of Civilizations, and is a member of the Soufan Group. **Tom Parker** has over fifteen years of experience in human rights and security issues. He has recently worked for the UN Counter-Terrorism Implementation Task Force and the Office of the High Commissioner for Human Rights, as well as for the UN Counter-Terrorism Centre, where he led a project on the development of national and regional counter-terrorism strategies in Southern and Central Africa, and worked on the development of the UN's Preventing Violent Extremism Plan of Action for the Office of the Secretary-General. Together, Richard Barrett and Tom Parker wrote **Chapter 6**, entitled **Acting ethically in the shadows: Intelligence gathering and human rights**, which sets out to explain the way in which State obligations under human rights law influence the information gathering activities of domestic and foreign intelligence services. The chapter convincingly argues that given the necessary secrecy surrounding their work, and the risk of weak public accountability and oversight mechanisms as a result, it is all the more important that the intelligence services are conversant with and observe the law. It notes that there are clear legal limits on intelligence gathering, whether undertaken directly by an intelligence agency or by someone acting on its behalf, as well as legal limits on the use of illegal techniques such as torture. With specific regard to intelligence related to terrorism, the chapter looks at ethical issues around tasking sources, their activities and the dissemination of their information. It highlights the limits on intelligence gathering, and very persuasively dismisses any justification of ticking bomb scenarios.

Ulrich Garms has extensive experience on human rights and counter-terrorism issues, having worked with the Human Rights Chamber for Bosnia and Herzegovina, the OHCHR and the Special Tribunal for Lebanon, which was the first international tribunal adjudicating terrorism cases. He currently works for the Terrorism Prevention Branch of the UN Office on Drugs and Crime (UNODC), where he provides advice to requesting States on their counter-terrorism legislation, and designs and delivers training on the investigation and prosecution of terrorism cases to investigators, prosecutors and judges, primarily in countries in Sub-Saharan Africa. He has led the development of several UNODC publications on human rights aspects of criminal justice in terrorism cases. Ulrich Garms wrote **Chapter 7**, entitled **The preventive criminal justice strategy against terrorism and its human rights implications**. The chapter first explains how the preventive criminal justice approach against terrorism is pursued by many States and promoted by the UN, the European Union and the Council of Europe because it promises to marry the prevention of acts of terrorism with the rule of law, due process and the human rights safeguards of the criminal justice system. Yet a preventive criminal justice strategy against terrorism requires, first, laws that criminalize conduct that takes place long before an attempt to commit a violent act has taken place, through 'advanced criminalization offences'. The chapter explores the criticisms put to these offences, as well as the legal policy questions and practical challenges they raise through an analysis of selected case law and of the debates surrounding the enactment of legislation creating new advanced criminalization offences in several countries. Second, a preventive criminal justice strategy against terrorism requires broad use of so-called 'special investigation techniques' and intelligence sources. The chapter discusses their impact on fair trial guarantees, and argues that their use inevitably requires the limitation of some fair trial safeguards. Garms convincingly concludes that the preventive criminal justice strategy against terrorism – inspired by the rule of law and human rights – does not come without side effects that are undesirable from a human rights perspective.

As advisor on human rights and security policies with the UN Office of the High Commissioner for Human Rights in Geneva, **Lisa N. Oldring** has been the principle author of UN reports on human rights and counter-terrorism legislation, policy and practice, global surveillance practices and the right to privacy in the digital age, on the use of force, foreign fighters, and other related issues. She has also been a legal advisor to International Commissions of Inquiry on Darfur, and on Lebanon, as well as the Special Advisor to Mary Robinson in her position as Chair of the GAVI Board, an attaché to the International Committee of the Red Cross; and human rights field officer with the UN field mission in Rwanda. In **Chapter 8**, entitled **Questions of accountability in countering terrorism**, Lisa Oldring examines the overarching questions for human rights violations in the context of countering terrorism, both as a question of moral effectiveness as well as legal duty. She focuses on three main challenges: the definition of terrorism and the legal framework applied by States in terrorism-related cases; the expansion of intelligence agencies' powers without effective oversight or safeguards against abuse; and the influence of national security considerations on criminal justice, notably through the expanded use of the state secrets' privilege.

1. Key trends in the fight against terrorism and key aspects of international human rights law

Manfred Nowak and Anne Charbord

The dramatic attacks of 11 September 2001 in the US, which consisted of the simultaneous hijacking of four planes, and resulted in thousands of victims[1] in the heart of New York and Washington, had an overwhelming impact on the world. The scale and nature of the attacks and the means used showed the strength and resolve of a terrorist group, the damage that can be caused by a few determined and organized individuals, the vulnerability of some of the world's key financial and defence centres, and the exposure of aviation transportation to terrorist attacks. Yet, in the immediate aftermath of the attacks, the response given to these unprecedented attacks was calm and a clear resolve from the world's leaders that such crimes, and those who caused them, would not prevail over 'shared values' of democracy, freedom, the rule of law and human rights.[2]

Unfortunately, the legal response that followed – from the Security Council to governments – was very different. It was soon argued that the new threat of terrorism from various groups in several parts of the world was such that it threatened the very existence of democracy. Countering terrorism was rebranded the 'war against terror' and the existing international legal framework was deemed insufficient to address the new paradigm. New rules, a new approach unconstrained by existing rules of international law, were necessary. The choice was clear: security or human rights. With the former clearly taking the lead to the detriment of

[1] The attacks resulted in the deaths of 2996 people, while more than 6000 were injured.

[2] See UN Security Council (2001), 'Security Council condemns "in strongest terms" terrorist attacks on United States', press release, 12 September, UN Doc. SC/7143, http://www.un.org/press/en/2001/SC7143.doc.htm, accessed 10 May 2017.

the latter, what followed was an overhaul of calmly, well established rules of international law: lines between legal regimes were blurred, 'exceptional' rules became the norm, and rules in violation of non-derogable human rights law, or outside the scope of any judicial review or control, were created. In turn, this opened the door to impunity for human rights violations, and lack of accountability from States committing them.

Yet, some sixteen years later, the threat of terrorism is as present as ever. New, more virulent and powerful terrorist groups have emerged, which control territory and are engaged in full-fledged armed conflicts; terrorist acts continue to take place, unabated; and a range of new phenomena have been identified, such as 'self-radicalized' individuals, 'lone wolves', and 'foreign terrorist fighters'. Following a short historical approach to the way in which terrorism has been dealt with by the United Nations (UN), this chapter will examine the developments and main trends in the 'fight against terrorism' since 2001, highlighting some of the key conceptual and legal fractures caused by the post-2001 approach and focusing on key tensions with international human rights law (IHRL). It will also recall some of the key aspects of the international human rights framework, most notably its ability to respond to serious threats faced by governments.

1. THE UNITED NATIONS RESPONSE TO TERRORISM

1.1 Prior to 2001

The General Assembly first dealt with the question of terrorism in 1972, following the kidnapping and killing of 11 Israeli athletes by the Palestinian 'Black September' group during the Munich summer Olympics. Resolution 3034 (1972)[3] was a sign of its times: entrenched in Cold

[3] Entitled 'Measures to prevent international terrorism which endangers or takes innocent human lives or jeopardizes fundamental freedoms, and study of the underlying causes of those forms of terrorism and acts of violence which lie in misery, frustration, grievance and despair and which cause some people to sacrifice human lives, including their own, in an attempt to effect radical changes'. In 1991, the series' name was shortened to 'measures to prevent international terrorism'.

War politics, as reflected by the voting pattern,[4] it became polarized on the question of national and liberation movements, and their link to terrorism. Instead of condemning terrorism, the resolution highlighted its underlying causes, namely misery, frustration, grievance and despair, focused on the right to self-determination and the legitimacy of the struggle of national and liberation movements, and endorsed the concept of 'State terrorism',[5] since then set aside.[6] It was not until 1985 that the General Assembly was able to depart from this position. Through resolution 40/61 (1985), adopted by consensus after the Achille Lauro hijacking by the Palestinian Liberation Front, the General Assembly affirmed that terrorist violence could not be justified under any circumstance,[7] and that the struggle of national liberation movements must be in accordance with the principles and purpose of the Charter and the Declaration on principles of international law concerning friendly relations and cooperation among States, a document which explicitly prohibits recourse to terrorist violence in the exercise of the right to self-determination.

Despite this resolution, the question of whether the definition of terrorism should cover acts of self-determination and liberation movements, or not, remained open, as revealed by a draft resolution put forward by Syria in 1987.[8] This question is still largely on the table, and

---

4 With 76 in favour, composed largely of the Eastern Group and the Group of 77, while 35 countries voted no, largely the Western Group. Seventeen countries abstained.

5 See also General Assembly (GA) resolution 39/159 of 17 December 1984, entitled 'Inadmissibility of the policy of State terrorism', 117 votes in favour, and 30 – western – countries abstained (no country voted against).

6 In 2005, the Secretary-General stated that it is 'time to set aside debates on so-called state-terrorism. The use of force by States is already regulated under international law' (UN General Assembly (2005), 'In larger freedom', UN Doc. A/59/2005, para. 91), while the chair of the Counter-Terrorism Committee clarified in 2002 that State-terrorism is not an international legal concept. In this reasoning, 'State terrorism' is in fact abuse of power and use of force by States, which is already regulated by international law, namely IHRL, IHL and international criminal law. The concept is no longer referred to in GA resolutions.

7 The resolution 'unequivocally condemns, as criminal, all acts, methods and practices of terrorism, wherever and by whom ever committed'. The qualification that terrorist acts are 'unjustifiable' was added with GA resolution 44/29 of 4 December 1989.

8 The draft resolution, presented by Syria and supported by the group of developing States called for an international conference to define terrorism and to differentiate it from the struggle of peoples for national liberation, which was

is one of the main stumbling blocks to the adoption of the International Convention on Terrorism.[9] While some may have seen elements of a definition in two Declarations contained in General Assembly resolutions,[10] which state that 'criminal acts intended or calculated to provoke a state of terror in the general public, a group of persons or particular persons for political purposes are in any circumstance unjustifiable, whatever the considerations of a political, philosophical, ideological, racial, ethnic, religious or any other nature that may be invoked to justify them', the reference to a political purpose makes this wording different to that contained in the UN Draft Comprehensive Convention, which does not require a political motive, and instead focuses on intimidation or coercion, and other international documents.[11] This suggests that the

---

never adopted. Instead, GA resolution 42/159 of 7 December 1987 requests the Secretary-General to 'seek the views of Member States on how to combat international terrorism, including through the possibility of convening an international conference to define terrorism and to differentiate it from the struggle of peoples for national liberation'. This much weaker wording left open the possibility that this conference not take place, thereby excluding that the 'struggle of peoples for national liberation' be excluded from the definition of terrorism.

[9] In 1996, General Assembly resolution 51/210 established an Ad Hoc Committee, which negotiated several texts resulting in the adoption of three treaties: the International Convention for the Suppression of Terrorist Bombings (GA resolution 52/164 of 15 December 1997); the International Convention for the Suppression of the Financing of Terrorism (GA resolution 54/109 of 9 December 1999); and the International Convention for the Suppression of Acts of Nuclear Terrorism (GA resolution 59/290 of 13 April 2005). In 2000, work had begun on a draft comprehensive convention on international terrorism to criminalize all forms of international terrorism and deny terrorists, their financiers and supporters access to funds, arms, and safe havens. While most of the text has been agreed, the outstanding issues are however key, and revolve around: (1) the definition (article 2); (2) the exclusionary clauses (article 3, former article 18), particularly on whether the text would be applicable to (a) the armed forces of a state in the exercise of their official duties and (b) to 'self-determination/resistance movements'. See also Ben Saul (2006), 'Defending "terrorism": Justification and excuses for terrorism in international criminal law', *Australian Yearbook of International Law*, **25**, 177–226.

[10] GA resolution 49/60 of 9 December 1994, which contains the Declaration to Eliminate International Terrorism, and GA resolution 51/210 of 17 December 1996, which contains the Declaration to Supplement the Declaration to Eliminate International Terrorism.

[11] See Ben Saul (2012), 'The Special Tribunal for Lebanon and terrorism as an international crime: Reflections on the judicial function', Legal Studies Research Paper No. 12/64, September, Sydney Law School, pp. 7 and 8.

legal definition of terrorism remains deeply contested, and that, at best, the definition reflects nascent political agreement on a shared concept of terrorism, but not legal agreement evidencing a customary crime.[12]

First attempts at addressing the question of terrorism and human rights also hit an ideological stumbling block, as evidenced by the short-lived 'Human Rights and Terrorism' resolutions.[13] The consensus over these resolutions fractured over the question of whether terrorist groups could commit 'gross human rights violations',[14] and whether terrorism itself could be considered as a violation of human rights. Many States argued that terrorism was a criminal act, not a violation of human rights; that only States could commit human rights violations; and that accepting otherwise would give terrorist groups a legitimacy that they might be looking for, but should not be granted. Following an increasing number of abstentions or votes against, the series was discontinued in 2005.[15] In a worrying development, Human Rights Council resolution 31/30 (2016), sponsored by Egypt, on 'the effects of terrorism on the enjoyment of all human rights', contains some of the same flaws. By overly focusing on the impact of terrorism, it 'instrumentaliz[es] victims of terrorism to weaken the international human rights system that is designed for their protection'. As noted by Belgium prior to the adoption of the resolution, '[w]e cannot be guided by fear, quite the opposite; our responsibility is to pursue a framework that preserves our values. We are convinced that the fight against terrorism, even in the most tragic moments must be undertaken with full respect for human rights and fundamental freedoms ... We have just been victims of a terrorist attack, but we call for you to

---

12 See Saul, ibid.

13 The first in this series started after the adoption of the Vienna Declaration and Plan of Action in 1993, with GA resolution 48/122 of 14 February 1994. The last was GA resolution 59/195 of 22 March 2005. In 1994, the UN Commission on Human Rights also started adopting resolutions on terrorism and human rights, which contained similar provisions.

14 See e.g. Preamble, UN Doc. A/RES/54/164.

15 See Kalliopi Koufa (2006), 'The UN, human rights and counter-terrorism', in Giuseppe Nesi (ed.), *International Cooperation in Counter-terrorism: The United Nations and Regional Organizations in the Fight Against Terrorism* (Aldershot: Ashgate), pp. 51 and 52. See also Economic and Social Council, 'Terrorism and human rights', Working paper submitted by Kalliopi K. Koufa in accordance with Sub-Commission resolution 1996/20, E/CN.4/Sub.2/1997/28.

vote against this text ... this sends the wrong message of the way in which we should tackle the issues facing us at the moment.'[16]

1.2 The Security Council Response Post-2001 and its Consequences

Prior to 2001, the Security Council had largely stayed away from the debate tainted by ideology that was taking place in the General Assembly, and the issue of terrorism had mostly taken the form of sanctions against States considered to have links to certain acts of terrorism.[17] Foreshadowing its post-2001 work on setting up an international counter-terrorism framework, in resolution 1269 (1999), the Security Council asked Member States to enhance international cooperation and co-ordination, and encouraged them to sign up and implement the counter-terrorism Conventions.

Following resolution 1368 (2001)[18] which stated that 'acts of international terrorism' were a threat to international peace and security, the UN Security Council adopted on 28 September 2001 resolution 1373, which is a key building block of the 'counter-terrorism framework' set up by the Council. The resolution was an immediate response to the terrorist attacks that took place on 11 September, but it was also a politically motivated, hastily adopted document that had a dramatic impact on human rights, whose consequences are still very largely felt today, in every corner of the world.

The resolution, adopted under Chapter VII of the Charter of the UN, required States to take a number of measures, including the criminalization of various acts of terrorism,[19] the prevention and suppression of the

---

[16] Article 19 (2016), 'UNHRC 31: States must reject flawed resolution on "terrorism"', 22 March, https://www.article19.org/resources.php/resource/38310/en/unhrc-31:-states-must-reject-flawed-resolution-on-, accessed 17 October 2017; International Service for Human Rights (2016), 'Counter-terrorism: Egyptian-led resolution sends wrong message at wrong time', 4 April, http://www.ishr.ch/news/counter-terrorism-egyptian-led-resolution-sends-wrong-message-wrong-time, accessed 17 October 2017.

[17] Libya, resolution 748 (1992); Sudan, resolution 1054 (1996) and the Taliban resolution 1267 (1999) expanded to include Al-Qaida by resolution 1333 (2000).

[18] 12 September 2001.

[19] It requires all States to criminalize terrorist acts (OP 2(e)); to penalize acts of support for or in preparation of terrorist offences (OP 2(e)); and to criminalize the financing of terrorism (OP 1(b)).

financing of terrorism[20] and the freezing of assets of individuals linked to terrorism. For the first time, the Security Council imposed on all UN Member States a number of general, permanent obligations, not connected to a specific conflict situation. The obligations laid out in the resolution contain no end in time or space and apply to any act of terrorism worldwide. In effect, this resolution amounted to the Council establishing new binding rules of international law. The legitimacy of the Council's so doing has been questioned.[21]

Yet, resolution 1373 mostly stood out for what it did not do: define terrorism, or make an explicit mention of the need to respect human rights in this context (except through a passing reference regarding refugee law). In turn, this empowered governments to take strong measures against terrorism – however they wished to define it – while disregarding their long-established human rights obligations. Many States understood this resolution as an obligation to adopt stringent counter-terrorism legislation, quickly, often under 'emergency' procedures, in the absence of sufficient consultations with key stakeholders and respect for thorough parliamentary procedures,[22] in a number of counter-terrorism areas. This impression was compounded by the accompanying monitoring mechanism set up by resolution 1373 whereby States were requested to report on their progress in the implementation of the resolution to the Counter-Terrorism Committee (CTC), with a first report due only ninety days after adoption of the resolution. Through State reporting, and later State visits and internal working documents to assess

[20] These obligations were already largely contained in the Convention on the Suppression of the Financing of Terrorism. As noted by Martin Scheinin, '[o]n 10 April 2002, after the 22nd ratification, the Convention entered into force and has by now obtained almost universal ratification (186 parties). Whatever criticisms we may have about resolution 1373, it was a success story in getting states on board to combat the financing of terrorism, and the emergency shortcut was remedied through subsequent action by states', Martin Scheinin (2014), 'A comment on Security Council Res 2178 (foreign terrorist fighters) as a "form" of global governance', Just Security, 6 October, https://www.justsecurity.org/15989/comment-security-council-res-2178-foreign-fighters-form-global-governance/, accessed 10 May 2017.

[21] For a detailed examination of all these developments, see Chapter 2 in this volume by Martin Scheinin.

[22] 'Special Rapporteur on human rights while countering terrorism', UN Doc. A/70/371, para. 13.

States' implementation of resolution 1373 (and later also 1624 (2005)),[23] the CTC evaluated States' implementation of the various requirements of the resolutions, and ranked their level of implementation. As the CTC largely failed to take human rights into consideration in carrying out its mandate, the stage was set for the widespread, hasty adoption of counter-terrorism legislation that often did not comply with IHRL.[24]

This top-down approach to the creation of an international counter-terrorism framework worked in combination with a lateral or horizontal approach,[25] in which States were inspired by, or simply copied, existing counter-terrorism legislation in other countries. This allowed certain governments to feel retroactively justified in their prior adoption of some rights-limiting counter-terrorism measures which had been criticized as not being compliant with the international human rights framework. This led, for example, former Egyptian Prime Minister Atef Abeid to offer that '[a]fter these horrible crimes committed in New York and Virginia, maybe Western countries should begin to think of Egypt's own fight against terror as their new model',[26] or the former Malaysian Minister of Justice to state, following a meeting with the former US Attorney General: 'I believe that (…) there will be no more basis to criticize each other's systems, specifically the [ISA – Internal Security Act], because if they do that, then the Patriot Act, which is quite similar in nature to the ISA, could come into a position of jeopardy itself.'[27] This also allowed

[23] See Preliminary Implementation Assessments, set up in December 2006, replaced in 2013 by an overview for implementation assessment and the detailed implementation assessment.

[24] For a detailed examination of all these developments, see Chapter 2 in this volume by Martin Scheinin.

[25] See Victor V. Ramraj (2012), 'The impossibility of global anti terrorism law', in Victor V. Ramraj, Michael Hor, Kent Roach and George Williams (eds), *Global Anti Terrorism Law and Policy*, 2nd edn (Cambridge: Cambridge University Press), pp. 44–66 at 48.

[26] See Human Rights Watch (HRW) (2001), 'Egypt: Human rights background', October, https://www.hrw.org/legacy/backgrounder/mena/egypt-bck-1001.htm, accessed 29 February 2016. See also Kent Roach noting that 'as with Egypt, Syria was able to proudly report the existence of offences to the CTC that before 9/11 would have been widely regarded within the UN and elsewhere as repressing political freedoms', in Kent Roach (2001), *The 9/11 Effect. Comparative Counter-Terrorism* (Cambridge: Cambridge University Press), p. 94.

[27] As quoted in Neil Hicks, Director of International Programs (2004), 'The impact of counter Terror on the Promotion and Protection of Human Rights: A Global Perspective', Human Rights First Paper prepared for 'Human Rights in an Age of Terrorism' a conference at the University of Connecticut, 9–11 September 2004.

States to justify some of the rights-limiting measures included in their new legislation by reference to what other States were doing. The impact of this subtle, non-prescriptive process is not negligible, and the particularly negative role of US and UK[28] legislation and practice on the rest of the world is a case in point. Combined with existing national differences in implementation of the rule of law, in institutional safeguards, in the role of and protection afforded to the judiciary, of human rights protection and of mechanisms to address alleged human rights violations, the emerging global counter-terrorism framework failed to take account of the political, institutional, legal, cultural, and religious differences in each State.

In this context, the need to respect individual rights and the international human rights framework in countering terrorism was relegated to a second zone, after the political imperatives of adopting counter-terrorism legislation to look strong in the face of the new terrorist threat, however defined, and to comply with new international obligations. At the most extreme end of the spectrum, human rights activists or members of the political opposition critical of this approach, were accused of assisting terrorists. For example, the US Attorney General John Ashcroft said in December 2001:

> [t]o those who scare peace-loving people with phantoms of lost liberty, my message is this: Your tactics only aid terrorists for they erode our national unity and diminish our resolve. They give ammunition to America's enemies and pause to America's friends. They encourage people of good will to remain silent in the face of evil.[29]

In the same vein, the Director of the Canadian Security Intelligence Service (CSIS) said:

> So why then, I ask, are those accused of terrorist offences often portrayed in media as quasi-folk heroes, despite the harsh statements of numerous judges? Why are they always photographed with their children, given tender-hearted

---

[28] See Kent Roach (2006), 'The post 9/11 migration of Britain's 2000 Terrorism Act', in Sudit Choudry (ed.), *The Migration of Constitutional Ideas* (Cambridge: Cambridge University Press).

[29] Testimony of Attorney General John Ashcroft, Senate Committee on the Judiciary, 6 December 2001, https://www.justice.gov/archive/ag/testimony/2001/1206transcriptsenatejudiciarycommittee.htm, accessed 7 May 2017. See also former Indian Deputy Prime Minister L.K. Advani, who in calling for the adoption of a new Prevention of Terrorism Act in November 2001, stated: 'If the opposition opposes the ordinance they will be wittingly or unwittingly helping terrorists', quoted in Hicks (n 27).

> profiles, and more or less taken at their word when they accuse CSIS or other government agencies of abusing them? It sometimes seems that to be accused of having terrorist connections in Canada has become a status symbol, a badge of courage in the struggle against the real enemy, which would appear to be, at least sometimes, the government. To some members of civil society, there is a certain romance to this. This loose partnership of single-issue NGOs, advocacy journalists and lawyers has succeeded, to a certain extent, in forging a positive public image for anyone accused of terrorist links or charges.[30]

More generally, former Egyptian President Hosni Mubarak was reported as saying that human rights arguments should not be put forward on all occasions, and that those who carry out terrorist acts have no claim to human rights,[31] a view which was largely shared.

As noted by the former UN Special Rapporteur on the promotion and protection of human rights while countering terrorism, Martin Scheinin, 'for a while, the global consensus about the imperative of combatting terrorism was so compelling that authoritarian governments could get away with their repressive practices simply by renaming political opponents as terrorists'.[32] Governments were able to prosecute dissidents and breach fundamental human rights with the apparent blessing of the UN Security Council, while the strong international stance against terrorism prevented the international community from being critical of governments that were carrying out these practices. One such example was the position of the EU in relation to Central Asian States, given their perceived importance in countering terrorism.[33]

---

[30] Remarks by Richard B. Fadden to the Canadian Association for Security and Intelligence Studies (CASIS) Annual International Conference, 20 October 2009, http://www.casis-acers.ca/wp-content/uploads/2014/06/Dick-Fadden-CSIS-Speech-To-CASIS-OCT-091.pdf, accessed 7 May 2017.

[31] See HRW (n 26).

[32] Martin Scheinin and Mathias Vermeulen, 'Unilateral exceptions to international law: Systematic analysis and critique of doctrines that seek to deny or reduce the applicability of human rights norms in the fight against terrorism', European University Institute Working Papers, Law, 2010/08, Paper delivered under the DETECTER project, p. 2.

[33] See Scheinin and Vermeulen, ibid., in relation to Uzbekistan, at p. 2. See also Gordon Crawford: 'The embrace of Central Asian states by the EU due to their strategic importance in combating perceived Islamist threats (…) can be manipulated by authoritarian rulers to provide them with enhanced legitimacy at home and a relatively free hand in repressing opposition political parties and non-governmental activist groups (…). Western support is more likely to result in rising authoritarian trends than in political liberalisation and democratisation'.

What resolution 1373 failed to mention in relation to human rights was remedied by resolution 1456 (2004). It stated that 'States must ensure that any measure taken to combat terrorism comply with international law, and should adopt such measures in accordance with international law, in particular international human rights, refugee, and humanitarian law'. All Security Council resolutions from thereon routinely included this, or other similar, language. However, as we will see, this was not sufficient to reverse the negative impact that resolution 1373, together with the lack of human rights interest of the CTC, had already had.

1.3 The General Assembly

In the post-2001 context, the General Assembly largely put aside its own internal conceptual differences to the question of terrorism, to address what some saw as the discriminatory and possibly counter-productive result of the Security Council approach. Putting itself forward as the sole body with universal legitimacy – 'the general organ having competence to consider measures to eliminate international terrorism'[34] – in 2003, it started focusing on the question of 'protection of human rights while countering terrorism', with a series of resolutions that address the human rights concerns posed by States' counter-terrorism measures.[35]

In 2004, the Panel on Threats, Challenges and Change recommended that the UN 'make better use of its assets in the fight against terrorism, articulating an effective and principled counter-terrorism strategy that is respectful of the rule of law and universal human rights'. The Panel noted 'the imperative to develop a strategy that addresses root causes and the rule of law and fundamental human rights', stating that what was required is a 'comprehensive strategy that incorporates but is broader than coercive measures'.[36] In 2005, through the World Summit Outcome Document, the General Assembly was charged with the development of a Strategy to promote comprehensive, coordinated and consistent responses, at the national, regional and international levels, to counter

---

Gordon Crawford (2008), 'EU human rights and democracy promotion in Central Asia: From lofty principles to lowly self-interests', *Perspectives on European Politics and Society*, **9** (2), 172–91.

[34] UN GA resolution 58/81 of 8 January 2004.

[35] UN GA resolution 57/219 of 27 February 2003. All these resolutions contain a human rights clause, and this series is still ongoing.

[36] Report of the Secretary-General's High Level Panel on Threats, challenges and change (2004), "A more secure world: Our shared responsibility"', UN Doc. A/59/565, para. 148.

terrorism, which also takes into account the conditions conducive to the spread of terrorism.[37] In May 2006, the UN Secretary-General's report 'Uniting Against Terrorism',[38] set forth elements for the Strategy, while noting the indispensability of the rule of law, nationally and internationally, in countering the threat of terrorism and the importance of human rights: 'Effective counter-terrorism measures and the protection of human rights are not conflicting goals, but complementary and mutually reinforcing ones. Accordingly, the defence of human rights is essential to the fulfillment of all aspects of a counter-terrorism strategy'.

Thus, between 2004 and 2006, the General Assembly, together with the Secretary-General, recalibrated the UN's approach to countering terrorism, away from coercive policies, and back towards the core values of the UN. These efforts culminated in the unanimous adoption, on 8 September 2006, of the UN Global Counter-Terrorism Strategy and Plan of Action (UN GCTS),[39] which can be seen as the General Assembly's answer to the Security Council's approach on the issue of countering terrorism. By stating that human rights are 'the fundamental basis of the fight against terrorism' and 'essential to all components of the Strategy', the Strategy places human rights at its centre, as the thread that runs through its entirety.[40] The Strategy also reaffirms the inextricable links between human rights and security, and places respect for the rule of law and human rights at the core of national and international counter-terrorism efforts. Since its adoption, the Strategy has been reviewed every two years by the General Assembly, and has – thus far – always been reaffirmed by consensus. In order to assist Member States in their implementation of the Strategy, and to provide a single UN interface on this issue, the Secretary-General set up the UN Counter-Terrorism Implementation Task Force (CTITF), an entity which comprises all the relevant UN secretariat branches and agencies that have a role to play in implementing the Strategy.[41] The CTITF has been severely criticized,

[37] UN Doc. A/RES/60/1, para. 82.

[38] UN Doc. A/60/825.

[39] UN GA resolution 60/288 of 20 September 2006.

[40] Composed of four Pillars, the first is devoted to addressing the conditions conducive to the spread of terrorism, while the fourth deals with measures to ensure respect for human rights for all and the rule of law as the fundamental basis of the fight against terrorism.

[41] To assist Member States in their implementation of the Strategy, and to provide a single UN interface, the Secretary-General set up the UN Counter-Terrorism Implementation Task Force. See https://www.un.org/counterterrorism/ctitf/en/about-task-force, accessed on 14 February 2016.

notably for its failure to give human rights the importance it deserves in light of its prominent role in the Strategy.[42]

1.4 A More Nuanced Approach

Following the General Assembly's new approach, the Security Council also started taking small steps to reintroduce human rights in what was essentially still a security-based approach to countering terrorism. In addition to the systematic inclusion of a human rights clause in its counter-terrorism resolutions, the Security Council also requested the CTC to adopt a more pro-active policy on human rights.[43] The big stride came in the fall of 2010, when in language that seemed directly borrowed from the UN GCTS, the Security Council recognized – for the first time – that 'terrorism will not be defeated by military force, law enforcement measures, and intelligence operations alone'. The Council underlined the need to address the conditions conducive to the spread of terrorism, including the need to promote the rule of law, the protection of human rights and fundamental freedoms, tolerance and inclusiveness to offer a viable alternative to those who could be susceptible to terrorist recruitment and to radicalization leading to violence. Further, the Security Council recognized that development, peace and security, and human rights are interlinked and mutually reinforcing.[44] This move – away from a pure security and law-enforcement approach to countering terrorism, now considered inadequate – was confirmed through resolution 2178 (2014), which recognized that 'terrorism will not be defeated by military force, law enforcement measures and intelligence operations alone', and underlined 'the need to address the conditions conducive to the spread of terrorism, as outlined in pillar I of the UN Global Counter-Terrorism Strategy (General Assembly resolution 60/288)'.[45]

Unfortunately, the Security Council's post-resolution 1373 interest in human rights has been insufficient to either correct the damage that had been done by the adoption of the first wave of counter-terrorism legislation, or to prevent States from adopting new counter-terrorism

[42] 'Special Rapporteur on human rights and counter-terrorism', UN Doc. A/HRC/34/61.

[43] See resolution 1535 (2004) and the CTC's May 2006 policy guidance for CTED in the area of human rights (see http://www.un.org/en/sc/ctc/rights.html, accessed 17 October 2017).

[44] UN Doc. S/PRST/2010/19 and UN Security Council resolution 1963 (2010).

[45] UN Doc. A/70/371 (n 22), para. 14.

legislation that included similar, as well as new, human rights shortcomings.[46] The more principled, long-term approach, which focuses on prevention, addressing the conditions conducive to terrorism, human rights and the rule of law, is a promising step in the right direction. Yet at present, the vagueness, broadness and overall lack of clarity of the concepts involved in 'preventing or countering violent extremism', a key aspect of the UN's post-2014 agenda,[47] renders any thorough analysis of measures that are adopted by States largely impossible. As a recent examination shows, such measures could have a negative impact on IHRL, while still failing to effectively counter terrorism.[48]

2. KEY TRENDS IN NATIONAL RESPONSES

In the immediate aftermath of the September 2001 terrorist attacks in the US, some governments were quick to argue that – given the renewed threat and new nature of terrorism – there was a need for stronger measures that could not be accommodated by the existing international framework. This scenario has unfortunately repeated itself, as exemplified by the reaction of the French government following the attacks in Paris in 2015. It appears that new terrorist attacks lead governments to adopt strong(er) measures against existing, and potential, terrorists, which vary in time and space – adapting and reacting to public revelations and change in public opinion, as well as to calls for accountability for human rights violations. For example, enhanced interrogation, secret detention and extraordinary rendition have given way to bulk surveillance and increased use of armed drones; and the moment at which governments start criminalizing preparatory acts of terrorism has moved forward in time, with recent measures that target 'extremism' in the absence of any link to violence.

In the wide array of measures that have been adopted to counter and prevent terrorist acts, some general, recurring trends and approaches can be found. This section will focus on the examination of a few, yet it is important to note that these are in no way exhaustive, nor do the examples reflect the number of States that are concerned by them. They

[46] See 'Report of the UN High Commissioner for Human Rights', UN Doc. A/HRC/28/28, paras. 21–30.

[47] 'Secretary General's plan of action to prevent violent extremism', UN Doc. A/70/674.

[48] 'Report of the Special Rapporteur on human rights while countering terrorism', UN Doc. A/HRC/31/65.

include: the use of the war paradigm in the context of countering terrorism (section 2.1); the externalization of counter-terrorism measures to limit the applicability of IHRL (section 2.2); attempts at circumventing the absolute nature of the prohibition of torture and refoulement (section 2.3); (ab)use of national security and reliance on intelligence information (section 2.4); and the instrumentalization of various branches of national and international law to counter terrorism (section 2.5).

2.1. The Use of the War Paradigm in the Context of Countering Terrorism

2.1.1 The US 'war against terror'

On 14 September 2001, the US Senate passed the Authorization for the Use of Military Force, which gave the President broad authority to use 'all necessary and appropriate force against those nations, organizations and persons he determines planned, authorized, committed or aided the terrorist attacks that occurred on September 11, 2001, or harbored such organizations or persons, in order to prevent future acts of international terrorism against the United States by such nations, organizations or persons'.[49] One day later, US President Bush declared: 'Everyone who wears the uniform should get ready. We're at war. There's been a war declared.'[50] A few days later, President Bush clarified that '[o]n September the 11th, enemies of freedom committed an act of war against our country. (…) Our war on terror begins with al-Qaeda, but it does not end there. It will not end until every terrorist group of global reach has been found, stopped and defeated.'[51]

From a legal perspective, the US considered itself 'engaged in a continuing armed conflict against Al-Qaida, the Taliban and other terrorist organizations supporting them', with troops on the ground in several places engaged in combat operations'.[52] The US government originally argued that this conflict was neither an international armed conflict

---

[49] Pub. L. 107-40, 115 Stat. 224.

[50] Ed Vulliamy, Peter Beaumont, Kamal Ahmed and Luke Harding (2001), 'Get ready for war, Bush tells America', *The Guardian, Observer Special*, 16 September, http://www.theguardian.com/world/2001/sep/16/terrorism.september11, accessed 4 March 2016.

[51] Address to a Joint Session of Congress and the American People, 20 September 2001, http://georgewbush-whitehouse.archives.gov/news/releases/2001/09/20010920-8.html, accessed 17 February 2016.

[52] 'Reply of the Government of the United States of America to the Report of the Five UNCHR Special Rapporteurs on Detainees in Guantanamo Bay',

governed by the Geneva Conventions, because Al-Qaeda was not a State party to the conventions, nor a non-international armed conflict (NIAC), because it exceeded the territory of one State.[53] The effect of such a statement was to exclude the armed conflict against 'Al-Qaida, the Taliban and other terrorist organizations supporting them' entirely from the protection of international humanitarian law (IHL).[54] Combined with arguments that IHRL obligations do not extend to extraterritorial actions,[55] this was an attempt to remove government measures against 'Al-Qaida, the Taliban and other terrorist organizations supporting them' in their entirety from the remit of international law. The US Supreme Court did not accept this position. Following its 2004 *Rasul* decision,[56] in which the Supreme Court affirmed the statutory jurisdiction of US federal courts to determine the legality of the detention of Guantanamo Bay detainees, in its 2006 *Hamdan* case, the Court ruled that the conflict was non-international in nature and governed by common article 3.[57] While this ruling importantly recalled the applicability of international law, it still had the effect of placing the US' counter-terrorism actions under the framework of IHL. In turn, this limited the applicability of IHRL in areas also governed by IHL, with severe consequences on individual rights.[58]

Cuba, 10 March 2006, http://www.state.gov/documents/organization/98969.pdf, accessed 15 February 2016.

[53] See White House Memorandum of 7 February 2002 on the 'Humane treatment of Taliban and Al Qaeda detainees', para. 2, http://www.pegc.us/archive/White_House/bush_memo_20020207_ed.pdf, accessed 16 February 2016. The US Supreme Court in *Hamdan* disagreed with this position. *Hamdan v. Rumsfeld*, 548 U.S. 557 (2006).

[54] See US government's argumentation in *Hamdan*, accepted by the Court of Appeal but rejected by the Supreme Court, 548 US 557, No. 04-5393, 15 July 2005.

[55] 'Reply of the Government of the United States of America to the Report of the Five UNCHR Special Rapporteurs on Detainees in Guantanamo Bay' (n 52).

[56] *Rasul v. Bush* (03-334) 542 U.S. 466 (2004).

[57] *Hamdan v. Rumsfeld* (n 53).

[58] Thus, individuals believed to belong to, or to be associated with terrorist groups were qualified as 'enemy combatants', even when arrested outside areas of armed conflict. See Military Commissions Act of 2006, Public Law 109–366 – 17 October 2006, para. 948a (preceded by the Military Order of 13 November 2001, Section 2).

2.1.2 Other uses of the war paradigm in a counter-terrorism context

The links between terrorism and armed conflict are complex and multifaceted. For example, one of the reasons why there is still no international definition of terrorism is that the UN draft Comprehensive Convention on International Terrorism has been stalled, inter alia, about whether and how acts committed in armed conflict should be excluded from its scope. The international terrorism conventions also are ambivalent about whether they apply in times of armed conflict, with some including exclusionary clauses and others not. Further, in situations of NIACs, States have often referred to their opponents as 'terrorists', and the various acts committed by them as 'acts of terrorism', partly to discredit their enemies and their actions, while prolonged unresolved conflicts have been unanimously recognized as a condition conducive to terrorism by the UN GCTS. Since September 2001, the perception that terrorism and armed conflict are distinct phenomena is progressively changing. The 'war on terror' was aimed at artificially broadening the scope of application of IHL, and in recent years, while the rhetoric has changed and the expression 'war on terror' is no longer favoured,[59] the use of the conflict paradigm in a counter-terrorism context continues. The US still considers itself at war with Al-Qaida, and former-US President Obama sought a new authorization to use force against ISIL from its parliament.[60] Immediately after the Paris attacks in November 2015, former President Hollande, declared itself at war with 'Islamist terrorism',[61] while after the attacks in Brussels in March 2016, the then French Prime Minister confirmed this position,[62] which remains vague and under theorized.

---

[59] See Toby Harnden (2010), 'Barack Obama declares the "War on Terror" is over', *The Telegraph*, 27 May: 'Yet this is not a global war against a tactic – terrorism – or a religion – Islam. (…) We are at war with a specific network, al-Qaeda, and its terrorist affiliates who support efforts to attack the United States, our allies, and partners'. In March 2009, it was already reported that the Obama administration wanted to stop using the expression 'war on terror'. Al Kamen (2009), 'The end of the global war on terror', *Washington Post*, 23 March.

[60] CNN (2015), 'Transcript: President Obama's address to the nation on the San Bernardino terror attack and the war on ISIS', 7 December.

[61] http://www.elysee.fr/declarations/article/discours-du-president-de-la-republique-devant-le-parlement-reuni-en-congres-3/, accessed 10 May 2017.

[62] See (2016), 'Attentats de Bruxelles: «Nous sommes en guerre», dit Manuel Valls', *Le Figaro*, 22 March, http://www.lefigaro.fr/flash-actu/2016/03/

Attempts at considering counter-terrorism operations under the framework of the law of armed conflict continue to be numerous and are multifaceted. They include, for example, the extraterritorial use of armed drones to carry out lethal operations against suspected terrorists. In recent years, lethal drone strikes have increased in numbers and expanded geographically. Indefinite detentions such as those in Guantanamo Bay continue. And even though the war paradigm usually covers extraterritorial actions by States, the use of military courts to try civilian suspects of acts of terrorism also aim at lowering the level of protection that the IHRL framework aims to afford all individuals. In the last few years, the deadliest terrorist groups are involved in armed conflict, either with the State or with other non-State armed groups.[63] This is the case of conflicts involving ISIL in Iraq and Syria, Boko Haram in Nigeria, the Taliban in Afghanistan, and the Al-Qaida 'network', including the Al-Nusra Front, AQAP, AQIM and Al-Shabaab. Their common denominator is that they entertain a certain conflation of legal regimes. Many of the legal questions will be discussed separately in later chapters; This chapter will simply bring some clarification and note a few of the key challenges.

2.1.3 The legal framework

Provided the legality of any action taken to counter terrorism depends on its evaluation within a specific legal framework, the determination of what legal framework is applicable, where and when, is essential. It is clear that in some cases, measures to counter terrorism do take place under the framework of IHL. And, provided that the Security Council itself can designate non-State armed groups as 'terrorist', a group can indeed be both. From a national legal perspective, in some States, jurisdiction can extend to acts of terrorism committed extraterritorially even in the context of an armed conflict while, in others, acts committed in the context of an armed conflict by any party to the conflict are excluded from the definition of terrorist acts. Consequently, any action that is taken under the rubric of 'terrorism' is not determinative, as the 'terrorism' legal framework can operate under the international umbrella of either IHL in conjunction with IHRL, or solely under the umbrella of

---

22/97001-20160322FILWWW00103-attentats-de-bruxelles-nous-sommes-en-guerre-dit-manuel-valls.php, accessed 10 May 2017.

63 Institute for Economics and Peace (2016), 'Global terrorism Index 2016', http://economicsandpeace.org/wp-content/uploads/2016/11/Global-Terrorism-Index-2016.2.pdf, accessed 17 October 2017.

IHRL. In this logic, what is determinative is whether the counter-terrorism action is taken under the framework of IHRL, tainted or untainted by IHL.

The International Committee of the Red Cross' (ICRC) position on the use of the expression 'war against terror' is that 'on the basis of an analysis of the available facts, [it] does not share the view that a global war is being waged and it takes a case-by-case approach to the legal qualification of situations of violence that are colloquially referred to as part of the 'war on terror'. Simply put, where violence reaches the threshold of armed conflict, whether international or non-international, IHL is applicable. Where it does not, other bodies of law come into play.'[64] In the same vein, five UN Special Rapporteurs noted in 2006 that 'the global struggle against international terrorism does not, as such, constitute an armed conflict for the purposes of the applicability of international humanitarian law'.[65]

It is important to clarify that certain conflicts that were placed under the banner of the 'global war against terror', did clearly qualify as armed conflicts for the purpose of the application of IHL. International armed conflicts included the October 2001 to June 2002 conflict in Afghanistan between the US-led coalition and the Taliban regime, and the 2003 international armed conflict in Iraq, between the US-led coalition and the Iraqi regime led by Saddam Hussein. NIACs included the one that started after the election of the Afghan government in June 2002, which opposed the Afghan government and the international forces against non-state armed groups, including the Taliban and Al-Qaeda, and the one in Iraq that started after the end of the formal occupation and the transfer of powers to the Iraqi government in 2004. More recently, the conflicts in Mali and Syria have been considered as NIACs.

Yet the US 'war against terror' encompassed more than these conflicts which qualified as armed conflicts for the purpose of the application of IHL, insofar as it opposed one country against a range of terrorist groups based in a number of other countries. More fundamentally, placing counter-terrorism operations and measures under a war paradigm raises one of the most contentious questions posed by developments since 9/11, which is whether there can exist a single, global or transnational NIACs between a State and one or several non-State armed groups that operate

---

64 See ICRC (2007), 'International humanitarian law and the challenges of contemporary armed conflicts', *International Review of the Red Cross*, **89** (867), 724–25.

65 'Report of the Five UN CHR Rapporteurs on the situation of detainees at Guantánamo Bay', UN Doc. E/CN.4/2006/120, para. 21.

out of a number of different territories – thus linking the applicability of IHL to the person (and their belonging to a group) rather than to the territory. This possibility was the one that was put forward in the 'war on terror', but is also the one used today to carry out lethal drone strikes in States where the threshold for armed conflict is not met (see Chapter 3).

Under IHL, NIACs are conflicts between a State and one or more non-State armed group, or between two or more non-State armed groups. The determination of the existence of a NIAC is made with reference to objective criteria based on facts on the ground, and the criteria to be considered are, first, its intensity and protraction[66] and, second, the degree of organization of the parties to the conflict.[67] Traditionally, there exists a presumption of territorial limitation to the existence of NIACs – because the intensity and protracted nature of a conflict is measured by analysing the frequency and severity of armed attacks within a geographically-limited area. Yet it is now increasingly recognized that it is at least theoretically possible to have a transnational, or global, NIAC with non-State armed groups.[68] However, where individual acts of terrorism take place outside the context of clearly defined armed conflicts, or where lethal drone attacks are carried out outside the context of an existing armed conflict, in practice they do not in themselves trigger the application of the IHL rules applicable to NIACs, because it is not possible to make the twofold demonstration that is required: first, show that intensity and protraction of violence has reached the necessary threshold and, second, show that the terrorist group responsible for the attacks or targeted by a strike is one and the same party to a pre-existing NIAC.[69] As highlighted by the International Criminal Tribunal for the former Yugoslavia (ICTY), these criteria allow to distinguish armed

---

66 International Criminal Tribunal for Rwanda, *Prosecutor v. Musema*, case No. ICTR-96-13-A, judgment of 27 January 2000, para. 248 and *Prosecutor v. Duško Tadić* (Trial Judgment) IT-94-1-T (7 May 1997), para. 562.

67 International Tribunal for the Former Yugoslavia, *Prosecutor v. Duško Tadić*, decision on the defence motion for interlocutory appeal on jurisdiction, case No. ICTY-94-1 (2 October 1995), para. 70.

68 See the written evidence from Christof Heyns, Dapo Akande, Lawrence Hill-Cawthorne and Thompson Chengeta to the UK Joint Committee on Human Rights for the UK Parliamentary Inquiry into UK Policy on the Use of Drones for Targeted Killings (DRO0024), December 2015, http://data.parliament.uk/writtenevidence/committeeevidence.svc/evidencedocument/human-rights-committee/the-uk-governments-policy-on-the-use-of-drones-for-targeted-killing/written/25641.html, accessed 17 February 2016.

69 See Jelena Pejic (2011), 'The protective scope of Common Article 3: More than meets the eye', *International Review of the Red Cross*, **93** (881),

conflict from, inter alia, 'terrorist activity, which are not subject to international humanitarian law'.[70]

Importantly, it has also been argued that accepting the existence of NIACs in these circumstances would also allow the whole world to be a potential battlefield, with the very severe consequences that this can have on all parties to the conflict. Indeed, not only does IHL allow for more flexibility regarding the use of force than the rules applicable outside an armed conflict, IHL is also based on the premise that certain acts of violence against military objectives are not prohibited, and provides for the possibility of proportionate civilian casualties, unlike other international legal frameworks. This should be borne in mind by those claiming the applicability of IHL on a global scale, as it could potentially put their armed forces at greater risk wherever they are located in the world, as well as allow the targeting of individuals in areas otherwise free of hostilities.[71]

It is also essential to bear in mind that in a situation of armed conflict, it is now well settled that IHRL continues to apply, and both IHRL and IHL frameworks act in a complementary and mutually reinforcing way.[72]

195–97. See also 'Special Rapporteur on human rights while countering terrorism', UN Doc. A/68/398, paras. 63–65. See also ICRC, 'much of the ongoing violence taking place in other parts of the world that is usually described as "terrorist" is perpetrated by loosely organized groups (networks), or individuals that, at best, share a common ideology. On the basis of currently available factual evidence it is doubtful whether these groups and networks can be characterised as party to any type of armed conflict, including 'transnational'". ICRC (2001), 'International humanitarian law and terrorism: questions and answers', 1 January, https://www.icrc.org/eng/resources/documents/faq/terrorism-faq-050504.htm, accessed 11 May 2017.

[70] ICTY, Opinion and judgment of 7 May 1997, *Prosecutor v. Dusko Tadic*, No. IT-94-1-T, para. 562.

[71] See International Commission of Jurists (2009), 'Assessing damage, urging action: Report of the eminent jurist panel on terrorism, counter-terrorism and human rights', http://www.un.org/en/sc/ctc/specialmeetings/2011/docs/icj/icj-2009-ejp-report.pdf, accessed 11 May 2017, p. 55, arguing that this is based on the IHL bedrock principle of equality of the parties. See also 'Special Rapporteur on human rights while countering terrorism', UN Doc. A/68/398, para. 63; Pejic (n 69), at 196; and ICRC (n 64), at 724.

[72] See International Court of Justice (1996), 'Legality of the Threat or Use of Nuclear Weapons, Advisory Opinion', I.C.J. Reports 1996, paras. 24 and 25; International Court of Justice (2004), 'Legal Consequences of the Construction of a Wall in the Occupied Palestinian Territory, Advisory Opinion', I.C.J. Reports 2004, para. 106. See also Human Rights Committee (2004), 'General Comment No. 31': 'the Covenant applies also in situations of armed conflict to which the

In addition, as IHRL applies at all times, inherently belongs to all individuals and is key to individual dignity, there is increasing recognition for the pragmatic position that not only State parties to a NIAC, but also non-State armed groups that control territories on which populations live, have human rights obligations.[73] As IHL is neither sufficient nor made to regulate many aspects of the relationship between the ruling authority and individuals within their power, this is a requirement for holding non-State armed groups accountable for the way in which they treat the populations under their control. From the perspective of the rights-holder, it does not matter whether their rights are guaranteed by the *de jure* government, or a non-State armed group, as long as they are able to live with the dignity to which they are entitled.[74]

Critically, the applicable framework is not the result of a choice by a State. As already noted, IHRL is applicable at all times, even in armed

---

rules of international humanitarian law are applicable. While, in respect of certain Covenant rights, more specific rules of international humanitarian law may be specially relevant for the purposes of the interpretation of Covenant rights, both spheres of law are complementary, not mutually exclusive'. UN Doc. CCPR/C/21/Rev.1/Add.13, para. 11.

[73] OHCHR (2011), 'Human rights in armed conflict', http://www.ohchr.org/Documents/Publications/HR_in_armed_conflict.pdf, accessed 17 October 2017, pp. 24 and 25; 'Special Rapporteur on human rights while countering terrorism', UN Doc. A/HRC/29/51, paras. 30 and 31. Note that a number of non-State armed groups have already been considered as holders of human rights obligations, including the Taliban: UNAMA/OHCHR (2013), 'Protection of civilians in armed conflict', February, p. 13; LTTE: 'Report of the Secretary-General's Panel of Experts on Accountability in Sri Lanka', 31 March 2011, para. 188, non-State armed groups in Libya: 'Report of the CoI on LAJ', UN Doc. A/HRC/17/44, 1 June 2011, para. 72. Note also that Article 11 of the Constitution of Abkhazia states that the 'Republic of Abkhazia shall recognize and guarantee the rights and freedoms proclaimed in the Universal Declaration of Human Rights, the International covenants of economic, social, cultural, civil and political rights and other universally recognized international legal instruments'. Already in the early 1990s, during the discussions in relation to the situation in Bosnia and Herzegovina, a member of the UN Human Rights Committee noted that 'thus [the Bosnian Serb authorities] might be asked to explain how they complied with the [ICCPR], not as a successor State, but as an authority in control of a territory'. See Decision on State Succession to the Obligations of the Former Yugoslavia under the International Covenant on Civil and Political Rights (separate opinion Mullerson), Human Rights Committee, in European Human Rights Reports 15 (1993), pp. 233–36.

[74] 'Special Rapporteur on human rights while countering terrorism', UN Doc. A/HRC/29/51, paras. 30 and 31.

conflict,[75] where it complements IHL. IHL applies only when there is a situation of armed conflict, whose existence is determined primarily on the basis of the situation on the ground, according to set criteria such as the intensity and protraction of the conflict and degree of organization of the parties. That the State decides to respond with military means to a terrorist threat, a group designated as terrorist, or one of its members, does not imply that IHL will apply, nor does it displace the applicability of IHRL. Similarly, that a State decides to deny the applicability of IHL to an armed conflict on the basis that non-State armed groups are designated as a terrorist organization, or that war crimes do not apply in NIACs where a person is a member of an organized armed group, does not mean that this is legally correct.[76]

Thus, plainly, attempts at lowering the protection that individuals deserve by artificially applying a war paradigm to measures to counter terrorism does not stand up to legal scrutiny. IHRL applies at all times, and IHL applies when and where there is an armed conflict; that is when the conditions for its existence and threshold are met. Absent an armed conflict, the main legal international framework that regulates the use of force is IHRL. Terrorism needs to be treated as a crime under domestic laws, and should be fought within a law-enforcement paradigm, on a national or international scale. This is the position that was adopted by many countries, which reacted against applying the 'war paradigm', even

---

[75] See 'Legality of the Threat or Use of Nuclear Weapons, Advisory Opinion' (n 72); 'Legal Consequences of the Construction of a Wall in the Occupied Palestinian Territory, Advisory Opinion' (n 72).

[76] See e.g. the adoption in Australia of a new text whose aim is to clarify that certain war crimes do not apply in NIACs where a person is a member of an organized armed group. Criminal Code Amendment (War Crimes) Bill 2016, adopted by both Houses of Parliament on 1 December 2016. Without defining who is a member of an organized armed group, or making a clear distinction between those directly or indirectly supporting organized armed groups, the text may lead to exclude from liability those responsible for the commission of war crimes against individuals who accompany or indirectly support such groups. This distinction is particularly important, and must take into careful consideration the particular role and substantial contributions of the person concerned to the activities of the group, particularly as in conflicts involving groups also qualified as terrorist there is a trend towards excluding such groups from the normal operation of the international humanitarian rights law framework. One aspect of this trend is to attempt to include all persons supporting the armed group – even indirectly – as targetable, even though many individuals who join terrorist groups also involved in armed conflicts will never hold any combat function.

after terrorist attacks had taken place on their soil, treating such acts, instead, as criminal acts.[77]

2.1.4 Use of military courts to try civilians

The 'war paradigm' has also led some States to bring home the militarization of the fight against terrorism, best illustrated by the use of military courts to try individuals accused of acts of terrorism. In the post-2001 context, the US has used Military Commissions to try persons suspected of acts of terrorism as 'enemy combatants', notwithstanding the circumstances of their arrest, in particular whether they were or not taking an active part in hostilities.[78] In turn, this was retroactively used as a justification by some States to continue their use of military or State courts to try civilians accused of acts of terrorism.[79]

While the International Covenant on Civil and Political Rights (ICCPR) does not prohibit the trial of civilians in military or special courts, the UN Human Rights Committee stated that 'military courts should not have the faculty to try cases which do not refer to offences committed by members of the armed forces in the course of their duties'.[80] UN Special Procedures mandate holders have also repeatedly made the more specific point that 'using military or emergency courts to

---

[77] See, for example, the statement of the former UK Director of Public Prosecutions: '... London is not a battlefield. Those innocents who were murdered on July 7, 2005 were not victims of war [...]. We need to be very clear about this. On the streets of London, there is no such thing as a "war on terror", just as there can be no such thing as a "war on drugs". [...] The fight against terrorism on the streets of Britain is not a war. It is the prevention of crime, the enforcement of our laws and the winning of justice for those damaged by their infringement'. International Commission of Jurists (n 71), at 51. See also International Commission of Jurists (n 71), at 54: 'The post September 11 terrorist bombings in London, Madrid and Bali were not treated as acts of war, but as criminal acts, and the authorities applied law enforcement, not military, means to address them'. In Norway, Anders Behring Breivik – who killed 77 people – was convicted of terrorism and premeditated murder by the Oslo District Court, and given the maximum sentence of 21 years' imprisonment in August 2012.

[78] The Special Rapporteur on human rights while countering terrorism has examined this question in depth, see UN Doc. A/HRC/6/17/Add.3.

[79] See International Commission of Jurists (n 71), at 137. On the use of military courts in Egypt until 2009, see 'Special Rapporteur on human rights while countering terrorism', UN Doc. A/HRC/13/37/Add.2.

[80] See UN Doc. CCPR/C/79/Add. 23, para. 9; see also Human Rights Committee (2007), 'General Comment No. 32', UN Doc. CCPR/C/GC/32, para. 22.

try civilians in the name of national security, a state of emergency or counter-terrorism is a regrettably common practice that runs counter to all international and regional standards and established case law'.[81] This potentially raises issues under the right to a fair trial, and particular concerns have been raised regarding the independence and impartiality of the judges; the possibility of full review – in law and fact – of the conviction and sentence; the broad discretion of the executive over these courts; the lower fair trial guarantees that often characterize such courts (prolonged periods of pre-charge and pre-trial detention with inadequate access to counsel, intrusion into the attorney-client confidentiality and strict limitations on the right to appeal and bail); and the lower procedural and evidential standards in these courts that often encourage systematic resort to extra-legal practices such as torture to extract confessions of alleged terrorist suspects. Thus, the use of military tribunals should be limited to trials of military personnel for acts committed in the course of military actions, and the trying of any civilians by military should take place only in limited exceptional situations where resort to such trials is necessary and justified by objective and serious reasons such as military occupation of foreign territory where regular civilian courts are unable to undertake the trials.[82] As noted by the Eminent Jurist Panel, there does not seem to be any convincing reason why military courts would be better equipped than civilian courts to deal with terrorism cases. Rather, the evidence suggests that military courts are used to bypass normal standards applicable in ordinary civilian courts, and to benefit from simplified rules that facilitate the conviction of accused persons.[83]

2.1.5 An emerging international 'terrorism' paradigm?

It is often the case that in NIACs, State parties refer to their opponents as 'terrorists', and the various acts committed by them as 'acts of terrorism'. Yet, the determination that a group is 'terrorist' is irrelevant for the purpose of the application of IHL, or for the evaluation of the lawfulness of the violence.[84] Such a qualification is often done for political reasons, in an effort to discredit the enemy and their actions. In the post 9/11

---

[81] See 'Special Rapporteur on the independence of judges and lawyers', UN Doc. A/68/285, para. 46.

[82] 'Special Rapporteur on human rights while countering terrorism', UN Doc. A/63/223, paras. 24–28.

[83] International Commission of Jurists (n 71), at 139.

[84] See Helen Duffy (2015), *The War on Terror and the Framework of International Law*, 2nd edn (Cambridge: Cambridge University Press), p. 346.

context, it has proven particularly effective, given that the priority of the fight against terrorism meant that in so doing, governments largely shielded their own actions against international criticism. It has been alleged that in the post-2001 context, internal armed conflicts have been redefined as 'wars against terrorism' in numerous countries, including, for example, China,[85] Colombia,[86] Thailand,[87] Macedonia and Russia, with Human Rights Watch noting that 'after September 11, governments from Skopje to Moscow scrambled to cast their own often brutal internal conflicts as part of the new international antiterrorist cause. With too few exceptions, this opportunism went unchecked.'[88]

Yet, in an interesting development, the Security Council is also entertaining a confusion between non-State armed groups parties to NIACs and 'terrorist groups' that commit acts of terrorism. This is particularly visible in the case of ISIL, regarding which the Security Council uses, on the one hand, language borrowed from the criminal law framework, and on the other hand, from the international humanitarian and human rights law framework,[89] the 'apex' of which is the use of the

---

See also Sandra Kraehenmann (2014), 'Foreign fighters under international law', Geneva Academy Briefing No. 7, October, p. 23.

[85] 'For China, the question was how a war on terrorism could be used to intensify a campaign against splittists in Xinjiang'. HRW (2002), 'Human Rights Watch World Report 2002', https://www.hrw.org/legacy/wr2k2/asia4.html, accessed 17 October 2017. See also Fu Hualing (2012), 'Responses to terrorism in China', where it is analysed that 'China responded to 9/11 actively and has used the event to highlight and magnify the terrorist threat in Xinjiang', in Victor V. Ramraj, Michael Hor, Kent Roach and George Williams (eds), *Global Anti-Terrorism Law and Policy*, 2nd edn (Cambridge: Cambridge University Press), p. 347.

[86] See International Commission of Jurists (n 71), at 65; see also Neil Hicks (n 27), 'The impact of counter terror on the promotion and protection of human rights: A global perspective', paper prepared for 'Human Rights in an Age of Terrorism' a conference at the University of Connecticut, 9–11 September, p. 3, which cites the former President of Colombia as saying in 2003 that Colombia's struggle against guerrilla forces is 'working to the same ends' as the US-led global war on terrorism.

[87] See Hicks (n 27), ibid.

[88] See HRW (n 85). Other examples, such as the Philippines and Nepal, may be given.

[89] See e.g. UN Security Council resolution 2170 (2014) and Security Council Presidential Statement on the situation in Syria, UN Doc. S/PRST/2013/15.

expression 'foreign terrorist fighter'.[90] Similarly to States' tactics, this aims at discrediting ISIL's actions, as well as applying the international terrorism sanctions framework to it.[91]

It is critical to ensure that the distinction between the IHL framework, and the 'terrorism' criminal law framework is maintained, as it can have very serious practical consequences, most notably for assessing the lawfulness of the use of force by a non-State armed group involved in an armed conflict.[92] Indeed, in situations short of armed conflict, where IHRL is the main applicable international framework, violence committed by non-State actors against either the State or other non-State actors that is qualified as 'terrorist' by domestic law will always be unlawful and criminal.

Most acts which are considered as terrorist outside the context of an armed conflict are also prohibited under IHL, such as attacks against civilians or civilian objects, or acts qualified by IHL itself as 'terrorist'.[93] Therefore, in situations of armed conflict, there is no legal significance in describing deliberate acts of violence against civilians or civilian objects as 'terrorist' because such acts would already be prohibited, and may even constitute war crimes.[94] However, in NIACs, acts of violence targeting military objectives, whether committed by a State's armed forces or by a non-State armed group party to a NIAC are not prohibited as a matter of IHL. Therefore, some acts which would be considered as terrorist if they were committed outside the context of an armed conflict may be considered as lawful. Should the targeting of legitimate military targets be considered as terrorist – in war as in peace – this would remove the whole *raison d'être* of IHL. Indeed, the distinction between civilian and military targets is at the core of IHL. Qualifying legitimate acts as terrorist would make them prohibited, and in turn would render IHL redundant.

---

90 See 'Special Rapporteur on human rights while countering terrorism', UN Doc. A/HRC/34/61.

91 See 'Special Rapporteur on human rights while countering terrorism', UN Doc. A/HRC/29/51, paras. 35–45.

92 For a full review of this question, see Kraehenmann (n 84), particularly p. 61 *et seq*.

93 Indeed, IHL also contains specific prohibitions that are qualified as acts of terrorism under IHL. For a full review, see Kraehenmann (n 84), at 24–31.

94 ICRC (2011), 'International humanitarian law and the challenges of contemporary armed conflicts', https://www.icrc.org/eng/assets/files/red-cross-crescent-movement/31st-international-conference/31-int-conference-ihl-challenges-report-11-5-1-2-en.pdf, accessed 18 October 2017, p. 50.

An important concern is that in the context of a NIAC, government authorities retain the power to prosecute and punish individuals that violate domestic law, including for acts of terrorism. This 'unfavourable' treatment is often presented as one of the reasons non-State armed groups are reluctant to abide by the rules of IHL, as they lack the incentive to do so. Consequently, adding the qualification of 'terrorist' to all acts committed in armed conflict, including to those that are not prohibited, reduces even more the chances that non-State armed groups party to a NIAC will comply with the rules of IHL.[95] It may also have serious consequences for those, particularly civil society, wishing to engage with them on humanitarian or human rights grounds, as it could be qualified as 'supporting' individuals or entities involved in acts of terrorism, and may also be criminalized under various national laws.[96] It is thus important to preserve the distinction between the IHL/IHRL and the criminal (or law enforcement) framework, as a conflation of these regimes would disserve IHL and, ultimately, the protection of civilians, which is one of IHL's main objectives.

These are not merely theoretical issues. The rhetoric in the Security Council regarding the armed conflict in Syria, particularly the situation in Aleppo where it was alleged that the indiscriminate air strikes carried out by government forces and their allies are war crimes and crimes against humanity,[97] is a cause of great concern. Both Syria's and Russia's representatives to the UN justified the attacks against the city as necessary in the fight against terrorism. In particular, the Russian representative stated that the humanitarian situation in Syria could not be discussed separately from the challenge of combating terrorism, and that easing civilians' suffering would not happen by ceasing counter-terrorism. The representative of Syria decried 'lightheaded' political practices that sent a message to terrorists and encouraged their acts.[98] Earlier, the President of the Russian Federation had said that 'Russia

[95] Id., at 49.

[96] See 'Special Rapporteur on human rights while countering terrorism' (n 22), UN Doc. A/70/371, paras. 31–44; and ICRC (n 64), 2011, p. 50.

[97] OHCHR (2016), 'Zeid tells Council siege and bombardment of Aleppo "constitute crimes of historic proportions"', 21 October, http://www.ohchr.org/EN/NewsEvents/Pages/HRCTacklesAleppoCrisis.aspx, accessed 18 October 2017; HRW (2016), 'Russia/Syria: War crimes in month of bombing of Aleppo', 1 December, https://www.hrw.org/news/2016/12/01/russia/syria-war-crimes-month-bombing-aleppo, accessed 18 October 2017.

[98] See https://www.un.org/press/en/2016/sc12605.doc.htm, accessed 10 May 2017.

would pursue "terrorists" even if they hid among civilians', because 'terrorists' can't be allowed to 'use people as human shields and blackmail the entire world', before adding that 'civilian deaths were the 'sad reality of war'.[99] On 5 December 2016, the Syrian representative described a vetoed draft resolution on a humanitarian ceasefire as one that 'would protect terrorism in Syria'.[100] That war crimes, or crimes against humanity, are committed in the name of countering terrorism is an extremely worrying development and a sharp reminder that for some States the fight against terrorism is a trump card that casts international law aside. It is important to note that IHRL and IHL exist primarily to protect individuals, and that neither are impediments to countering terrorism. That force is used against a group that has been determined to be 'terrorist', even by the UN, does not impact on the applicability of principles of IHL, which primarily aim to protect the civilian population living under its aegis.

2.2 The Externalization of Measures to Limit the Applicability of International Human Rights Law

In the post 9/11 context, some States externalized, or internationalized, some of their counter-terrorism measures, while at the same time positing that human rights obligations are territorial in scope. Through this construction, they attempted to circumvent both their human rights obligations and any accountability for human rights violations caused by their counter-terrorism measures. This position is meant to generally endorse the idea that a State is able to do abroad what it cannot do at home.

Examples abound. This was the construction put forward by the US when placing persons detained in the context of its war on terror in locations outside US territory, such as Guantanamo Bay,[101] to prevent the

---

[99] BBC News (2016), 'Syria conflict: Russian war crimes claim "rhetoric" says Putin', 13 October, http://www.bbc.co.uk/news/world-middle-east-37633256, accessed 18 October 2017.

[100] See http://www.un.org/press/en/2016/sc12609.doc.htm, accessed 10 May 2017.

[101] 'Reply of the Government of the United States of America to the Report of the Five UNCHR Special Rapporteurs on Detainees in Guantanamo Bay, Cuba' (n 52). By simultaneously arguing (until the *Hamdan* overruling in 2006) that IHL did not apply either, the US administration sought to create a 'legal black hole', to which no international or national law applied (see *Rasul v. Bush* (n 56) and *Boumediene v. Bush*, 553 U.S. 723 2008).

application of cruel, inhuman and degrading treatment provisions[102] or access to judicial review of their detention,[103] and the position of some States regarding occupied territories.[104] It was also the argument put forward by States to limit the accountability of troops using lethal force in foreign countries.[105] Following a short reminder of the international legal framework regarding extraterritorial obligations, two examples will be examined: detention and non-refoulement obligations when operating abroad.

2.2.1 Legal framework

Article 2(1) of the ICCPR provides that '[e]ach State party to the Covenant undertakes to respect and to ensure to all individuals within its territory and subject to its jurisdiction the rights recognized in the present Covenant'.[106] This is generally interpreted as meaning that wherever a State exercises jurisdiction, or powers that affect the rights protected by the Covenant, it must comply with the Covenant.[107] The Human Rights Committee has noted, in particular that:

---

[102] This 'loophole' was closed by the US Detainee Treatment Act adopted in 2005, 42 U.S.C. § 2000dd: US Code – Section 2000DD: Prohibition on cruel, inhuman, or degrading treatment or punishment of persons under custody or control of the US government. See also David Luban (2014), 'Just looking for loopholes', Just Security, 19 October, https://www.justsecurity.org/16540/just-loopholes/, accessed 30 March 2016.

[103] Access to habeas corpus was granted through two US Supreme Court rulings: *Rasul v. Bush* (n 56) and *Boumediene v. Bush* (n 101).

[104] See UN Doc. CCPR/C/ISR/CO/3.

[105] See the UK government's position in the European Court of Human Rights in the Grand Chamber case of *Al-Skeini and others v. UK*, App. no. 55721/07 (ECtHR 7 July 2011), paras. 109–119. See also House of Lords judgment, *Al-Skeini v. Secretary of State* [2007] UKHL 26.

[106] For an overview, see Marko Milanovic (2011), *Extraterritorial Application of Human Rights Treaties: Law, Principles and Policy* (Oxford: Oxford University Press).

[107] 'Legal Consequences of the Construction of a Wall in the Occupied Palestinian Territory, Advisory Opinion' (n 72), at p. 136, para. 10; UN Committee against Torture (2004), 'Conclusions and recommendations: United Kingdom of Great Britain and Northern Ireland', UN Doc. CAT/C/CR/33/3, 10 December, para. 4(b); UN Committee against Torture (2006), 'Consideration of Reports Submitted by States Parties under Article 19 of the Convention, United States of America', UN Doc. CAT/C/ USA/CO/2, 25 July, para. 14.

> States Parties are required ... to respect and to ensure the Covenant rights to all persons who may be within their territory and to all persons subject to their jurisdiction. This means that a State party must respect and ensure the rights laid down in the Covenant to anyone within the power or effective control of that State Party, even if not situated within the territory of the State Party.[108]

This must be done without any discrimination of any kind, such as race, colour, sex, language, religion, political or other opinion, national or social origin, property, birth or other status. The Committee against Torture (CAT Committee) stated on several occasions that the Convention against Torture (CAT) applies in any territory under a State party's jurisdiction which is to be understood to include 'all areas under the effective de facto control' of the State party, and 'all persons under the effective control of its authorities, of whichever type, wherever located in the world.'[109] This is also the position of regional human rights bodies.[110] The notions of 'power' and 'effective control' are indicators of whether a State is exercising 'jurisdiction' or governmental powers, the abuse of which human rights protections are intended to constrain.[111]

---

108 Human Rights Committee, 'General Comment No. 31' (n 72), UN Doc. CCPR/C/21/Rev.1/Add.13, para. 10. See also UN Docs. CCPR/CO/78/ISR, para. 11; CCPR/CO/72/NET, para. 8; CCPR/CO/81/BEL, para. 6; UN Human Rights Committee (1981), 'Views of 29 July 1981, *López Burgos v. Uruguay*', Communication No. 52/1979. See also Manfred Nowak (2005), *U.N. Covenant on Civil and Political Rights: CCPR Commentary*, 2nd rev. edn (Kehl: N.P. Engel), pp. 43–5.

109 UN Doc. CAT/C/CR/33/3, para. 4 (b); UN Doc. CAT/C/USA/CO/2, para. 20.

110 Inter-American Commission on Human Rights (IACHR) (2002), 'Request for precautionary measures in favour of detainees being held by the United States at Guantánamo Bay' (12 March), *I.L.M.*, **41**, 532–35. See also IACHR (2002), 'Report on terrorism and human rights', OAS Doc. OEA/Ser.L/V/ 11.116, Doc. 5 rev. 1 corr., 22 October. See also for the European Court of Human Rights which covers overall control over a territory and over an individual: *Loizidou v. Turkey*, App. no. 15318/89 (ECtHR 28 November 1996); *Issa v. Turkey*, App. no. 31821/96 (ECtHR, 16 November 2004); *Bankovic and Others v. Belgium and 16 Other Contracting States*, App. no. 52207/99 (ECtHR, 12 December 2001); *Al-Skeini and Others v. UK*, App. no. 55721/07 (ECtHR, 7 July 2011); *Hirsi Jamaa et al. v. Italy*, App. no. 27765/09 (ECtHR, 23 February 2012).

111 See UN High Commissioner for Human Rights (2014), 'The right to privacy in the digital age', UN Doc. A/27/37, para. 33.

2.2.2 Detentions abroad and non-refoulement obligations

The US argued that human rights law did not apply to persons detained in the context of its war on terror in locations outside US territory,[112] such as Guantanamo Bay.[113] However, according to a correct application of the principles spelt out above, instead of being placed out of reach of international law, IHRL – operating alone or together with the relevant IHL in the case of detainees captured during an armed conflict – apply to all those detainees that were, or still are, detained.[114] All those detained must have access to a judicial authority, to review the legality of their detention,[115] and those that weren't captured in the course of an armed conflict can only be considered to be arbitrarily detained under IHRL.[116] Continued, indefinite detention is arbitrary, and the right of access to courts – with all fair trial guarantees provided by article 14 of the ICCPR – must be provided.

Further, some States that maintained detention facilities outside their territories, such as the UK and the US, in Iraq or Afghanistan, have claimed that the non-refoulement principle was not applicable to the detainees held there, as it is restricted to their own territories. Thus, they transferred detainees to the domestic authorities of Iraq or Afghanistan without assessing any risk of torture.[117] The prohibition of refoulement is

---

[112] 'Reply of the Government of the United States of America to the Report of the Five UNCHR Special Rapporteurs on Detainees in Guantanamo Bay, Cuba' (n 52). By simultaneously arguing (*Hamdan* in 2006) that IHL did not apply either, the US administration sought to create a 'legal black hole', to which no international or national law applied.

[113] Thousands of persons have reportedly been detained by the US as 'enemy combatants', including 779 held at Guantánamo since the prison opened on 11 January 2002. Of those, as at January 2016, 678 have been released or transferred, one was transferred to the US to be tried, and nine have died. Ninety-one men are still held, and 34 of these men have been recommended for release by high-level governmental review processes. See: http://www.closeguantanamo.org/Prisoners#sthash.P4icsZpe.dpuf, accessed on 22 February 2016.

[114] See 'Special Rapporteur on human rights while countering terrorism: Mission to the United States of America', UN Doc. A/HRC/6/17/Add.3, 22 November 2007.

[115] See Article 9(4) ICCPR, and ICRC, 'Customary IHL, Rule 99, Deprivation of Liberty', https://www.icrc.org/customary-ihl/eng/docs/v1_cha_chapter32_rule99, accessed 18 October 2017.

[116] See 'Report by five Special Rapporteurs on the situation of detainees at Guantanamo Bay', UN Doc. E/CN.4/2006/120, paras. 25 and 26. See also Human Rights Committee (2014), 'General Comment No. 35', UN Doc. CCPR/C/GC/35, paras. 15, 24, 32, 36 and 37.

[117] 'Special Rapporteur on torture', UN Doc. A/HRC/13/39/Add.5, para. 241.

also applicable to transfers of detainees in custody beyond the State territories. Otherwise this would give States the possibility to circumvent their obligations by transferring a person to one of their own detention facilities abroad, prior to transferring them to national authorities.[118]

2.2.3 Extraordinary renditions and proxy detention

Since 2005, the details of a related, even more disturbing, practice[119] started to emerge, in which the US – in addition to secretly capturing, transferring and detaining people itself, was also transferring people (so-called 'extraordinary renditions') to other States with poor human rights records and 'harsher' interrogations methods than those applied in the US detention facilities at Guantanamo Bay, Abu Ghraib, Bagram Air Base and similar detention centres abroad, for the purpose of interrogation or detention without charge. Further, terrorist suspects were kidnapped in third States and brought to countries where they were exposed to interrogations involving torture and ill-treatment.[120] This practice, known as 'proxy detention' involves the responsibility of both the State that is detaining the victim and the State on whose behalf or at whose behest the detention takes place. The Central Intelligence Agency (CIA) appears to have been generally involved in the capture and transfer of prisoners, as well as in providing questions for those held in foreign prisons.[121] In some cases, persons have been rendered to other countries precisely to circumvent the absolute prohibition of torture in international

---

118 See 'Special Rapporteur on torture: Study on the phenomena of torture, cruel, inhuman or degrading treatment or punishment in the world, including an assessment of conditions of detention', UN Doc. A/HRC/13/39/Add.5, para. 241.

119 See 'Joint study on global practices in relation to secret detention in the context of countering terrorism of the Special Rapporteur on the promotion and protection of human rights and fundamental freedoms while countering terrorism, Martin Scheinin; the Special Rapporteur on torture and other cruel, inhuman or degrading treatment or punishment, Manfred Nowak; the Working Group on Arbitrary Detention represented by its vice-chair, Shaheen Sardar Ali; and the Working Group on Enforced or Involuntary Disappearances represented by its chair, Jeremy Sarkin', UN Doc. A/HRC/13/42, para. 36.

120 See 'Special Rapporteur on torture', UN Doc. A/HRC/13/39/Add.5, para. 244.

121 See 'Joint study on secret detention' (n 119), paras. 36 and 141.These foreign prisons were allegedly in Jordan, Egypt, Morocco, the Syrian Arab Republic, Pakistan, Ethiopia and Djibouti and likely in Uzbekistan. See 'Joint study on secret detention' (n 119), para. 143.

law[122] ('outsourcing of torture'). A very large number of States have been found complicit in these practices.[123]

The UN Special Procedures mandate holders that examined the practice of secret detention determined that the removal of a person to a State for the purpose of holding that person in secret detention, or the exclusion of the possibility of review by domestic courts of the sending State, can never be considered compatible with the obligation laid down in article 2(2) of the ICCPR.[124] Extraordinary rendition for the purpose of torturing individuals is to be condemned as a clear violation of international law and the non-refoulement principle in particular.[125] In addition, the CAT and other cruel, inhuman or degrading treatment or punishment not only expressly bans torture, but article 4(1) also implicitly prohibits complicity in acts of torture, as it requires each State party to ensure that all acts of torture, including those acts by any person that constitute complicity or participation in torture, are criminal offences under its criminal law. In particular, the CAT Committee has considered complicity to include acts that amount to instigation, incitement, superior order and instruction, consent, acquiescence and concealment.[126] A State is therefore responsible when it was aware of the risk of torture and ill-treatment, or ought to have been aware of the risk, inherently associated with the establishment or operation of such a facility or a given transfer to the facility, and did not take reasonable steps to prevent it.[127] Such practices can amount to a violation of the State's obligation under customary international law of non-refoulement.[128]

The European Court of Human Rights (ECtHR) has taken the international judicial lead in addressing the impunity that continues to surround these practices, with some assistance – mainly at regional level[129] – to address the question of State responsibility, as well as ensure

---

122 See 'Joint study on secret detention' (n 119), para. 287.

123 Including the UK, Germany, Canada and Australia. See 'Joint study on secret detention' (n 119), para. 159.

124 See 'Joint study on secret detention' (n 119), para. 38.

125 See 'Special Rapporteur on torture', UN Doc. A/HRC/13/39/Add.5, para. 245.

126 See 'Joint study on secret detention' (n 119), para. 39.

127 See 'Joint study on secret detention' (n 119), para. 40.

128 See 'Joint study on secret detention' (n 119), para. 43.

129 See 'Alleged secret detentions in Council of Europe member States' ('Marty Report'), AS/Jur (2006) 03 rev, and the follow-up report 'Secret detentions and illegal transfers of detainees involving Council of Europe member States: second report', Doc. 11302 rev.; 'Secretary General's report under article 52 of the European Convention on Human Rights on the question of secret

State accountability for participation in extraordinary rendition. Four cases have addressed the role and responsibility of Council of Europe (CoE) Member States in international, cross-border illegal counter-terrorism operations that are clear, blatant violations of human rights. Thus far, the Court has found three CoE member States – namely Macedonia,[130] Poland[131] and Italy[132] – responsible for their participation in recent past abuses in the context of the 'war on terror', including for

detention and transport of detainees suspected of terrorist acts, notably by or at the instigation of foreign agencies' (SG/Inf (2006) 5, 28 February 2006) and his supplementary report on the subject (SG/Inf (2006) 13, 14 June 2006); European Commission for Democracy through Law (Venice Commission) (2006), 'Opinion on the international legal obligations of Council of Europe members States in respect of secret detention facilities and inter-State transport of prisoners', 17–18 March, Opinion No. 363/2005, CDL-AD(2006)009; Council of Europe (COE) (2007), 'Secret detentions and unlawful inter-state transfers of detainees involving Council of Europe Member States: Second report', Doc. 11302 rev., 11 June, Rapporteur Dick Marty; EP Directorate-General for Internal Policies (2012), 'The results of inquiries into the CIA's programme of extraordinary rendition and secret prisons in European states in light of the new Legal framework following the Lisbon Treaty', May, PE 462.456; EP Committee on Foreign Affairs (2012), 'Opinion on the alleged transportation and illegal detention of prisoners in European countries by the CIA, 6 July, Rapporteur Sarah Ludford, AD/908016EN.doc; CoE (2011), 'Abuse of state secrecy and national security: obstacles to parliamentary and judicial scrutiny of human rights violations', 16 September, Doc. 12714. At the time of writing, the full US Senate Select Committee on Intelligence (SSCI) summary report of the study of the programme of detention and interrogation operated by the Bush-era CIA has still not been made public (SSCI (2014), 'Committee Study of the Central Intelligence Agency's detention and interrogation program', released on 9 December 2014, http://www.intelligence.senate.gov/study2014/sscistudy1.pdf, accessed 8 May 2017), the Council of Europe's Secretary General decided to close, in February 2016, its Article 52 inquiry into European States' roles in the CIA rendition and secret detention. Despite some national inquiries, no one with responsibility for the serious violations has been held accountable; and no effective investigations have taken place at national level. This has led the European Parliament to recently express 'serious concern about the apathy shown by Member States and EU institutions with regards to recognizing the multiple fundamental rights violations and torture which took place on European soil between 2001 and 2006, investigating them and bringing those complicit and responsible to justice'.

130 *El-Masri v. Former Yugoslav Republic of Macedonia*, App. no. 39630/09 (ECtHR, 13 December 2012).

131 *Al Nashiri v. Poland*, App. no. 28761/11 (ECtHR, 16 February 2015); *Husayn (Abu Zubaydah) v. Poland*, App. no. 7511/13 (ECtHR, 16 February 2015).

132 *Nasr and Ghali v. Italy*, App. no. 44883/09 (ECtHR, 23 February 2016).

torture, extraordinary rendition, arbitrary detention and hosting a CIA black site (in the case of Poland).

2.2.4 Surveillance

In respect of mass electronic surveillance and interception, there is increasing evidence emerging regarding the practice of States to outsource surveillance tasks to others. There is credible information to suggest that some governments have systematically routed data collection and analytical tasks through jurisdictions with weaker safeguards for privacy. Reportedly, some governments have operated a transnational network of intelligence agencies through interlocking legal loopholes, involving the coordination of surveillance practice to outflank the protections provided by domestic legal regimes.[133] Both the UN General Assembly and the Human Rights Council have addressed this issue, particularly by affirming that the same rights that people have offline must also be protected online, including the right to privacy.[134]

A continuing issue of serious concern is that of extraterritorial mass surveillance programmes, and the proliferation of laws that authorize asymmetrical protection regimes for nationals and non-nationals. The German parliament recently adopted a text that allows for the bulk surveillance on broad grounds and without judicial supervision of non-German citizens by the Federal Intelligence Service from within Germany.[135] In France, a law on the surveillance of international communications was adopted in 2015,[136] authorizing the mass surveillance of broad categories of persons or geographic areas, providing for long, renewable periods of surveillance and even longer periods of retention, absent judicial supervision. In the US, extraterritorial mass surveillance programmes are still in place, notably those under Section 702 of the Foreign Intelligence Surveillance Amendments Act,[137] and those under Executive Order 12333,[138] which is the primary authority

---

[133] See Report of the UN High Commissioner for Human Rights (2014), 'The right to privacy in the digital age' (n 111), UN Doc. A/HRC/27/37, para. 30.

[134] See GA resolution 68/167 of 18 December 2013 and UN Doc. A/HRC/DEC/25/117.

[135] 'Gesetz zur Ausland-Ausland Fernmeldeaufklaerung des Bundesnachritendienstes', adopted on 21 October 2016.

[136] Loi no. 2015-1556 du 30 novembre 2015 relative aux mesures de surveillance des communications électroniques internationales.

[137] Has been renewed for four years by the FISA Amendments Reauthorization Act of 2017 (H.R. 4478).

[138] Signed by US President Ronald Reagan on 4 December 1981.

under which the National Security Agency (NSA) gathers foreign intelligence, without sufficient safeguards, supervision or oversight.[139] The UN Special Rapporteur on human rights and counter-terrorism has recalled that differential treatment of nationals and non-nationals is incompatible with the principle of non-discrimination, itself inherent in any proportionality assessment. States are legally bound to afford the same protection to nationals and to non-nationals, and to those within and outside their jurisdiction, which is also the position of the UN Human Rights Committee.[140]

In relation to these emerging practices, the UN High Commissioner for Human Rights has noted that:

> [a] State cannot avoid its human rights responsibilities simply by refraining from bringing those powers within the bounds of law. To conclude otherwise would not only undermine the universality and essence of the rights protected by international human rights law, but may also create structural incentives for States to outsource surveillance to each other.[141]

In applying the principles relating to States' extraterritorial obligations, the High Commissioner concluded that:

> digital surveillance may engage a State's human rights obligations if that surveillance involves the State's exercise of power or effective control in relation to digital communications infrastructure, wherever found, for example, through direct tapping or penetration of that infrastructure. Equally, where the State exercises regulatory jurisdiction over a third party that physically controls the data, that State also would have obligations under the Covenant. If a country seeks to assert jurisdiction over the data of private companies as a result of the incorporation of those companies in that country,

---

139 See Faiza Patel (2015), 'Bulk collection under Section 215 has ended … What next?', Just Security, 30 November, https://www.justsecurity.org/27996/bulk-collection-ended-whats-next/, accessed 11 May 2017; Electronic Frontier Foundation (2014), 'A primer on Executive Order 12333: The mass surveillance starlet', 2 June, https://www.eff.org/deeplinks/2014/06/primer-executive-order-12333-mass-surveillance-starlet, accessed on 11 May 2017; ACLU (2016), 'ACLU comments to the Privacy and Civil Liberties Oversight Board on its review of Executive Order 12333', 13 January, https://www.aclu.org/letter/aclu-comments-privacy-and-civil-liberties-oversight-board-its-review-executive-order-12333, accessed 11 May 2017.

140 See 'Special Rapporteur on human rights and counter-terrorism', UN Doc. A/HRC/34/61, para. 33. In relation to the Human Rights Committee, see UN Docs. CCPR/C/GBR/CO/7, para. 24(a), CCPR/C/USA/CO/4, para. 24(a).

141 See Report of the UN High Commissioner for Human Rights (n 111), 'The right to privacy in the digital age', UN Doc. A/HRC/27/37, para. 33.

> then human rights protections must be extended to those whose privacy is being interfered with, whether in the country of incorporation or beyond. This holds whether or not such an exercise of jurisdiction is lawful in the first place, or in fact violates another State's sovereignty.[142]

The specific issue of extraterritorial surveillance and interception of communications has a particular importance in this question. Indeed, the US, appears to make a distinction between the surveillance of US citizens and individuals in US territory, and non-US citizens abroad. While this position which is linked to the question of extraterritorial application of IHRL may be in the process of evolving,[143] the UN Human Rights Committee has articulated concerns that non-US persons enjoy only limited protection against excessive surveillance, and has recommended that measures be taken to ensure that any interference with the right to privacy complies with the principles of legality, proportionality and necessity, regardless of the nationality or location of the individuals whose communications are under direct surveillance.[144]

2.2.5 International intelligence cooperation

The need for international cooperation in the fight against terrorism of a transnational nature has long been recognized.[145] When it became known that the 11 September attacks were in part prepared in Western Europe and that some of the individuals allegedly involved in its preparation were under observation by some European intelligence agencies, the need for more effective and coordinated cooperation between intelligence agencies was widely acknowledged.[146] Yet this type of cooperation – while certainly necessary and legitimate – can pose serious human rights concerns. The imperative of gaining information where terrorist cells are based may lead some States to work with other States that have lower human rights standards, where intelligence agencies are given many (unregulated) powers, or where torture, ill-treatment and other human rights violations are routine. At the receiving end, the shared information

---

142 (n 111), para. 34.

143 For a full review, see Marko Milanovic (2015), 'Human rights treaties and foreign surveillance: Privacy in the digital age', *Harvard Law Review*, **56** (1), 81–146.

144 UN Doc. CCPR/C/USA/CO/4, para. 22.

145 See the pre-2001 GA resolutions entitled 'Measures to eliminate international terrorism', e.g. resolution 46/51 of 9 December 1991.

146 See 'Special Rapporteur on human rights while countering terrorism', UN Doc. A/HRC/10/3, para. 47. This was also a key element of UN Security Council resolution 1373 (2001).

can be used without knowledge of how it was obtained, or with the knowledge that in its collection other States violated IHRL.

The secrecy that surrounds the collection and dissemination of the information,[147] the principles that underlie most intelligence-sharing agreements,[148] the overwhelming need to maintain this type of co-operation with certain States, combined with the limited mandates of national oversight bodies, are all impediments to proper accountability. Yet in the current counter-terrorism context, which includes a manifold increase in reliance on intelligence information as the basis for a number of varied and serious legal and operational measures that can have very serious impacts on the rights of the individuals concerned, such as arrest and detention, decisions on immigration and asylum status, decisions to carry out drone strikes, to restrict freedom of expression or to ban non-governmental organizations (NGOs) and websites – there is a need for a clear legal framework to regulate the sharing of intelligence information between States.

Where States routinely exchange information from countries with poor human rights records, regarding which it is known that they, or their intelligence agencies, routinely engage in human rights violations, such as torture, ill-treatment or arbitrary detention, they are likely to be complicit in the human rights violations in question.[149] Any defence based on the difficulties assessing the origin of the information must be discarded as simply allowing governments to deny responsibility for using information that has been obtained in breach of international law.[150] There is further agreement that the differentiation that is sometimes made between the 'operational' and the 'legal' uses of the information is both unhelpful and unnecessary for the purpose of responsibility. Indeed, not only does it further undermine the absolute prohibition of torture,[151] the mere reliance on information that has been obtained through human rights violations – even for operational

[147] See the references to the agreements within NATO and the Shanghai Cooperation Organisation in the report of the 'Special Rapporteur on human rights while countering terrorism', UN Doc. A/HRC/10/3, para. 49.

[148] See the references to the 'need to know' approach to intelligence distribution and the policy of 'originator control' in 'Special Rapporteur on human rights while countering terrorism' (n 146), UN Doc. A/HRC/10/3, para. 48.

[149] See International Commission of Jurists (n 71), at 85; 'Special Rapporteur on human rights while countering terrorism' (n 146), UN Doc. A/HRC/10/3, para. 55.

[150] 'Special Rapporteur on human rights while countering terrorism' (n 146), UN Doc. A/HRC/10/3, para. 56.

[151] International Commission of Jurists (n 71), at 85.

purposes – inevitably implies a 'recognition of lawfulness' of such practices and can trigger State responsibility.[152] Further, given the wide range of measures that can be impacted by intelligence information, particularly given the increased use of administrative measures in countering terrorism, as well as the increased reliance even in court proceedings on classified information, it is at best naïve to accept this differentiation as a basis for limiting or absolving responsibility. In sum, according to the former Special Rapporteur on human rights and counter-terrorism, it would be contrary to the rule of law for States or their intelligence services to request a foreign entity to undertake activities in their jurisdiction that they could not lawfully undertake themselves. National law should contain an absolute prohibition on intelligence services cooperating with foreign entities in order to evade legal obligations that apply to their own activities.[153]

2.3 Attempts at Circumventing the Absolute Nature of the Prohibition of Torture and Refoulement

In their fight against terrorism, States have repeatedly tried to circumvent the absolute prohibition of torture and of refoulement. As seen, the deliberate internationalization of counter-terrorism measures combined with claims of territorial limitations of the human rights framework through the use of proxy detention, extraordinary rendition, and transfer to other States from detention centres located abroad was one means, another being the simple acceptance, as described above, of information or evidence obtained through torture in foreign countries.

In his capacity as Special Rapporteur on torture, one of the authors of this chapter was struck, during his tenure, at how 'ticking bomb scenarios', no matter how unlikely, appeared to have become the guiding cognitive frame when it came to upholding the protection of human dignity. While fully respecting and understanding the fundamental security challenges with which many States are confronted, and expressing his full support for their legitimate and lawful endeavours to protect their citizens, it was somewhat astounding to see how many alleged 'exceptional circumstances' and 'unique situations' were presented to him. A number of government officials indicated that their country was currently

[152] 'Special Rapporteur on human rights while countering terrorism' (n 146), UN Doc. A/HRC/10/3, para. 55.

[153] 'Special Rapporteur on human rights while countering terrorism: Good practices on legal and institutional frameworks for intelligence services and their oversight', UN Doc. A/HRC/14/46, para. 50.

confronted with an unrivalled and critical security challenge which included the 'global war on terror', and officials of all ranks at least implicitly put the absoluteness and non-derogability of the torture prohibition into question and on some occasions portrayed it as an academic or theoretical, if not naïve, ideal which lacked applicability and a sense of realism. He noted that this is the first time the absolute and non-derogable nature of the prohibition of torture was put into question since the existence of the UN, even in democratic States. He also stressed that there are good philosophical and historical reasons for States agreeing in the aftermath of the Nazi Holocaust that the prohibition of torture should be guaranteed under IHRL as one of the few absolute and non-derogable rights. History, including the recent context of the global 'war on terror' shows that putting the absolute prohibition of torture in question means opening Pandora's box. It will take many years until the global damage that was inflicted on the prohibition of torture as a rule of *jus cogens* is repaired.[154]

2.3.1 The legal framework

The prohibition of torture is one of the few absolute and non-derogable human rights. Article 2(2) CAT holds in unambiguous terms that '[n]o exceptional circumstances whatsoever, whether a state of war or a threat of war, internal political instability or any other public emergency, may be invoked as a justification of torture.'[155] The absolute nature of the prohibition of torture means that the right to personal integrity and dignity – the freedom from torture – cannot be balanced against any other right or concern. Torture must not be balanced against national security interests or even the protection of other human rights. No limitations are permitted on the prohibition of torture. Even under exceptional circumstances such as 'war or a threat of war, internal political instability or any other public emergency', the prohibition of torture remains untouchable (article 4(2) ICCPR).[156]

The principle of non-refoulement is an important principle of international law prohibiting the expulsion, return or extradition of a person to another State where there are substantial grounds for believing that he or

154 'Special Rapporteur on torture' (n 125), UN Doc. A/HRC/13/39/Add.5, paras. 43–45.

155 See also articles 4 and 7 ICCPR. The prohibition against torture is also a part of customary international law, and a norm of *jus cogens.*

156 'Special Rapporteur on torture' (n 125), UN Doc. A/HRC/13/39/Add.5, paras. 40–42.

she would face the risk of being tortured.[157] It is codified in international conventions (article 3 CAT, article 33 Refugee Convention) and considered a part of the prohibition of torture and ill-treatment (article 7 ICCPR, article 3 European Convention on Human Rights (ECHR)) according to the well-established case law of the Human Rights Committee[158] and the ECtHR.[159] Furthermore, it is considered as part of international customary law, thus binding all States irrespective of the ratification of any of the mentioned treaties.[160] As a consequence, States are not only prohibited from subjecting persons to torture by its own authorities but also from sending them to a State where they run the risk of being tortured. This includes the sending of aliens to a State that will send them to a third State where they risk being tortured, so called indirect or 'chain-refoulement'. It is therefore the responsibility of the sending State to assess the general situation in the receiving State and the risk of the particular individual concerned upon return. In sum, the non-refoulement principle is absolute and applies irrespective of the victim's conduct. As noted by the International Court of Justice's (ICJ) Eminent Jurist Panel, some States see non-refoulement as an impediment to effectively fighting terrorism. However, it would be more correct to say that torture and other serious human rights violations are an impediment to refoulement.[161]

2.3.2 Disingenuous Legal Interpretations

In their fight against terrorism, some States have tried to introduce the notion that the protection of national security from the threat of terrorism is a trump card that allows *all* human rights, even those that are absolute, to be weighed against that imperative. States have argued that when fighting terrorism, no right is absolute; all rights can be tempered by the requirement to protect individuals from the threat of terrorism, including absolute rights.

---

[157] See 'Special Rapporteur on torture' (n 125), UN Doc. A/HRC/13/39/Add.5, para. 238.

[158] See e.g. UN Doc. CCPR/C/48/D/470/1991, para. 13.2; UN Doc. HRI/GEN/Rev.7, p. 150 *et seq.*, para. 9.

[159] *Jabari v. Turkey*, App. no 40035/98 (ECtHR, 11 July 2000), para. 38.

[160] Nowak (n 108), Art. 7, para. 45; UN Declaration on Territorial Asylum 1967; GA resolutions 37/95 of 13 December 1982, 48/116 of 20 December 1993; Sanremo Declaration on the Principle of Non-Refoulement; UNHCR ExCom Conclusions on International Protection No. 25 (1982), No. 55 (1989), No. 79 (1996).

[161] International Commission of Jurists (n 71), at 102.

In the US, the initial 'torture memos'[162] argued that the prohibition of torture required the intentional infliction of severe pain of the level associated with death and organ failure (a standard imported from a health benefits statute having no relevance to the issue at hand, and aimed at highlighting that only an extraordinarily high degree of pain amounts to torture); that an interrogator could inflict even that level of severe pain as long as he did not 'specifically intend' to do so; that no criminal law could constrain the president as commander in chief, and that he could order outright torture; and that an interrogator who engages in torture could defend his behaviour by claiming that it was done because of 'necessity' or because it was required for self-defence – of the nation, not of the interrogator himself – even where no imminent threat was posed. A review of the legality of these memos in 2005[163] concluded that the CIA could continue to engage in whatever coercive tactics it requested, that it did not need to change its practices, despite the fact that the law, at least for public consumption, had grown increasingly restrictive with respect to interrogation tactics. The Legal Advisor reasoned that the relevant standard under US law for what constitutes 'cruel, inhuman, or degrading' is whether government conduct 'shocks the conscience', a due process test, which amounts to the exercise of power without any reasonable justification in the service of a legitimate government objective and concluded that the CIA enhanced interrogation programme would not shock the conscience as no government objective can be more compelling than the security of the nation, which is that pursued by interrogators. He also noted that not all conduct could be justified by sufficiently weighty government interest, but that in the present case, not only the techniques do not amount to torture the government also sought to 'minimize the risk of injury or any suffering that does not further the Government's interest in obtaining actionable intelligence'.[164] This amounts to saying that 'whether prisoner abuse is cruel, inhuman or

---

[162] Referred to as three documents prepared by the Office of the Legal Counsel at the United States Department of Justice and signed in August 2002 ('Yoo, Bybee, Bradbury Memos').

[163] May 2005, issued by the Office of the Legal Counsel and signed by Stephen Bradbury.

[164] See David Cole (2010), 'The sacrificial Yoo: Accounting for torture in the OPR Report', Georgetown Public Law and Legal Theory Research Paper No. 10-73, J. *Nat'l Security L. & Pol'y*, **4**, 455–64, at 457–60; Manfred Nowak (2006), 'What practices constitute torture? US and UN Standards', *Human Rights Quarterly*, **28**, 809–41.

degrading depends not on the abuse, but on the motive of the interrogator'.[165] These practices were stopped first by the 2005 Detainee Treatment Act, as well as through President Obama's Executive Order 13491 on Ensuring Lawful Interrogations.

Other States argued that it is necessary to deport dangerous individuals in order to protect their communities from terrorist threats.[166] They thus tried to introduce a test of reasonableness applicable to terrorist suspects, balancing the absolute rights of the individual against the threat to national security. While this approach has had some support, for example, from the Canadian Supreme Court in its 2002 *Suresh* judgment, where it was accepted that refoulement could occur in exceptional circumstances if a substantial risk to the national security of the State was proven,[167] it has been rejected by the CAT Committee, which confirmed the absolute nature of article 3 on numerous occasions.[168] Similarly, the ECtHR has discarded any 'balancing act'. In the case of *Saadi v. Italy*, the UK made a third party intervention, in which it claimed that the security risk posed by an individual's dangerousness ought to be weighed against the risk to the individual in the receiving State. It was argued that where an individual is suspected of involvement in terrorism, the standard of proof that expulsion would constitute a breach of article 3 ought to be the 'more likely than not' standard rather than the 'real risk' standard currently applied. The Court, however, rejected this reasoning. While recognizing the danger of terrorism and the 'immense difficulties' for States to protect their communities, it has stated that this 'must not, however, call into question the absolute nature of Article 3'.[169] The Court qualified the possible 'balancing' exercise as misconceived, noting that:

---

[165] See also David Luban (2014), 'Just looking for loopholes' (n 102), Just Security, 19 October.

[166] See 'Special Rapporteur on torture' (n 122), UN Doc. A/HRC/13/39/Add.5, para. 240.

[167] Supreme Court of Canada, *Manickavasagam Suresh v. Canada (Minister of Citizenship and Immigration)* 2002 SCC 1. File No.: 27790. No Canadian court has found that such 'exceptional circumstances' exist.

[168] See e.g. UN Doc. CAT/C/18/D/39/1996, para. 14.5; UN Doc. CAT/C/SR.652, para. 59; UN Doc. CAT/C/NPL/CO/2, para. 17; UN Doc. CAT/C/FRA/CO/3, para. 6. In *Tapia Paez v. Sweden*, the Committee stated that '[t]he nature of the activities in which the person concerned engaged cannot be a material consideration when making a determination under article 3 of the Convention', UN Doc. CAT/C/18/D/39/1996, 28 April 1997, para. 14.5.

[169] *Saadi v. Italy*, App. no. 37201/06 (ECtHR, 28 February 2008), para. 137. Note, that in a later case with a similar outcome, Lithuania, Portugal, Slovakia

> [t]he concepts of 'risk' and 'dangerousness' in this context do not lend themselves to a balancing test because they are notions that can only be assessed independently of each other. Either the evidence adduced before the Court reveals that there is a substantial risk if the person is sent back, or it does not. The prospect that he may pose a serious threat to the community if not returned does not reduce in any way the degree of risk of ill treatment that the person may be subject to on return.[170]

2.3.3 Diplomatic assurances

In order to circumvent the absolute prohibition of torture in cases where an individual would normally be at risk of torture if deported to a third country, some States have relied on 'diplomatic assurances' obtained from foreign authorities that they would refrain from torturing an individual upon return. In some cases, general Memoranda of Understanding have been concluded with third countries.[171] This practice raises a number of serious human rights concerns. The UN High Commissioner for Human Rights has emphasized that, as a practical matter, these arrangements do not work as in reality they do not provide adequate protection against torture and other ill-treatment, nor, as a legal matter, can they nullify the obligation of non-refoulement.[172] In one of the author's capacity as Special Rapporteur on the question of torture, the practice of diplomatic assurances has been repeatedly criticized as 'nothing but attempts to circumvent the absolute prohibition of torture and non-refoulement'.[173] Indeed, diplomatic assurances are an unreliable and ineffective instrument for the protection against torture, as witnessed by numerous cases where suspected terrorists were subjected to torture upon return despite of given assurances and guarantees.[174]

---

and the UK made similar arguments. See *A. v. the Netherlands*, App. no. 4900/06 (ECtHR, 20 July 2010).

170 *Saadi*, ibid., para. 139.

171 The UK has signed such agreements with Jordan, Libya, Lebanon and Algeria. See generally on this: 'Special Rapporteur on torture' (n 125), UN Doc. A/HRC/13/39/Add.5, para. 244; UN Doc. E/CN.4/2006/6, para. 29; Manfred Nowak and Elizabeth McArthur (2008), *The International Convention Against Torture, A Commentary* (New York: Oxford University Press), p. 216, fn. 474.

172 See, for example, 'Report of the UN High Commissioner for Human Rights', UN Doc. A/HRC/4/88 and the High Commissioner's statement on Human Rights Day, December 2005, http://www.ohchr.org/EN/NewsEvents/Pages/DisplayNews.aspx?NewsID=2117&LangID=E, accessed 1 March 2016.

173 See 'Special Rapporteur on torture' (n 125), UN Doc. A/HRC/13/39/Add.5, para. 243; UN Doc. E/CN.4/2006/6, para. 32; UN Doc. A/HRC/10/44/Add.2, para. 68.

174 See also Committee against Torture, views on communication No. 233/2003, *Agiza v. Sweden*, 20 May 2005 (A/60/44, annex VIII, s. A), and

The main concerns are that the assurances are sought mostly from countries with a proven record of torture and mostly in relation to persons belonging to a high-risk group (e.g. 'Islamic fundamentalists'). Assurances are not legally binding and thus unlikely to be complied with by States who otherwise violate their binding violations under international law. In addition, the authority providing the assurance might not have the power to enforce their compliance vis-à-vis its own security forces. Diplomatic assurances cannot be and are often not securely monitored, as even the best monitoring mechanisms (e.g. ICRC, European Committee for the Prevention of Torture and Inhuman or Degrading Treatment or Punishment) are no guarantee against torture. They neither provide for sanctions nor for recourses for the victims in case of a violation.[175] In sum, this practice leads to an erosion of the principle of non-refoulement. It encourages States to seek an exception to their obligation instead of using all their diplomatic and legal powers as States parties to hold other States parties accountable for their violations. In cases of violations of the principle upon return, despite given assurances, both the sending and receiving States have a common interest in denying it and exert pressure to blur accountability.[176]

The CAT Committee, the Human Rights Committee, and the ECtHR have not generally opposed diplomatic assurances in principle. They have nonetheless clarified that they do not absolve a State from its obligation to assess the risk of torture in the individual circumstances of the case. In the highly publicized case of *Othman* (Abu Qatada)[177] regarding the envisaged deportation of an individual to Jordan, the ECtHR accepted the deportation of the individual in question, despite noting that '[a]ssurances are not in themselves sufficient to ensure adequate protection against the risk of ill-treatment'[178] and that 'the picture painted by the reports of United Nations bodies and NGOs of torture in Jordanian prisons is as consistent as it is disturbing (...) torture remains (...) "widespread and routine"'.[179] The Court noted that it did not 'consider that the general

Human Rights Committee, views on communication No. 1416/2005, *Alzery v. Sweden*, 25 October 2006 (A/62/40 (vol. II), annex VII).

[175] 'Special Rapporteur on torture, Report to the Commission on Human Rights', UN Doc. E/CN.4/2006/6, 23 December 2005, para. 31.

[176] 'Special Rapporteur on torture' (n 125), UN Doc. A/HRC/13/39/Add.5, para. 243.

[177] *Othman (Abu Qatada) v. the UK*, Appl. no. 8139/09 (ECtHR 17 January 2012).

[178] Ibid., at para. 187.

[179] Id., at para. 191.

human rights situation in Jordan excludes accepting any assurances whatsoever from the Jordanian Government. Instead, the Court considers the UK and Jordanian governments have made genuine efforts to obtain and provide transparent and detailed assurances to ensure that the applicant will not be ill-treated upon return to Jordan.'[180] In such circumstances, one is left to wonder in what cases the Court would give no weight whatsoever to such assurances. The Court's reasoning sits rather uncomfortably with the CAT Committee's recommendations that diplomatic assurances should only be relied upon with regard to States which do not systematically violate the UN CAT's provisions.[181]

2.4. Increased Reliance on Intelligence Information and (Ab)use of National Security

2.4.1 Intelligence information as a basis for rights-limiting measures

Another defining feature of the post-2001 context has been the increased use of intelligence information as a basis for various rights-limiting counter-terrorism measures. This is due, first, to the view of some States that 'traditional' law-enforcement is useless in the face of the new terrorist threat. This is what Vice President Cheney meant when he referred to the need to increasingly work on 'the dark' side.[182] Perhaps another way of putting this argument is that given the potentially devastating effect of any terrorist attack, there is a need to take effective, flexible and speedy measures to prevent the occurrence of acts of terrorism. And preventive information-gathering on international terrorist groups will often be the result of transnational intelligence cooperation. Given the complexities of international inquiries and prosecutions, particularly when much of the information comes from foreign intelligence agencies, States have attempted, where possible, to use the information collected through intelligence or received through intelligence sharing as

---

180 Id., at para. 194.

181 UN Doc. CAT/C/USA/CO/2, para. 21.

182 'We also have to work, through, sort of the dark side, if you will. We've got to spend time in the shadows in the intelligence world. A lot of what needs to be done here will have to be done quietly, without any discussion, using sources and methods that are available to our intelligence agencies, if we're going to be successful. That's the world these folks operate in, and so it's going to be vital for us to use any means at our disposal, basically, to achieve our objective'. US Vice-President Dick Cheney (2001), 'Meet the press', interview by Tim Russert, NBC News, 16 September.

such, without needing to 'transform' it into hard evidence that can be used in a court of law. Consequently, in the post-9/11 context, there has been a surge in the use of executive decisions based on confidential intelligence information against individuals regarding whom there is an alleged suspicion of involvement in acts of terrorism or who are vaguely defined as a threat to national security. The administrative nature of these measures allows States to by-pass more stringent criminal law procedures, protect sources, and maintain good diplomatic relations with other States with which information is exchanged.

A broad range of counter-terrorism measures are concerned, from detention (i.e. preventive administrative detention on grounds of national security; administrative detention for extradition purposes); to measures that limit freedom of movement within and limit entry or departure from a State (control orders, retention of travel documents), measures to limit spoken or written expression (measures that prevent certain individuals from speaking in public, or that allow executive authorities to block websites in the absence of any initial judicial control or ex-post facto judicial recourse[183]), as well as measures to block financial resources (the listing of terrorist suspects). These measures can have a very serious impact on the individuals to whom they apply and their families. They can also have a much broader negative impact, as unjustified or secret measures may give the impression that they are arbitrary, regardless of whether they are or not. In turn, this can alienate certain particularly targeted communities,[184] or even withdraw the trust that societies place in their governments that they are rightly and fairly countering terrorism.

Another issue at least worth mentioning is the strong link between the work of intelligence bodies, whose aim is to detect potential national security threats, including terrorist threats, by gathering data and information in such a way as not to alert those targeted, through a range of special investigative techniques such as secret surveillance, interception and monitoring of (electronic) communications, secret searches of premises and objects, the use of infiltrators,[185] and the increased criminalization of preparatory activities, which can be several steps away from the actual commission of acts of terrorism. The further away these inchoate offences are from the criminal terrorist act, the more they rely on *mens rea* rather than *actus reus* and, as no act of terrorism has been committed,

---

183 'Special Rapporteur on human rights while countering terrorism', UN Doc. A/HRC/31/65, UN Doc. para. 40.

184 International Commission of Jurists (n 71), at 92.

185 'Special Rapporteur on human rights while countering terrorism', UN Doc. A/HRC/10/3, para. 26.

their discovery heavily relies on intelligence information. In turn, this can blur the lines between intelligence information and the collection of evidence.

It is clear that under IHRL, States have not only a right, but a duty, to prevent acts of terrorism. Indeed, States have an obligation to take positive measures to protect the lives and security of individuals under their jurisdiction.[186] At the same time, all of the measures adopted that impact on individual human rights must comply with the international human rights framework; in particular, they must be provided by law, strictly necessary and proportionate, and must not be discriminatory. In addition, as often the only way to ensure compliance with these requirements is to ensure a possibility of judicial review, such an option must be open, preferably ex-ante and ex-post facto, with all the guarantees that are attached to such review under IHRL. It appears however that, often, administrative counter-terrorism measures taken on the basis of intelligence information do not comply with such requirements; in some cases, they even seem to be adopted precisely to by-pass the judicial process altogether, and allow for simplified, expeditious, less stringent procedures, where executive authorities are able to act on the basis of suspicion rather than evidence.

This increased use of intelligence information raises two main issues. First, when the authorities assert the confidential nature of the information used as a basis for the adoption of rights-limiting administrative measures – either because it is too vague to be used in court, or because sources and methods of work must be protected – the possibility for individuals concerned to be able to defend themselves of the actions for which they are sanctioned is extremely challenging. Second, the mere existence of administrative measures rooted in intelligence information creates an ever-more important need for information that can be used in this way. In turn, this has led to increased powers given to intelligence agencies. In many States, intelligence agencies have been allowed to detain and interrogate individuals, powers that traditionally lie with law-enforcement agencies. Unfortunately, this increase in power has rarely been combined with a simultaneous import of the checks and balances that are normally associated with law-enforcement powers. Due to the low levels of oversight of intelligence agencies, any increase in their powers creates a risk for human rights protection.

---

[186] Office of the High Commissioner for Human Rights (2008), 'Terrorism, counter-terrorism and human rights, Fact Sheet No. 32', July, pp. 1 and 8.

The former Special Rapporteur on human rights and counter-terrorism has shown concern that in several countries the power shift from law enforcement agencies to intelligence agencies for countering and preventing terrorist threats was accomplished precisely to circumvent the necessary safeguards in a democratic society, thereby abusing the usually legitimate secrecy of intelligence operations. He noted that this shift could ultimately endanger the rule of law, as the collection of intelligence and the collection of evidence about criminal acts becomes more and more blurred. In particular, he highlighted that this can lead to a situation where States begin preferring to use undisclosed evidence gathered by intelligence agents in administrative proceedings over attempts to prove guilt beyond reasonable doubt in a criminal trial.[187] In this respect, a good practice is that '[i]f intelligence services possess powers of arrest and detention, they comply with international human rights standards on the rights to liberty and fair trial, as well as the prohibition of torture and inhuman and degrading treatment'.[188]

2.4.2 Administrative detention

As former UN High Commissioner Louise Arbour noted:

> [a]dministrative measures are used to effect the detention of an individual much earlier in an investigation than would be required under criminal law principles such as the presumption of innocence. In my view, the onus should be squarely on governments to establish that the procedures used in 'standard' criminal investigations (…) which allow the arrest to be made close to the charge, are unsuitable to their counter-terrorism efforts.[189]

Indeed, in their counter-terrorism efforts, States have increased their use of two specific kinds of detention, which are both outside the criminal justice process and can therefore both be qualified as administrative detention: (1) the detention of individuals in the context of deportation and extradition,[190] and (2) the preventive detention on grounds of

---

[187] 'Special Rapporteur on human rights while countering terrorism' (n 146), UN Doc. A/HRC/10/3, para. 37.

[188] 'Special Rapporteur on human rights while countering terrorism', UN Doc. A/HRC/14/46, Practice 29.

[189] Louise Arbour (2006),'In our name and on our behalf', Chatham House, 15 February.

[190] See e.g. UK's Part IV of the 2001 Anti-Terrorism, Crime and Security Act, s. 23(1), which allowed the indefinite detention of non-UK citizens who could not be deported; Canada's 'Security Certificates', Immigration and Refugee Protection Act, S.C. (2001), c.27, s. 34.

national security.[191] While many States already had in their legal arsenal some form of administrative preventive detention on national security grounds, other States have introduced or increased the detention of individuals on the grounds that they are suspected of being engaged in terrorist activities or are a danger to national security following a determination by one or several members of the executive in the post-2001 context. Such detention can be easily abused, and is permitted under the ICCPR in very limited circumstances 'where the person concerned constitutes a clear and serious threat to society that cannot be contained in any other manner'.[192] The ECHR, for its part, does not allow for such detention, and the ECtHR has on a number of occasions found 'internment and preventive detention without charge to be incompatible with the fundamental right to liberty (...), in the absence of a valid derogation under Article 15'.[193] The former Special Rapporteur on human rights while countering terrorism has highlighted that the use of 'administrative detention' as a counter-terrorism tool against persons on the sole basis of a broadly formulated element of suspicion that a person forms a 'threat to national security' or similar expressions that lack the level of precision required by the principle of legality was of special concern, particularly as much of the information concerning the reasons for such detention is often classified, so that the detainee and his or her

191 See Singapore's Internal Security Act (ISA), in force since Singapore's independence in 1965, which allows preventive detention where the president is subjectively satisfied that the detention is necessary for the purposes of national security, public order or essential services. See Chapter 143, s. 8 of the ISA; Israel's 1979 Emergency Powers (Detention) Law, which allows for the detention of individuals by the executive for State or public security, renewable on a six-month basis; Australia's Control Orders, s. 104.4 of the Criminal Code (amendments 2005); In the UK, the Prevention of Terrorism Act 2005 allowed the Home Secretary to restrict an individual's liberty for the purpose of 'protecting members of the public from a risk of terrorism'.

192 Human Rights Committee, *David Alberto Campora Schweizer v. Uruguay*, Communication No. 66/1980, para. 18.1.

193 *A and Others v. UK*, App. no. 3455/05 (ECtHR, 19 February 2009), para. 172. In this case, the British government argued that 11 individuals were detained on national security grounds with a view to deportation in their home country (i.e. detention of aliens under article 5(1)(f)). The European Court requalified the legal basis for detention (para. 191) and noted that '[I]t is, instead, clear (...) that the applicants were certified and detained because they were suspected of being international terrorists and because it was believed that their presence at liberty in the United Kingdom gave rise to a threat to national security'.

lawyer have no access to this information and thereby no effective means of contesting the grounds of the detention.[194]

Access to courts is essential in this context. It is important to recall that all persons who are detained, whatever the reason or legal basis for their detention, and wherever they are detained, must have access to courts to review the legality of their detention.[195] The Court must be able to carry out a substantive review. Even though the ECHR does not apply to the specific context of preventive security on grounds of national security, the ECtHR provides interesting and useful guidance on the review procedure and the use of secret intelligence information regarding detention in the context of deportation and extradition. The ECtHR notes that although there is no uniform standard to be applied irrespective of the context, '[t]he reviewing court must not have merely advisory functions, but must have the competence to "decide" on the "lawfulness" of the detention and to order release if detention is unlawful'.[196] In all cases, the proceedings must be adversarial and must always ensure equality of arms between the parties.

This requirement is particularly relevant, as increased reliance on intelligence for countering terrorism has often been done without adequate consideration for the due process safeguards necessary to protect against abuses. Not only can the information used be partial, overstated, misunderstood, incomplete, or simply wrong, but in the absence of publicity of the 'information' neither the judge nor the individual concerned may be in a position to rectify the facts.[197] The ECtHR has admitted the use of intelligence in principle, but noted that '(…) there may be restrictions on the right to a fully adversarial procedure where strictly necessary in the light of a strong countervailing public interest, such as national security, the need to keep secret certain police methods of investigation or the protection of the fundamental rights of another person. There will not be a fair trial, however, unless

---

194 'Special Rapporteur on human rights while countering terrorism', UN Doc. A/63/223, paras. 19 and 20.

195 Article 9(4) ICCPR, which contains a broad right of *habeas corpus.* See also article 5(4) ECHR, and Article 7 American Convention on Human Rights.

196 *A and Others v. UK* (n 193), App. no. 3455/05 (ECtHR, 19 February 2009), para. 202.

197 As noted by the Supreme Court of Canada: 'The judge (…) is not in a position to identify errors, find omissions, or assess the credibility and truthfulness of the information in the way the named person would be'. Supreme Court of Canada, *Charkaoui v. Canada (Minister of Citizenship and Immigration)*, 2007 SCC 9, para. 63.

any difficulties caused to the defendant by a limitation on his rights are sufficiently counterbalanced by the procedures followed by the judicial authorities'.[198] Whether the review procedure provides sufficient guarantees to protect the detainees' rights despite the use of secret information must be examined on a case-by-case basis, but various elements to be considered include whether the judges are able to consider both the 'open' and 'closed' material, whether the applicant can appoint or have appointed a 'security-cleared counsel' who is able to consider the 'closed' material, and act on the defendant's behalf, and whether recommendations can be made regarding the need to de-classify some of the material.

In sum, the detention of terrorist suspects on grounds of national security is problematic. On the practical side, given that in order to be legal such detention can only be temporary, its benefits outside the context of true emergencies that threaten the existence of the nation must be questioned. Where individuals have committed crimes of terrorism, they should be tried in proceedings to which all fair trial guarantees apply. It is indeed argued that the right to a fair trial enshrined in all international and regional human rights instruments also includes the right *to* a trial. States should not be allowed to circumvent the safeguards protecting criminal defendants by detaining them as terrorist suspects without charging them.[199] In addition, given the very serious impact that detention can have on individuals, their families, their communities and society as a whole, full respect for due process and the rule of law not only reduces the threat of terrorism by showing that the criminal justice system is capable of punishing those responsible for violations of the law, it also increases the State's credibility in enforcing the law, and ensures that the fragile trust that the individuals place in their authorities that they are not taking arbitrary, overly broad or discriminatory measures in countering terrorism is maintained.

---

198 *A and Others v. UK* (n 193), para. 205.

199 This is the point made by the UN Working Group on Arbitrary Detention in the case of *Satray v. Malaysia* (Opinion No. 32/2008, U.N. Doc. A/HRC/13/30/Add.1 at 123 (2010)), in which the Working Group noted that Mr Satray had been detained for more than six and a half years without any charges being brought against him, and without the possibility of a fair and public hearing by an independent and impartial tribunal. During this time, the government had not produced any evidence to substantiate its accusation that he was a member of the Jemaah Islamiyyah. Based on Article 10 Universal Declaration of Human Rights (UDHR), the Working Group considered that no one should be detained without trial.

2.4.3 State secrecy provisions

Another key issue has been the broad invoking of national security concerns as a blanket bar to access to justice.[200] This issue will be addressed in greater detail in the chapter on accountability (Chapter 8), but also needs to be mentioned in the present context due to its close ties with ways in which States have broadly responded in a post-9/11 context. As already noted, there are many reasons why a State would want to keep its intelligence information confidential, notably to protect the methods of its intelligence agencies, to protect its agents on the ground, and to protect its diplomatic relations with other States with which it is cooperating on intelligence matters. For example, when asked to release documents on the detention and interrogation of Binyam Mohamed, regarding which there had been allegations that the UK government had been involved in his ill-treatment, the UK refused at first, arguing that releasing the documents without US permission would damage the UK's relationship with the US, and that the US would cut intelligence-sharing ties with the UK. This reasoning was rejected by UK courts, which instead highlighted the important role played by the UK in Binyam Mohamed's interrogation, and decided that the information concerning his treatment – including information received from the CIA – was evidence of the UK government's complicity in his torture, and should thus be de-redacted. The government was prohibited from using secret evidence in its defence, and it was required that allegations of wrong-doing be heard in public.[201] In the same vein, some States that entirely depend on other States for their access to intelligence are very concerned about protecting the confidential information that is provided to them. Canada is a case in point.[202] Due to its special relationship in intelligence cooperation, and long borders with the US, as well as fears about its security expressed by the US as revealed by Canada being singled out in the US' Patriot Act,[203] Canada's response in a post-9/11 context has been

---

200 U.N. Doc. A/63/223, para. 13.

201 For a summary of this case, see Open Society Justice Initiative (OSI) (2013), 'Globalizing torture: CIA secret detention and extraordinary rendition', OSI, https://www.opensocietyfoundations.org/sites/default/files/globalizing-torture-20120205.pdf, accessed 13 May 2013, pp. 115–17.

202 See the analysis of Canada's response to 9/11: Kent Roach (2011), 'Canada responds: Border and human security', in Roach (n 26), at 361–425.

203 See Uniting And Strengthening America By Providing Appropriate Tools Required To Intercept And Obstruct Terrorism (USA Patriot Act) Act of 2001, 115 STAT. 272 PUBLIC LAW 107–56—OCT. 26, 2001, Title 4, Subsection A, 'Protecting the Northern Border'.

to assuage the concerns of its southern neighbour.[204] In doing so, it enhanced its intelligence cooperation in various ways,[205] as well as its secrecy provisions as part of its 2001 anti-terrorism legislation.[206]

While States may limit the disclosure to the general public of specific information which is important for the protection of national security, for instance about the sources, identities and methods of intelligence agents, many States have gone far beyond what is absolutely necessary. State secrecy doctrines have been used to conceal illegal acts from judicial authorities. As noted by the ECtHR, '[t]he concept of "State secrets" has often been invoked to obstruct the search for the truth'.[207] In the case of *Nasr*, the Court noted that the legitimate principle of 'State secrecy' had clearly been applied in order to ensure that those responsible did not have to answer for their actions.[208] Secrecy can lead to impunity and a lack of accountability for serious human rights violations, which can frustrate the victims' right to truth. The former UN High Commissioner for Human Rights importantly noted that legitimate national security considerations do not include governmental interests and activities that constitute grave crimes under IHRL, let alone policies that are precisely calculated to evade the operation of human rights law.[209]

2.5 The Instrumentalization of Various Branches of National and International Law to Counter-Terrorism

One of the key defining trends of the fight against terrorism since 11 September 2001 has been the use by States of various parts of their legal arsenal to counter-terrorism. In many States, counter-terrorism measures have not remained confined to criminal law. Rather, States have

---

204 Roach (n 26), at 361.

205 See in particular the case of Maher Arar, in which the Canadian Police Force passed on inaccurate information to its American counterparts, which eventually contributed to Arar's detention and subsequent rendition to Syria, where he was detained and tortured for almost a year. See the Dennis O'Connor (2006), 'Report of the Commission of Inquiry into the Actions of Canadian Officials in Relation to Maher Arar, Analysis and Recommendations', Government of Canada Publications.

206 Roach (n 26), at 387–89.

207 *El-Masri v. Macedonia* (n 130), App. no. 39630/09 (ECtHR, 13 December 2012), paras. 191–93.

208 *Nasr and Ghali v. Italy* (n 132), App. no. 44883/09 (ECtHR, 23 February 2016), para. 272.

209 Observations on behalf of the High Commissioner for Human Rights to the European Court of Human Rights in *El-Masri* (n 130), ibid.

used their immigration laws, citizenship laws, banking laws, and laws applicable to civil society to address the threat posed by terrorism. Measures have been adopted in the field of development, humanitarian assistance, but also education and health, for example. The seeping of measures to counter-terrorism in almost all areas regulated by the State can have very serious human rights consequences. This section will focus on three examples: the use of immigration laws; the regulation of civil society through laws to address the financing of terrorism; and impact of counter-terrorism legislation on the right to development.

2.5.1 Immigration law

States have increasingly placed their immigration policies and laws at the centre of their counter-terrorism strategies. This was partly to respond to Security Council resolution 1373, which required States to ensure that terrorists do not abuse refugee status.

As examined in greater detail by Ben Emmerson in Chapter 3, with terrorist groups gaining control of territory and participating in armed conflicts in a number of regions, and governments, international organizations and civil society increasingly concerned about violent extremism and how to tackle it, there is a growing perception that the movement of people is a threat to national security. It is not disputed that States have a right to determine who is entitled to enter and stay on their territory. At the same time, they also have an obligation to respect, protect and fulfil the human rights of all individuals in their jurisdiction, regardless of their nationality, origin and immigration status, as well as their specific obligations under international refugee law. It is legitimate for States to want to increase border security through border controls to identify security threats before an individual enters their territory. Yet 'Maritime interception operations' or 'push back operations', as well as bilateral or multi-lateral readmission agreements, such as the EU-Turkey Statement, agreed on 18 March 2016, which provides for the blanket return of all migrants crossing from Turkey to Greece, pose specific challenges as they may amount to collective expulsion[210] and violations of the principle of non-refoulement.[211]

---

[210] HRW (2016), 'EU: Turkey mass-return deal threatens rights, would harm refugees, undermine EU's principles', press release, 15 March.

[211] Amnesty International (2015), 'Europe's gatekeeper: Unlawful detention and deportation of refugees from Turkey', 16 December, EUR 44/3022/2015; Amnesty International (2016), 'Turkey "safe country" sham revealed as dozens of Afghans forcibly returned hours after EU refugee deal', press release, 23 March; Amnesty International (2016), 'EU-Turkey deal: Greek decision

The administrative detention of foreign nationals considered to be a security threat has been a recurrent approach of States. As former UN High Commissioner for Human Rights Louise Arbour noted already in 2006:

> countries are using various laws at their disposal – asylum, immigration, extradition and so on – to remove persons alleged to constitute national security threats from their territories. In particular one sees an attempt to avoid the heavy due process requirements of the criminal system by turning instead to the administrative law framework.[212]

That tendency was observable in Canada's certificates under the Immigration and Refugee Protection Act 2001 for detention of foreign nationals for up to 120 days without review, followed by removal; and in the UK's indefinite detention of foreign terror suspects under the Anti-terrorism, Crime and Security Act 2001. These schemes were deemed by national and international courts to be unconstitutional, and/or discriminatory, and/or in breach of fundamental rights. It is crucial that, amidst mounting terrorism concerns and increased numbers of migrants moving into foreign territories, States do not resort to similar measures that violate human rights. States have a right to detain foreigners prior to deportation and extradition.[213] But detention should always be a last resort and must comply with the principle of legality. Continued detention in this context can become arbitrary where the State does not have any intention of deporting or extraditing the individual; where the State is not diligent enough in carrying out the proceedings, or where the proceedings take too long; and where there are legal or practical reasons the deportation or extradition becomes impossible, such as a risk of violation of the absolute prohibition of refoulement should the individual be returned. In these cases, the individual must be released. Further, the detention of children can never ever be in their best interest: alternatives

---

highlights fundamental flaws', press release, 20 May, on the appeal won by a Syrian national who arrived in Greece, against a decision that would have led to his forcible return to Turkey; HRW (2016), 'Turkey: border guards kill and injure asylum seekers', 10 May, https://www.hrw.org/news/2016/05/10/turkey-border-guards-kill-and-injure-asylum-seekers, accessed 19 October 2017.

[212] Speech by Louise Arbour, UN High Commissioner for Human Rights, Chatham House, Wednesday 15 February 2006, https://www.chathamhouse.org/sites/files/chathamhouse/public/Research/International%20Law/ilparbour.pdf, accessed 24 October 2017.

[213] See Article 9 ICCPR and e.g. Article 5 ECHR.

to detention must be provided to unaccompanied migrant children and families with children.

In sum, from a 'macro-legal' perspective, a State should not place immigration laws at the centre of their counter-terrorism strategies. This response is both an ineffective way to respond to the threat of terrorism, as its ultimate outcome is the export of the threat; it also lacks the capacity of criminal law in showing exemplar rigour in punishing individuals for wrongdoing. It is thus important that the State responds to criminal acts with criminal law, while immigration laws should serve to regulate immigration. From a more 'micro-legal' perspective, given the impact that such removal measures can have on the individuals, it is important that the individuals are given the opportunity to challenge the lawfulness of their detention,[214] and that the State includes appropriate safeguards before any deportation takes place, including to ensure that the deportation is not used a as form of administrative detention based on discriminatory grounds; to consider any risk of ill-treatment of the individual upon return to prevent any violation of the absolute prohibition of refoulement and to give any appeal a preventive effect, so as to avoid a violation of this absolute prohibition.

2.5.2 Regulation of civil society through laws to address the financing of terrorism

Measures to counter the financing of terrorism[215] have had an important impact on civil society. This is largely due to the very important impact of a (rather unknown) international organization, the Financial Action Task Force (FATF),[216] which has made a critical link between the two.

---

[214] See Human Rights Committee (2004), *Ahani v. Canada*, Communication No. 1051/2002 UN Doc. CCPR/C/80/D/1051/2002 (2004) '[G]iven that an individual under a security certificate has neither been convicted of any crime nor sentenced to a term of imprisonment, an individual must have appropriate access, in terms of Article 9(4) to judicial review of the detention, that is to say review of the substantive justification of the detention as well as sufficiently frequent review'.

[215] International Convention for the Suppression of the Financing of Terrorism, adopted by the General Assembly of the UN in resolution 54/109 of 9 December 1999, entered into force on 10 April 2002, and Security Council resolution 1373 (2001).

[216] See 1989 G-7 Economic Declaration. FATF is an intergovernmental organization to develop policies to combat money laundering and, since 2001, the financing of terrorism. According to its mandate (2012–2020), current objectives are to set standards and to promote effective implementation of legal, regulatory and operational measures for combating terrorist financing, and to

Indeed, FATF has affirmed that it has been 'demonstrated that terrorists and terrorist organizations exploit the non-profit organization (NPO) sector to raise and move funds, provide logistical support, encourage terrorist recruitment, or otherwise support terrorist organizations and terrorist activity'.[217] FATF has thus required States to review their legislation pertaining to NPOs[218] to ensure that they cannot be misused (a) by terrorist organizations posing as legitimate entities; (b) to exploit legitimate entities as conduits for terrorist financing, including for the purpose of escaping asset-freezing measures; and (c) to conceal or obscure the clandestine diversion of funds intended for legitimate purposes to terrorist organizations'.[219] States are thus required to adopt a number of measures regarding the supervision and monitoring of the entire NPO sector, while for NPOs that 'account for a significant portion of the financial resources under control of the sector and a substantial share of the sector's international activities', States are required to adopt more extensive specific standards.[220] States' implementation of the recommendations is monitored through a Mutual Evaluation process, and non-compliance with FATF recommendations can be damaging for a country, in particular for its financial and business sector.

FATF has highlighted the 'vital role' of NPOs, and noted that '[m]easures adopted by countries to protect the NPO sector from terrorist abuse should not disrupt or discourage legitimate charitable activities', and actions taken by governments should 'to the extent reasonably possible, avoid any negative impact on innocent and legitimate beneficiaries of charitable activity'. Unfortunately, this positive statement is accompanied by an important caveat: 'this interest cannot excuse the need to undertake immediate and effective action to advance the immediate interest of halting terrorist financing or other forms of support by NPOs'.[221] This statement, in fact, maintains the perception that the fight

---

identify national-level vulnerabilities with the aim of protecting the international financial system from misuse (20 April 2012, Washington, DC).

[217] See FATF (2012), 'Interpretative Note to Recommendation 8', http://fatfplatform.org/wp-content/uploads/2015/02/Interpretive-Note-to-Recommendation-8.pdf, accessed 19 October 2017. See also FATF (2014), 'FATF report: Risk of terrorist abuse in non-profit organizations', FATF/OECD, paras. 13, 75 and 91–124.

[218] This chapter will refer to NPOs when referring to FATF (as this is the language FATF uses), otherwise it will use the term NGOs, as preferred human rights language.

[219] FATF, Recommendation 8, on NPOs.

[220] Ibid.

[221] See FATF (2012), 'Interpretative Note to Recommendation 8' (n 217).

against terrorism is a trump card within the existing human rights and humanitarian law framework.

As stressed by Ben Emmerson, the former Special Rapporteur on Human Rights while countering terrorism,[222] while opportunities for abuse exist[223] and there are examples in which the financing of terrorism through civil society have been established,[224] abuse is in fact rare in the NPO sector[225] and represents only a small part of the total funds managed by civil society.[226] States should 'avoid rhetoric that ties NPOs to terrorism financing in general terms because it overstates the threat and unduly damages the NPO sector as a whole'.[227] Regarding the measures adopted to implement the FATF recommendation on abuse of NPOs, in fact, 'very few, if any, instances of terrorism financing have been detected as a result of [civil society organization]-specific supervisory measures'.[228]

In fact, the FATF requirements relating to the financing of terrorism and NPOs have been a useful tool for a number of States to clamp down on civil society.[229] In implementing these requirements, States have adopted legislation that strictly regulates, limits, restricts and controls civil society. Such legislation typically includes an obligation to register, with burdensome and complex procedures for the registration, which in

---

222 See report, UN Doc. A/70/371 (n 22), para. 22.

223 See CTITF (2009), 'CTITF Working Group Report: Tackling the financing of terrorism', http://www.un.org/en/terrorism/ctitf/pdfs/ctitf_financing_eng_final.pdf, accessed 15 May 2017, paras. 63 and 64.

224 See Emile van der Does de Willebois (2010), 'Nonprofit organizations and the combatting of terrorism financing, A proportionate response', World Bank Working Paper No. 208, Ch. 2; FATF (2014), 'Risk of terrorist abuse in NPOs', FATF/OECD, Ch. 3.

225 Joint Select Committee (2015), 'Draft Protection of Charities Bill', 23 February, para. 37.

226 van der Does de Willebois (n 224). See also CTITF (n 223), para. 64. and Recommendation 65.

227 Ibid.

228 'Special Rapporteur on the rights to freedom of peaceful assembly and of association', UN Doc. A/HRC/23/39, para. 25. See also 'Special Rapporteur on human rights while countering terrorism', UN Doc. A/70/371 (n 22), paras. 23 and 24.

229 See 'Special Rapporteur on the rights to freedom of peaceful assembly and of association' who warned against 'the implementation of restrictive measures – such as FATF Recommendation 8 – which have been misused by States to violate international law', UN Doc. A/HRC/23/39, para. 25. See also 'Special Rapporteur on human rights while countering terrorism', UN Doc. A/HRC/70/371 (n 22), para. 24.

turn enhance the possibility that the registration be denied, often coupled with limited ability to appeal the refusal; limited ability to obtain funding from abroad; and criminalization of various forms of membership of unregistered groups.[230] The absence in the FATF recommendation of any reference to the rights to freedom of association and its corollary, the ability to access financial resources, nor to the need to respect the principles of legality, proportionality, necessity and non-discrimination, has leant legitimacy to States which adopt legislation without due respect for the right to freedom of association. In fact, the views of several UN special procedures mandate holders is that the FATF recommendation 'fails to provide for specific measures to protect the civil society sector from undue restrictions to their right to freedom of association by States asserting that their measures are in compliance with FATF Recommendation 8'.[231]

It should be noted, however, that in 2015 – for the first time – FATF stated that 'as a matter of principle, complying with the FATF recommendations should not contravene a country's obligations under (…) international human rights law to promote universal respect for, and observance of, fundamental human rights and freedoms, such as freedom of expression, religion, or belief, and freedom of peaceful assembly and of association'.[232] Yet, many States have already adopted rights-limiting legislation to comply with – or abuse – FATF's recommendations, largely without FATF's monitoring bodies raising any concerns regarding the lack of human rights compliance.[233] Thus, while this is a very positive development, it will be difficult to fully repair the damage that has been done to civil society through counter-terrorism legislation to comply with FATF recommendations on NPOs.

[230] For an overview, see Ben Hayes (2012), 'Counter-terrorism, "policy laundering" and the FATF: Legalising surveillance, regulating civil society', Transnational Institute/Statewatch, https://www.tni.org/en/publication/counter-terrorism-policy-laundering-and-the-fatf, accessed 15 May 2017.

[231] 'Special Rapporteur on freedom of association and assembly', UN Doc. A/HRC/23/39, para. 25 and 'Special Rapporteur on human rights while countering terrorism', UN Doc. A/HRC/70/371 (n 22), para. 26.

[232] FATF, Best Practices, 2015, para. 22.

[233] Special Rapporteur on human rights while countering terrorism, A/HRC/70/371 (n 22), para. 26.

2.5.3 Impact of counter-terrorism legislation on humanitarian assistance and the right to development

Since 2001, a complex legal framework to criminalize or limit various acts of support to terrorism has been set up, involving all levels of government. From the Security Council, with resolution 1373,[234] and the International Convention for the Suppression of the Financing of Terrorism, to national legislation that prohibits various forms of support to terrorism,[235] the inclusion by donors of counter-terrorism related clauses in humanitarian grant and partnership agreement contracts to help ensure that their funds are not used to benefit terrorists or to support acts of terrorism,[236] an intricate web of obligations at all levels that impacts on civil society acting domestically and abroad has been set up. This complexity is compounded by the lack of clarity and broadness of the laws themselves and their varying scope of application, as well as by case-law relating to material support.[237] In turn, civil society's ability to operate, with the constant Damocles sword of possible prosecution for material support hanging over its head has been, rightly or wrongly, constrained. This fear of being sanctioned for carrying out its activities has a very serious impact on recipients and beneficiaries.[238]

Understandably, the complexities and risks of sanctions linked to operating in certain areas or with certain groups has had a chilling effect[239] on many civil society actors. By way of example, humanitarian

[234] UN Security Council resolution 1373 (2001), para. 1(d). Resolution 1373 has also been the basis for national and regional sanction regimes, see para. para. 1(c).

[235] For a thorough examination, see Kate Mackintosh and Patrick Duplat (2013), 'Study of the impact of donor counter-terrorism measures on principled humanitarian action', July, https://docs.unocha.org/sites/dms/documents/ct_study_full_report.pdf, accessed 15 May 2017 and Harvard Program on Humanitarian Policy and Conflict Research (2011), HPCR Working Paper: Humanitarian action under scrutiny: Criminalizing humanitarian engagement', http://c0186748.cdn1.cloudfiles.rackspacecloud.com/HPCR%20CHE%202011.pdf, accessed 17 May 2017.

[236] See Mackintosh and Duplat, ibid., at p. 47 *et seq.*

[237] See the US Supreme Court case of *Holder v. Humanitarian Law Project*, 561 U.S. 1 (2010), 130 S. Ct, 2705.

[238] For an overview of the complexities of the legal frameworks, and the risks for civil society, see 'Special Rapporteur on human rights while countering terrorism', UN Doc. A/70/371 (n 22), paras. 31–36.

[239] See Press Conference, Special Rapporteur on human rights while countering terrorism, Martin Scheinin, 26 October 2010, cited in HCPR Working Paper (2011), http://www.un.org/press/en/2010/101026_Scheinin.doc.htm, accessed 15 May 2017.

NGOs have reoriented their operations to areas where there are no designated terrorist groups, or shifted their priorities to ensure first and foremost that they limit their contacts with, or bring indirect support to, any designated terrorist group. In turn, this has meant that responding to humanitarian needs can become a secondary concern, and has thus seriously impacted their ability to remain neutral, impartial, and independent. Others have simply refused to take funding from certain donors, which has affected their ability to access financial resources.

Specific counter-terrorism measures have also affected civil society's perceived independence, neutrality and impartiality, and have thus impacted its ability to work with certain groups, governments, or in certain areas.[240] That certain NGOs are asked by the Security Council to report to the UN on groups and beneficiaries to which humanitarian assistance is being delivered[241] gives the impression that even humanitarian actors are being co-opted into the UN's broader counter-terrorism agenda. Policies such as the vetting of NGOs by donors also have an impact on NGOs' independence, and ability to work in a climate of trust with local implementing partners.[242]

---

240 For a general discussion, see Annyssa Bellal and Stuart Casey-Maslen (2011), 'Rules of engagement: Protecting civilians through dialogue with non-state actors', Geneva Academy of International Humanitarian and Human Rights Law, https://nlbcdytz.preview.infomaniak.website/joomlatools-files/docman-files/Research%20documents/Rules-of-Engagement-EN.pdf, accessed 19 October 2017, pp. 15 and 16. See also Mackintosh and Duplat (n 235), at 81; Harvard Program on Humanitarian Policy and Conflict Research (n 235), at 32; and Jessica Burniske with Naz Modirzadeh and Dustin Lewis (2014), 'Counter-terrorism laws and regulations: What aid agencies need to know', Humanitarian Practice Network at ODI Number 79 (November), p. 3 and Ashley Jackson and Abdi Aynte (2013), 'Talking to the other side: Humanitarian negotiations with Al-Shabaab in Somalia', HPG Working Paper (December), https://www.odi.org/sites/odi.org.uk/files/odi-assets/publications-opinion-files/8744.pdf, accessed 15 May 2017, p. 6.

241 See e.g. UN Security Council resolution 1916 (2010), para. 11. See also 'Special Rapporteur on human rights while countering terrorism' (n 22), UN Doc. A/70/371, para. 31.

242 See Burniske et al. (n 240), at 6. See also Neal Cohen, Robert Hasty and Ashley Wonton (2014), 'Implications of the USAID partner vetting system and state department risk analysis and management system under European Union and United Kingdom data protection and privacy law, counterterrorism and humanitarian engagement project', Counterterrorism and Humanitarian Engagement Project, Research and Policy Paper, March.

Civil society's ability to operate has been impacted by restrictions in available funding in areas where terrorist groups are active,[243] as well as by an increased reliance from donors on what may be seen as 'safe' implementing partners, such as UN agencies, other international or regional organizations, and large NGOs, to the detriment of smaller or local NGOs.[244] In addition, counter-terrorism legislation has also affected NGOs' access to financial services.[245] To protect themselves from any risk of liability under counter-terrorism legislation,[246] some banks have refused to process transactions involving 'high-risk' environments or actors.[247] NGOs have found that their ability to access financial services, including banking services, has been reduced, while other NGOs have seen their bank accounts altogether closed.

Given the importance of civil society in addressing the conditions conducive to the spread of terrorism, countering the appeal of violent extremism, protecting and promoting human rights and the rule of law, and delivering humanitarian relief, counter-terrorism measures that have a negative impact on the ability of the NGO sector to operate effectively and independently can ultimately be counterproductive in reducing the

---

[243] Mackintosh and Duplat (n 235), at 82 for an example in Somalia, where following the listing of Al-Shabaab as a terrorist organization in 2008, 'a single instance of diverted aid or payments to local authorities was now potentially a crime under US law for which both USAID and its implementing partners could be held accountable'.

[244] Mackintosh and Duplat (n 235), at 104.

[245] Human Rights Council resolution 27/21:'*Concerned* that unilateral coercive measures have, in some instances, prevented humanitarian organizations from making financial transfers to States where they work'.

[246] 'The limited revenue that most INGOs may generate for a bank is not sufficient to justify the risks that banks believe doing business with INGOs will expose them to'. See Victoria Metcalfe-Hough, Tom Keatinge and Sara Pantuliano (2015), 'UK humanitarian aid in the age of counter terrorism: Perceptions and reality', Humanitarian Policy Group, ODI, https://www.odi.org/sites/odi.org.uk/files/odi-assets/publications-opinion-files/9479.pdf, accessed 15 May 2017, p. 13.

[247] See Martin Arnold and Sam Fleming (2014), 'Regulation: bank counts the risks and rewards', *Financial Times*, 14 November, https://www.ft.com/content/9df378a2-66bb-11e4-91ab-00144feabdc0, accessed 19 October 2017. On the risks of these practices for money laundering and counter terrorist financing, see The Commonwealth and La Francophonie (2015), 'Walking a tightrope: AML/CTF regulation, financial inclusion and remittances', Annual Commonwealth & Francophonie Dialogue with the G20 Discussion Paper, 3.9, April.

threat posed by terrorism.[248] In addition, this lacks coherence: the ability of civil society actors to be effective in countering terrorism and violent extremism depends in part on its ability to engage with communities in proximity to a terrorist threat, whether that is in areas where terrorist groups are active, or where the risk of radicalization has been demonstratively proven. NGOs cannot be asked to contribute to mitigating the risk while at the same time risking prosecution when they do so.

The preventing or countering violent extremism agenda, which has gained momentum in the past few years, and was fully consecrated by the Secretary-General's Plan of Action to Prevent Violent Extremism[249] contains the seeds of the risk of instrumentalization of various fields of State involvement – such as human rights promotion and protection, development, education, gender issues, and democracy. While the Secretary-General is right in stressing that individuals are often not drawn to terrorist violence in a vacuum and thus that it is essential to take seriously the so-called 'conditions conducive to the spread of terrorism' contained in Pillar I of the UN GCTS,[250] it is just as important to ensure that they remain long-term objectives in their own right, and not just as a part of the broader State agenda to counter or prevent violent extremism.[251] While human rights violations may be a factor conducive to violent extremism, the State must respect, protect and promote the rights of all individuals, of all ages, genders, ethnic or religious belonging without discrimination, regardless of any broader agenda, including the prevention and countering of violent extremism. Ending prolonged conflicts, fighting against impunity must be pursued as ends in themselves, and not only because they might be used by violent groups to recruit individuals to their cause, at the risk of undermining the *raison d'être* of international law, humanitarian values, or the UN itself.

---

[248] 'Special Rapporteur on human rights while countering terrorism' (n 22), UN Doc. A/70/371, para. 45.

[249] UN Doc. A/70/674 (n 47).

[250] The conditions conducive of Pillar I include but are not limited to prolonged unresolved conflicts, dehumanization of victims of terrorism in all its forms and manifestations, lack of the rule of law and violations of human rights, ethnic, national and religious discrimination, political exclusion, socio-economic marginalization and lack of good governance.

[251] 'Special Rapporteur on human rights while countering terrorism', UN Doc. A/31/65, para. 50.

3. HUMAN RIGHTS WHILE COUNTERING TERRORISM: THE DEBATE, THE FRAMEWORK AND THE CHALLENGES

3.1 The Debate: Terrorism or Human Rights Versus Terrorism and Human Rights

As noted at the beginning of this chapter, the post-11 September 2001 context has brought with it a discourse of 'exceptionalism'. After initial statements promoting values such as human rights, the rule of law and democracy, the fear of terrorist attacks and the need to look tough on terror soon led governments to argue that the new terrorist threat was such that there was a stark choice to be made between guaranteeing national security on the one hand and preserving individual freedoms and liberty on the other. In this Hobbesian perspective, preserving security was prioritized over the protection of human rights. The assault on human rights went even further, as human rights were also portrayed as an *impediment* to security. States whose human rights records were far from stellar were able to proudly display as exemplary their rights-limiting measures, using terrorism as their new justification, while States that had proudly upheld human rights attempted to evade their human rights obligations through various legal constructions. Throughout, human rights advocates were often accused of being irresponsibly soft on terrorism. All of this was apparently done to comply with Security Council resolutions, and much of the legislation was adopted in the absence of criticism from international monitoring bodies (CTC or FATF monitoring mechanisms). A rollback phenomenon was observed post-2006 largely led by the General Assembly, national courts, and civil society. Yet it is clear that with each new wave of terrorist attack or threat, in new regions and by new terrorist groups, new rights-limiting measures are adopted with little consideration for human rights, as the new State of emergency proclaimed in France shows, or various statements referring to a 'war' being waged.

Yet this doesn't need to be so. It may be a commonplace, but it is worth bearing in mind that the modern international human rights framework, embodied in the Universal Declaration of Human Rights, was born in 1948, after some of the most brutal atrocities of the twentieth century. The international framework that was built upon in the next fifty years, which includes a set of binding international treaties and monitoring mechanisms, was not built in a vacuum by idealists who had no foot in reality. The framework itself is not only rooted in genocidal atrocities but developed in an era that had as its backdrop the Cold War, a number of brutal conflicts in many regions of the world and the existence of terrorist threats and terrorist attacks in all regions of the world. The framework itself is realist and flexible, and rooted in the common belief that security can only be achieved where the dignity of all human beings was to be respected, where no one is unworthy of human rights protection.

There is truth in the fact that it is easier to point to how the post-9/11 framework has harmed the human rights framework than it is to show the successes that it has had in effectively countering terrorism. This is largely due to the secretive nature of national security, which means that successes remain secret.[252] Yet, it is also true that counter-terrorism measures are, and must remain, a subject of legal and societal debate among States' citizens, and it has never been compellingly argued that the post-2001 context is different in nature or intensity to past threats to national or international security, nor have any convincing results been presented of how the post-2001 security approach, which weighed the threat of terrorism against human rights, has produced effective results. In fact, a bird's view would show that some sixteen years after 9/11, the security approach to countering terrorism has not been as effective as it was promised to be, with the threat of terrorism looming large, the emergence of new and more virulent terrorist groups, and the commission of acts of terrorism in all regions of the world on an almost daily basis. The UN Secretary-General made that clear in his Plan of Action to Prevent Violent Extremism, where he stated: 'Over the past two decades, the international community has sought to address violent extremism [that leads to terrorism] primarily within the context of security-based counter-terrorism measures adopted in response to the threat posed by Al-Qaida and its affiliated groups. However, with the emergence of a new generation of groups, there is a growing international consensus that such counter-terrorism measures have not been sufficient to prevent the spread of violent extremism (…). There is a need to take a more comprehensive approach which encompasses not only on-going, essential security-based counter-terrorism measures, but also systematic preventive measures which directly address the drivers of violent extremism that have given rise to the emergence of these new and more virulent groups (…). I am convinced that the creation of open, equitable, inclusive and pluralist societies, based on the full respect of human rights and with economic

252 Roach (n 26), at 431.

opportunities for all, represents the most tangible and meaningful alternative to violent extremism and the most promising strategy for rendering it unattractive'.[253]

Terrorism, together with the new concept of violent extremism, are highly complex phenomena. While much more work and study needs to be carried out about what brings any individual to turn to terrorist groups and commit acts of terrorist violence, the links between human rights and these phenomena are emerging. There is general consensus that human rights violations are one of the conditions that are conducive to terrorism. This was already made clear in the UN GCTS, and recalled by the Secretary-General in his Plan of Action to Prevent Violent Extremism: 'we must also acknowledge that [violent extremism that leads to terrorism] does not arise in a vacuum. Narratives of grievance, actual or perceived injustice, promised empowerment and sweeping change become attractive where human rights are being violated, good governance is being ignored and aspirations are being crushed (…)'.[254] There is also agreement that the fight against terrorism is itself a fight for human rights and fundamental freedoms, democratic values, the rule of law, and pluralism. These humanistic, universal values cannot be defended through means that are contrary to them, as that would render their defense meaningless. Finally, to come full circle, there is also consensus that countering terrorism without respecting human rights can be counterproductive, as human rights violations are one of the conditions conducive to terrorism. This is what the General Assembly meant in the UN GCTS when it reaffirmed that 'the promotion and protection of human rights for all and the rule of law is essential to all components of the Strategy, recognizing that effective counter-terrorism measures and the protection of human rights are not conflicting goals, but complementary and mutually reinforcing.'[255]

3.2 The Right Framework: Counter-Terrorism and Human Rights

The apparent dichotomy between human rights and security was made possible through the opposition of two seemingly contrary State obligations: its obligation to protect individuals from acts of terrorism, and its

[253] UN Doc. A/70/674 (n 47), paras. 4–7.

[254] See UN GA UN GCTS, Pillar I and 'Secretary General's plan of action to prevent violent extremism', UN Doc. A/70/674 (n 47), paras. 3 and 7.

[255] UN Doc. A/RES/60/288, Pillar 4 of the Plan of Action.

obligation to respect IHRL.[256] Yet it is important to note that States' duty to protect individuals under their jurisdiction from terrorist attacks is itself an obligation that arises out of human rights law. Indeed, States have not only a general duty to protect individuals under their jurisdiction against interference in the enjoyment of human rights,[257] but a more specific duty to ensure respect for the right to life[258] and the right to security of every person within its territory.[259] This includes an obligation to take all appropriate and necessary steps to safeguard the lives of those within their jurisdiction. States must put in place effective criminal justice and law enforcement systems, such as measures to deter the commission of offences and investigate violations where they occur; ensure that those suspected of criminal acts are prosecuted; provide victims with effective remedies; and take other necessary steps to prevent

---

[256] Each State has a duty to respect, protect and fulfil human rights, arising out of their specific treaty obligations (core human rights treaties include the International Covenant on Economic, Social and Cultural Rights, and the ICCPR and their Optional Protocols; the International Convention on the Elimination of All Forms of Racial Discrimination; the Convention on the Elimination of All Forms of Discrimination against Women and its Optional Protocol; the Convention against Torture and other Cruel, Inhuman or Degrading Treatment or Punishment and its Optional Protocol; the Convention on the Rights of the Child and its two Optional Protocols; the International Convention on the Protection of the Rights of All Migrant Workers and Members of Their Families; the International Convention for the Protection of All Persons from Enforced Disappearance, and the Convention on the Rights of Persons with Disabilities and its Optional Protocol. There are also various regional treaties on the protection of human rights and fundamental freedoms), or out of customary international law (these bind all States even if they are not party to a particular treaty. Some of the rights set out in the UDHR are widely regarded to hold this character, as well as some rights included in the ICCPR). In addition, some rights are recognized as having a special status as *jus cogens* (peremptory norms of customary international law), which means that there are no circumstances whatsoever in which derogation from them is permissible. According to the International Law Commission's articles on State responsibility, these include the prohibitions of torture, slavery, genocide, racial discrimination, crimes against humanity, and the right to self-determination.

[257] On all this section, see Office of the High Commissioner for Human Rights (n 186), at 8 and 9.

[258] This right is protected in most human rights treaties, and has been described as the 'supreme right', without which others are without meaning. See Human Rights Committee (1982), 'General Comment No. 6' and Nowak (n 108), at 121.

[259] See Human Rights Committee, views on communication No. 859/1999, *Luis Asdrúbal Jiménez Vaca v. Colombia*, 25 March 2002, para. 7.3.

a recurrence of violations. In addition, international and regional human rights law has recognized that, in specific circumstances, States have a positive obligation to take preventive operational measures to protect an individual or individuals whose life is known or suspected to be at risk from the criminal acts of another individual,[260] which certainly includes terrorists. Also important to highlight is the obligation on States to ensure the personal security of individuals under their jurisdiction where a threat is known or suspected to exist.[261] It can thus be said that the provision of security from terrorist attacks and the protection of human rights are not separate obligations, but are in fact part of one and the same obligation; which in turn triggers another requirement: that all measures taken to counter terrorism also comply with human rights.

One has to be cognizant of the difficulties inherent in the propositions made above. It can be very challenging for States to adopt effective counter-terrorism measures that fully comply with the international human rights framework. Yet the human rights framework, with its in-built flexibilities, was specifically conceived to enable States to address their changing security needs. As noted by the ICJ's Eminent Jurist Panel:

> [h]uman rights and humanitarian law were not drafted with peace and political stability in mind. Rather, the very raison d'être of this legal system is to provide States with the framework that allows them to respond effectively to even the most serious of crises. Accordingly, human rights are not, and can never be, a luxury to be cast aside in times of difficulty. International law is the bulwark that will help States respond effectively whatever difficulties arise.[262]

IHRL thus allows for two types of restrictions to rights: limitations to a number of qualified rights and, in a very limited set of exceptional circumstances, derogations. States may also legitimately limit the exercise of certain rights, including the right to freedom of expression, to freedom of association and assembly, to freedom of movement and to respect for private and family life. In order to fully respect their human rights obligations while imposing such limitations, States must respect a number of conditions: the limitations must be prescribed by law, they

---

260 *Kiliç v. Turkey*, App. no. 22492/93 (ECtHR, 28 March 2000), para. 62. See also Inter-American Court of Human Rights, *Velásquez Rodríguez v. Honduras*, judgment of 29 July 1988, para. 174.

261 Human Rights Committee, views on communication No. 195/1985, *Delgado Páez v. Colombia*, 12 July 1990 (A/45/40 (vol. II), annex IX, s. D.

262 International Commission of Jurists (n 71), at 18.

must be in a pursuit of a legitimate aim, and they must respect the principles of proportionality and non-discrimination. In the case of rights-limiting measures taken to counter terrorism, respect for the principle of legality is critical. It is important to bear in mind that the law must be accessible, precise and respect the principle of certainty of the law. Criminal laws must also comply with the principle of non-retroactivity: conduct that occurred prior to its entry into force as applicable law must not be criminalized and any penalties must be limited to those applicable at the time that any offence was committed, unless the law provides for a lighter penalty. There is little doubt that the countering of terrorism is an important objective which can, in principle, permit the limitation of certain rights. Yet States must not use this justifiable objective as a pretext to broaden State powers in other areas.[263] Finally, it should be noted that the principle of proportionality has a critical link to the effectiveness of any counter-terrorism measure. States that adopt rights-limiting measures must be prepared to bring evidence of their effectiveness, as an ineffective measure will likely not comply with the principle of proportionality.

In addition, in genuine emergencies which threaten the life of the nation, States may derogate from certain human rights provisions under the ICCPR. Article 4 of the ICCPR sets out the formal and substantive requirements which a State party must fulfil to derogate legitimately from certain obligations under the Covenant. In addition to the need to immediately inform the other States Parties to the Covenant, through the intermediary of the UN Secretary-General, of the provisions from which it has derogated and of the reasons by which it was actuated, a state must fulfil a number of substantive conditions. Derogations must only take place in a time of 'public emergency which threatens the life of the nation'. In its General Comment No. 29, the Human Rights Committee has stated that such an emergency is one of an exceptional nature. While it is theoretically possible that this be triggered by terrorist acts or by the threat of terrorism, this must be assessed on a case-by-case basis. Any derogation under article 4(1) of the Covenant may only be 'to the extent strictly required by the exigencies of the situation'. Derogations must thus be understood as exceptional, temporary measures, and the restoration of a state of normalcy where full respect for the Covenant can again be secured must be the predominant objective of the derogating State. In

---

[263] Offences created under counter-terrorist legislation, along with any associated powers of investigation or prosecution, must be limited to countering terrorism. See 'Special Rapporteur on human rights while countering terrorism', UN Doc. E/CN.4/2006/98, para. 47.

addition, any derogating measure must comply with the principles of necessity and proportionality. A rational link must exist between the derogating measure and the objective pursued and the measure must be the least intrusive on the right derogated from as possible. Finally, derogations must not be discriminatory.

A State may, however, never derogate from certain rights, which are considered so important that regardless of the nature of the threat they can never be set aside. Article 4(2) of the ICCPR identifies as non-derogable the right to life, freedom from torture or cruel, inhuman or degrading treatment or punishment, the prohibition against slavery and servitude, freedom from imprisonment for failure to fulfil a contract, freedom from retrospective penalties, the right to be recognized as a person before the law, and freedom of thought, conscience and religion. In its General Comment No. 29, the Human Rights Committee has also emphasized that the Covenant's provisions relating to procedural safeguards can never be made subject to measures that would circumvent the protection of these non-derogable rights. In addition, article 4(1) of the ICCPR specifies that any derogating measures must not be inconsistent with obligations under international law which, as the Human Rights Committee has pointed out in its General Comment No. 29, includes obligations under IHRL, IHL and international criminal law. The Committee also identified rights and freedoms under customary international law that may not be derogated from even if not listed in article 4(2): The right of all persons deprived of their liberty to be treated with humanity and with respect for the inherent dignity of the human person; the prohibitions against the taking of hostages, abductions or unacknowledged detention; the international protection of the rights of persons belonging to minorities; the deportation or forcible transfer of population without grounds permitted under international law; and the prohibition against propaganda for war or in advocacy of national, racial or religious hatred that would constitute incitement to discrimination, hostility or violence.

In light of these flexibilities, the choice, then, for a State with a demonstrated need to adapt the level of human rights protection is not to choose between respect for human rights on the one hand and security on the other. Rather, the State must work within the human rights framework to adapt the level of protection to the needs of the State, be it protecting populations during a high-profile event such as the World Cup, to protect the methods used by intelligence agencies during the trial of an individual accused of acts of terrorism, or to protect its population after a series of terrorist attacks on its territory and a risk of more to come. As noted by the former Special Rapporteur on the promotion and protection of human rights while countering terrorism:

> [t]hrough the careful application of human rights law it is possible to respond effectively to the challenges involved in the countering of terrorism while complying with human rights. There is no need in this process for a balancing between human rights and security, as the proper balance can and must be found within human rights law itself. Law is the balance, not a weight to be measured.[264]

3.3 The Challenge: Upholding Human Rights While Countering Terrorism

In the post-9/11 context, the judiciary and civil society[265] have played a particularly important role in reintroducing human rights law where it had been cast aside, as well as in assisting governments and parliaments in finding human rights-compliant ways to counter-terrorism. Some of the most emblematic cases have already been referred to, such as the US Supreme Court case of *Holder*, where the court simply reintroduced international law where the government had attempted to create a new legal framework from which international law was absent. In the cases of *Rasul* and *Boumediene*, the same court gave detainees at Guantanamo Bay access to courts for a judicial review of their detention, despite the fact that US Congress had denied them this right. In the case of *Charkaoui*,[266] the Canadian Supreme Court declared that an important part of Canada's counter-terrorism architecture, its regime of Security Certificates violated the right to security of the person as protected by the Canadian Charter. Indeed, the Court noted the existence of a number of other, less rights-limiting alternatives through which the information serving as the basis for the certificates could be protected while at the same time affording the individuals subject to the certificates greater right of defence, and noted – through an evaluation of the necessity of the measures – that less restrictive means existed to protect the sensitive information, and thus that the infringement to the individual's rights could not be justified. Other examples abound. In addition to the

---

[264] 'Special Rapporteur on human rights while countering terrorism', UN Doc. A/HRC/16/51, para. 12.

[265] David Cole (2016), 'Engines of liberty: How civil society helped restore constitutional rights in the aftermath of 9/11', Just Security, 28 March, https://www.justsecurity.org/30249/engines-liberty-civil-society-helped-restore-constitutional-rights-aftermath-911/, accessed 15 May 2017.

[266] *Charkaoui v. Canada (Minister of Citizenship and Immigration)* (n 197).

ECtHR's progressive jurisprudence relating to accountability to victims in the context of the 'war of terror', notably *El-Masri*, *Al-Nashiri* and *Nasr and Ghali*, a number of national courts have also held the executive to account for human rights abuses committed in the name of national security and counterterrorism.[267]

In the context of mass data surveillance, the Court of Justice of the European Union (CJEU)[268] outlawed bulk access to contents data,[269] by stating that access on a generalized basis to the content of electronic communications compromises the 'essence' of the fundamental right to respect for private life.[270] Further, following its decision that the mandatory retention of metadata relating to a person's private life and communications is in itself an interference with the right to privacy,[271] the CJEU ruled that national legislation which provides for 'general and indiscriminate retention of all traffic and location data of all subscribers and registered users relating to all means of electronic communication' is contrary to EU law.[272] The ECtHR, for its part, has developed the requirement of 'reasonable suspicion' in the context of bulk interception,[273] noting that the entity authorizing interception must be 'capable of verifying the existence of a reasonable suspicion against the

---

[267] E.g, High Court of Kenya, *Salim Awdah Salim et al. v. Commissioner of Police and al*, Petition No. 822 of 2008, 31 July 2013.

[268] Case C-362/14, *Maximilian Schrems v. Data Protection Commissioner* (CJEU, 6 October 2015).

[269] Martin Scheinin (2015), 'Mass surveillance and the right to privacy: Adding nuance to the Schrems case', Just Security, 13 October 2015, https://www.justsecurity.org/26781/adding-nuance-context-max-schrems-case-safe-harbor/, accessed 15 May 2017.

[270] The Court also noted that the simple access to personal data by public authorities, even in the absence of any further processing of that data, was an interference into the right to privacy. This welcome position is also that taken in the US Court of Appeal for the Second Circuit, *ACLU v. Clapper*, no. 14-42-cv, 2015 WL 2097814, (2d Cir. 2015), 7 May 2015 and in UK Investigatory Powers Tribunal, *Privacy International v. Secretary of State for Foreign and Commonwealth Affairs and Others* [2016] UKIPTrib 15_110-CH.

[271] Joined Cases C-293/12 and C-594/12, *Digital Rights v. Ireland* (CJEU, 8 April 2014). On the decisions's impact, see e.g. District Court of the Hague striking down the Dutch data retention legislation NL:RBDHA:2015:2498, District Court of the Hague, 11 March 2015, Case no. C/09/480009/KG/ZA 14/.

[272] Joined Cases C-203/15 *Tele2 Sverige AB v. Post-ochtelestyrelsen* and C-698/15 *Secretary of State for Home Department v. Tom Watson and Others* (CJEU, 21 December 2016).

[273] *Szabo and Vissy v. Hungary*, App. no. 37138/14 (ECtHR, 12 January 2016) and *Zakharov v. Russia*, App. no. 47143/06 (ECtHR, 4 December 2015).

person concerned', that the authorization itself must 'clearly identify' a specific person or a single set of premises, and that there must be the 'ability to verify whether sufficient reasons for intercepting a specific individual's communications exist in each case'.[274] At national level, the US' bulk telephone metadata collection programme under Section 215 of the Patriot Act[275] was declared illegal through the case of *ACLU v. Clapper*.[276] In the UK, the Investigatory Powers Tribunal held, on 17 October 2016,[277] that the regime for obtaining bulk communications data and for the retention of bulk personal datasets (prior to government acknowledgement in 2015), could not be 'foreseeable by the public when it was not explained to parliament'.[278] In Germany, the Constitutional Court ruled that screening data across several private and public databases in order to find potential terrorists ('sleepers') was illegal.[279] Regarding international cooperation between intelligence agencies, the UK's Investigatory Powers Tribunal ruled that the intelligence-sharing agreements between the UK's GCHQ and the US' NSA pertaining to their UPSTREAM and PRISM programmes were unlawful prior to 5 December 2014, due to their secrecy.[280] Through these rulings, which

---

[274] See also in Canada: case of *R v. Rogers*, 2016 ONSC 70, in which the Court produced a set of guidelines to ensure that orders to obtain customer information from telecommunications providers are proportionate.

[275] Using section 215 of the Patriot Act, the NSA requested that the telephone metadata associated with telephone calls made by and to American citizens be turned over in bulk by phone companies to be collected and aggregated into a repository or data bank that could later be queried.

[276] *ACLU v. Clapper* (n 270).

[277] *Privacy International v. Secretary of State for Foreign and Commonwealth Affairs and Others* (n 270). See also the critical 'Review of Directions given under Section 94 of the Telecommunications Act 1984', July 2016 by the Interception of Communications Commissioner (IOCCO). See also the application to Strasbourg, *10 Human Rights Organisations v. the UK*, App. no. 24960/15, particularly the applicants' reply to observations of the government of the UK, September 2016.

[278] This case focused on the quality of the law, without considering whether the bulk data collection regimes were proportionate, per se. Note that the operational case for the use of bulk powers was examined by the Independent Reviewer of Terrorism Legislation, David Anderson (2016), 'Bulk powers review – Report', August.

[279] German Constitutional Court, 1 BvR 518/02, 22 May 2016.

[280] They were considered lawful thereafter, as certain of the policies had been made public during the case before the Tribunal. Investigatory Powers Tribunal, *Liberty/Privacy Cases*, 6 February 2015 [2015] UKIPTrib 13_77-H, and 5 December 2014, [2014] UKIPTrib 13_77-H., application to Strasbourg, *10*

require governments to provide a human rights justification for the use of mass surveillance technology and reaffirm the applicability of the key human rights principles of legality, necessity and proportionality to interferences to the right to privacy, courts have actively curtailed mass surveillance programmes.

A most emblematic example of a progressive dialogue between courts and governments on finding counter-terrorism measures that satisfy a human rights framework is to be found in the UK's attempt at finding a solution to its administrative detention of foreigners regarding whom there is an alleged risk of being linked to terrorism, but who cannot be deported without a risk of refoulement. In 2001, the UK adopted the Antiterrorism, Crime and Security Act, which included, in its now infamous Part IV, the indeterminate detention of non-citizens regarding whom removal or deportation was not possible without violating the absolute prohibition of refoulement. The power to detain applied where the Secretary of State issued a certificate indicating his belief that the person's presence in the UK was a risk to national security and that he suspected the person of being an international terrorist. In order to act fully within the human rights framework, which included both the absolute prohibition of refoulement and ECHR requirement that such detention was possible only 'with a view to deportation or extradition,'[281] the UK accompanied this provision with a derogation from the ECHR. In addition, by including this power under immigration law rather than criminal law, the UK was able to use secret evidence, which would not have been allowed under criminal law, where the use of electronic surveillance is prohibited. Indeed, this provision was to be administered by a specialized tribunal, the Special Immigration Appeal Commission, which was allowed to consider both 'open' materials (that can be made public) and 'closed' materials (that – for reasons of national security – cannot be made public) through the appointment of security cleared counsels ('Special advocates') to challenge the evidence without such evidence being disclosed to the applicant.

During the lifetime of the legislation, only 16 individuals were certified under this provision and detained. Yet some of these individuals contested their detention, and in the *Belmarsh case*,[282] the House of Lords found that although there was a public emergency that threatened the life of the nation, the detention regime under Part IV of the 2001 Act

Human Rights Organisations v. the UK (n 277), particularly the applicants' reply to observations of the government of the UK, September 2016.

[281] See Article 5(1)(f) ECHR.

[282] *A. v. Secretary of State* [2004] UKHL 56, 16 December 2004.

and the use of immigration law as a tool to counter-terrorism was a disproportionate and non-rational response to the threat to security. The grounds for reaching their conclusion included first, that the legislation was discriminatory, because it only affected non-nationals, while the terrorist threat also came from British nationals; and, second, that it left individuals suspected of being international terrorists at liberty to leave the UK and continue their activities abroad.[283] The House of Lords thus made a declaration of incompatibility, which is not binding on the parties, and which meant that the applicants remained in detention. The case eventually made it to the ECtHR,[284] which concluded like the House of Lords that the derogating measures were disproportionate in that they discriminated unjustifiably between nationals and non-nationals.

In March 2005, the UK government replaced Part IV with 'control orders'[285] which could be made on the basis of intelligence leading to a reasonable suspicion of involvement of any individual in terrorism-related activities. Such activities were broadly defined,[286] and while courts could review control orders, they could only quash them if they were 'obviously flawed'. Control orders stopped short of the criticisms that applied to Part IV: they were not discriminatory, affecting nationals and foreigners alike, and stopped short of outright detention. They could nonetheless result in punitive house arrests, limit places of residence, and require individuals to surrender their passports. They have been challenged at national level for violating the right to liberty as well as the right to a fair trial, although they were never challenged before the ECtHR. On the right to liberty, the House of Lords concluded that although an 18-hour curfew was excessive, a 14-hour curfew did not

---

283 Lord Bingham noted that 'the choice of an immigration measure to address a security problem had the inevitable result of failing adequately to address that problem', ibid., para. 43.

284 *A. and Others v. UK* (n 193) App no. 3455/05 (ECHR, 19 February 2009).

285 Prevention of Terrorism Act 2005, Chapter 2.

286 See Terrorism Act 2000 which includes 'serious damage to property'. This is at variance with the Special Rapporteur on human rights while countering terrorism's proposed definition that terrorism only applies where there is serious harm to human beings. See UN Doc. A/HRC/16/51, Model provision 7. See also other terrorist offences included in the 2005 Act, which are also considered as overly broad by the Special Rapporteur, UN Doc. E/CN.4/2006/98/Add.1, para. 18.

violate the right to liberty.[287] On the question of the right to a fair trial, notably the use of secret evidence and the Special advocates, the Lords relied on the reasoning of the ECtHR.[288] In 2011, control orders were abandoned and replaced by terrorism prevention and investigation measures that did not allow the imposition of house arrests or relocation orders.[289]

While not subject to outright judicial condemnation, control orders could be seen as another example of a State attempting to circumvent the normal functioning of criminal law. Some have highlighted that because the link to any possibility of deportation or removal was gone, they were more akin to 'preventive justice', 'future law' and 'pre-punishment', where courts blindly accept the State's characterization of such interventions as civil and preventive when they have effects that are similar to criminal punishments, and where imprecise tools like intelligence are used for imposing legal consequences.[290] Their effectiveness was questioned. Indeed, seven individuals placed under control orders absconded, and while curfews did sufficiently prevent contact with others to be effective in countering acts of terrorism, they did prevent the gathering of evidence of crimes based on preparations for terrorism. In turn, this raises the question of their proportionality as a counter-terrorism measure, as discussed earlier. It seems – like in the case of preventive detention – that a more effective and fairer solution would have been found in prosecution of these individuals: those guilty of acts of terrorism, including inchoate offences, should be punished accordingly, while those against whom there is little to no evidence should be released. Yet, control orders could also be seen as an example of a State attempting to find a human rights compliant solution in response to a series of condemning rulings, to an identified and complex counter-terrorism requirement, within the framework of its national legislation (whose criminal law did not permit the use of intercept evidence).

This is also the position one can have vis-à-vis another aspect of this question, which relates to diplomatic assurances. Othman (Abu-Qatada) had been detained under a Part IV order, before being subject to a control

---

287 *Secretary of State for the Home Department v. JJ and Others* [2007] UKHL 45; *Secretary of State for the Home Department v. MB and AF* [2007] UKHL 46; *Secretary of State for the Home Department v. E and S* [2007] UKHL 47.

288 See *A. and Others v. UK* (n 193).

289 Terrorism Prevention and Investigation Measures Act 2011.

290 See Lucia Zedner's analysis discussed in Roach (n 26), at 281. See more broadly on this question, Kent Roach's analysis (n 26), at 280–87.

order. In 2005, he was due to be deported to Jordan, based on a memorandum of understanding (MoU) signed between the UK and Jordan, which was seen as a way to deport those the UK wanted out of its territory, while circumventing the absolute prohibition of refoulement. The ECtHR ruled that while the MoU sufficiently mitigated the risk of ill-treatment upon return, for the first time the Court ruled that – due to a real risk that in any retrial in Jordan, evidence obtained in breach of the absolute prohibition of torture would be used against him – there was a real risk of flagrant denial of justice. This meant that the individual could still not be returned to Jordan. The UK government complied with the ruling, despite serious opposition at home, then negotiated a specific treaty, which stipulated that if there was 'a real risk' that a statement was obtained through torture, it could not be admitted as trial evidence unless the prosecutor first proved 'beyond any doubt' that it was not coerced. It was on this basis that the applicant was sent back to Jordan. While this treaty has been criticized as being worthless,[291] this entire episode throughout which the UK has tried to solve one of its main counter-terrorism and human rights challenges, namely how to deal with individuals regarding whom there is intelligence-based information that they are somehow linked to terrorism, without violating the absolute prohibition of refoulement, and maintaining its own internal prohibition on the use of electronic surveillance as evidence, does highlight how a constructive human rights-based and solutions-oriented dialogue can take place to address States' concerns in this field.

4. CONCLUSION

The link between terrorism and human rights violations, armed conflict, migration, marginalization, discrimination and impunity is increasingly apparent. There is now ample evidence that responses to terrorism adopted outside the international legal framework are not only ineffective but can also be counter-productive. Yet, in addressing new terrorist threats, States have continued to adopt measures that still do not comply with the international human rights, humanitarian and refugee law framework, despite the progressive jurisprudence from national and regional courts that reaffirm the applicability of IHRL in the context of countering terrorism. There is an undeniable need to understand that to

[291] See HRW (2014), 'Abu Qatada trial showed UK/Jordan Torture Treaty is worthless', 11 July, https://www.hrw.org/news/2014/07/11/abu-qatada-trial-showed-uk/jordan-torture-treaty-worthless, accessed 19 October 2017.

break the cycle of terrorist violence, counter-terrorism strategies must not only go beyond a strict security approach to countering terrorism, but must also respect all human rights, as an element of comprehensively addressing all the conditions conducive to terrorism and violent extremism that may lead to terrorism. Human rights law, humanitarian and refugee law are not impediments to effectively countering terrorism. Security and the protection of the rights and dignity of all individuals are complementary and mutually reinforcing. It is thus essential that any measure to counter terrorism be grounded in, and fully respect, international law.

2. Impact of post-9/11 counter-terrorism measures on all human rights

Martin Scheinin

My tenure as the first Special Rapporteur on the promotion and protection of human rights while countering terrorism, appointed first by the Commission on Human Rights, then by the Human Rights Council (2005–2011), allowed first-hand exposure to the colossal negative and lasting impact that counter-terrorism measures can have on a whole range of human rights, including political, civil, economic, social and cultural rights. Counter-terrorism measures can affect everyone but they have overwhelmingly affected minorities, indigenous groups, political dissidents and human rights defenders.

The negative impact of counter-terrorism measures can either be the result of deliberate government policy, which aims to counter terrorism only in name but in fact pursues a political agenda, or be the unintentional consequence of badly conceived national, regional or international measures adopted to fight terrorism. Either way, the effect of these post-2001 measures has been a huge drawback for human rights, and in the space of fourteen years, very little effort has been made to return to a situation that is more favourable to human rights protection. On the contrary, also recent measures adopted by States to respond to a real or perceived terrorist threat continue to affect more and more human rights, such as the right to privacy or the right to not be rendered stateless.

This chapter aims (1) to explain the change of paradigm which occurred after the 11 September 2001 attacks in the United States, in particular with the UN Security Council taking decisive action to counter terrorism, and (2) to highlight some key trends in national responses which have impacted on a broad range of human rights.

1. UN SECURITY COUNCIL COUNTER-TERRORISM FRAMEWORK

The post-9/11 counter-terrorism framework has been very largely defined by the measures adopted by the Security Council. Key resolutions in the setting up of this framework include Security Council resolution 1373 (2001) which legislated on legal obligations of Member States in the combat against terrorism and set up a Counter-Terrorism Committee to oversee the national legislative changes and other measures. Another key resolution is the much newer resolution 2178 (2014) on foreign terrorist fighters, which expanded the legal obligations of Member States in the fight against terrorism. Already before 9/11, resolution 1267 (1999) had set up a sanctions mechanism which, together with subsequent resolutions, now includes an arms embargo, a travel ban and an asset freeze against individuals and entities even loosely related to Al-Qaida. Having determined that international terrorism is a threat to international peace and security, the Security Council was able to adopt most resolutions that deal with counter-terrorism under Chapter VII of the Charter of the United Nations. Therefore, many States and their international lawyers claim that States' counter-terrorism obligations would enjoy primacy in respect of human rights obligations, pursuant to Article 103 of the UN Charter.

1.1 UN Security Council Resolutions 1373 and 2178: General Counter-Terrorism Framework

In the immediate aftermath of the 11 September 2001 terrorist attacks on the New York World Trade Centre, the UN Security Council adopted resolution 1373 (2001). Acting under Chapter VII of the Charter, the Security Council required all States to criminalize terrorist acts; to penalize acts of support for or in preparation of terrorist offences; to criminalize the financing of terrorism; to exclude terrorist offences from the category of political crimes; to freeze funds of persons who commit or attempt to commit terrorist acts; and to strengthen international cooperation in criminal matters. This was the first time that the Security Council imposed on all UN Member States a number of general, permanent obligations, not connected to a specific conflict situation. In addition, the resolution set up the Counter-Terrorism Committee, to monitor States' implementation of resolution 1373.

Through this resolution, the Security Council established new binding rules of international law. Indeed, the obligations laid out in resolution

1373 contain no end in time, are not limited to a specific geographic area, and apply to any act of 'terrorism' committed worldwide. In my capacity as Special Rapporteur, I took the view that in adopting this resolution, the Security Council was acting ultra vires, exceeding the powers granted to it in the UN Charter.[1]

The UN Charter strikes a careful balance between the powers of various UN organs, and in particular between the General Assembly and the Security Council.[2] While the General Assembly, responsible inter alia for the development of international law and the adoption of new legally binding treaties, represents traditional modes of decision-making in international organizations and respect for the sovereign equality of states, the Security Council is in charge of addressing specific threats to international peace and security, through political action by a small number of states including the five major victors of World War II and, if necessary, through supranational enforcement. With resolution 1373, the Security Council identified international terrorism as a threat to peace and security, and took for itself 'legislative powers', powers which inherently belong to the General Assembly.[3] In addition, while the Security Council is granted a great deal of discretion to determine what amounts to a threat to peace, this determination must always be linked to a specific concrete situation, as opposed to an abstract problem or hypothetical future situation. Finally, measures adopted by the Security Council under Chapter VII should be taken on a case-by-case basis, according to the principle of proportionality,[4] to ensure that its exceptional powers are used solely to take measures deemed indispensable to countering a specific threat to peace and security. In contrast, the legal regime established by Security Council resolution 1373 has been maintained beyond any reasonable crisis situation that had emerged in September 2001.[5]

In 2014, the Security Council adopted resolution 2178 (2014) under Chapter VII of the UN Charter. This resolution, the adoption of which was driven by the flow of foreign fighters to join groups like ISIL in Iraq

---

1 See 'Report of the Special rapporteur on human rights and counter-terrorism', UN Doc. A/65/258.

2 Ibid., para. 38.

3 See Martin Scheinin (2014), 'Back to post-9/11 panic? Security Council resolution on foreign terrorist fighters', *Just Security*, 23 September, https://www.justsecurity.org/15407/post-911-panic-security-council-resolution-foreign-terrorist-fighters-scheinin/, accessed 5 June 2017.

4 See A/65/258 (n 1), para. 36.

5 See Scheinin (n 3).

and Syria, is another 'legislative' resolution, with 'teeth', which also includes wide-ranging legally binding obligations for States.[6] It requires States, inter alia, to prevent and suppress the recruiting, organizing, transporting or equipping of individuals who travel to engage in terrorist acts or terrorist training, and the financing of their travel and of their activities, as well as to ensure that domestic legislation establishes as serious criminal offences which duly reflect the seriousness of the offence, to travel, provide funds, organize or recruit individuals for the purpose of engaging in terrorist acts or training. It imposes upon all Member States far-reaching new legal obligations without any effort to limit its scope of application *racione loci*, or *ratione temporis*.

In terms of legal doctrine, there is a significant difference between resolution 1373 and resolution 2178. Resolution 1373 was adopted after the adoption by the General Assembly of the International Convention for the Suppression of the Financing of Terrorism (1999), and because it contained equivalent provisions, had the effect of speeding up its implementation and ultimately also its universal ratification process.[7] Resolution 2178 is different, in that it imposes totally new legislative obligations upon Member States without the existence of a preceding treaty adopted by the General Assembly, and there is no way States could regularize the legal basis for their action by ratifying an existing treaty. As such, resolution 2178 is worse – indeed, far worse – than resolution 1373 from the perspective of the international rule of law.

There is another key difference between the two resolutions. Resolution 1373 makes only one passing reference to human rights, in the very specific context of refugee status. Since then, several Security Council resolutions[8] refer to human rights through a so-called human rights clause, which prescribes that States must ensure that any measure taken to combat terrorism comply with all their obligations under international law, and should adopt such measures in accordance with international law, in particular international human rights, refugee and humanitarian law. Crucially, resolution 2178 contains this human rights clause in its

---

6 Ibid.

7 See Martin Scheinin (2014), 'A comment on Security Council Res 2178 (foreign terrorist fighters) as a "form" of global governance', *Just Security*, 6 October, https://www.justsecurity.org/15989/comment-security-council-res-2178-foreign-fighters-form-global-governance/, accessed 5 October 2017.

8 See, inter alia, UN Security Council resolutions 1456 (2003) – where the Security Council met at ministerial level and for the first time included this clause – and 1535 (2004).

preamble.[9] It should however be noted that in some other resolutions, the Security Council specifies that *all* actions taken to counter terrorism – and not only State action – must comply with international human rights law.[10] This more progressive wording thus includes UN action. This is not the formulation included in resolution 2178.

There is also a significant similarity between resolutions 1373 and 2178: they both aim to criminalize a phenomenon without defining it – namely 'terrorism'. In the light of the persistent problem of the lack of a universal, comprehensive and precise definition of 'terrorism' it was in 2001, and remains possibly even more acutely, problematic for binding permanent measures to be imposed by the Council on all Member States on the basis of hypothetical future acts falling under such a controversial and internationally undefined notion as terrorism.[11] As I highlighted already in 2005, when I took up my position as Special Rapporteur,[12] the international framework on counter-terrorism imposes obligations and issues instructions to States on the question of terrorism without there being a comprehensive definition of the term. This is not only problematic for States in their ability to determine levels of proper compliance with the framework, posing difficulties for extradition and mutual legal assistance, but also has adverse consequences for human rights. Calls by the international community to combat terrorism, without defining the term, has meant that individual States have been free to define what is meant by the term, as they wish. In turn, this has resulted in the international legitimization of conduct undertaken by oppressive regimes.

---

9 Operative clause (OP) 7: 'Reaffirming that Member States must ensure that any measures taken to counter terrorism comply with all their obligations under international law, in particular international human rights law, international refugee law, and international humanitarian law, underscoring that respect for human rights, fundamental freedoms and the rule of law are complementary and mutually reinforcing with effective counter-terrorism measures, and are an essential part of a successful counter-terrorism effort and notes the importance of respect for the rule of law so as to effectively prevent and combat terrorism, and noting that failure to comply with these and other international obligations, including under the Charter of the United Nations, is one of the factors contributing to increased radicalization and fosters a sense of impunity'.

10 See, e.g., Security Council resolution 1822 (2008) and General Assembly resolution 62/272 (2008). This formulation includes UN action to counter-terrorism.

11 See A/65/258 (n 1), para. 37.

12 'Report of the Special rapporteur on the promotion and protection of human rights and fundamental freedoms while countering terrorism', UN Doc. E.CN/4/2006/98, paras. 26 and 27.

Indeed, the Security Council has delivered the message that the international community wants strong action against 'terrorism' however defined.[13] By placing such a strong obligation on States, without defining the key term or providing an adequate framework, and with only a passing reference to human rights, resolution 1373 has been a handy tool for repressive regimes around the world. It has led to much abuse, and its consequences are still felt today. Governments have been very largely free to resort to vague and broad definitions of terrorism, which stigmatize as 'terrorism' whatever they do not like. This has included political opposition, trade unions, religious movements, minority and indigenous groups, and human rights defenders.

Resolution 2178 provides repressive and oppressive regimes with similar tools, and greater ground for action. If a country applies an abusive definition of terrorism that includes organized non-violent campaigns of indigenous groups towards self-determination, the criminalization of the provision of training to empower these groups, including in the field of human rights, would render this training illegal. The State could refer to its obligations under the UN Charter to justify a crackdown upon travel, training and funding of organizations and movements said to constitute a threat to the oppressive regime itself – even when totally non-violent. Both of these resolutions potentially allow States to breach fundamental rights all while seemingly complying with Security Council obligations.

The Security Council Counter-Terrorism Committee (CTC), set up by resolution 1373 to oversee the implementation of the resolution at the national level, could have contributed to mitigating this problem.[14] However, two factors prevented this from being the case. First, the mere existence of the mechanism was understood by many States as an obligation to take expansive counter-terrorism measures, even where the threat of terrorism was very limited. The second factor was the CTC's own dismissive approach to human rights. The CTC's initial policy on human rights was expressed by its first Chairman in a briefing to the

---

[13] Ibid.

[14] The CTC was established to monitor, including by considering reports of State parties, the implementation of the resolution. Over the years, its role has expanded. In particular, resolution 1535 (2004) established the Counter-Terrorism Committee Executive Directorate (CTED), and a greater role given to the CTC in determining where technical assistance in the field of counter-terrorism was needed for States. With this, the CTC began undertaking country visits, upon invitation by Member States.

Security Council on 18 January 2002: 'The Counter-Terrorism Committee is mandated to monitor the implementation of resolution 1373. Monitoring performance against other international conventions, including human rights law, is outside the scope of the Counter-Terrorism Committee's mandate.' Given the broad nature of resolution 1373, the fact that the definition of terrorism is a key condition to the effects of any counter-terrorism legislation, and that any counter-terrorism legislation will necessarily impact upon a range of human rights, such as the right to liberty and security, the absolute prohibition of torture and other ill-treatment, to a fair trial, to freedom of expression, religion and belief, to name a few, this approach was limiting and biased. It was however a clear reflection of the Security Council's general approach at the time, that human rights were secondary to the imperative of fighting terrorism.

While the CTC has since progressively introduced human rights standards in its daily work,[15] most notably through the 2006 conclusions for policy guidance regarding human rights which guide the Counter-Terrorism Committee Executive Directorate (CTED) in its daily work[16] as well as through its preliminary implementation assessments relating to resolution 1373,[17] and set up a working group on the human rights aspect of counter-terrorism within CTED,[18] the commitment to human rights

---

[15] For a first step, see UN Security Council resolution 1535 (2004) which set up the CTED and mandated it to liaise with the Office of the United Nations High Commissioner for Human Rights (OHCHR) and other human rights organizations in matters related to human rights in the context of countering terrorism.

[16] This document states that CTED should (1) Provide advice to the Committee, including for its ongoing dialogue with States on their implementation of resolution 1373 (2001), on international human rights, refugee and humanitarian law, in connection with identification and implementation of effective measures to implement resolution 1373 (2001); (2) Advise the Committee on how to ensure that any measures States take to implement the provisions of resolution 1624 (2005) comply with their obligations under international law, in particular international human rights law, refugee law, and humanitarian law; and (3) Liaise with the OHCHR and, as appropriate, with other human rights organizations in matters related to counter-terrorism. UN Security Council (2006), 'Conclusions for policy guidance regarding human rights and the CTC', UN Doc. S/AC.40/2006/PG.2.

[17] Commonly referred to as PIAs, they are documents prepared in advance of CTC visits to make a preliminary assessment and highlight possible problem areas, country visits and other interactions with Member States.

[18] As endorsed by Security Council resolution 1805 (2008). The working group's main objectives are to enhance expertise and develop common approaches by CTED staff on these issues, as well as to consider ways in which

needs to be translated into the practice of the Committee. In my capacity as Special Rapporteur, I conducted a study to assess the human rights implications of the questions and comments between Member States and the Committee regarding the reports submitted by Member States pursuant to resolution 1373. I examined approximately 100 reports submitted between November 2005 and May 2010. The results of this study showed that while the CTC never asked questions that were openly in opposition with human rights standards, there were many instances in which the questions posed seemed to promote counter-terrorism measures which could interfere with the enjoyment of specific human rights. This approach reflected a lack of sensitivity to a number of potentially affected rights and risked giving States the impression that turning a blind eye to international human rights standards was acceptable in this context. While we still do not know what is being discussed confidentially between the CTC and Member States, what is publicly available from State reports leaves room for improvement in a number of key areas. This includes the guarantees of due process that should accompany the freezing of the funds of individuals suspected of being linked to terrorism; the right to seek asylum and to non-refoulement obligations, with often too broad an approach being taken by the Committee on the issue of exclusion, suggesting that national security or public order are sufficient grounds to exclude a refugee; and freedom of association, with the Committee asking questions about States monitoring the activities of charitable organizations and non-governmental organizations, without mention of international freedom of expression and freedom of association standards, which in turn risks providing oppressive States with further pretexts to crack down on human rights defenders. Finally, there is no public record of the interest of the CTC in curtailing politically inspired over-inclusive national definitions of terrorism that pose a threat both to human rights and to the efficiency of proper counter-terrorism

---

the Committee might more effectively encourage Member States to comply with their international obligations in this area. See also UN Security Council resolution 1963 (2010) in which the Security Council for the first time adopts UN Global Counter-Terrorism Strategy and Plan of Action language and states that effective counter-terrorism measures and respect for human rights are complementary and mutually reinforcing, and are an essential part of a successful counter-terrorism effort. It also notes the importance of respect for the rule of law so as to effectively combat terrorism and 'thus encourages CTED to further develop its activities in this area, to ensure that all human rights issues relevant to the implementation of resolutions 1373 (2001) and 1624 (2005) are addressed consistently and even-handedly including, as appropriate, on country visits that are organized with the consent of the visited member State'.

measures. Consequently, some States have used this mechanism to obtain international recognition – even a stamp of approval – for rights-limiting measures which thcy would possibly not have otherwise taken, or not otherwise have adopted so openly.

1.2 The Al-Qaida Sanctions Regime

The second main aspect of the Security Council's counter-terrorism regime is a sanctions mechanism.

1.2.1 Key characteristics

Security Council Resolution 1267 (1999) was adopted following the bombing of the US Embassy in Kenya. It established the 1267 Al Qaida and Taliban Sanctions Regime. This resolution[19] adopted under Chapter VII of the UN Charter required all States to take a number of measures, an asset freeze, a travel ban and an arms embargo[20] in connection with any individual or entity 'associated with' Al-Qaida and the Taliban, as designated by the Sanctions Committee, and placed on the Al-Qaida Sanctions List. In 2011, the original procedure stopped dealing with the Taliban, to only include individuals and entities associated with Al-Qaida, while a separate committee was created to deal exclusively with the Taliban.[21] Resolutions 2170 (2014) and 2178 (2014) added new responsibilities to the Committee, in particular to report on the threat posed by groups like ISIL associated with Al-Qaida and on foreign terrorist fighters and make recommendations on potential responses.

1.2.2 Key concerns

Even though the number of listed individuals and entities was always rather small, these sanctions have had a huge impact on the human rights[22] of the individuals listed. There are two key concerns linked to this regime: whether the system is compatible with the powers of the

---

[19] Together with other numerous resolutions which have modified the system drastically, including: resolutions 1333 (2000), 1390 (2002), 1455 (2003), 1526 (2004), 1617 (2005), 1735 (2006), 1822 (2008), 1904 (2009), 1989 (2011) and resolution 2083 (2012).

[20] It also provided for a mechanism of humanitarian exemptions – to assist in the basic needs of human life – which are authorized on a case-by-case basis.

[21] Security Council resolutions 1989 (2011), and 1988 (2011), which created a new committee to only deal with the Taliban.

[22] Listings at the regional or national levels – which find their legal basis in Security Council resolution 1373 (2001), can have a similar impact on those listed.

Security Council under Chapter VII; and whether the regime complies with basic principles of due process, applicable to all individuals, including those suspected of terrorism-related activities.

1.2.2.1 Compatibility with the Security Council's powers under Chapter VII of the UN Charter I concluded in 2011 that the 1267 regime amounts to action ultra vires[23] by the Security Council. The modifications brought to the regime by resolution 1390 (2002) following the defeat of the Taliban rule in Afghanistan constitute the first example of an open-ended resolution on sanctions, adopted under Chapter VII, without any link to a specific territory or State. While resolution 1267 (1999) could be seen as a temporary emergency measure by the Security Council, using its Chapter VII powers to address a specific threat to peace and security, from 2002 the regime was no longer limited in time or space. Meanwhile, the rapid progress in State ratifications of the International Convention for the Suppression of the Financing of Terrorism provides a proper legal basis for States' obligations in this field. Further, the actual effectiveness of the listing created pursuant to resolution 1267 in targeting appropriate persons for sanctions is far from proven. Furthermore, while the sanctions regime of the Security Council that imposes severe sanctions upon named individuals can be said to have judicial or quasi-judicial character, the role of the Security Council under the UN Charter requires that any legal determinations by it should always be limited to a particular situation and should be interpreted as being of a preliminary rather than a final character. The Security Council powers under this regime are thus difficult to reconcile with the legal order of the Charter, and the provisions of its article 41.[24]

1.2.2.2 Compliance with basic principles of due process Targeted sanctions under the regime have come under frequent criticism by legal scholars and in the reports commissioned by international organizations, and they have been challenged in a number of legal proceedings, at international, regional and national level. Most concerns have been raised about procedural fairness and the absence of effective means for an individual to challenge a listing decision once made.

The 2005 World Summit Outcome document called upon the Security Council, with the support of the Secretary-General, to ensure that fair and

---

[23] See Martin Scheinin and Lisa Ginsborg (2011), 'You can't always get what you want: The Kadi II conundrum and the Security Council 1267 Terrorist Sanctions Regime', *Essex Human Rights Review*, **8**, 7–19.

[24] See A/65/258 (n 1), para. 52.

clear procedures existed for placing individuals and entities on sanctions lists and for removing them, as well as for granting humanitarian exemptions.[25] On 29 June 2010, the Security Council held a debate on the promotion and strengthening of the rule of law in the maintenance of international peace and security and addressed also the efficiency and credibility of sanctions regimes.[26] As Special Rapporteur, I also expressed concern that the listing practice created pursuant to resolution 1267 (1999) has had a serious impact on due process-related rights for individuals suspected of terrorism, as well as their families, and highlighted that as the Security Council had taken on quasi-judicial functions, the procedure for de-listing needed to meet the standards required to ensure a fair and public hearing by a competent, independent and impartial tribunal established by law.[27]

The greatest challenges to the system, however, have been the various international, regional and national rulings that have concluded that the consequences of the system were in violation of the rights of defence, the right to be heard and the right to an effective judicial review as well as to the right to freedom of movement, private life, honour and reputation, and to property.[28] These cases were quite damaging for the Security Council. In addition to lowering the effectiveness of the system and undermining its authority, the European decisions bound two States that were also permanent members of the Security Council. Numerous

---

[25] See General Assembly resolution 60/1 (2005), para. 109.

[26] See UN Security Council Presidential Statement (2010), UN Doc. S/PRST/2010/11, 29 June.

[27] See 'Report of the Special Rapporteur on the protection of human rights and fundamental freedoms while countering terrorism', UN Doc. A/63/223, para. 16; UN Doc. and A/65/258 (n 1), paras. 51–58.

[28] See Joined Cases C-402/05 P and C-415/05 P, *Yassin Abdullah Kadi and Al Barakaat International Foundation v. Council of the EU and Commission of the EC* (ECJ, 3 September 2008), in which the Court found a violation of the applicants' rights of defence, right to be heard and right to an effective judicial review. See also UN Human Rights Committee, *Sayadi and Vinck v. Belgium*, Communication No. 1472/2006, UN Doc. CCPR/C/94/D/1472/2006, 29 December 2008, in which the Committee found a violation of the applicants' freedom of movement (Article 12 ICCPR) and right to privacy and protection against unlawful attacks on their honour and reputation (Article 17 ICCPR). See also Joined Cases C-584/10 P, C-593/10 P and C-595/10 P, *Commission and Others v. Kadi* (Grand Chamber, 18 July 2013), in which the Court found a violation of the applicant's rights of defence, right to effective judicial review and right to property. See also *Nada v. Switzerland*, App. no. 10593/08 (ECtHR, 12 September 2012), in which the Court found a violation of the applicant's right to respect for his private life and right to an effective domestic remedy.

improvements were therefore gradually brought to the regime, notably in respect of the status of affected individuals, such as the notification of listed individuals,[29] the dissemination of statements[30] and narrative summaries of reasons for listing,[31] and the mandatory review of all entries on the list,[32] as well as in respect of the procedures for listing and de-listing, including the establishment of an Office of the Ombudsperson to receive requests from individuals and entities seeking to be removed from the list and that nowadays has de facto de-listing powers, even if accompanied by a *de jure* power of Security Council members to block the de-listing.[33]

There are in my view three key issues that remain: first, the question of the criteria for placement on the list, second, the duration of the listing, and third, the question of the evidence used. On the first point, the criteria for placement on the list, resolution 1989 (2011) refers to the possibility of including on the list any individual or entity designated by the Security Council's Sanctions Committee as 'associated' with Al-Qaida. This includes those that finance, plan, facilitate, prepare or perpetrate activities or acts in conjunction with Al-Qaida, under its name, on its behalf, or in its support; those that supply, sell, transfer arms to Al-Qaida, recruit for Al-Qaida, or support acts or activities of Al-Qaida or any cell, affiliate, splinter group or derivative thereof.[34] Resolution 2083 (2012) clarified that the criteria for listing covers resources used for the provision of internet hosting and related services in support of Al-Qaida and those associated with it,[35] the use of proceeds from drug cultivation, production and trafficking,[36] and to the payment of ransoms to those placed on the Al-Qaida Sanctions List.[37] Finally, resolution 2178 (2014) adds that it also applies to funds, financial assets or economic resources made available to or for the benefit of listed individuals in connection with their travel, including costs incurred with respect to

---

29 See Security Council resolution 1735 (2006), paras. 10 and 11.
30 See Security Council resolution 1735 (2006).
31 See Security Council resolution 1822 (2008), para. 12.
32 See Security Council resolution 1822 (2008), paras. 25 and 26.
33 See Security Council resolutions 1904 (2009), 1989 (2011), 2083 (2012) and 2161 (2014).
34 See Security Council resolution 1989 (2011), para. 4.
35 See Security Council resolution 2083 (2012), para. 4.
36 See Security Council resolution 2083 (2012), para. 5.
37 See Security Council resolution 2083 (2012), para. 6.

transportation and lodging.[38] The reference to the *payment* of ransom alone in the above list demonstrates how far 'association' can be stretched.

Both the practice of the 1267 Committee in listing, and what we know of the type of the organizational structure of Al-Qaida, reveal the breadth of the targeting criteria set forth by the Security Council. As is now well known, Al-Qaida has for the past ten years been more a cult or an idea than an organization with a chain of command and a clear membership.[39] In turn, this has given a wide margin of manoeuvre to the Committee in determining who could be on the list. This is compounded by what we know of the practice of the Committee regarding its procedure for placing individuals and entities on the list, which is (1) based on confidential information often solely shared at capital level directly between intelligence agencies, not at the diplomatic UN level of the Committee, which has too diverse a membership for such confidential information to be shared, and (2) following an 'I agree to list without questions asked provided you reciprocate' no objection procedure. The listing procedure thus has great potential for unintended errors, or for deliberate abuse by certain States to place on this list groups or individuals they do not like. It was, and remains, a political decision taken by diplomatic representatives of States within political bodies, not necessarily shared between the deciding States. One striking example of the breadth of the listing is the fact that ISIL is included in the Al-Qaida Sanctions list, as an alias of Al-Qaida in Iraq, despite a very public disavowal of ISIL by Al-Qaida's leader in February 2014.

Regarding the question of the duration of the listing, I noted already in 2008 that because of the indefinite freezing of the assets of those listed, the listing amounted to a 'criminal charge' in the human rights law meaning of the term, owing to the severity of the sanction. As the European Union General Court said in 2010, '[i]n the scale of a human life, 10 years in fact represent a substantial period of time and the question of the classification of the measures in question as preventative or punitive, protective or confiscatory, civil or criminal seems now to be

---

[38] See Security Council resolution 2178 (2014), para. 6.

[39] See Patrick Cockburn, 'Al-Qa'ida is an idea rather than an organization, and this has long been the case. For a five-year period after 1996, it did have cadres, resources, and camps in Afghanistan, but these were eliminated after the overthrow of the Taliban in 2001. Subsequently, al Qa'ida's name became primarily a rallying cry, a set of Islamic beliefs (...)'. Patrick Cockburn (2014), *The Jihadis Return, ISIS and the New Sunni Uprising*, New York and London: OR Books, p. 39.

an open one'.[40] While the original 1267 resolution could be seen as a temporary emergency measure by the Security Council, using its Chapter VII powers to address a specific threat to peace and security, the process is now unlimited in time and space. While the stated objective of the sanctions imposed under the 1267 regime may be preventive and deterrent, their actual impact on designated individuals and entities is comparable in nature to a penal sanction. And this, in turn, calls for a strict application of the standards required to ensure a fair and public hearing by a competent, independent and impartial tribunal established by law. Despite the improvements brought to the system, this requirement is in my view still not met. In particular, there is still no right to an effective remedy.[41] As stated by the Ombudsperson herself, 'while the Ombudsperson process remains a robust one, there are limitations to its fairness and effectiveness arising principally from a lack of transparency of procedures, especially in the latter stages of the process'.[42]

The third key remaining issue, disclosure of evidence, is at the heart of the legal problems arising out of the sanctions regime. Indeed, as seen, the listing is based on secret communication that may or may not contain factual evidence and which is often not shared even between Committee member States, and therefore will also not easily be shared with any body in charge of reviewing the lawfulness and legality of the listing, whether at the level of the UN, or by national, regional or international courts. Without this information, any review procedure will fall short of the necessary requirements to ensure a fair and public hearing. This is what was meant by the European Union General Court when it said 'the review carried out by the Community judicature of Community measures to freeze funds can be regarded as effective only if it concerns, indirectly, the substantive assessments of the Sanctions Committee itself and the evidence underlying them'. This position was echoed by the European

[40] Case T-85/09, *Yassin Abdullah Kadi v. Commission* (CJEU, 30 September 2010), para. 150.

[41] See 'Report of the Special Rapporteur on the promotion and protection of human rights while countering terrorism', UN Doc. A/63/233, for an overview of the applicable legal framework relating to the right to a fair trial. Notably, in *Sayadi and Vinck v. Belgium* (n 28), the Human Rights Committee dismissed a complaint that the listing resulted in a breach of Article 14 ICCPR (fair trial), as in the Committee's views the sanctions did not amount to a 'criminal charge'. This outcome is, however, difficult to reconcile with the Committee's own General Comment No. 32 on fair trial.

[42] See (2015), 'Ninth report of the Ombudsperson to the Security Council', UN Doc. S/2015/80, para. 56.

Court of Human Rights. This is also the problem faced by the Ombudsperson, as she highlighted in her ninth report to the Security Council in early 2015. In light of these various issues, I remain of the opinion that this sanction mechanism should be replaced with a system whereby the UN and the Security Council would continue to be involved through, inter alia, assistance and advice, while the actual listing of individuals would be done by Member States, accompanied by adequate procedural guarantees.[43]

2. KEY HUMAN RIGHTS CONCERNS POSED BY THE POST-2001 COUNTER-TERRORISM REGIME

The regime set forth by the Security Council has, by its very existence, undermined the protection of human rights. States often took the 90-day deadline included in resolution 1373 (2001) to report on their implementation of the resolution as a deadline to adopt legislation. As a result, States have adopted legislation in a rushed manner, often using exceptional powers or procedures, without sufficient consultation, all while seemingly abiding by their international obligations. In this legislation, States have ill-defined terrorism, which has had consequences on the entire gamut of rights, and individuals, that can be, are, and have been, affected by counter-terrorism measures.

At the same time, the role of the Security Council should not be overstated, either. In many States, emergency counter-terrorism legislation pre-dated the requirements set forth by the Security Council, while in other cases, such rights-limiting legislation would have been adopted regardless of Security Council involvement. A common defining element, however, is that the existence of harsh counter-terrorism measures was regarded by the international community as a positive value. The fact that it eroded human rights and had a very negative impact on individuals, communities, ethnic and religious groups was not taken into consideration – except by a few lone voices – until a few years later.

2.1 Definition of Terrorism and Related Offences

Counter-terrorism laws, policies and practices must be limited to the countering of terrorism, as properly defined. The approach taken by most

43 'Report of the Special Rapporteur on the promotion and protection of human rights and fundamental freedoms while countering terrorism', 22 December 2010, UN Doc. A/HRC/16/51, para. 33.

States is to link terrorist offences to a stand-alone definition of 'terrorism', a 'terrorist act', 'terrorist activity' or similar terms. Such definitions are very often also linked to the listing of proscribed organizations, and are the trigger for special powers of arrest, questioning and investigation, alterations in the rules concerning detention and trial, and administrative measures, such as deportation procedures and the forfeiting of property.[44] The legislation introduced to combat terrorism, or legislation on national security, or in some cases legislation on asylum, which can indirectly deal with counter-terrorism as it applies to non-nationals, often affords lower levels of protection to individuals suspected of acts of terrorism. This includes precluding or limiting recourse to an independent judiciary,[45] extending periods of police and pre-trial detention,[46] and limiting access to a lawyer.[47] Counter-terrorism legislation can also include recourse to military or special tribunals for terrorism-related cases, which can have a serious impact on the independence, impartiality and competence of the judiciary, as well as lower fair trial guarantees.[48] Consequently, the adoption of overly broad definitions of terrorism carries the potential for deliberate misuse of the term. It can overly impact on, or stigmatize, certain individuals or groups or, where such laws and measures restrict the enjoyment of human rights and freedom, or offend the principles of necessity and proportionality that govern the permissibility of any restriction of human rights.[49]

One Security Council resolution needs to be mentioned as representing a positive approach that respects international rule of law. In the absence of a universally agreed upon, comprehensive and concise definition of terrorism, counter-terrorism laws and policies must be limited to the countering of offences that correspond to the characteristics of conduct to be suppressed in the fight against international terrorism, as identified by the Security Council in its resolution 1566 (2004), paragraph 3.[50] While

---

44 Id., para. 26.
45 See A/63/223 (n 27), para. 13.
46 See A/63/223 (n 27), para. 18.
47 See A/63/223 (n 27), paras. 68 and 69.
48 See A/63/223 (n 27), paras. 23–28.
49 See A/HRC/16/51 (n 43), para. 26.
50 'criminal acts, including against civilians, committed with the intent to cause death or serious bodily injury, or taking of hostages, with the purpose to provoke a state of terror in the general public or in a group of persons or particular persons, intimidate a population or compel a government or an international organization to do or to abstain from doing any act, act, which constitute offences within the scope of and as defined in the international conventions and protocols relating to terrorism'.

the international community is concerned with international terrorism, individual States may in my view also legitimately include in their terrorism definitions conduct that corresponds to all elements of a serious crime as defined by their national law, when combined with the other cumulative characteristics of resolution 1566. In addition, definitions of terrorism and associated offences must be accessible, formulated with sufficient precision, non-discriminatory and non-retroactive.[51] Besides the characteristics included in resolution 1566, States may also refer to the motivation of actors to advance a political, religious, or ideological cause. While acts of terrorism are under no circumstances justifiable, reference to these motivations can assist in further narrowing the scope of application of the definition of terrorism.[52]

In my capacity as Special Rapporteur, I offered the following definition of terrorism as a model:

> Terrorism means an action or attempted action where:
>
> (1) the action:
> (a) constituted the intentional killing of hostages; or
> (b) is intended to cause death or serious bodily injury to one or more members of the general population or segments of it; or
> (c) involved lethal or serious physical violence against one or more members of the general population or segments of it;
>
> *and*
>
> (2) the action is done or attempted with the intention of:
> (a) provoking a state of terror in the general public or segments of it; or
> (b) compelling a government or international organization to do or abstain from doing something;
>
> *and*
>
> (3) the action corresponds to:
> (a) the definition of a serious offence in national law, enacted for the purpose of complying with international conventions and protocols relating to terrorism or with resolutions of the Security Council relating to terrorism; or
> (b) all elements of a serious crime defined by national law.[53]

---

[51] See Article 15 ICCPR, General Assembly resolution 63/185 para. 18, and 'Report of the Special Rapporteur on the promotion and protection of human rights and fundamental freedoms while countering terrorism', UN Doc. E/CN.4/2006/98, para. 49.

[52] See A/HRC/16/51 (n 43), para. 26.

[53] See A/HRC/16/51 (n 43), para. 28.

2.2 Increased Powers for Executive Authorities: Intelligence Information and Administrative Measures

Counter-terrorism legislation adopted in the post-9/11 context often also affords greater powers to the executive, through the use of various mechanisms which limit judicial involvement altogether. This increase in administrative powers is often heavily reliant on the security services. Since September 2001, some governments insisted that clear distinctions between intelligence and law enforcement powers were no longer tenable, arguing that the extraordinary character of the contemporary terrorist threat demands that intelligence agencies acquire new powers to interrogate, arrest and detain people. Such powers are not per se in violation of international law, provided those agencies to which the powers are given comply with all relevant human rights standards, as well as domestic constitutional and other provisions prescribed for ordinary law enforcement agencies.

However, in certain cases, these powers were granted to intelligence agencies precisely to circumvent these safeguards. This is an abuse of the legitimate secrecy of intelligence operations, which in turn can endanger the trust that individuals place in their intelligence agencies in a democratic society, but also at a more practical level it can endanger the rule of law, as the line between collection of evidence in a criminal setting and the collection of intelligence becomes more blurred. This can lead to a situation where States begin preferring to use undisclosed evidence gathered by intelligence agents in administrative proceedings over attempts to prove guilt beyond reasonable doubt in a criminal trial.[54]

2.2.1 Powers to detain and interrogate

In some cases, intelligence agencies have legally acquired the power to detain people who are expected to have information about terrorist activities. While such preventive detention for public security reasons may in exceptional cases be a proportionate interference with the right to liberty, there are situations where individuals are detained for a long period of time for the sole purpose of intelligence gathering or on broad grounds in the name of prevention. These situations constitute arbitrary deprivation of liberty. The mere administrative detention of a person, for the sole purpose of gathering information, is unlawful.[55] The lack of

---

[54] 'Report of the UN Special Rapporteur on the promotion and protection of human rights and fundamental freedoms while countering terrorism', UN Doc. A/HRC/14/46, para. 37.

[55] See A/HRC/10/3 (n 54), para. 38.

effective judicial oversight over the actions of intelligence services, which can result in impunity for their actions, is also a cause for concern.[56] Any power of detention and interrogation of the intelligence services must find its basis in the law,[57] and must be under the strict and effective control of ordinary civilian authorities. Intelligence agencies must at all times operate with full respect of international human rights law.[58] In addition, they must be held accountable for any violations of international law, including for gross human rights violations, such as extraordinary renditions, torture, disappearances or secret detention.[59]

2.2.2 Intelligence cooperation

To fully gauge the impact of the use of intelligence information in countering terrorism on human rights, it is necessary to examine the issue of intelligence cooperation. While such cooperation is necessary, because terrorist operations can be, and often are, mounted transnationally,[60] it is also susceptible to lead to serious human rights violations in the absence of stringent safeguards and accountability mechanisms. As became clear through the comprehensive system of extraordinary renditions and prolonged secret detention, joint operations can lead to serious human rights violations. Such a system required an international web of exchange of information, some of which was corrupted, shared systematically with partners in the war on terror through intelligence cooperation.[61] Such a system was only made possible through the collaboration of many States, either through the provision of information, the facilitation of renditions through the provision of individuals, airspace or airports, or the hosting of secret detention centres.[62]

All States are responsible when they knowingly engage in, render aid or assist in the commission of internationally wrongful acts, including violations of human rights. Grave human rights violations by States such as torture, enforced disappearances or arbitrary detention should place

---

56 See A/HRC/10/3 (n 54), para. 39.

57 See A/HRC/10/3 (n 54), para. 40.

58 See A/HRC/10/3 (n 54), para. 69.

59 See A/HRC/10/3 (n 54), para. 72.

60 It became clear, soon after the events of 11 September 2001, that the attacks were prepared in part in Western Europe, and that some of the terrorists apparently involved in the attack were under observation by, inter alia, the French and German intelligence agencies. See A/HRC/10/3 (n 54), para. 47. For more on this issue, see id., paras. 47–54.

61 A/HRC/10/3 (n 54), para. 51.

62 A/HRC/10/3 (n 54), para. 52.

constraints on policies of cooperation by States, including between their intelligence agencies, with States that are known to violate human rights. The prohibition against torture is an absolute and peremptory norm of international law. States must not aid or assist in the commission of acts of torture, or recognize such practices as lawful by relying on intelligence information obtained through torture. Safeguards to prevent intelligence agencies from making use of such intelligence must be introduced.[63]

Another cause for concern is the participation of foreign agents in the interrogation of persons held in situations that violate international human rights standards. The active participation through the sending of interrogators or questions, or even the mere presence of intelligence personnel at an interview with a person who is being held in places where his rights are being violated can be reasonably understood as implicitly condoning such practices. The continuous engagement and presence of foreign officials has in some cases constituted a form of encouragement or even support. In my view, State responsibility may be triggered also by even more passive and geographically distant forms of creating a demand for intelligence information obtained through internationally wrongful means. The active or passive participation by States in the interrogation of persons held by another State constitutes an internationally wrongful act if the State knew or ought to have known that the person was facing a real risk of torture or other prohibited treatment, including arbitrary detention.[64]

Finally, regarding the sending and receiving of intelligence for operational use, at a minimum States that know or ought to know that they are receiving intelligence obtained through violations of human rights, and are either creating a demand for such information or elevating its operational use to a policy are complicit in the human rights violations in question. Indeed, reliance on information from torture in another country, even if the information is obtained only for 'operational purposes', inevitably implies the 'recognition of lawfulness' of such practices and therefore triggers the application of principles of State responsibility. States that receive information obtained through torture or inhuman or degrading treatment are complicit in the commission of internationally wrongful acts. This is also irreconcilable with the obligation *erga omnes* of States to cooperate in the eradication of torture.[65]

---

[63] A/HRC/10/3 (n 54), para. 53.
[64] A/HRC/10/3 (n 54), para. 54.
[65] A/HRC/10/3 (n 54), para. 55.

2.2.3 Rights-limiting administrative measures

States have also increased their reliance on information provided by the security services for the adoption of rights-limiting administrative measures, which by nature limit the involvement of the judiciary.

2.2.3.1 'Terrorist' listings and sanctions The first type of such measure includes the use of targeted sanctions through the listing of terrorist suspects. Typically, such listings result in a denial of access by listed individuals to their own property, a refusal of social security benefits, limitations on their ability to work and restrictions on their ability to travel domestically and internationally. They can impact on the entire family, when the individual listed is the sole working member of the family, or because of the reputational cost of the listing. As such, they significantly interfere with the right to freedom of movement, property rights, the right to privacy, the right to work, to health and the right to family life. I have noted that the implementation of any sanctions against individuals or entities listed as terrorist must comply with the following minimum safeguards: (1) Sanctions against the individual or entity are based on reasonable grounds to believe that the individual or entity has knowingly carried out, participated in or facilitated a terrorist act; (2) The listed individual or entity is promptly informed of the listing and its factual grounds, the consequences of such listing and the matters in items (3) to (6) below; (3) The listed individual or entity has the right to apply for de-listing or non-implementation of the sanctions, and has a right to court review of the decision resulting from such application, with due process rights applying to such review, including disclosure of the case against him, her or it, and such rules concerning the burden of proof that are commensurate with the severity of the sanctions; (4) The listed individual or entity has the right to make a fresh application for delisting or lifting of sanctions in the event of a material change of circumstances or the emergence of new evidence relevant to the listing; (5) The listing of an individual or entity, and the sanctions resulting from it, lapse automatically after 12 months, unless renewed through a determination that meets the requirements of items (1) to (3) above; and (6) Compensation is available for persons and entities wrongly affected, including third parties.

2.2.3.2 Administrative detention on grounds of national security These administrative measures also include greater use of administrative detention on national security grounds,[66] often combined with immigration or deportation measures, based on an element of suspicion that a person forms a 'threat to national security' or similar expressions that lack the level of precision required by the principle of legality.[67] States have increasingly placed their immigration policies and laws at the centre of their counter-terrorism strategies: it is indeed 'easier' to deport individuals that they consider as a threat, and detain them prior to deportation, than try them before a court. This way, States can rely on the less stringent safeguards applicable to deportations rather than the strict fair trial standards applicable to criminal proceedings.

States are allowed to detain foreigners for the purpose of deportation and extradition for as long as is necessary to carry out proceedings. Under the European Convention on Human Rights (ECHR), the detention of foreigners is one of the specifically listed grounds for detention under Article 5. However, where the State does not have any intention of deporting or extraditing the individuals, or where there are legal or practical reasons the deportation or extradition becomes impossible – such as respect for the absolute prohibition of *refoulement* – the continued detention of the foreigner not charged with a serious crime will become arbitrary. Also, such detention is only lawful as long as the State undertakes proceedings to that effect; where the State is not diligent enough in carrying out the proceedings, or where the proceedings take too long, the continued detention will become unreasonable and will therefore be considered arbitrary. It is not disputed under either the International Covenant on Civil and Political Rights (ICCPR) or the ECHR that States have a right to determine who is entitled to enter and stay on their territory, nor is it disputed that they have the right to detain foreigners prior to deportation. However, a State should not place immigration laws at the centre of their counter-terrorism strategies. Terrorists are criminals, and should be dealt with as such, whereas immigration laws should serve to regulate immigration. Given the impact of removal measures, it is important that the State includes appropriate safeguards before any deportation takes place, including to ensure that the deportation is not used as a form of administrative detention based on discriminatory grounds and to consider any risk of ill-treatment of the individual upon return to prevent any violation of the absolute prohibition of *refoulement*.

---

66 See A/63/223 (n 27), para. 19.
67 Ibid.

Detention on grounds of national security often means that one or several members of the executive decide to detain individuals on the grounds that they are suspected of being engaged in terrorist activities, are therefore a danger to national security, and must be detained to prevent them from carrying out their terrorist activities. This is also referred to as preventive detention on national security grounds. This can lead to serious abuse, especially where either the definition of acts of terrorism is itself overly broad to encompass actions which are not terrorist per se, or where the deciding authority need not bring evidence that the individual is a risk to national security. As noted by the Human Rights Committee, such detention is permitted by Article 9 of the ICCPR under very limited circumstances 'where the person concerned constitutes a clear and serious threat to society that cannot be contained in any other manner'.[68] It is noteworthy that the ECHR does not allow detention on such grounds. The European Court of Human Rights (ECtHR) has on a number of occasions found 'internment and preventive detention without charge to be incompatible with the fundamental right to liberty under Article 5 § 1, in the absence of a valid derogation under Article 15'.[69] This position was restated again in the case of *A v. UK* (2009) in which the British Government argued that 11 individuals were detained on national security grounds with a view to deportation to their home country, as permitted under Article 5(1)(f) of the ECHR. The European Court, instead of accepting this, noted that 'it is, instead, clear (…) that the applicants were certified and detained because they were suspected of being international terrorists and because it was believed that their presence at liberty in the United Kingdom gave rise to a threat to national security',[70] and concluded the detention was not allowed under the ECHR, unless the UK had validly derogated from the Convention.

The detention of terrorist suspects on grounds of national security is problematic outside the context of true emergencies that threaten the life of the nation, from both a practical and a legal perspective. On the practical side, unless detention is permanent – which is clearly contrary to international human rights law – the individual will need to be released. This raises doubts of the benefits of such detention from the State's point of view, and begs the question: wouldn't it be more useful to

---

[68] Human Rights Committee (1990), *David Alberto Campora Schweizer v. Uruguay*, Communication No. 66/1980, UN Doc. CCPR/C/OP/2 at 90, para. 18.1.

[69] See *A and Others v. UK*, App. No. 3455/05 (ECtHR, 19 February 2009), para. 172.

[70] Id., at para. 191.

try an individual who is truly dangerous and involved in acts of terrorism than to detain him for a period of time, and then have him released? From a legal perspective, it is also argued that the right to a fair trial enshrined in all international and regional human rights instruments also includes the right to a trial. States should not be allowed to circumvent the safeguards protecting criminal defendants by detaining them as terrorist suspects without charging them. This is the point made by the UN's Working Group on Arbitrary Detention in the case of *Satray v. Malaysia*.[71]

Regarding the right of access to courts for individuals in detention, international law is very clear: All persons who are detained, whatever the reason or legal basis for their detention, and wherever they are detained, must have access to courts to review the legality of their detention.[72] As such, individuals who are detained administratively on grounds of security pursuant to an executive decision, or who are detained in the context of immigration, deportation or removal, or pending extradition must be given the opportunity to challenge the lawfulness of their detention.[73] The court in charge of the habeas corpus

---

71 UN Working Group on Arbitrary Detention (2010), in the case of *Satray v. Malaysia* Opinion No. 32/2008, UN Doc. A/HRC/13/30/Add.1 at 123. Mr Satray was arrested in April 2002 and was still detained in 2008, when the Working Group examined his case. He was detained under the Internal Security Act, under suspicion of being a member of the 'Jemaah Islamiyyah', which allowed for potentially indefinite detention, based on a suspicion that the person 'has acted or is about to act or is likely to act in any manner prejudicial to the security of Malaysia'. The Working Group noted that Mr Satray had been detained for more than six and a half years, without any charges being brought against him, and without the possibility of a fair and public hearing by an independent and impartial tribunal. During this time, the government had not produced any evidence to substantiate its accusation that he was a member of the Jemaah Islamiyyah. The Working Group considered that no one should be detained without trial, based on Article 10 Universal Declaration on Human Rights (UDHR): 'Everyone is entitled in full equality to a fair and public hearing by an independent and impartial tribunal, in the determination of his rights and obligations and of any criminal charge against him'. Therefore, an arrest carried out in virtue of the sole decision of police officers and a detention stemming from an order issued by an Executive authority, like the Minister of Home Affairs and Internal Security, and not by a judge or magistrate, is not in conformity with the UDHR.

72 This is enshrined in Article 9(4) of the ICCPR which contains a broad right of habeas corpus, as well as in Article 5(4) ECHR, and Article 7 of the American Convention on Human Rights.

73 Let's illustrate the application of this Article to administrative detention with the Human Rights Committee (2004), *Ahani v. Canada*, Communication

review must have the ability to carry out a substantive review.[74] The jurisprudence of the ECtHR is very useful in providing additional clarity on this issue. It has summarized its own case law by stating: 'Article 5(4) does not guarantee a right of judicial review of such a scope as to empower the court, on all aspects of the case (…) to substitute its own discretion for that of the decision-making authority. The review should, however, be wide enough to bear on those conditions which are essential for the "lawful" detention of a person (…). The reviewing court must not have merely advisory functions, but must have the competence to "decide" on the "lawfulness" of the detention and to order release if detention is unlawful'.[75]

The ECtHR also noted that there is no uniform, unvarying standard to be applied irrespective of the context, facts and circumstances. However, in all cases, the court must (1) have a judicial character; (2) provide guarantees appropriate to the type of deprivation of liberty in question; (3) the proceedings must be adversarial and must always ensure equality of arms between the parties. The requirement of equality of arms is particularly relevant in the context of administrative detention, because of the frequent use of intelligence information – which will be kept secret – as a basis for the detention. The ECtHR has admitted the use of intelligence in principle by saying that:

> [T]here may be restrictions on the right to a fully adversarial procedure where strictly necessary in the light of a strong countervailing public interest, such as national security, the need to keep secret certain police methods of

---

No. 1051/2002, UN Doc. CCPR/C/80/D/1051/2002. Mr Ahani was an Iranian national who had obtained asylum in Canada but was placed in mandatory detention for nine years prior to his deportation, following certification by two ministers that there were reasonable grounds to believe that he would engage in terrorist activities. Mr Ahani waited four years to have the lawfulness of the certification determined by Canadian courts. The Human Rights Committee found a violation of Article 9(4):'[D]etention (…) on national security grounds does not result ipso facto in arbitrary detention contrary to Article 9(1) [ICCPR]. However, given that an individual under a security certificate has neither been convicted of any crime nor sentenced to a term of imprisonment, an individual must have appropriate access, in terms of Article 9(4) to judicial review of the detention, that is to say review of the substantive justification of the detention as well as sufficiently frequent review'. The Canadian Security Certificates have since been found unconstitutional by the Canadian Supreme Court (Supreme Court of Canada, *Charkaoui v. Canada (Minister of Citizenship and Immigration)*, 2007 SCC 9).

[74] See Article 9(4) ICCPR and Article 5(4) ECHR.

[75] *A and Others v. UK* (n 69).

> investigation or the protection of the fundamental rights of another person. There will not be a fair trial, however, unless any difficulties caused to the defendant by a limitation on his rights are sufficiently counterbalanced by the procedures followed by the judicial authorities.[76]

In determining the level of guarantees for the review to comply with Article 5(4) ECHR, the European Court examines, on a case-by-case basis: the length of the detention; whether the judges are able to consider both the 'open' and 'closed' material; whether the applicant can appoint or have appointed a 'security-cleared counsel' who is able to consider the 'closed' material, and act on the defendant's behalf; and whether recommendations can be made regarding the need to declassify some of the material. Detentions that are mostly based on closed material are more likely to be arbitrary than those that are not. In addition, the right must be exercised 'without unreasonable delay', which is to be determined on a case-by-case basis. The Human Rights Committee noted, however, that in case of a long period of administrative detention, the review must be sufficiently frequent to assess whether the reasons for detention are still present.[77]

In my capacity as Special Rapporteur, I identified the following as core elements of best practice in the arrest and interrogation of terrorist suspects: (1) Any form of secret or unacknowledged detention is prohibited; (2) Every person has the right to contact a lawyer of his or her choice from the moment of arrest or detention. The scope of such choice may be restricted for genuine reasons of national security; (3) Any form of torture or other cruel, inhuman or degrading treatment or punishment is prohibited. Compliance with this prohibition shall be effectively monitored; (4) Information obtained through torture or other cruel, inhuman or degrading treatment or punishment, anywhere in the world, shall not be used in any proceedings and shall never be solicited or condoned; (5) Anyone arrested as a terrorist suspect who would face a real risk of torture or other cruel, inhuman or degrading treatment or punishment shall enjoy the right of non-refoulement, and may not be extradited, expelled or otherwise formally or informally removed to a country or area if the foreseeable consequence of that measure is the person's exposure to such a risk.[78]

---

[76] ECtHR, *Rowe and Davis v. the United Kingdom*, [GC], no. 28901/95, §§ 60–63.

[77] See *Ahani v. Canada*, Communication No. 1051/2002, UN Doc. CCPR/C/80/D/1051/2002 (2004).

[78] See A/HRC/16/51 (n 43), para. 38.

2.2.3.3 Measures regarding foreign terrorist fighters More recently, several States have adopted legislation to implement the requirements relating to the travel of 'foreign terrorist fighters' found in Security Council resolution 2178 (2014). These powers include seizure and retention of passports and identity cards where there is a suspicion that an individual will engage in terrorism-related activity abroad, or temporary exclusion from a country, as well as various forms of house arrests; even the stripping of citizenship can be envisaged. These measures can have a serious impact on freedom of movement, the prohibition of arbitrary deprivation of nationality or on the absolute prohibition of *refoulement*, the right to work, to a family life, to education, to health; as well as the right to safety and security, and they highlight, once more, an increased reliance on intelligence information, as decisions are often taken by members of the executive based on secret intelligence information.

2.2.4 Increased surveillance measures

In my capacity as Special Rapporteur I also expressed serious concern that in the name of countering terrorism, States have expanded initiatives to identify, scan and tag the general public through the use of multiple techniques which might violate an individual's right to privacy.[79] When surveillance is of places and large groups of people, it is typically subject to weaker regimes for authorization and oversight. Human rights standards have been tested, stretched and breached through the use of stop-and-search powers, notably through racial profiling in breach of the prohibition of discrimination; or the compilation of lists and databases to calculate the probability of suspicious activities and identify individuals seen as worthy of further scrutiny. This includes the techniques such as 'no-fly/selectee' lists, which are circulated to airlines and security officials with instructions to detain and question any passenger with a certain name. Such lists often contain a number of errors, and raise privacy concerns, as they are often kept secret, but subject individuals to continuous surveillance without their knowledge. More advanced techniques have also been introduced, such as the collection of biometrics or the use of body scanners that can see through clothing. I am particularly concerned that biometrics are often collected in a centralized database,

---

[79] 'Report of the UN Special Rapporteur on the promotion and protection of human rights and fundamental freedoms while countering terrorism UN Doc. A/HRC/13/37.

which increases information security risks, including error rates. In turn, this can result in the wrongful criminalization of individuals, or social exclusion.

Surveillance measures adopted as anti-terrorism measures have had a profound, chilling effect on other fundamental rights. In addition to constituting a right in itself, privacy serves as a basis for other rights and without which the other rights would not be effectively enjoyed. Privacy is necessary to create zones to allow individuals and groups to be able to think and develop ideas and relationships. Mass surveillance and online monitoring have a particularly chilling effect on freedom of expression, with users afraid to visit websites, express their opinions or communicate with other persons for fear they will face sanctions. This is particularly relevant for individuals wishing to dissent and might deter some of these persons from exercising their democratic right to protest against government policy. The rights to freedom of association and assembly are also threatened by the use of surveillance. These freedoms often require private meetings and communications to allow people to organize in the face of governments or other powerful actors. Expanded surveillance powers have sometimes led to a 'function creep', when police or intelligence agencies have labelled other groups as terrorists in order to allow the use of surveillance powers which were given only for the fight against terrorism. Freedom of movement can also be substantially affected by surveillance. The creation of secret watch lists, excessive data collection and sharing and imposition of intrusive scanning devices or biometrics, all create extra barriers to mobility. However, one of the most serious effects of surveillance measures is that they may lead to miscarriages of justice and violate due process guarantees. The challenge of gaining access to judicial review is that some legal regimes may prevent access to the courts unless individuals can show that interference has taken place, which is precluded by the secretive nature of the surveillance programmes. Individuals may not be able to prove or demonstrate that they are actually under surveillance. As a result, individuals may not be able to appeal to courts for remedy.

There is well-founded concern that there is a trend towards extending State surveillance powers beyond terrorism. Following the events of 11 September 2001, a number of legislatures introduced sunset clauses into and reviews of anti-terrorism legislation, as it was assumed that extraordinary powers may be required for a short period of time to respond to the then danger. These sunset clauses and reviews were not included in some areas of policymaking and, in later policies, were not considered at all. Many of the investigative powers given to law enforcement agencies under anti-terror laws are granted to these agencies to conduct investigations unrelated to terrorism. Meanwhile, States are following each other's lead on policy without considering the human rights implications. Many of the policies that seriously impact on the right to privacy were introduced first as extraordinary, but then became regional and international standards. Collectively, such interference is having significant negative impacts on the protection of the right to privacy, as there is limited access to legal safeguards. Without a rigorous set of legal safeguards and a means to measure the necessity, proportionality, or reasonableness of the interference, States have no guidance on minimizing the risks to privacy generated by their new policies. In my capacity as Special Rapporteur, I identified a set of best practices. These include, first, the principle of minimal intrusiveness, which require States to have exhausted less-intrusive techniques before resorting to others. This will assist in ensuring that the policies are both necessary and proportionate. Second, States should respect the principle of purpose specification restricting secondary use of personal data. Information collected for one purpose must be protected from being used for another. States must be obliged to provide a legal basis for the re-use of information, in accordance with constitutional and human rights principles, in particular when the information is shared between intelligence and law enforcement agencies within a State or across borders. Third, States need to respect the principle of oversight and regulated authorization of lawful access. Judicial authorization and review for access to personal information must exist, and internal oversight bodies within government agencies must be given an increased role. In addition, as the application of secrecy privileges for surveillance systems inhibit the ability of legislatures. Judicial bodies and the public to scrutinize State powers, States must respect the principle of transparency and integrity, which requires openness and communication about surveillance practices. Open debate and scrutiny is essential to understanding the advantages and limitations of surveillance techniques, so that the public understands the necessity and lawfulness of surveillance. Finally, the principle of effective modernization must be introduced. Tools such as privacy impact assessments may help inform the public about surveillance practices, while instilling a culture of privacy within government agencies as they develop new surveillance systems to combat terrorism. International standards must also be adopted to require States to enhance their safeguards to reflect technological change.

After finishing as Special Rapporteur in July 2011, much of my academic work has focused on surveillance and its impact upon privacy and other human rights. The revelations by former Central Intelligence Agency and National Security Agency contractor Edward Snowden in

2013 brought to the attention of the public at large the scope and pervasiveness of modern methods of electronic mass surveillance, including by the United States and some of its closest allies. Within the EU-funded research project SURVEILLE, we have developed a multidimensional and multidisciplinary methodology for assessing the security benefit, the cost efficiency, the moral hazards and the human rights impact of any given surveillance technology.[80] The most important finding that emerged from this line of research was that electronic mass surveillance has failed on all counts: its actual capacity to deliver better security is minimal, or even counterproductive due to the misallocation of resources and attention, while the resulting intrusions into privacy and other human rights are disproportionate and often affect the essential inviolable core of privacy. Recent rulings by the Court of Justice of the European Union on data retention and on data transfers from Europe to the United States corroborate and confirm our assessments.[81]

2.2.5 Increased criminalization of preparatory offences

In the post-2001 context, many States have developed new offences which criminalize preparatory activities to acts of terrorism, some even several steps away from the commission of an act of terrorism. The arguments in favour of the introduction of inchoate offences, such as encouraging terrorism, apology or glorification of terrorism, planning on going abroad to join a terrorist group, can be found in the need to prevent the commission of acts of terrorism, given the immense harm that they can cause, rather than deal with the perpetrators once the harm has occurred. The criminalization of such offences, however, raises particular difficulties. Regarding matters of pure legal construction, by displacing criminal liability away from the actual commission of a terrorist act, the *mens rea* is given more importance than the *actus reus*. This in turn impacts on the protection of fundamental rights. As the *actus reus* is often innocuous, it is coupled with other – often 'secret' – information which would be used to reconstruct the intention of the individual, and

80 The outcomes of the FP7 research project SURVEILLE (Surveillance: Ethical Issues, Legal Limitations, and Efficiency) are available on the project website at http://www.surveille.eu, accessed 5 October 2017. Under 'Publications', see, in particular, project Deliverable D4.10 and the two Papers based on D2.8. For a concise presentation of the methodology, see the SURVEILLE Briefing Note, also available on the project website.

81 Joined Cases C-293/12 and C-594/12, *Digital Rights v. Ireland* (CJEU, 8 April 2014); Case C-362/14, *Maximilian Schrems v. Data Protection Commissioner* (CJEU, 6 October 2015).

both of these elements, together, would constitute the commission of the offence. The use of repressive law-enforcement powers would therefore be triggered at an early stage, and where the information forming the basis for the *mens rea* could not be made public, administrative measures on national security grounds would be applied, with limited judicial involvement.

In my capacity as Special Rapporteur, I have highlighted the value of a proactive approach to the countering of terrorist acts and the prevention of violent radicalization. As such, the establishment of a separate offence of incitement to terrorism – as is required by Security Council resolution 1624 (2005) in a State's counter-terrorism arsenal – is important and allows States to ensure that terrorist offences are punishable by sentences heavier than those imposable under national law for similar offences committed without a terrorist intent. A model definition for such an offence, endorsed by myself as Special Rapporteur, is 'It is an offence to intentionally and unlawfully distribute or otherwise make available a message to the public with the intent to incite the commission of a terrorist offence, where such conduct, whether or not expressly advocating terrorist offences, causes a danger that one or more such offences may be committed'.[82]

2.2.6 Impact of counter-terrorism measures on humanitarian action

A number of counter-terrorism measures, adopted at national, regional or international level, can have a serious impact on principled humanitarian action. Humanitarian principles require that assistance be brought to those suffering wherever they may be found, and that such assistance be brought impartially, without discrimination, solely on the basis of need. However, a number of counter-terrorism measures can seriously impair such humanitarian action.[83]

Terrorist listings can raise serious problems for humanitarian actors. While they often include provisions regarding humanitarian exemptions from the prohibition of financial transactions with listed groups, there may be a real or perceived opacity about which groups, individuals or entities are included in the lists (Security Council resolution 1373 leaves it to national authorities to determine which groups should be included on terrorist lists at the national level, while as we have seen the UN-level Al-Qaida Sanctions list has broad criteria for inclusion), or about how to

[82] A/HRC/16/51 (n 43), para. 32.
[83] See also Chapter 3 in this volume.

deal with humanitarian exemptions. National legislation can also be problematic. In a number of States, national laws criminalize various interactions with groups that have been qualified as terrorist. It should be noted that where non-State armed groups designated as terrorist, which control parts of territories where civilians live, any humanitarian action will necessarily involve some form of engagement, such as discussions to negotiate humanitarian access, the logistics of humanitarian delivery, etc., with these groups. National legislation varies, and various forms of engagement with designated armed groups and their members that are designated as terrorists can engage humanitarian actors with criminal liability.

In any event, the lack of clarity regarding counter-terrorism requirements, the existence of numerous national and international provisions across the globe, together with the use in such legislation of overly broad or vague terms, can act as an inhibiting factor for humanitarian engagement, and donors and other humanitarian actors can be led to self-censor. In turn, this can lead to reduced humanitarian engagement or even a lack of humanitarian action where groups designated as terrorist are active. This often, unfortunately, coincides with areas where populations are in dire need of assistance.

3. CONCLUSION

This chapter has taken stock of the wide range of negative impacts upon human rights that post-9/11 counter-terrorism measures have had. Some of those impacts can be categorized as permissible limitations upon human rights, some as potentially lawful derogations from human rights treaties during a state of emergency, and some as outright human rights violations. Even where the measures as such might be lawful or at least potentially lawful if proper human rights guarantees are introduced, it has to be stated that the breadth and severity of human rights violations caused by counter-terrorism measures is alarming. Many issues and many human rights were covered above but there are also other negative human rights impacts that were not even addressed.[84]

The international human rights community, and the broader international community of States and international organizations, needs to

---

[84] For instance, see my reports as Special Rapporteur on the impact of counter-terrorism measures upon economic, social and cultural rights (UN Doc. A/HRC/6/17), and on gender analysis of counter-terrorism measures (UN Doc. A/64/211).

remain vigilant concerning the negative effect of counter-terrorism measures upon the enjoyment of human rights. The terrorist attacks of 9/11 were a moment of horror in the history of humankind but also a moment that casts a long shadow.

3. New counter-terrorism measures: Continuing challenges for human rights

Ben Emmerson QC

The challenges posed by global and national counter-terrorism measures are complex and evolving, and their impact on the protection of human rights is significant. Many of the measures making up the current counter-terrorism framework were adopted, perhaps in haste, immediately after 2001 and UN Security Council resolution 1373 (2001). The social and political context of their adoption meant that many of the measures were introduced without due regard to international law requirements, including (but not limited to) international human rights obligations. The erosion of liberties that has resulted has been pervasive and, in many cases, counter-productive. There is emerging evidence that military and law enforcement responses to terrorism, which disregard individual rights, cannot defeat (and may in fact create conditions conducive to) terrorist activity.[1] That is borne out by the fact that new terrorist threats and terror groups have emerged since 2001, even in parts of the world where counter-terrorism resources have been heavily deployed.[2]

What happened in 2001 remains true today: when terrorist acts occur, the outrage of the international community and States affected tends to

[1] See the UN Global Counter-Terrorism Strategy, UN Doc. A/RES/60/288: 'Recognizing also that terrorism will not be defeated by military force, law enforcement measures, and intelligence operations alone, and underlining the need to address the conditions conducive to the spread of terrorism, as outlined in Pillar I of the United Nations Global Counter-Terrorism Strategy'. See also the inclusion by the Security Council of a human rights clause, e.g. UN Security Council resolution 1456 (2003), para. 6, and UN Security Council's recognition that terrorism will not be defeated by strength alone, see Resolution 2178 (2014).

[2] See 'Report of the Special Rapporteur on human rights and counter-terrorism', UN Doc. A/HRC/29/51.

precipitate a hurried response that leads to the adoption of often ill-conceived counter-terrorism measures.[3] Governments, desperate to avoid further attacks 'on their watch', understandably (but short-sightedly) see the introduction of more draconian counter-terrorism measures as the most appropriate reaction. The population of an affected State, reeling from the effects of a terrorist attack and fearful of further such attacks, tend to offer little opposition to incursions of civil liberties. Accordingly, counter-terrorism measures have brought about a slow but steady attrition of fundamental human rights.

A number of recent developments in the field pose particular threats to human rights: the increased use of remotely piloted aircrafts ('drones') in counter-terrorism operations; mass digital surveillance for counter-terrorism purposes; the question of 'foreign terrorist fighters'; measures to counter the financing of terrorism which seriously impact on civil society; measures to counter-terrorism which impact on the human rights of migrants; and measures to address 'violent extremism' which can also adversely impact on a range of human rights.

1. THE USE OF REMOTELY PILOTED AIRCRAFTS IN COUNTER-TERRORISM OPERATIONS

An important development in the past few years has been the use of drones in lethal, extraterritorial counter-terrorism operations. The technology is predominantly used for intelligence, surveillance and reconnaissance purposes, but can also be weaponized and used for targeted attacks. The tactical military advantage of arming drones is considered to be the speed of response from the moment of sighting a target to the delivery of deadly force by precision-guided missile.

States known to use drones as part of their overseas counter-terrorism operations include the United States, the United Kingdom, and Israel. Although the use of drones to target individuals is shrouded in secrecy, drone strikes are known to have taken place in Afghanistan, Gaza, Iraq, Pakistan, Somalia, Syria and Yemen. Civilian casualties are an inherent risk in such actions, amounting to a potential breach of international humanitarian and human rights law.

---

[3] International Commission of Jurists (2009), 'Assessing damage, urging action', Report of the Eminent Jurist Panel on Terrorism, Counter-Terrorism and Human Rights, http://www.un.org/en/sc/ctc/specialmeetings/2011/docs/icj/icj-2009-ejp-report.pdf (accessed 11 May 2017).

In 2013, in my capacity as Special Rapporteur, I launched an inquiry into the use of drones in extraterritorial lethal counter-terrorism operations, and in the context of asymmetrical armed conflict. The objectives of the inquiry were to evaluate allegations that the increasing use of drones had caused disproportionate civilian casualties, and to make recommendations concerning the duty of States to investigate such incidents. From a sample of 37 strikes for which some information was available, I concluded that in 30 cases the State's duty of investigation and transparency had not been met.[4] The use of drones in a military context is not inevitably unlawful but, in a climate in which drone technology continues to advance, in which increasing numbers of States (and non-State actors) seek to acquire the technology, and in which the prevalence of drone use in more recent theatres of operations, such as the wars in Iraq and Syria, had increased, the principles and obligations circumscribing the use of drones must be clear and public.[5]

1.1 The Human Rights Impact of Drone Strikes

The discussion about the legality of the use of drones to target individuals in international law should always have as its starting point the grave impact that drone strikes have on individuals and their communities, whether the strikes take place in the context of an armed conflict or not. The obvious impact is the loss of life: of the targeted person and, often, bystanders. But another serious impact is the psychological trauma occasioned by drone strikes on individuals living in regions subject to strikes. The anxiety that is generated translates into the interruption of education, as families keep children home from schools out of fear of attacks; the undermining of religious and cultural practices, as community members avoid gathering in groups; and a reluctance to assist the victims of drone strikes for fear of being caught in secondary strikes. Strikes prevent men and women from going to work, to a doctor, and from visiting relatives and friends. As such, drone strikes can

---

4 See 'Report of the Special Rapporteur on human rights and counter-terrorism', UN Docs A/68/389 and A/HRC/25/59.

5 See also 'Report of the Special Rapporteur on extra-judicial, summary or arbitrary executions', UN Doc. A/68/382 and Human Rights Council (2014), 'Summary of the Human Rights Council interactive panel discussion of experts on the use of remotely piloted aircraft or armed drones in compliance with international law, Report of the Office of the United Nations High Commissioner for Human Rights', UN Doc. A/HRC/28/38.

seriously affect economic, social and cultural rights, as well as fundamental freedoms: the right to freedom from arbitrary or unlawful interference with privacy, family and home, the right to peaceful assembly, the right to freedom of association, the right to freedom of religion, the right to education, the right to health and the right to work. The right to a fair trial, due process and the presumption of innocence may also be compromised.[6]

A related concern is that drone strikes may in fact undermine an effective counter-terrorism strategy. In probably the most expansive research to date into drone strikes in Pakistan, New York University (NYU) and Stanford University found that drone strikes breed resentment and discontent towards the United States, and that there is evidence to suggest that the strikes have aided militant recruitment and motivated terrorist activity.[7] The report further notes that '[m]any of the journalists, NGO and humanitarian workers, medical professionals, and Pakistani governmental officials with whom we spoke expressed their belief that, on balance, drone strikes likely increase terrorism'.[8] In addition, it found that strikes by the United States have contributed to the delegitimization of non-governmental organizations (NGOs) that are perceived to be Western, or that receive US aid, including those providing much-needed services such as access to water, education, and vaccines. That perception has been exploited by Taliban forces.[9] In the same vein, the Recommendations and Report of the Stimson Task Force on US Drone Policy noted in April 2015 that '[c]ivilian casualties, even if relatively few, can anger whole communities, increase anti-US sentiment and become a potent recruiting tool for terrorist organizations. Even strikes that kill

---

[6] The UN Global Counter-Terrorism Strategy recalls that that States (1) have a duty to bring to justice, on the basis of extradite or prosecute, any person who supports, facilitates, participates or attempts to participate in the financing, planning, preparation or perpetration of terrorist acts or provides safe havens; and (2) must ensure the apprehension and prosecution or extradition of perpetrators of terrorist acts, in accordance with the relevant provisions of national and international law, in particular human rights law, refugee law and international humanitarian law.

[7] International Human Rights and Conflict Resolution Clinic (Stanford Law School) and Global Justice Clinic (NYU School of Law) (2012), 'Living under drones: Death, injury and trauma to civilians from US drone practices in Pakistan', September, https://law.stanford.edu/wp-content/uploads/sites/default/files/publication/313671/doc/slspublic/Stanford_NYU_LIVING_UNDER_DRONES.pdf (accessed 6 October 2017), p. 132.

[8] Id., p. 134.

[9] Id., pp. 139–40.

only terrorist operatives can cause great resentment, particularly in contexts in which terrorist recruiting efforts rely on tribal loyalties or on an economically desperate population'.[10]

1.2 The Importance of the Determination of the Applicable Legal Frameworks

International human rights law prohibits the arbitrary deprivation of life, in any circumstance and at all times. International human rights law countenances the intentional use of lethal force by a State only as a last resort: if strictly necessary and proportionate, if aimed at preventing an immediate threat to the life of another, and only if there is no other means of preventing the threat from materializing, such as restraint, capture, and the graduated use of force.[11]

For this reason, outside of an armed conflict, lethal drone attacks will rarely be lawful. In situations of armed conflict, where international humanitarian law operates alongside (and in a complementary fashion to) international human rights law, there may be occasions in which a lethal drone strike would be a lawful operation according to the applicable targeting rules of international humanitarian law.[12] Whether, and what kind of, an armed conflict exists will therefore be a critical feature to identify in order to assess the legality of a drone strike.

1.3 Contentious Areas Regarding the Applicability of International Humanitarian Law

Non-international armed conflicts (NIACs) are conflicts between a State and one or more non-State armed groups, or between two or more non-State armed groups. The generally accepted criteria for the existence of such conflicts are the intensity and protraction of the conflict and the

---

[10] Stimson Centre (2015), 'Recommendations and Report of the Task Force on US Drone Policy', 2nd edn, https://www.stimson.org/sites/default/files/file-attachments/recommendations_and_report_of_the_task_force_on_us_drone_policy_second_edition.pdf, accessed 22 January 2018, p. 29 *et seq*.

[11] Code of Conduct for Law Enforcement Officials, art. 3. See also *McCann and Others v. United Kingdom*, App. no. 18984/91 (ECtHR, 27 September 1995), paras. 203–14; Human Rights Committee (1982), *Maria Fanny Suárez de Guerrero v. Colombia*, Communication No. R.11/45, 31 March, para. 13.2.

[12] *Legality of the Threat or Use of Nuclear Weapons*, Advisory Opinion (ICJ Reports 1996), paras. 24 and 25; *Legal Consequences of the Construction of a Wall in the Occupied Palestinian Territory*, Advisory Opinion (ICJ Reports 2004), para. 106.

degree of organization of the parties.[13] International humanitarian law applies to NIACs, but it is not always easy to tell whether a particular context amounts to a NIAC, particularly where non-State armed groups tend no longer to operate within territorial boundaries (which used to be a defining characteristic of NIACs). The International Committee of the Red Cross (ICRC) has underlined that international humanitarian law does not permit the targeting of persons who are located in non-belligerent States even if they are directly participating in hostilities, to avoid the whole world becoming a battlefield (a 'transnational' non-international armed conflict). Contrary to this, States engaged in NIAC with a transnationally operating non-State armed group often consider the traditional geographical limitation of conflict to be irrelevant in the modern context. By such an approach, the scope of application of international humanitarian law is *ratione personae* rather than *ratione loci*.

1.3.1 Degree of organization of the non-State armed group

For a NIAC to exist, one of the parties to the armed conflict must be an organized non-State armed group, which implies at minimum a common command structure, adequate communications, joint mission planning and execution, and cooperation in the acquisition and distribution of weaponry. It is only if this criterion is fulfilled and demonstratively proven that a group may be targeted for attack under international humanitarian law targeting rules. States that export national concepts such as 'associated forces' to the international forum must also demonstratively show that these other forces have a sufficient degree of organization with the group to which they are affiliated and which itself is a party to a NIAC to satisfy the requirements of international humanitarian law for lawful targeting.

1.3.2 Intensity of hostilities

While some States support the idea that non-State armed groups engaging in infrequent attacks may still be engaged in armed conflict, a long period without any serious attack is likely to undermine a claim that the situation amounts to a NIAC.

---

[13] See *Prosecutor v. Dusko Tadic*, case No. IT-94-1-T (ICTY, 2 October 1995), para. 70.

1.3.3 Legitimate targets in a non-international armed conflict

Properly determining who takes part directly in hostilities is critical to a proper application of the principles of distinction, proportionality and precaution, which are cornerstones of international humanitarian law. According to the ICRC,[14] individuals may be considered to be members of a non-State armed group, and therefore targeted at any time, only if they have assumed a 'continuous combat function' within that group – a lasting integration into an armed group. If this criterion is not met, an individual who is otherwise affiliated with an armed group can be regarded as having protected civilian status and may be targeted with deadly force only if, and as long as, the individual is directly participating in hostilities. Some States, however, argue that all members of an armed group are legitimate targets at all times, and that a requirement that individuals be targeted with lethal force only if, and as long as, they are directly participating in hostilities creates a near-insurmountable operational hurdle. It is clear that disclosure by States of the criteria they adopt to determine direct participation in hostilities is critical to achieving transparency as to what conduct might expose a civilian to deadly force, for evaluating whether any attack is lawful under international law, and for assessing the number of civilian casualties resulting from an attack. Concepts such as 'signature strikes', 'hit lists', 'high value targets' or 'pre-identified targets' have no legal basis in international law, and may therefore be legal or illegal depending on whether they satisfy general rules of international humanitarian law.

1.4 Transparency and Accountability

The current lack of transparency around the use of drones creates an accountability vacuum and affects the ability of victims to seek redress.[15] Insufficient transparency has obscured details of the circumstances in which armed drones have been used, the number of casualties incurred, State policies on the use of armed drones, and the legal basis on which they are used. It has also hindered evaluation of the impact of drone strikes and created obstacles to determining the content of, and compliance with, the applicable legal framework. It hampers the delivery of

---

[14] See Nils Melzer (2009), 'Interpretive guidance on the notion of direct participation in hostilities under international humanitarian law', ICRC (May), https://www.icrc.org/eng/assets/files/other/icrc-002-0990.pdf (accessed 6 October 2017).

[15] See the address of the former UN High Commissioner for Human Rights to the Security Council, 18 August 2013.

justice and redress for victims, and acts as a barrier to preventing violations from occurring in the first place. Accountability requires public access to relevant information.

Under international human rights law, the duty to investigate alleged violations of the right to life is a component of the right itself. Therefore, a failure to investigate and, where applicable, to punish those responsible for a violation of the right to life constitutes a violation of the right to life itself.[16] States therefore have an obligation to carry out prompt, independent and impartial investigations whenever there are credible indications of a serious violation of international human rights law, including from an alleged drone strike. As an inherent part of the right to life, international human rights law requires accountability for violations of that right.

International humanitarian law also places an onus on any State using lethal force to account for civilian casualties. The State is under an obligation to conduct a prompt, independent and impartial fact-finding inquiry and provide a detailed public explanation.[17] This obligation is triggered whenever there is a plausible indication from any source that civilian casualties may have been sustained, including where the facts are unclear or the information is partial or circumstantial. The obligation arises whether the attack was initiated by remotely piloted aircraft or other means, and whether it occurred within or outside an area of active hostilities. Given the international humanitarian law obligation of accountability, there is no legal justification for States to keep secret their own estimates of the number of civilian casualties inflicted by drone strikes. To entrust methods of warfare to secret intelligence agencies that by nature neither confirm nor deny the existence of their operations necessarily frustrates the duties of accountability and transparency. Military activity that claims the lives of human beings can never satisfy the legal requirements of accountability and transparency if it is carried out by secret intelligence agencies.

---

16 Human Rights Committee (2004), General Comment No. 31, para. 15; *McCann and others v. United Kingdom* (n 11), para. 169.

17 Based on the findings of the Public Commission to Examine the Maritime Incident of 31 May 2010, the Turkel Commission, http://www.turkelcommittee.gov.il/files/wordocs/8808report-eng.pdf (accessed 5 June 2017).

2. MASS DIGITAL SURVEILLANCE FOR COUNTER-TERRORISM PURPOSES

2.1 From Targeted to Bulk Interception: State Justification

The exponential growth in States' technological capabilities over the past decade has improved the capacity of intelligence and law enforcement agencies to carry out surveillance of individuals and organizations. Most States now have the capacity to intercept and monitor calls, read text messages, monitor online activity, penetrate databases and cloud facilities, and use malware systems to infiltrate individual computers or smartphones, to override their settings and to monitor their activity. Taken together, these forms of surveillance provide a mosaic of data from multiple sources that can generate valuable intelligence about particular individuals or organizations.

The targeted interception of communications can provide a valuable source of information for States to investigate, forestall and prosecute acts of terrorism and other serious crime. In many cases, the interception of communications by the State requires prior suspicion of criminality of the targeted individual or organization. In such cases, the almost invariable practice of States is to require prior judicial or executive authorization. In some States, there is an additional tier of *ex post facto* independent review. These stages of review provide an opportunity for scrutiny of the basis for the alleged suspicion, and for an assessment of the legality and proportionality of surveillance measures in a particular case. In cases such as these, it is therefore possible to make an objective assessment of the necessity and proportionality of the contemplated surveillance, weighing the degree of the proposed intrusion against its anticipated value to a particular investigation.

Some States are able to secure bulk access to communications and content data without prior suspicion. States with high levels of Internet penetration can gain access to the telephone and email data of an effectively unlimited number of users and maintain an overview of Internet activity associated with particular websites, without any prior suspicion related to a specific individual or organization. In some States, authorities can apply automated 'data mining' algorithms to dragnet a potentially limitless universe of communications traffic. By placing taps on fibre-optic cables through which the majority of digital communications travel, relevant States have thus been able to conduct mass surveillance of communications content and metadata, providing intelligence and law enforcement agencies with the opportunity to monitor and record not only their own citizens' communications, but also the communications of individuals located in other States. This capacity is typically reinforced by mandatory data retention laws that require telecommunications and Internet service providers to preserve communications data for inspection and analysis. The use of scanning software, profiling criteria and specified search terms enables the relevant authorities to filter vast quantities of stored information in order to identify patterns of communication between individuals and organizations.

Since 2013, the nature and extent of some States' surveillance programmes has been increasingly revealed. It has become apparent that the communications of literally every Internet user are potentially open for inspection by intelligence and law enforcement agencies in the States concerned. That amounts to a systematic interference with the right to respect for the privacy of communications, which requires a correspondingly compelling justification. States have nonetheless largely maintained that the secrecy of these programmes and the level of interference with the right to privacy were essential for effective counter-terrorism responses.

2.1.1 Required secrecy

Following the disclosure of mass surveillance programmes, the States involved argued that the disclosures had damaged national security by alerting potential terrorists to the fact that their communications were under surveillance. The value of mass interception technology as a counter-terrorism and law enforcement tool thus rests in the fact that users of the Internet assume their communications are confidential.

Some have argued that users of the Internet have no reasonable expectation of privacy, and must assume that their communications are available to be monitored by corporate and State entities alike. This suggestion is plainly unwarranted. First, it does not take into consideration the fact that digital communications have become part of everyday life, and that anyone who wishes to participate in the exchange of information and ideas in the modern world is nowadays obliged to use transnational digital communications technology. The Internet is not a purely public space; it is composed of many layers of private, social and public realms. Those making informed use of social media platforms in which messages are posted in full public view obviously have no reasonable expectation of privacy. Those sending private messages by email – encrypted or not – certainly do have that expectation. A general principle of international human rights law is that individuals can be regarded as having given up a protected human right only through an express and unequivocal waiver, voluntarily given on an informed basis.

Merely using the Internet as a means of private communication cannot constitute an informed waiver of the right to privacy under article 17 of the International Covenant on Civil and Political Rights (the ICCPR).

2.1.2 Required level of intrusion

It has also been argued that the added value of mass surveillance technology derives from the very fact that it permits the surveillance of the communications of individuals and organizations who have not previously come to the attention of the authorities. The public interest benefit in bulk access technology is said to derive precisely from the fact that it does not require prior suspicion, and so contributes to the identification and interruption of potential terrorist activity that would otherwise not have come to the authorities' attention at an early stage.

The potential efficacy of mass interception does not provide an adequate human rights law justification for its use. The fact that it is technically feasible and that it may sometimes yield useful intelligence does not by itself mean that it is either reasonable or lawful. To comply with article 17 of the ICCPR, any interference with the right to privacy must be prescribed by law and must be a necessary and proportionate means of achieving a legitimate public policy objective. It is a central axiom of proportionality that the greater the interference, the more compelling the justification must be if it is to meet the requirements of the Covenant.

2.2 An Online Right to Privacy

In resolution 68/167 (2013), the General Assembly reaffirmed the right to privacy, according to which no one shall be subjected to arbitrary or unlawful interference with his or her privacy, family, home or correspondence, and the right to the protection of the law against such interference, as set out in article 12 of the Universal Declaration of Human Rights and article 17 of the ICCPR. Importantly, the General Assembly also stated that there is a legal right to respect for the privacy of digital communications, by affirming that that the same rights that people have offline must also be protected online.

Consequently, States' obligations under article 17 of the ICCPR include the obligation to respect the privacy and security of digital communications. In principle, therefore, individuals have the right to share information and ideas with one another without interference by the State, secure in the knowledge that their communication will reach and be read by the intended recipients alone. Measures that interfere with this right must be authorized by domestic law that is accessible and precise and that conforms with the requirements of the ICCPR. Such laws must also pursue a legitimate aim and meet the tests of necessity and proportionality.[18] Following a review of national practices and legislation, the UN High Commissioner for Human Rights concluded that international human rights law provides a clear and universal framework for the promotion and protection of the right to privacy, including in the context of domestic and extraterritorial surveillance, the interception of digital communications and the collection of personal data. The practice of many States has, however, revealed a lack of adequate national legislation and/or enforcement, weak procedural safeguards, and ineffective oversight, all of which have contributed to a lack of accountability for arbitrary or unlawful interference with the right to privacy.[19]

The adoption of mass surveillance technology undoubtedly impinges on the very essence of the right to privacy. Bulk access to all digital communications traffic eradicates the possibility of any individualized proportionality analysis because there is no target-specific justification. The proportionality analysis thus shifts from the micro level (assessing the justification for invading a particular individual's or organization's privacy) to the macro level (assessing the justification for adopting a system that involves wholesale interference with the individual and collective privacy rights of all Internet users). The sheer scale of the interference with privacy rights calls for a competing public policy justification of analogical magnitude.

As an absolute minimum, article 17 ICCPR requires States who use mass surveillance technology to give a meaningful public account of the tangible benefits that accrue from its use. Without such a justification, there is simply no means to measure the compatibility of this emerging State practice with the requirements of the ICCPR. An assessment of proportionality in this context involves striking a balance between the societal interest in the protection of online privacy, on the one hand, and the counterweighing interest in effective counter-terrorism and law enforcement, on the other. Determining where that balance is to be struck

---

[18] For a detailed examination of the components of the right to privacy as well as the requirements for any interference to be lawful, see 'Report of the Special Rapporteur on the promotion and protection of human rights and fundamental freedoms while countering terrorism', UN Doc. A/69/397 and 'Report of the Office of the United Nations High Commissioner for Human Rights, Right to Privacy in the Digital Age', UN Doc. A/HRC/27/37.

[19] 'Right to Privacy in the Digital Age', ibid., para. 47. Note that the UN Human Rights Council through resolution A/HRC/28/L.27 adopted without a vote, decided to appoint a Special Rapporteur on the right to privacy.

requires an informed public debate to take place within and between States. This assessment must also take into consideration the fact that the Internet is now the primary mode of communication for many millions of people around the world.

The truth is that the use of mass surveillance technology effectively does away with the right to privacy of communications on the Internet altogether. It is potentially inconsistent with the core principle that States should adopt the least intrusive means available when interfering with protected human rights, and it excludes any individualized proportionality assessment. The secrecy enshrouding it renders impossible any more generalized proportionality analysis, and the States engaging in mass surveillance have neither provided a detailed or evidence based public justification for its necessity, nor have they enacted explicit domestic legislation to authorize its use. This comes close to derogating from the right to privacy altogether in relation to digital communications, which presents a serious challenge to an established norm of international law.

In a recent case, an individual requested that the EU's Data Protection Commissioner prohibit Facebook from transmitting his personal data to the United States on the grounds that many IT firms there had cooperated with the National Security Agency. The Court of Justice of the European Union[20] examined the question under article 7 of the EU Charter of Fundamental Rights, which protects right to respect for one's private life in identical terms to article 8 of the European Convention on Human Rights. The Court held that the mere access by public authorities to confidential or group-specific communications data constitutes an intrusion into the right to privacy, even without any further processing of that data. This is an important, yet unsurprising, finding. More significant is the Court's conclusion that while indiscriminate intrusion into 'metadata' may constitute a particularly serious intrusion into the right to privacy, access to 'content' data will affect the essence of the right to privacy.[21] An infringement that affects the essence of a protected human right can never be lawful. Where the infringement is such that the essence of the

---

[20] Case C–362/14, *Maximilian Schrems v. Data Protection Commissioner* (CJEU, 6 October 2015).

[21] *Maximilian Schrems*, ibid., para. 94. See also Martin Scheinin (2015), 'The essence of privacy, and varying degrees of intrusion', VerfBlog, 7 October, http://www.verfassungsblog.de/en/the-essence-of-privacy-and-varying-degrees-of-intrusion/ (accessed 5 June 2017) and Martin Scheinin (2015), 'Mass surveillance and the right to privacy: Adding nuance to the Schrems case', *Just Security*, 13 October, https://www.justsecurity.org/26781/adding-nuance-context-max-schrems-case-safe-harbor/ (accessed 15 May 2017).

right is affected, the red line of unlawfulness has necessarily been crossed, with no scope for justification on proportionality grounds.[22]

A State's duty to protect against the threat of terrorism should never be used as a Trojan horse to usher in wider powers of surveillance for unrelated governmental functions. There is an ever-present danger of 'purpose creep', by which measures justified on counter-terrorism grounds are made available for use by public authorities for much less weighty public interest purposes. There is clearly an onus on States deploying bulk access surveillance technology to explain promptly, precisely and publicly why this wholesale intrusion into collective privacy is justified for the prevention of terrorism or other serious crime.

3. FOREIGN TERRORIST FIGHTERS

The issue of foreign terrorist fighters is not a new one,[23] but it gained a new prominence as a feature of the armed conflicts in Iraq and Syria.[24] The Security Council attempted to address the issue in resolution 2178 (2014).[25] That resolution defined 'foreign terrorist fighters' as 'individuals who travel to a State other than their State of residence or nationality for the purpose of the perpetration, planning or preparation of, or participation in, terrorist acts or receiving of terrorist training, including in connection with armed conflict'. The resolution requested that Member States prevent the travel of 'foreign terrorist fighters'; bring them to justice; and criminalize their travel, its funding, and its organization or facilitation through recruitment.

Crucially, the resolution includes a strong human rights clause. The Council reaffirmed that any measure taken to counter terrorism must respect States' international human rights obligations and noted the importance of respect for the rule of law in the prevention and combating of terrorism, not least because failure to do so can contribute to increased radicalization and impunity. The resolution also noted that terrorism will

---

22 See also European Court of Human Rights, *Big Brother Watch and others v. United Kingdom*, App. no. 58170/13, lodged on 4 September 2013.

23 See Sandra Kraehenmann (2014), 'Foreign fighters under international law', Geneva Academy Briefing No. 7 (October).

24 See 'Report of the Special Rapporteur on the protection and promotion of human rights while countering terrorism', UN Doc. A/HRC/29/51.

25 See also Security Council resolution 2170 (2014), which specifically addressed the flow of fighters to join ISIL and other individuals, groups and entities associated with Al-Qaida in Iraq and Syria.

not be defeated by military, law enforcement and intelligence operations alone, but requires action to address the conditions conducive to terrorism set out in Pillar I of the UN Global Counter-Terrorism Strategy.[26]

Despite the attention given in the resolution to protection of human rights, a number of concerns have been raised about it.[27] One of those is that the Security Council has taken on the role of legislator by requesting States to adopt a number of open-ended binding measures in their national legal arsenal. Another is that the resolution calls upon Member States to require airlines to provide advance passenger information to detect individuals who may fall under the definition of foreign terrorist fighters. While the resolution is clear that this should not be done by resorting to discriminatory profiling, its practical implementation has prompted concern, including about the serious impact it can have on a person's right to privacy.

A further concern relates to the broad nature of some of the provisions, and the lack of clarity of certain terms including the lack of definition of 'terrorism' or 'extremism'. The risk is that States create their own definitions that incorporate non-violent dissenters and take repressive steps with the apparent endorsement of the Security Council. The lack of clarity also creates legal uncertainty about to whom the Security Council intended the resolution to apply: members of all non-State armed groups, those defined as terrorist groups under national law or international law, or both. States should only introduce national measures to implement resolution 2178 (2014) that comply with their international human rights obligations, and that apply only to those individuals who are conclusively shown to meet the criteria laid down by the Council. Implementing measures must satisfy the principle of legality, as enshrined in article 15 of the ICCPR, which requires that criminal liability, and any definition, must be precise, certain, and not subject to interpretation which would unduly broaden the scope of the proscribed conduct. Vague provisions

---

26 A/RES/60/288.

27 See 'Report of the United Nations High Commissioner for Human Rights on the protection of human rights and fundamental freedoms while countering terrorism', UN Doc. A/HRC/28/28, paras. 46 and 47. See also Martin Scheinin (2014), 'Back to post-9/11 panic? Security Council resolution on foreign terrorist fighters', *Just Security*, 23 September, https://www.justsecurity.org/15407/post-911-panic-security-council-resolution-foreign-terrorist-fighters-scheinin/ (accessed 5 June 2017) and Martin Scheinin (2016), 'A comment on Security Council Res 2178 (foreign terrorist fighters) as a "form" of global governance', *Just Security*, 6 October, https://www.justsecurity.org/15989/comment-security-council-res-2178-foreign-fighters-form-global-governance/ (accessed 10 May 2017).

such as 'advocating terrorism' or 'hostile activity' or provisions which rely on the subjective interpretation of an executive authority such as 'serious reasons to believe' that an individual plans to leave the country to engage in terrorist activity, may fall short of these requirements.

A number of rights may be affected by national legislation introduced to implement Security Council resolution 2178. Measures such as seizure and retention of passports or identity cards may impact on freedom of movement; the stripping of citizenship can impact on the prohibition of arbitrary deprivation of nationality or on the absolute prohibition of *refoulement*; restrictions on travel, or bans from entering one's country can impact on the right to work, to a family life, to health; various types of house arrest or preventive detention can impact on the right to liberty, safety and security. The right to a fair trial in its different components can be affected by preventive measures imposed on the basis of classified information, in secret proceedings, or in the absence of adequate judicial review or without adequate legal representation.

Effective prosecutions for the acts covered by resolution 2178, while central to States' overall approach to the issue of foreign terrorist fighters, are extremely difficult to achieve. The use of the Internet and social media adds complexity, as do the short time frame within which individuals act, and the diversity of individuals concerned, with an increasing number of women and minors involved. Alleged events may have taken place abroad, with key evidence to be obtained from other countries, including some involved in an armed conflict. States must make a particular effort to ensure the fairness of proceedings at all stages leading to the trial and the trial itself. To protect the presumption of innocence, States must ensure that the burden of proof be placed on the prosecution to prove all the essential elements of the crime, as set out in General Comment No. 32 of the Human Rights Committee. A presumption that an individual travelling to an area of armed conflict will engage in or support terrorist activity, unless they can prove otherwise, may not meet this criterion. It is also critical that prosecutors and judges ensure that any evidence that may have been obtained in violation of human rights law, in particular as a result of torture, inhuman or degrading treatment, be excluded from the proceedings. Finally, it is essential that where returning foreign fighters are suspected of having committed war crimes or other international crimes, such as crimes against humanity, this is the basis on which they should be prosecuted. While procedurally quicker and politically more expedient to prosecute them under 'ordinary' counter-terrorism legislation, individuals who may be guilty of international crimes should not remain unpunished for those crimes.

4. NEGATIVE IMPACT OF MEASURES TO COUNTER SUPPORT TO TERRORISM ON CIVIL SOCIETY

It is a worrying trend that measures introduced by States to counter terrorism have had a negative impact on civil society and the space in which it operates.[28] The concern is all the greater given the important role that civil society can play in countering terrorism and violent extremism, and the indispensable contribution it can make to counter-terrorism initiatives. Civil society has the unique ability to reach out to local communities; to provide assistance in protecting and promoting human rights; to give a voice to disaffected and marginalized sections of society; to promote the needs of those who are politically, economically or socially excluded; to deliver humanitarian relief in areas affected by conflict; and to play an integral part in the realization of longer term development goals. In a very tangible sense, therefore, the work of civil society groups makes a direct contribution to addressing the conditions conducive to the spread of terrorism, as identified in the Global Counter-Terrorism Strategy.

4.1 Impact of Provisions on Countering the Financing of Terrorism

It is an international legal obligation for States to adopt national legislation to combat the financing of terrorism.[29] It is in part because of a perceived risk that civil society groups can be used, wittingly or unwittingly, as a means of providing support to terrorist organizations, that measures impacting civil society have been introduced. The potential connection was first raised in an Interpretative Note to Recommendation 8 issued by the Financial Action Task Force (FATF)[30] on the financing of

---

[28] For a detailed analysis, see 'Report of the Special Rapporteur on human rights and counter-terrorism', UN Doc. A/70/371.

[29] See International Convention for the Suppression of the Financing of Terrorism Adopted by the General Assembly of the United Nations in resolution 54/109 of 9 December 1999, entered into force on 10 April 2002. See also Security Council resolution 1373 (2001).

[30] FATF is an opaque and largely unaccountable intergovernmental organization whose current objectives are inter alia to set standards and to promote effective implementation of measures for combating terrorist financing, and to protect the international financial system from misuse. Its 40 Recommendations are to be implemented at the national level through legislation and other legally binding measures, and are complemented by Interpretative Notes, Best Practices, and a Handbook for Countries and Assessors.

terrorism and non-profit organizations (NPOs),[31] which states, in its original form, that it has been 'demonstrated that terrorists and terrorist organizations exploit the NPO sector to raise and move funds, provide logistical support, encourage terrorist recruitment, or otherwise support terrorist organizations and terrorist activity'.[32]

FATF's Recommendation 8 deals specifically with NPOs. It requires States to undertake a review of their legislation pertaining to NPOs to ensure that they cannot be misused: (a) by terrorist organizations posing as legitimate entities; (b) to exploit legitimate entities as conduits for terrorist financing, including for the purpose of escaping asset-freezing measures; and (c) to conceal or obscure the clandestine diversion of funds intended for legitimate purposes to terrorist organizations. In order to prevent abuse of NPOs, as well as to identify and take effective action against those NPOs that are exploited or actively support terrorists or terrorist organizations, States are required to adopt a number of measures commensurate with the risks identified through a domestic review of the NPO sector and a national risk assessment.

Recommendation 8 addresses terrorist financing and the provision of 'material support' to terrorists.[33] In the response it suggests, however, it does not focus on financing per se, but recommends regulation of the functioning of civil society through a range of measures which largely impact on freedom of association. According to FATF, the regulation of NPOs should depend on variables such as size, wealth, and potential for abuse. In practice, such distinctions may be difficult to implement, as many NGOs, including human rights NGOs, do not fall squarely into a single category. Some States have adopted wholesale measures that strictly regulate civil society. Such legislation typically includes an obligation to register by way of burdensome, complex or inconsistent

---

[31] Defined as 'a legal person or arrangement or organization that primarily engages in raising or disbursing funds for purposes such as charitable, religious, cultural, educational, social or fraternal purposes, or for the carrying out of other types of "good works"'. See FATF Glossary.

[32] Specifically, FATF identified five categories of possible abuse of NPOs by terrorist entities. See FATF (2014), *Risk of Terrorist Abuse in Non-Profit Organisations* (Paris: FATF), p. 5, and paras. 75 and 91–124.

[33] See the references to 'funds and other assets' in the Interpretative Note to Recommendation 8, as well FATF, *Risk of Terrorist Abuse in Non-Profit Organisations*, ibid., para. 29, which states: 'Recommendation 8 does not limit itself to a narrow definition of terrorism financing, but also focuses on what is described as material support – as defined in the FATF definition of "funds and other assets", which includes "financial assets, economic resources, property of every kind"'.

procedures, which in turn increase the likelihood that the registration be denied, often coupled with limited ability to appeal the refusal; a limitation on obtaining funding from abroad; and the criminalization of various forms of membership of unregistered groups.[34]

It is clear that opportunities for abuse exist, and there are established examples of terrorist financing occurring through civil society. Nevertheless, the amounts involved represent only a fraction of a percentage of total NPO funds.[35] The Government of the United Kingdom, in 2007, noted that 'the scale of terrorist links to the charitable sector is extremely small in comparison to the size of the charitable sector'[36] and, in 2015, the Joint Committee on the Draft Protection of Charities Bill confirmed that '[t]he consensus of opinion is that abuse, distinct from honest mistakes and persistent mismanagement, is rare in the charity sector'.[37] For its part, the UN Counter-Terrorism Implementation Task Force's Working Group on Tackling the Financing of Terrorism noted that '[i]t is important to be realistic about the actual use of this sector for terrorism financing. As a percentage of the total NPO financial flows, [terrorism financing]-related funds are very small'.[38] It further recommended that States 'avoid rhetoric that ties NPOs to terrorism financing in general terms because it overstates the threat and unduly damages the NPO sector as a whole'.[39]

The Special Rapporteur on the rights to freedom of peaceful assembly and association has noted that 'very few, if any, instances of terrorism

---

[34] For an overview, see Ben Hayes (2012), 'Counter-terrorism, "policy laundering" and the FATF: Legalising surveillance, regulating civil society", Transnational Institute/Statewatch, https://www.tni.org/en/publication/counter-terrorism-policy-laundering-and-the-fatf (accessed 15 May 2017).

[35] Emile van der Does de Willebois (2010), 'Nonprofit organizations and the combatting of terrorism financing: A proportionate response', World Bank Working Paper No. 208, Ch. 3.

[36] United Kingdom Home Office and HM Treasury (2007), 'Review of Safeguards to protect the charitable sector (England and Wales) from terrorist abuse summary of responses and next steps', December, http://webarchive.nationalarchives.gov.uk/+/http:/www.homeoffice.gov.uk/documents/cons-2007-protecting-charities/cons-2007-charities-responses?view=Binary (accessed 5 October 2017).

[37] Joint Committee on the Draft Protection of Charities Bill (2015), 'Draft Protection of Charities Bill', February, para. 37.

[38] UN CTITF Working Group (2009), 'Tackling the financing of terrorism', October, para. 64.

[39] Id., Recommendation 65.

financing have been detected as a result of [civil society organization]-specific supervisory measures', and stated that 'Recommendation 8 does not adequately take into account that States already have other means, such as financial surveillance and police cooperation, to effectively address the terrorism financing threat'.[40] A 2014 FATF study corroborates this analysis,[41] by concluding that 'the detection of terrorist abuse and risk within the NPO sector is essentially accomplished by accessing and assessing different types of information from different sources', including most commonly NPO regulatory information. There is thus no compelling argument to justify the extensive additional measures that States must introduce to comply with FATF Recommendation 8. Indeed, despite FATF's recognition of the importance of the role of civil society and its insistence that the measures adopted should not disrupt or discourage legitimate charitable activities,[42] FATF Recommendation 8 has proved to be a useful tool for a number of States as a means of limiting civil society space and suppressing political opposition.[43]

The absence in Recommendation 8 of any reference to the right of freedom of association (and its corollary, the ability to access financial resources), nor to the need to respect the principles of legality, proportionality, necessity and non-discrimination, has leant a veneer of legitimacy to States that have adopted restrictive legislation without due respect for their international human rights obligations. It is clear that Recommendation 8 'fails to provide for specific measures to protect the civil

---

[40] 'Report of the Special Rapporteur on the rights to peaceful assembly and association', UN Doc. A/HRC/23/39, para. 25.

[41] FATF, *Risk of Terrorist Abuse in Non-Profit Organisations* (n 32), Ch. 4.

[42] See Interpretative Note to Recommendation 8, which highlights the 'vital role' of NPOs, in particular their efforts in providing 'essential services, comfort and hope to those in need around the world', the need to ensure measures 'do not disrupt or discourage legitimate charitable activities', and to 'the extent reasonably possible, avoid any negative impact on innocent and legitimate beneficiaries of charitable activity'. See also UN CTITF (2011), 'Expert Working Group meeting on preventing abuse of the non-profit sector for the purposes of terrorist financing, key observations of the organizers', 18–20 January, Lancaster House, London, at para. 7, and FATF (2015), *Best Practices on Combating the Abuse of Non-Profit Organisations*, June (Paris: FATF), para. 18; see also FATF Recommendation 1, which recommends that the measures adopted be commensurate to the risks.

[43] See 'Report of the Special Rapporteur on Freedom of Association and Assembly', UN Doc. A/HRC/23/39, para. 25, in which the Special Rapporteur warns against 'the implementation of restrictive measures – such as FATF Recommendation 8 – which have been misused by States to violate international law'.

society sector from undue restrictions to their right to freedom of association by States asserting that their measures are in compliance with FATF Recommendation 8'.[44] In addition, while FATF's monitoring bodies could have played a key mitigating role by highlighting in their mutual evaluations areas where national legislation is at variance with international human rights law, in practice, in its peer review processes, FATF has rarely criticized over-regulation or lack of respect for human rights,[45] focusing instead on cases of insufficient regulation.[46]

FATF has very recently adopted a more nuanced approach in its revised Best Practices for the implementation of Recommendation 8. For the first time FATF has stated that 'as a matter of principle, complying with the FATF recommendations should not contravene a country's obligations under (…) international human rights law to promote universal respect for, and observance of, fundamental human rights and freedoms, such as freedom of expression, religion, or belief, and freedom

---

[44] 'Special Rapporteur on Freedom of Association and Assembly', ibid., para. 25. See also Thomas Carothers and Saskia Brechenmacher (2014), 'Closing space: Democracy and human rights support under fire', Carnegie Endowment for International Peace, http://carnegieendowment.org/2014/02/20/closing-space-democracy-and-human-rights-support-under-fire-pub-54503 (accessed 5 June 2017), p. 29.

[45] For an example where the reviewing body highlighted the State's 'blanket approach' as not being justified by assessed terrorism financing risks, see ESAAM (2015), 'Mutual Evaluation Report, Ethiopia', May, para. 142. On the legislation, see UN High Commissioner for Human Rights (2014), 'Ethiopia: Pillay condemns crackdown on journalists, increasing restrictions on freedom of expression', press release, 2 May, https://reliefweb.int/report/ethiopia/pillay condemnscrackdownjournalistsincreasingrestrictionsfreedomexpression (accessed 20 January 2018).

[46] See e.g. FATF/GAFI (2008), 'Second Mutual Evaluation Report – Anti-money laundering and combating the financing of terrorism – Russian Federation', para. 720, as well as Inara Gulpe-Laganovska (2008), *Choking on Bureaucracy, State Curbs on Independent Civil Society Activism*, vol. 20, no. 1(d) (New York: Human Rights Watch). See also Human Rights Committee (2009), 'Concluding observations', UN Doc. CCPR/C/RUS/CO/6, para. 26. See also MENA FATF (2010), 'Mutual Evaluation Report, Kingdom of Saudi Arabia', para. 798. See Amnesty International (2014), 'Saudi Arabia's ACPRA: How the Kingdom silences its human rights activists', MDA 23/025/2014, October, p. 5 and INCL (2017), 'NGO Law Monitor: Saudi Arabia', http://www.icnl.org/research/monitor/saudiarabia.html (accessed 5 October 2017). See also the 'Report of the Working Group on the Universal Periodic Review', UN Doc. A/HRC/11/23, para. 35.

of peaceful assembly and of association'.[47] This significant development should be welcomed: States should be urged to take the revised Best Practices into consideration in adopting any legislation to regulate civil society, and FATF monitoring bodies should rely on this guidance in evaluating the way in which States have domestically implemented Recommendation 8.

4.2 The Impact of Laws Criminalizing Material Support for Terrorism

The adoption of binding international and regional instruments proscribing material support for terrorism, together with overbroad domestic legislation implementing those obligations or otherwise criminalizing such support, can pose a significant threat to civil society organizations, some of whose activities may – unwittingly – constitute indirect material support according to the definitions adopted. NGOs have been constrained by real or perceived threats of prosecution, which in turn can have a serious impact on recipients and beneficiaries.

Both UN Security Council resolution 1373 (2001)[48] and the International Convention for the Suppression of the Financing of Terrorism require States to adopt measures at the national level to prohibit funding and material support being made available for the purposes of carrying out terrorist acts. Resolution 1373 has also been the basis on which national governments and regional entities have set up sanction regimes applicable to individuals and entities designated as terrorist,[49] which supplement the UN 1267/Al-Qaida Sanctions Regime.[50] Importantly, the 1267/Al-Qaida Sanctions Regime provides for humanitarian exemptions on a case-by-case basis, whereas resolution 1373 does not mention any such exemptions, thus leaving it to individual States to decide whether to include them in their own national regimes.

Many States have now adopted legislation criminalizing material support.[51] As a result, donors now frequently include counter-terrorism clauses in humanitarian grant and partnership agreement contracts,

---

47 FATF, *Best Practices* (n 42), para. 22.

48 UN Security Council resolution 1373, para. 1(d).

49 UN Security Council resolution 1373, para. 1(c).

50 See 'Report of the Special Rapporteur on human rights and counter-terrorism', UN Docs A/HRC/29/51 and A/67/396.

51 For a thorough examination, see Kate Mackintosh and Patrick Duplat (2013), 'Study of the impact of donor counter-terrorism measures on principled humanitarian action', July, https://docs.unocha.org/sites/dms/documents/ct_

requiring NGOs to provide onerous guarantees that their funds are not used to benefit terrorists or to support acts of terrorism.[52] Vetting processes have also been introduced,[53] and NGOs acting domestically and abroad are subject to a complex array of different counter-terrorism laws and approaches.[54]

Exemptions for humanitarian purposes exist under some, but not all, legal regimes.[55] In certain jurisdictions, it is possible to obtain a licence from national authorities to deal with proscribed groups for the purpose of providing humanitarian aid.[56] In other cases, the government can waive some its provisions to allow humanitarian operations for certain organizations.[57]

---

study_full_report.pdf (accessed 15 May 2017) and Harvard Program on Humanitarian Policy and Conflict Research (2011), 'Humanitarian action under scrutiny: Criminalizing humanitarian engagement', HPCR Working Paper (February), http://c0186748.cdn1.cloudfiles.rackspacecloud.com/HPCR%20CHE%202011.pdf (accessed 17 May 2017).

52 See Mackintosh and Duplat (n 51), pp. 47 *et seq.*

53 See Harvard Program on Humanitarian Policy and Conflict Research (n 51), p. 23.

54 'In the name of security, counterterrorism Laws worldwide since September 11'.

55 See Part 5.3 Division 102.8 of the Australian Criminal Code. See Sections 9 and 10 of the New Zealand Suppression of Terrorism Act 2002. In the United States, the provisions on providing material support to terrorists (18 USC 2339A) and to designated foreign terrorist organizations (18 USC 2339B) both provide for an exception for 'medicine or religious materials' (see 18 USC 2339A (b)(1) and 18 USC 2339B (g)(4)). For a discussion on this exception, see Mackintosh and Duplat (n 51) and Harvard Program on Humanitarian Policy and Conflict Research (n 51). See also attempts at broadening humanitarian exemption, with the draft Bill 'Humanitarian Assistance Facilitation Act', https://www.govtrack.us/congress/bills/113/hr3526/summary (accessed 5 October 2017).

56 For Australia, see Section 22, Part 4 of the UN Charter Act. For New Zealand, see Section 10 of the New Zealand Suppression of Terrorism Act 2002.

57 The Office of Foreign Assets Control (OFAC) of the United States Treasury Department can issue exemptions for humanitarian action in the form of general or specific licences, but they do not provide immunity against the criminal prohibition on providing material support or resources to terrorists. See Jessica Burniske with Naz Modirzadeh and Dustin Lewis (2014), 'Counterterrorism laws and regulations: What aid agencies need to know', Humanitarian Practice Network at ODI Number 79 (November). For the specific example of Somalia, see Mackintosh and Duplat (n 51), pp. 79 and 80; and Harvard Program on Humanitarian Policy and Conflict Research (n 51), p. 21.

While the practical challenges encountered by NGOs working in areas controlled by designated terrorist groups – such as Mali, Nigeria, Pakistan, the Philippines, Somalia, Palestine and more recently in Syria – may be similar, the legal situation can vary greatly according to the overlapping and inconsistent requirements of different applicable regimes. Variables include: whether the non-State armed groups in control of territory are on terrorism sanction lists; whether a humanitarian exemption has been granted directly by the UN Security Council;[58] where the NGO is registered, and what the nationality of its staff is; where it conducts its operations; and where its funding comes from (noting that funding may come from various sources, each with its own requirements, and may also have been passed on from intermediary partners).

Many civil society groups fear that the laws on providing support to terrorism are often so broad and vague that they will be sanctioned for carrying out their activities, even though they have taken every feasible precaution to avoid policies that are capable of providing indirect support to terrorist groups. This concern has been reinforced by the case of *Holder v. Humanitarian Law Project*,[59] in which the US Supreme Court by a 6-3 majority confirmed the constitutionality of the primary US material support statute.[60] The Court held that the provision of training on humanitarian and international law, petitioning various representative bodies (including the UN), and engaging in political advocacy, to organizations designated by the Department of State as Foreign Terrorist Organizations,[61] constituted 'material support'. In a ruling that has had a chilling effect on NGO operations, Chief Justice Roberts held that 'material support' included initiatives that were intended to promote peaceable, lawful conduct because such assistance could be 'diverted' to advance terrorist objectives. Consequently, irrespective of their nationality, individuals working for civil society organizations anywhere in the world may now be prosecuted in the United States and incur up to 15 years' imprisonment if they engage in one of the acts listed in the material support statute with an entity they knew was a designated foreign terrorist organization, or engaged in terrorist activity or acts of

[58] Such as through Resolution 1916 (2010). See Mackintosh and Duplat (n 51), pp. 75 and 76.

[59] *Holder v. Humanitarian Law Project*, 561 U.S. 1 (2010) 130 S. Ct, 2705.

[60] This case dealt with material statute under 18 U.S.C. 2339B, but material support contains the same elements under 2339A.

[61] The Kurdish Workers Party (PKK) and the Liberation Tigers of Tamil Eelam (LTTE).

terrorism.[62] That is despite the fact that engagement with such organizations for humanitarian purposes is recognized under international law,[63] and humanitarian access is now commonly included in UN Security Council resolutions.[64] Such engagement is often necessary when designated terrorist groups control territory, in order for humanitarian organizations to secure access to civilians living in the area (for example, by the payment of fees for visa entries) or to reduce the risk of harm to civilians in armed conflict. Such activity should not be criminalized, and the potential chilling effect of the *Holder* decision on the work of humanitarian, human rights, and advocacy organizations around the world is troubling.[65]

As highlighted by the UN Secretary-General, '[a]t the absolute minimum, it is critical that Member States support, or at least do not impede, efforts by humanitarian organizations to engage armed groups in order to seek improved protection for civilians – even those groups that are proscribed in some national legislation'.[66] As the Secretary-General went on to point out, the increasing appreciation by Member States of the importance of engagement for humanitarian purposes has yet to translate 'into a willingness to refrain from adopting measures that impede, or in some cases, criminalize engagement with non-State armed groups'.[67]

One of the most worrying consequences of these developments is that humanitarian NGOs have been impacted in their ability to adhere to the guiding principles of neutrality, impartiality, and independence. The parameters of humanitarian action have been shifted so that programmes that are specifically designed to avoid contact with a designated group

---

[62] With the exceptions referred to earlier.

[63] See Harvard Program on Humanitarian Policy and Conflict Research (n 51), pp. 4 *et seq.*

[64] See UN Security Council resolution 2139 (2014).

[65] See Harvard Program on Humanitarian Policy and Conflict Research (n 51), pp. 18–21, Mackintosh and Duplat (n 51), pp. 40–42. Additionally, it is of note that in the case of *United States v. Shah*, the Court seems to make a distinction between the provision of medicine and the provision of medical treatment; 474 F.Supp.2d 492 (SDNY 2007). See also BBC Radio 4, 'A deadly dilemma', transcript available at: http://www.bbc.co.uk/programmes/b047zk6z (accessed 5 October 2017), para. 45; and Ashley Jackson and Abdi Aynte (2013), 'Talking to the other side', Humanitarian negotiations with Al-Shabaab in Somalia, HPG Working Paper, December, p. 7.

[66] 'Report of the Secretary-General on the protection of civilians in armed conflict', UN Doc. S/2009/277, para. 45.

[67] 'Report of the Secretary-General on the protection of civilians in armed conflict', UN Doc. S/2010/579, para. 55.

(so as to limit the organization's exposure to criminal liability) are preferred over programmes that are designed to respond most directly and effectively to humanitarian needs.[68]

Counter-terrorism measures have thus contributed to a self-imposed restriction by civil society actors of their own space.[69] It is unsurprising that, given the complexities involved in operating in or around areas where terrorist groups are active, some NGOs have preferred to re-orient their operations to areas where there are fewer risks of prosecution or have refused to take funding from certain donors. Increased guidance, transparency and clarity on the scope and impact of counter-terrorism laws and policies[70] are necessary for NGOs to be able to decide whether to undertake certain programs, and to develop appropriate risk-mitigating procedures.[71]

Some measures at the international and national levels have also contributed to a perception that NGOs have been co-opted into official counter-terrorism initiatives, thereby limiting their ability to operate in certain areas, with certain governments, or with certain groups.[72] These include reporting requirements such as those imposed by resolution 1916 (2010), as they involve NGOs in the sanctions process against designated terrorist groups, which undermines their actual or perceived neutrality;[73] and the vetting of NGOs by donors, which impacts on their perceived independence and their ability to work in a climate of trust with local

---

68 See Mackintosh and Duplat (n 51) pp. 72 and 84.

69 See Press Conference, Special Rapporteur on Human Rights and Counter-Terrorism, Martin Scheinin, 26 October 2010, cited in HCPR Working Paper, 2011, available at: http://www.un.org/press/en/2010/101026_Scheinin.doc.htm (accessed 5 October 2017).

70 See Burniske with Moziradeh and Lewis (n 57), p. 7. See also Joint Committee on the Draft Protection of Charities Bill (n 37), paras. 187–192.

71 See Burniske with Moziradeh and Lewis (n 57), p. 7, and Mackintosh and Duplat (n 51), p. 81 and Harvard Program on Humanitarian Policy and Conflict Research (n 51), p. 114.

72 For a general discussion, see Annyssa Bellal and Stuart Casey-Maslen (2011), 'Rules of Engagement: Protecting Civilians through Dialogue with Non-State Actors', Geneva Academy of International Humanitarian and Human Rights Law, pp. 15–16. See also Mackintosh and Duplat (n 51), p. 81; Harvard Program on Humanitarian Policy and Conflict Research (n 51), p. 32; Burniske with Moziradeh and Lewis (n 57), p. 3; and Jackson and Aynte (n 65), p. 6.

73 Mackintosh and Duplat (n 51), p. 81 and Harvard Program on Humanitarian Policy and Conflict Research (n 51), p. 31.

implementing partners.[74] NGOs are increasingly being drawn into a broader counter-terrorism infrastructure, and in turn this further constricts the space in which civil society groups are able to operate.[75]

On a very practical level, NGO operations are increasingly constrained by restrictions on available funding in areas where terrorist groups are active,[76] and by increased reliance on the part of donors on 'safer' implementing partners such as UN agencies, and other international organizations, to the detriment of smaller or local NGOs.[77] Civil society groups have highlighted the financial and resources implications of the increased time that is now spent on administrative requirements, complying – and proving compliance – with counter-terrorism material support legislation,[78] which, in turn, has an inevitable impact on their operational capabilities.[79]

Further, counter-terrorism concerns have affected civil society access to financial services.[80] Many banks have implemented risk-averse protocols that go beyond the specific requirements of the FATF recommendations in order to shield themselves from any possible risk of liability under counter-terrorism legislation.[81] In effect, this means no longer processing transactions involving high-risk environments or actors.[82] Some NGOs have found that their ability to access financial services,

---

74 See Burniske with Moziradeh and Lewis (n 57), p. 6. See also Neal Cohen, Robert Hasty, Ashley Wonton (2014), 'Implications of the USAID partner vetting system and state department risk analysis and management system under European Union and United Kingdom data protection and privacy law', Counterterrorism and Humanitarian Engagement Project, Research and Policy Paper, March.

75 See, e.g., David Anderson, transcript of the evidence before the Committee on 2 December 2014 on the effect of anti-terrorism laws on charities, Q195.

76 Mackintosh and Duplat (n 51), p. 82 for an example in Somalia.

77 Mackintosh and Duplat (n 51), p. 104.

78 Mackintosh and Duplat (n 51), pp. 72 and 103.

79 Mackintosh and Duplat (n 51), p. 103.

80 Human Rights Council resolution 27/21: 'Concerned that unilateral coercive measures have, in some instances, prevented humanitarian organizations from making financial transfers to States where they work'.

81 See Victoria Metcalfe-Hough, Tom Keatinge and Sara Pantuliano (2015), 'UK humanitarian aid in the age of counter terrorism: Perceptions and reality', Humanitarian Policy Group, ODI, https://www.odi.org/sites/odi.org.uk/files/odi-assets/publications-opinion-files/9479.pdf (accessed 15 May 2017), p. 13.

82 See Martin Arnold and Sam Fleming (2014), 'Regulation: bank counts the risks and rewards', *Financial Times*, 14 November, http://www.ft.com/cms/s/0/9df378a2-66bb-11e4-91ab-00144feabdc0.html#axzz3J2G48VEu (accessed 7 June 2017).

including banking services, has been severely impaired, while others have seen their bank accounts closed altogether. For NGOs operating in areas of conflict, the inability to access financial services can have very severe consequences, including delayed aid delivery and increased physical risk to staff and offices (with larger amounts of cash being transported and used). Moreover, transactions outside the banking sector are more difficult to trace and account for.[83] The FATF has underlined that financial institutions should not view NPOs as automatically high risk simply because they operate in cash-intensive environments or in countries of great humanitarian need.[84]

Financial services restrictions on NGOs operating in sensitive contexts threaten both the operations of organizations and even their very existence. The denial of banking facilities without reasonable suspicion that the targeted organization or transaction constitutes support of terrorism or money laundering is incompatible with the right to freedom of association. Singling out organizations on the basis of stereotypical assumptions relating to characteristics such as religion or the predominant race of the organization's membership or beneficiaries constitutes unjustified discrimination and is prohibited under international law.[85] The risk that material support provisions – or over-cautious responses to them – will bring about such infringements is significant.

5. MEASURES THAT IMPACT ON THE RIGHTS OF MIGRANTS

According to reliable sources, at the end of 2015, a total of 65.3 million individuals had been displaced by conflict and persecution, representing one in every 113 individuals on the planet.[86] During the course of 2015, over 1 million individuals entered Europe.[87] At the same time, information from Member States and UN Reports indicate that between

[83] See Burniske with Moziradeh and Lewis (n 57), pp. 8 and 9 and Metcalfe-Hough, Keatinge and Pantuliano (n 81), pp. 6 and 7.

[84] FATF, *Best Practice* (n 42), paras. 68–70.

[85] 'Report of the Special Rapporteur on the rights to freedom of peaceful assembly and of association', A/HRC/23/39/Add.1, paras. 84 and 85.

[86] UNHCR (2015), 'Global trends: Forced displacement in 2015', http://www.unhcr.org/576408cd7 (accessed 5 October 2017).

[87] European Agency for the Management of Operational Cooperation at the External Borders of the Member States of the European Union (FRONTEX) (2016), 'Risk analysis for 2016', http://frontex.europa.eu/assets/Publications/Risk_Analysis/Annual_Risk_Analysis_2016.pdf (accessed 11 June 2017).

25 000 to 30 000 individuals from more than 100 Member States had travelled to join groups associated with Al-Qaida, ISIL and others, and that the numbers of such fighters had increased by 71 per cent between mid-2014 and March 2015.[88] This led the UN Secretary-General to note that '[m]illions of people have fled the territory controlled by terrorist and violent extremist groups. Migratory flows have increased both away from and towards the conflict zones, involving those seeking safety and those lured into the conflict as foreign terrorist fighters, further destabilizing the regions concerned'.[89]

Possibly helped by the link between terrorism and refugees made through UN Security Council resolution 1373 (2001),[90] it was not long until all movements of migrants were seen as a threat to national security. This perception was assisted by numerous sensational but unproven media reports, including that a Syrian passport was 'found' on one of the individuals who carried out the attack in November 2015 in Paris,[91] or that ISIL fighters disguise themselves as women in burkas,[92] which have sowed fears that members of terrorist groups 'infiltrate' migratory flows to carry out acts of terrorism, or 'radicalize' nationals, without proper screening or controls at international borders. At the same time, politicians referred to the 'absolute link between migration and terrorism';[93] warned of 'sleeper cells' coming to Europe,[94] of the 'considerable risk of terrorists infiltrating immigration flows',[95] and of boats 'full of terrorists'

---

[88] UNODC (2016), 'Discussion guide for the thematic discussion on criminal justice responses to prevent and counter terrorism in all its forms and manifestations', UN Doc. E/CN.15/2016/6, paras. 41 and 42.

[89] 'UN Secretary-General Plan of Action to Prevent Violent Extremism', UN Doc. A/70/674, para. 2.

[90] States were requested to take appropriate measures before granting refugee status for the purpose of ensuring that the asylum-seeker had not planned, facilitated or participated in the commission of terrorist acts. UN Security Council resolution 1373 (2001), para. 3(f).

[91] Marcus Walker and Noemie Bisserbe (2015), 'Paris stadium attacker got to Europe using fake Syrian passport', *Wall Street Journal*, 16 November.

[92] Sara Malm (2016), 'Humiliated ISIS fighter is paraded by Egyptian soldiers after disguising himself as a burka-clad WOMAN in desperate bid to defect from terrorists', *Mail Online*, 7 April.

[93] Deutsche Welle (2016), 'Slovak prime minister blames migrants for terror threat', 30 July and Deutsche Welle (2016), 'Czech president warns of migrants' "barbaric acts", 2 August.

[94] Katrin Bennhold (2015), 'As migrants reach Europe, fears may be misplaced', *New York Times*, 20 October.

[95] Neil Arun (2015), 'Militants, migrants and the Med', *BBC News*, 24 February.

coming to Europe.[96] Others have suggested the 'total and complete shutdown of Muslims entering the [national territory]'[97] before actively attempting to prevent nationals from several countries from entering national territory, in a discriminatory and unlawful move.[98] The perception that irregular migration can increase the terrorist threat has also been given credence by official assessments that '[the November 2015 Paris attacks] clearly demonstrated that irregular migratory flows could be used by terrorists to enter the EU'.[99] Official statements by European leaders also made a clear link between strengthening border controls and terrorist attacks,[100] while the spectre of refugee camps as recruiting grounds for terrorist groups (as in Pakistan and Yemen)[101] or the radicalization of migrants by 'homegrown radicals'[102] was raised. Migrants, including asylum seekers and refugees, have thus been 'stigmatized and labelled as terrorists'.[103] While in 2016 the numbers of migrants entering into Europe dropped significantly to approximately 382 000,[104] many of the measures that States had set up to address this so-called 'migration crisis' are still in place, and have a serious impact on the human rights of all migrants.

---

96 Ibid.

97 Jenna Johnson (2015), 'Trump calls for "total and complete shutdown of Muslims entering the United States"', *The Washington Post*, 7 December.

98 Press Release by UN Special Rapporteurs on migrants, human rights and counter-terrorism, racism and freedom of religion, 'New policy breaches Washington's human rights obligations', Geneva, 1 February 2017.

99 FRONTEX, 'Risk analysis for 2016' (n 87).

100 Conclusions of the Council of the EU and of the Member States meeting within the Council on Counter-Terrorism, 20 November 2015, point 4. c) and d).

101 Khalid Koser (2016), 'Migration, violent extremism and terrorism: Myths and realities', World Bank Blog, Migration and Violent Extremism in Contemporary Europe, 16 March, http://blogs.worldbank.org/peoplemove/migration-and-violent-extremism-contemporary-europe (accessed 12 June 2017).

102 Guy Chazan (2016), 'Germany fears influence of homegrown militants on Syrian refugees', *Financial Times*, 29 March.

103 UNHCR presentation to the Joint Seminar of the Strategic Committee on Immigration, Frontiers and Asylum (SCIFA) and Committee on Article 36 (CATS) organized by the Slovenian EU Presidency, Ljubljana, 17–18 January 2008, remarks by Vincent Cochetel, 'Terrorism as a global phenomenon'.

104 FRONTEX (2017), 'Risk analysis for 2017', http://frontex.europa.eu/assets/Publications/Risk_Analysis/Annual_Risk_Analysis_2017.pdf (accessed 12 June 2017).

There is, to date, little hard evidence to show that terrorists take advantage of mass migration flows to carry out acts of terrorism,[105] or that migrants are somehow more prone to radicalization than others. Instead, much of the discussion is based on inaccurate information,[106] or is simply alarmist in the absence of a clearer understanding of 'radicalization' processes.[107] Research shows that very few refugees have actually carried out acts of terrorism.[108] As noted by an Office of the UN High Commissioner for Refugees representative, 'there is a clear perception in some quarters that asylum is misused to hide or provide safe haven for terrorists. Such perceptions are analytically and statistically unfounded, and must change',[109] while the UN Secretary-General warned against 'misplaced suspicions about migrants and refugees (...), which only play into the hands of terrorists trying to sow divisions and fear'.[110]

It is critical to bear in mind that in the clear majority of cases, migrants are populations at risk rather than populations posing a risk. These individuals are themselves escaping persecution, armed conflict and violence, including terrorist acts, often fleeing areas where terrorist groups are most active. Indeed, terrorist activity is a significant driver of refugee activity and internal displacement, and the countries that are the greatest sources of refugees and internally displaced persons also suffer the most from acts of terrorism.[111] Where migrants are themselves

---

[105] UNHCR (2015), 'UNHCR chief says it is 'absolute nonsense' to blame refugees for terror', press release, 17 November.

[106] Ishaan Tharoor (2015), 'Were Syrian refugees involved in the Paris attacks? What we know and don't know', *The Washington Post*, 17 November 2015.

[107] 'Report of the Special Rapporteur on human rights and counter-terrorism', UN Doc. A/HRC/31/65.

[108] Kathleen Newland (2015), 'The US record shows refugees are not a threat', Migration Policy Institute, October, http://www.migrationpolicy.org/news/us-record-shows-refugees-are-not-threat (accessed 5 October 2017).

[109] Remarks by Vincent Cochetel (n 103).

[110] UN Secretary-General (2015), 'Secretary-General's remarks to the General Assembly meeting on global awareness of the tragedies of irregular migrants in the Mediterranean Basin with specific emphasis on Syrian asylum seekers', 20 November, https://www.un.org/sg/en/content/sg/statement/2015-11-20/secretary-generals-remarks-general-assembly-meeting-global-awareness (accessed 12 June 2017).

[111] Of the 11 countries that had more than 500 deaths from acts of terrorism in 2014, ten generated the highest levels of refugees and internally displaced persons in the world. Further, over 16 million refugees and internally displaced persons came from the five countries with the highest levels of terrorism in 2014, and approximately 70 per cent of UNHCR's total population of concern came

victims of terrorist violence,[112] either because they are forced to flee as a direct consequence of the actions of a terrorist group or of the failure of the State to protect them (such as the Yezidis and Christians in areas under ISIL control or individuals fleeing Boko Haram's kidnappings of women, forcible recruitment of children and men in Northern Nigeria) or because they are escaping conflict, lack of opportunities or prospects for themselves and their families,[113] they must be granted the protection that victims of terrorism are entitled to, rather than be ostracized as potential terrorists. This approach is the only one that is consistent with Security Council resolutions that show grave concern at the devastating humanitarian impact on the civilian populations caused by some terrorist groups,[114] including gross, systematic and widespread abuses of human rights and violations of international humanitarian law,[115] which have led to the displacement of hundreds of thousands of people.[116]

The fears that migrants pose a terrorist threat have been used to garner support for restrictive migration policies in which security concerns seem to trump humanitarian and protection considerations.[117] These have included stricter border controls (or their reintroduction where there were none), preventing individuals of named nationalities from entering their territory, building fences to keep migrants out,[118] engaging in push back operations, detention and refoulement at borders, or the criminalization of irregular migration.

---

from the 20 countries with the highest number of terrorism-related fatalities. Institute for Economics and Peace (2015), 'Global Terrorism Index 2015', http://economicsandpeace.org/wp-content/uploads/2015/11/Global-Terrorism-Index-2015.pdf (accessed 12 June 2017), pp. 59 *et seq.*

[112] 'Report of the Special Rapporteur on human rights and counter-terrorism', UN Doc. A/HRC/20/14, paras. 11–16.

[113] Khalid Koser and Amy E. Cunningham (2015), 'Migration, violent extremism and terrorism: Myths and realities', in Institute for Economics and Peace (2015), 'Global Terrorism Index 2015', https://www.files.ethz.ch/isn/194968/Global-Terrorism-Index-2015.pdf (accessed 12 June 2017), p. 83.

[114] UN Security Council resolution 2170 (2014).

[115] Ibid.

[116] UN Security Council resolution 2258 (2015).

[117] See the address to the 44th INTERPOL Regional European Conference in Prague by the Assistant High Commissioner (Protection) on 18 May 2016, http://www.unhcr.org/admin/dipstatements/573c8e987/security-international-refugee-protection-unhcrs-perspective-volker-turk.html (accessed 5 October 2017).

[118] George Jahn (2015), 'Austria joins other EU nations to build fence along borders to slows migrant flow', *The Star*, 28 October.

International borders are not zones of exclusion or exception for human rights obligations. States must, of course, exercise jurisdiction at their international borders, but they must do so in light of their human rights obligations and they should ensure that human rights are at the centre of the migration governance at international borders.[119] The human rights of all persons at international borders must be respected in the pursuit of border control, law enforcement, and other State objectives, regardless of which authorities perform border governance measures and where such measures take place.[120]

In light of this, some key principles can be drawn:

(1) Migration is not a crime.[121] Accordingly, the term 'illegal migrants' should not be used to refer to migrants in an irregular situation,[122] States should not criminalize irregular entry, the attempt to enter in an irregular manner, or irregular stay,[123] and asylum seekers should not be penalized for illegal entry.[124] States should ensure that all measures aimed at addressing migration, including irregular migration, do not adversely impact on the human rights and dignity of migrants[125] or contribute to their stigmatization.

(2) All border governance measures should comply with the principles of legality, proportionality, necessity and non-discrimination. Enhanced screening processes at international borders based on broad profiles or stereotypical assumptions that persons of a certain racial, national or ethnic origin, or religion are particularly likely to commit crimes are likely to be incompatible with the principle of non-discrimination,[126] while the blanket imposition of additional

---

[119] UN OHCHR, 'Recommended principles and guidelines on human rights at international borders', II.A.2.

[120] UN OHCHR, 'Recommended principles and guidelines on human rights at international borders', I.A.1.

[121] See e.g. Statement by the UN Special Rapporteur on the human rights of migrants, 'Mainstreaming a human rights-based approach to migration within the High Level Dialogue', PGA Plenary Session – Criminalization of Migrants, 2 October 2013.

[122] UN General Assembly resolution 3449 (9 December 1975).

[123] OHCHR, 'Recommended principles and guidelines on human rights at international borders' Guideline 2.4.

[124] Article 31 Convention Relating to the Status of Refugees 1951.

[125] OHCHR, Recommended principles and guidelines on human rights at international borders' Guidelines, II.A.5.

[126] 'Report of the Special Rapporteur on human rights and counter-terrorism', UN Doc. A/HRC/4/26.

barriers to entry or screening measures for particular groups of people based on grounds prohibited under international human rights law may also constitute disproportionate interferences with human rights.[127] Conversely, border authorities must be trained properly on the risks, limitations and human rights impacts of the technology, so that its use does not result in reduced exercise of judgment in screening processes.[128] Further, any information gathered about migrants should not be shared with third countries that might expose the individuals to human rights violations, including refoulement or inhuman treatment, and that personal data is collected, stored and shared with sufficient safeguards to ensure that the rights engaged are respected.[129]

(3) International refugee law is not an obstacle to an effective counter-terrorism strategy. Where properly applied, refugee law takes into account the security interests of States and of host communities while at the same time protecting the rights of refugees.[130] A fair and effectively managed system of asylum does not shield individuals suspected of acts of terrorism from prosecution; on the contrary, international refugee law provides for the identification of those who have committed heinous acts or serious crimes and their exclusion from refugee status.[131] However, while the presence of an individual on a list of terrorist suspects or a member of a designated terrorist organization at the international, regional or national levels may trigger consideration of the applicability of clauses relating to exclusion from refugee status, it does not in itself constitute

---

[127] Screening Procedures for Syrian Refugees Compiled by the House Democratic Caucus. See also press release by UN Special Rapporteurs on migrants, human rights and counter-terrorism, racism and freedom of religion (n 98). And also 'Report of the Special Rapporteur on human rights and counter-terrorism', ibid., paras. 35 and 36.

[128] OHCHR, Recommended principles and guidelines on human rights at international borders' Guideline 6 (3) and (4).

[129] European Union Agency for Fundamental Rights (2013), 'Fundamental rights at Europe's southern borders', http://fra.europa.eu/sites/default/files/fundamental-rights-europes-southern-sea-borders-jul-13_en.pdf (accessed 5 October 2017), pp. 60 *et seq.*

[130] See the address to the 44th INTERPOL Regional European Conference in Prague by the Assistant High Commissioner (Protection) (n 117).

[131] Remarks by Vincent Cochetel (n 103). See also 'Report of the Special Rapporteur on human rights and counter-terrorism', UN Doc. A/62/263, para. 35.

sufficient evidence to justify exclusion.[132] An assessment must be carried out on a case-by-case basis to give careful consideration to the particular role, personal involvement and substantial contributions of the person concerned to the activities of the organization.[133]

(4) The absolute prohibition of refoulement, which applies irrespective of the individual's conduct, and does not yield to the imperative of fighting terrorism, must be respected at all times, regardless of the manner in which the transfer occurs, or where it occurs, as it applies extraterritorially.[134] Any State that engages in 'maritime interception operations', 'push back operations' and 'search and rescue operations' on the high seas, such as in the Mediterranean and the Indian Ocean,[135] including those that aim to carry out blanket returns of rescued migrants to one country,[136] is bound by it.[137]

---

132 UNHCR, 'Statement on Article 1F of the 1951 Convention, July 2009, pp. 8 and 30.

133 Ibid., pp. 9, 12, 23–25.

134 *Hirsi Jamaa v. Italy*, App. no. 27765/09 (ECtHR, 23 February 2012). See also UNHCR, 'Advisory Opinion on the Extraterritorial Application of Non-Refoulement Obligations Under the 1951 Convention Relating to the Status of Refugees and its 1967 Protocol' (26 January 2007) and UNHCR, 'Legal Position: Despite court ruling on Sri Lankans detained at sea, Australia bound by international obligations' (4 February 2015). *A contrario*, see *Haitian Centre for Human Rights v. United States*, Case No. 10.675, Inter-Am. Comm. H.R., Report No. 51/96, OEA/Ser.L/V/II.95 Doc. 7 rev. (1997), at 550, para. 157.

135 'Report of the Special Rapporteur on human rights and counter-terrorism' UN Doc. A/62/263.

136 See Niels Franze (2016), 'NATO expands Aegean Sea migrant patrols into Turkish and Greek territorial waters – Rescued Migrants to be automatically returned to Turkey', *Migrants at Sea*, 7 March, https://migrantsatsea.org/2016/03/07/nato-expands-aegean-sea-migrant-patrols-into-turkish-and-greek-territorial-waters-rescued-migrants-to-be-automatically-returned-to-turkey/ (accessed 12 June 2017).

137 In the landmark *Hirsi Jamaa* ruling (n 134), the European Court of Human Rights noted that such operations could also violate the prohibition of collective expulsion, which imposes a duty of due process. Push back operations without an individualized assessment are thus generally illegal, regardless of whether there is a risk of refoulement or not. See Jan Arno Hessbruegge (2012), 'European Court of Human Rights protects migrants against "push back" operations on the high seas', *Insights*, **16** (14), 1.

(5) States must ensure that bilateral or multi-lateral readmission agreements and bilateral, regional and international cooperation agreements, arrangements or laws or policies do not have a deleterious effect on the human rights of migrants at borders. Any agreement on border governance should be made public and transparent, and should not be entered into with countries unable to demonstrate that they respect, protect and fulfill their human rights obligations at international borders.[138] Accountability and oversight mechanisms should also be included.[139]

(6) While it is not disputed that States have the right to detain foreigners prior to deportation and extradition, detention should always be a last resort. Detention must always comply with the principle of legality, and the grounds for detention must be exhaustively listed. Deterring irregular migrants can never be considered as a legitimate ground for detention. In all cases, to avoid detention from becoming arbitrary, detention must be necessary, reasonable and proportionate. As such, indefinite or mandatory detention – which also contributes to the stigmatization of migrants and foreigners – should be prohibited.

It is clear that there should be no avenue for those supporting or committing acts of terrorism to secure access to territory, whether to find a safe haven, avoid prosecution, or to carry out further attacks. An effective response to possible security threats should not, however, solely come from measures seeking to restrict the movement of refugees and migrants and further limit access to territory at the expense of human rights, justice, accountability, human dignity, equality, and non-discrimination. This simply diverts migrant movements along other routes, aggravates their situation, and contributes to the flourishing business of smugglers and traffickers.[140]

---

[138] OHCHR, Recommended Principles and Guidelines on human rights at international borders, Guideline 10.4 and 10.5.

[139] OHCHR, Intervener Brief in the case of *N.D. and N.T. v. Spain*, App. nos. 8675/15 and 8697/15 (ECtHR, 9 October 2015).

[140] UNHCR (2015), 'Addressing security concerns without undermining refugee protection – UNHCR's perspective', Rev. 2, 17 December.

6. MEASURES TO COUNTER AND PREVENT VIOLENT EXTREMISM

The increasing recognition that a strict security approach to countering terrorism has not only failed to prevent the spread of terrorism and the proliferation of terrorist groups, but has in some cases been counter-productive, is seen as the basis for the adoption of a more paused and principled approach firmly grounded in prevention, and in addressing the underlying grievances that may lead individuals to make the wrong choices. This approach – broadly referred to as preventing or countering violent extremism – is now firmly placed on the international community's agenda and represents a very significant development.

On 24 September 2014, at a high-level meeting of the UN Security Council, resolution 2178 (2014) was unanimously adopted. This resolution includes a section on countering violent extremism in order to prevent terrorism, as an integral part of addressing the threat to international peace and security posed by foreign terrorist fighters. This resolution, adopted under Chapter VII of the UN Charter, is particularly indicative of the shift in the approach taken by the UN to counter terrorism, based on the recognition that a response confined to security alone is insufficient.[141] Importantly, it contains a strong human rights clause which links the failure to respect human rights and the rule of law to increased radicalization,[142] and recalls the need to address the conditions conducive to the spread of terrorism as outlined in the Global Counter-Terrorism Strategy to defeat terrorism.[143]

On 7 January 2016, the UN Secretary-General presented his Plan of Action to Prevent Violent Extremism to the General Assembly.[144] Almost ten years after the unanimous adoption by the General Assembly of the UN Global Counter-Terrorism Strategy,[145] this key document recognizes that addressing violent extremism primarily within the context of security-based counter-terrorism measures has been insufficient to prevent the spread of violent extremism, as demonstrated by the emergence of new, more virulent, violent extremist groups. Importantly, the

---

141 'Report of the Special Rapporteur on human rights while countering terrorism', UN Doc. A/70/371, para. 14. See also Security Council resolution 2129 (2013), para. 19.

142 Security Council resolution 2178 (2014), PP 8.

143 Security Council resolution 2178 (2014), PP 15.

144 'UN Secretary-General Plan of Action to prevent violent extremism', A/70/674; Considered by the General Assembly on 15 January 2016.

145 A/RES/60/288.

Secretary-General acknowledges the centrality of human rights to the question of violent extremism. He recalls the critical role of respect for all human rights in preventing violent extremism, and places human rights as a red thread throughout his Plan. In particular, he highlights the negative impact that violent extremism itself has on human rights,[146] the role that human rights violations can play in leading to violent extremism,[147] the role that individual human rights violations can play in the process of radicalization,[148] and the importance of respecting human rights in adopting measures to prevent violent extremism.[149]

A first main challenge relating to preventing or countering violent extremism is that of the lack of definition of the terms at the international level. While both the Security Council and the Secretary-General call for Member States to address the phenomena of 'violent extremism' and 'radicalization', both fail to provide any comprehensive definition of the terms. The term 'extremism' was used by several States prior to the adoption of resolution 2178 as an offence in itself,[150] and, in that context, has attracted well-founded concern that its vagueness could lead to its use against members of religious minorities, civil society, human rights defenders, peaceful separatist and indigenous groups and members of political opposition parties.[151] This concern has been reiterated in the

---

146 'UN Secretary-General Plan of Action to prevent violent extremism', UN Doc. A/70/674, paras. 18–20.

147 Id., paras. 3 and 27–29.

148 Id., paras. 33 and 34.

149 Id., paras. 20 and 50.

150 SOVA Center for Information and Analysis (2010), 'The structure of Russian anti-extremist legislation', November, http://www.europarl.europa.eu/meetdocs/2009_2014/documents/droi/dv/201/201011/20101129_3_10sova_en.pdf (accessed 5 October 2017). See also Inter-parliamentary Assembly of Member Nations of the Commonwealth of Independent States, Model law on Countering Extremism, http://cis-legislation.com/document.fwx?rgn=30827 (accessed 5 October 2017).

151 'Report of the Working Group on arbitrary detention', UN Doc. A/HRC/16/53/Add.1 paras. 99–106; 'Report of the Special Rapporteur on human rights and counter-terrorism', UN Doc. A/HRC/10/3, para. 35. See also Fédération Internationale des Droits de l'Homme (FIDH) (2012), 'Shanghai Cooperation Organisation: A vehicle for human rights violations', September, https://www.fidh.org/IMG/pdf/sco_report.pdf (accessed 5 October 2017). See also Article 19, 'Amendments to Extremist legislation further restricts freedom of expression', 19 July 2007, on Russia's law on 'Counteracting Extremist Activity', adopted in 2002. See also Human Rights Committee, General Comment 34, CCPR/C/GC/34, para. 46, which stresses that offences such as 'extremist

current context,[152] and well illustrated by a number of recent cases, where legislation relating to extremism was used against non-violent groups, their activities,[153] religious texts,[154] or journalists and political activists critical of State policy.[155] The past few years have shown that counter-terrorism measures have often been too liberally applied to conduct that should not qualify as terrorism per se due to overly broad and vague definitions of terrorism. In the absence of a clear definition of violent extremism, and considering that measures to prevent violent extremism may also have a serious impact on human rights, the introduction of new terminology alone does not provide any guarantee against abusive application and the adoption of sweeping measures to counter violent extremism. Given the absence of any attempt at a definition at the international level,[156] the use of the term as a basis for the adoption of new strategies, measures and legislation may prove significantly more dangerous for human rights than the term terrorism. Similarly, the term 'radicalization' as the process through which individuals become 'violent extremists' has been criticized as overly simplistic, ungrounded in

---

activity' must be clearly defined to ensure that they do not lead to unnecessary or disproportionate interference with freedom of expression.

[152] ACLU, Article 19 and Brennan Centre for Justice at the NYU Law School, letter to Ben Emmerson, 24 December 2015, on file. See also Article 19, 'UN HRC: Resolution on Violent Extremism undermines clarity', 8 October 2015, stating that 'extremism' and 'radicalization' are 'poorly defined concepts which open the door to human rights abuses'. Several governments already routinely label political opponents and journalists as terrorists. Identifying 'extremism' as the problem only provides more grounds to crush dissent'.

[153] SOVA Center for Information and Analysis (2015), 'Misuse of anti-extremism legislation in November 2015', 17 December, http://www.sova-center.ru/en/misuse/news-releases/2015/12/d33482/ (accessed 5 October 2017).

[154] Ibid. See also Global Freedom of Expression, 'The case of "Prayers to God: its purpose and place in Islam" book being extremist', https://globalfreedomofexpression.columbia.edu/cases/the-case-of-prayers-to-god-its-purpose-and-place-in-islam-book-being-extremist/ (accessed 5 October 2017).

[155] 'Boris Stomakhin', https://en.wikipedia.org/wiki/Boris_Stomakhin (accessed 5 October 2017). See also Boris Stomakhin (2015) 'Russia's Supreme Court upholds 7-year sentence for journalist for inciting terrorism', *RAPSI*, 23 July, http://rapsinews.com/judicial_news/20150723/274250392.html (accessed 5 October 2017).

[156] Whereas for terrorism at the international level, there are 12 'Sectoral' conventions, a draft definition in the draft Comprehensive Convention on International Terrorism, as well as Security Council resolution 1566 (2005).

empirical scientific studies on which to base programmes to address this phenomenon.[157]

A second main concern, which is a direct consequence of the first, is that given the elasticity of the various concepts involved, measures taken by States to counter or prevent violent extremism, or extremism, whether to operationalize UN Security Council Resolution 2178 (2014) or otherwise, include a wide array of legislative, administrative and policy measures, which target a range of activities, individuals and communities. This may lead some States to implement highly intrusive, disproportionate or discriminatory measures which can have lasting effects on affected individuals and communities. States can, and have, included in this category measures that criminalize preparatory offences to terrorism and measures that target 'extremist' speech, groups, individuals or online content. Some States include programmes involving individual interventions and counseling, and others include engaging with, and building the capacity of, certain communities, with the government, the police, or through religious authorities.

Particularly concerning from a human rights perspective are measures that target specific individuals or groups based on a determination that they are particularly 'at risk' of violent extremism, as they can be discriminatory and stigmatize various minority, ethnic, religious or indigenous groups. Effective strategies and programmes should not be based on pre- or mis-conceptions of which groups are most susceptible to radicalization or violent extremism, but should rely on evidence to ensure a proper understanding of the national and local issues that impact on the radicalization process. This will not only contribute to ensuring that all at-risk communities are adequately impacted by strategies and programmes to prevent or counter violent extremism, but also that entire communities, ethnic or religious groups are not stigmatized by their

[157] Arun Kundnani (2015), *A Decade Lost: Rethinking Extremism and Radicalisation* (London: Claystone), p. 15; Faiza Patel (2011), 'Rethinking radicalization', Brennan Center for Justice; Peter Romaniuk (2015), 'Does CVE work? Lessons learned from the global effort to counter violent extremism', Global Center on Cooperative Security (September); and Lynn Davies, Zubeda Limbada, Laura Zahra McDonald, Basia Spalek and Doug Weeks (2015), 'Formers and families: Transitional journeys in and out of violent extremism in the UK', Connect Justice, http://www.connectjustice.org/UK-Formers-&-Families.pdf (accessed 5 October 2017); Louise Richardson (2006), *What Terrorists Want* (London: John Murray), pp. 60 *et seq*. For a pre-2001 account: Martha Crenshaw (1981), 'The causes of terrorism', *Comparative Politics*, **13** (4), 379–99.

implementation.[158] There can also be a perception amongst communities that countering or preventing violent extremism is simply another vehicle for the State to implement the security aspects of its counter-terrorism strategy. If substantiated, such approaches can violate the right to privacy and, by further stigmatizing certain groups and undermining community trust in law enforcement, can be both ineffective and counter-productive.[159] To be effective, a clear distinction needs to be made between measures to counter or prevent violent extremism and the security aspect of countering terrorism, which involves law enforcement and security services.

7. CONCLUSION

This chapter has highlighted various 'new' areas of counter-terrorism that pose challenges for compliance with international human rights law. In some cases, States are still attempting to act outside any legal framework, by keeping their actions as opaque as possible and citing national security as a reason for blanket secrecy around their programmes. In a continuing alarming development, a growing number of States, under the pretext of national security concerns, are abusing counter-terrorism measures to restrict civil society and stifle legitimate opposition. As the Secretary-General has recently pointed out, a vibrant civil society is crucial to countering violent extremism, promoting dialogue, defending human rights and enhancing social cohesion. As has been the case for many of the measures adopted in haste after 2001, hindsight will undoubtedly show that the adoption of counter-terrorism measures in disrespect of human rights continues to be at best, ineffective, at worst, counter-productive.

---

[158] Arun Kundnani (2009), 'Spooked! How not to prevent violent extremism', Institute of Race Relations, October; Romaniuk, ibid., pp. 16–18; UK Prevent Strategy, para. 3.25.

[159] Michael Price (2015), 'Community outreach or intelligence gathering? A closer look at "countering violent extremism" programs', Brennan Center for Justice at New York School of Law, January; Kundnani, ibid. See also UK BBC Radio 4, 'The Report: Changing Jihadi minds', aired on 3 December 2015, http://www.bbc.co.uk/programmes/b06qmpr0 (accessed 5 October 2017).

4. The complexity and challenges of addressing the conditions conducive to terrorism

Fionnuala Ní Aoláin*

Terrorism is paradoxically both an epiphenomenal and constant phenomena. In its micro practice terrorism's predictability, durability and pathways are inconsistent, capricious, and defy easy capture. Terrorism has a long history. In fact, terrorism has long been experienced in national and international systems, a potent example being the murder of the Austrian Crown Prince by a Serbian nationalist triggering the outbreak of the First World War.[1] States, scholars, and commentators have consistently struggled to define precisely what constitute the conditions that produce violence that, inter alia, primarily targets civilians and civilian objects to achieve its objectives. Despite decades of labeling the acts of various groups and organizations as 'terrorist' in multiple parts of the globe, we are no closer to a comprehensive and agreed definition of terrorism by states. In spite of considerable state and international efforts being spent to regulate terrorist groups and individuals labeled as terrorists, much less

* Fionnuala Ní Aoláin, Robina Chair in Law, Public Policy, and Society, University of Minnesota Law School and Professor of Law, Transitional Justice Institute, University of Ulster. My thanks to Griffin Ferry, Ami Hutchinson and Dane Rockow for research assistance. The analysis in section 1 of this chapter relies in part on my historical analysis of the interface between emergency powers and anti-terrorist law in: Oren Gross and Fionnuala Ní Aoláin (2006), *Law in Times of Crisis: Emergency Powers in Theory and Practice* (New York: Cambridge University Press).

[1] *See* Charles A. Russell, Leon J. Barket Jr and Bowman H. Miller (1979), 'Out-inventing the terrorist', in Alexander Yonah, David Carlton, and Paul Wilkinson (eds), *Terrorism: Theory and Practice* (Boulder, CO: Westview); Sharon Harzenski (2003), 'Terrorism, a history: Stage 1', *Journal of Transnational Law and Policy*, **12** (2). We do not suggest that every act of political assassination constitutes a terrorist act, as there may be multiple causalities for such (illegal) actions.

substantive scrutiny has been directed to defining and separating out the causes of terrorism. Astonishingly, any basic literature review reveals that scholars, policy-makers, and regulators spend far more time thinking about 'defeating', 'ending', and 'managing' terrorism than they do reflecting on the individual, communal, institutional, and structural cases that enable and produce terrorism. At a minimum, the limits of our collective knowledge should force some uncomfortable conversations about the efficacy of legal and policy solutions to terrorism.

This chapter seeks to survey that terrain with a particular understanding of the causes of terrorism as defined and understood by states, inter-state agreement, and international institutional definitions. Section 1 addresses some of the challenges in defining terrorism. These challenges underscore how difficult it may be to hone in on the core phenomenon addressed by this book, and thereby avoid a larger penumbra of regulatory issues associated with other forms of individual and collective violence. Addressing the causes of terrorism is easier, if one has a clear understanding of the phenomena in question. Section 2 sets out in broad scope some of the sketchily agreed-upon conditions conducive to the production of terrorism. The analysis cautions against linear overreaching on defining what constitutes the causes of terrorism. I argue that we should not circumvent the inevitable realization that causalities overlap, and that there are intersectional explanations clarifying the phenomena of terrorism. Thus, identifying broad causes are a necessary but not sufficient means to explain the resort to terrorist violence in particular cases and geographies. Section 3 addresses individual mobilization to terrorism through the lens of empirical analysis combined with the theoretical lens of masculinities. Section 4 offers some conclusions and presses for greater empirical sophistication and theoretical attention to understanding the contexts and conditions that produce terrorism.

1. DEFINITIONAL CLARITY

To explore the causes underlying the resort to terrorist violence I start from an elucidation of the term terrorism. The contemporary political climate in which sweeping categorizations about the nature and form of all forms of violence that are directed against states, discourages any attempts to disaggregate the phenomenon of terrorism from other forms of violence.[2]

[2] I note however that empirical analysis has sought to disaggregate certain key features of terrorism. *See, e.g.*, the International Terrorism: Attributes of Terrorist Events (ITERATE) dataset which has coded many variables (e.g.

Cogent examples of this phenomena are the persistent descriptions of the moderate Syrian opposition as 'terrorists' by the Russian government and Assad regime,[3] and the depiction of the Kurdish Peshmerga as terrorists by Turkey and 'military fighters' by Iraqi Kurds.[4] Historically, terrorism was viewed by many states as a temporary and finite phenomenon. Another generally salient feature of terrorism was its national or nationalistic characteristic notwithstanding that, in practice, terrorist groups and individuals may have operated outside the state against which their actions were generally directed, and may have directed violence against other states to achieve the ends sought. This territorially-based presumption has been severely weakened by the emergence of highly fluid transnational and networked terrorist groupings,[5] whose ideologies are less geographically fixed and whose capabilities across borders have increased.

The preoccupation with the challenges posed by violent actors has long existed for many states, whether such actors are characterized as terrorists, insurgents, non-state, or paramilitary actors. The use of the terms 'terrorism' and 'counterterrorism' pose some conceptual and methodological challenges. The term 'terrorism' has become ubiquitous in contemporary state conversations to describe the actions and views of those who disavow the state or use violent methods to advance their political beliefs and ideologies. The term is provocative and generally intentionally pejorative, as it places those included within its ambit as outside the

---

incident date, country location, target entity, attack type, casualties, perpetrators' nationalities, terrorist group, victims' nationalities, and logistical outcome).

[3] *See, e.g.*, (2015), 'Syrian president Bashar al-Assad: Facing down rebellion', BBC News, 21 October, http://www.bbc.com/news/10338256, accessed 10 October 2017; Liz Sly and Suzan Haidamous (2017), 'At Russia-led talks, Syrian rebels and government meet for the first time', *Washington Post*, January, https://www.washingtonpost.com/world/at-russia-led-talks-syrian-rebels-and-government-meet-for-the-first-time/2017/01/23/e6373d5e-df65-11e6-8902-610fe486791c_story.html, accessed 10 October 2017.

[4] *See, e.g.*, Greg Myre (2014), 'Why does the U.S. like Iraq's Kurds, but not Syria's?', NPR, September, http://www.npr.org/sections/parallels/2014/09/23/350579007/why-does-the-u-s-like-the-kurds-in-iraq-but-not-in-syria, accessed 10 October 2017.

[5] While some have viewed this transnational vista as a post-9/11 phenomena, the ITERATE data has tracked this dimension of transnational terrorist attacks from 1968 to the mid-1980s, confirming a rise during this period. Despite the trend in more transnational incidents, the overwhelming majority of terrorist incidents remain domestic. Todd Sandler (2014), 'The analytical study of terrorism: Taking stock', *Journal of Peace Research*, **51** (2), 257–71; Khusrav Gaibulloev, Todd Sandler and Charlinda Sanifort (2011), 'Assessing the evolving threat of terrorism', *Global Policy*, **3**, Paper 146.

realm of acceptable behavior, and signals their exclusion from the agreed upon social and communal boundaries of the state and the community.[6] The term precludes deeper conversations about the causalities of violence, as well as reflection on the conditions within the state conducive to engendering violent acts. Much of the legal and political literature is rife with sweeping generalizations about the nature and form of all types of violence directed against states, discouraging any attempts to disaggregate the phenomenon of terrorism from other forms of violence.[7] It is not the goal of this chapter to revisit the lack of definitional and legal clarity surrounding 'terrorism', but rather to acknowledge that the absence of such precision influences how we understand who constitutes a terrorist actor and how we assess the kinds of human rights harms that result from counterterrorism response.

For feminist national security scholars like myself, reflection on the ways in which a focus on particular acts of violence – generally to the body and to property – avoids state engagement with structural and pervasive violence ought to give momentary pause on the adoption of the terrorism category itself. At the very least, it might prompt critical reflection on the need to judiciously tease out the category specifically – moving to an emphasis on precision and nuance in application, and a focus on acts of terrorism –in the sense of civilian targeting as the core to which the legal concept should be applied. Equally as important, the rhetorical slide from acts of terrorism to global 'war on terror', provokes similar concern about the expansion of the terrorism category in a way that undermines the rule of law, enables legal 'black holes' to emerge,[8] and creates conceptual and practical fuzziness around the obligations and limitations of states when addressing politically motivated violence.

As a practical legal matter, the term 'terrorism' operates to shut down conversations about legitimate uses of force by non-state actors in the context of wars of national liberation, occupation, and armed conflicts falling within the protective mandate of the 1977 Protocol Additional to the Geneva Conventions of 1949. It has also become extremely challenging to connect conversations concerning terrorism to the general legal

---

[6] US Congress, Senate, Committee on the Judiciary, 'Antiterrorism Policy: Hearing before the Senate Comm. On the Judiciary', 107th Cong., 1st sess., 2001, 309–64 (testimony of Attorney Gen. J. Ashcroft).

[7] John Mueller and Mark Stewart (2016), 'Conflating terrorism and insurgency', Lawfare (blog), 28 February, https://www.lawfareblog.com/conflating-terrorism-and-insurgency, accessed 7 June 2017.

[8] Lord Johan Steyn (2003), 'Guantanamo Bay: The legal black hole', lecture, Twenty-Seventh F.A. Mann Lecture, London, England, 25 November.

framework governing self-determination under international human rights law.[9] It is unfailingly difficult in any jurisdiction to activate a conversation about how, why, and with what baggage we use the term 'terrorism'. Doing so puts one in the category of a seeming apologist for unacceptable acts, while not doing so invites intellectual dishonesty and a superficiality of engagement with what is ultimately an 'essentially contested concept'.[10] Moreover, as the application of the term has widened to include criminalization of those who provide 'material support' to designated terrorist groups,[11] the space between legitimate freedom of speech and association in relationship to terrorism practice has narrowed.

There has long existed deep disagreement within national and international legal communities concerning the legal definition of terrorism.[12] As early as 1937 the League of Nations had drafted the *Convention for the Prevention and Punishment of Terrorism.*[13] Upon its creation the United Nations (UN) inherited and sought to advance this work. In parallel, a number of regional international organizations have addressed the manifestations of terrorism at a national and regional level. These

---

[9] *See* Monica Duffy Toft (2012), 'Self-determination, secession and civil war', *Terrorism and Political Violence*, **24** (4), 581–600 (showing, for example, that Article 1 of the Covenant on Civil and Political Rights and Article 1 of the Covenant on Economic, Social and Cultural Rights affirm the right to self-determination).

[10] W.B. Gallie (1969), 'Essentially contested concepts', in Max Black (ed.), *The Importance of Language* (Ithaca: Cornell University Press), pp. 121–46.

[11] *See Holder v. Humanitarian Law Project*, 561 U.S. 1 (2010) 130 S. Ct, 2705.

[12] Hans-Peter Gasser (2002), 'Acts of terror, "terrorism" and international humanitarian law,' *International Review of the Red Cross*, **84** (847), 552–54; *see United States v. Yousef*, 327 F.3d 56, 106 (2nd Cir. 2003) ('"Terrorism" is a term as loosely deployed as it is powerfully charged. ... Indeed, the nations of the world are so divisively split on the legitimacy of such aggression as to make it impossible to pinpoint an area of harmony or consensus.') (citing *Tel-Oren v. Libyan Arab Republic*, 726 F.2d 774, 795 (D.C. Cir. 1984).

[13] International Conference on the Repression of Terrorism, Geneva, 1937; *Convention for the Prevention and Punishment of Terrorism* (Geneva, 16 November 1937); *see also* M. Cherif Bassiouni (1999), 'International terrorism', in M. Cherif Bassiouni (ed.), *International Criminal Law* (Leiden, The Netherlands: Koninklijke Brill NV), p. 765.

include the Council of Europe,[14] the European Union (EU), the Organization for Security and Co-operation in Europe, the African Union, and the Organization of American States.[15] Much of the work by these bodies can be defined as attempts to agree on Suppression Conventions as well as co-operative regional action on a multitude of fronts.

A post-9/11 Report by the Inter-American Commission on Human Rights usefully breaks down the concept of terrorism in international law into five distinct categories.[16] It includes *Actions* (including forms of violence); *Actors* (including persons or organizations); *Causes or Struggles* (where the cause or the struggle may be so marked by terrorist violence as to be indistinguishable from it, or where isolated terrorist violence may take place as part of the cause or struggle); *Situations* (where terrorist violence is particularly serious or widespread in a state or region); and *Armed Conflicts* (in the sense of terrorism being used during the course of an armed conflict (international or internal) as set out by the Geneva Conventions and Additional Protocols).[17] Despite elucidation of these valuable categories, broad consensus on an international legal classification has remained elusive, although in practice this space is narrowing.[18] This formal lack of consensus is most potently illustrated by the lack of an agreed definition of terrorism within the UN General Assembly's Ad Hoc Committee on Terrorism as well as within the working group of the General Assembly's Sixth Committee, in the

---

[14] *See Conseil de l'Europe, La Lutte Contre le Terrorisme: Les Normes Du Conseil de l'Europe* (2007) (Strasbourg Cedex: Council of Europe) (also available in English).

[15] Inter-American Convention Against Terrorism (Treaty Doc. 107-18), 6 March 2002, AG/Res. 1840 (XXXII-O/02); Inter-American Committee Against Terrorism (2003), 'Declaration of San Salvador on strengthening cooperation in the fight against terrorism', 24 January, www.state.gov/p/wha/rls/59249.htm; The Council of the European Union, Council Framework Decision of 13 June 2002 on the European arrest warrant and the surrender procedures between Member States, 13 June 2002, 2002/584/JHA; Organization for Security and Cooperation in Europe, Charter on Preventing and Combating Terrorism, 7 December 2002, MC(10).JOUR/2; African Union, Declaration of the Second High-Level Intergovernmental Meeting on the Prevention and Combating of Terrorism in Africa, 13–14 October 2004, Mtg/HLIG/Conv.Terror/Decl (II) Rev.2.

[16] Inter-American Commission on Human Rights (2002), 'Report on terrorism and human rights', 22 October, OEA/Ser.L/V/II.116.

[17] Ibid., para. 12.

[18] There now seems to be a regional European Agreement on a definition of terrorism, which speaks to the potential for broader international consensus. Protocol Amending the European Convention on the Suppression of Terrorism, 15 May 2003, E.T.S. No. 190.

context of a comprehensive treaty regulating state responses to and responsibility for terrorism.[19] A draft Terrorism Convention remains in negotiation, but is bogged down on whether to exempt activities of the states' armed forces and whether the convention should apply to armed resistance groups who are fighting against colonial or foreign occupation.[20] The amount of concerted political energy expended on defining terrorism may provide some clues as to why there has been comparatively little enthusiasm for addressing the causes of terrorism. Existentially, if we don't agree what the object is, addressing how it has come into being (and preventing that birth) is both a conceptual and practical stretch.

Lack of agreement on a comprehensive definition does not mean that there is no consensus at all between states on what constitutes terrorism. In fact, and definitionally jumpstarted by September 11, the international community has identified certain acts of violence that are generally considered to be forms of terrorism. In this ever-expanding list are included such acts as the hijacking of civilian airplanes and taking the lives of hostages, the primary purpose of which could be said to be to spread terror among the civilian population both in times of armed conflict and in peacetime. Moreover, when we look at the wide range of international definitions (as provided by regional bodies and/or the UN) we can identify certain common characteristics to be seen in incidents of terrorism. For example, the UN General Assembly has a working definition of terrorism for general use in resolutions and declarations on terrorism. Namely, '[c]riminal acts intended or calculated to provoke a state of terror in the general public, a group of persons or particular persons, for political purposes [which] are in any circumstances unjustifiable, whether on the considerations of a political, philosophical, ideological, racial, ethnic, religious or any other nature that may be used to

---

[19] *See* UN General Assembly Ad Hoc Committee on International Terrorism (1973), 'Observations of states submitted in accordance with General Assembly Resolution 3034', 16 May, A/AC.160/1.

[20] *See e.g.*, United Nations, General Assembly (2002), 'Report of the Ad Hoc Committee by the General Assembly Resolution 51/510 of 17 December 1996', 28 January–1 February, U.N. Doc. a/57/37, para. 5-22; UN General Assembly (2005), 'Ad hoc body elaborating comprehensive convention on terrorism to reconvene early next year, sixth committee decides', press release, 29 November, http://www.un.org/News/Press/docs/2005/gal3292.doc.htm, accessed 10 October 2017.

justify them'.[21] The Inter-American Commission Report again usefully identifies certain common characteristics, including the nature and identity of the perpetrators of terrorism, the nature and identity of the victims of terrorism, the objectives of terrorism, and the measures employed to perpetrate terrorism.[22] The key to many of these partially agreed-upon definitions is the understanding that the targeting of civilians is per se unacceptable. While the protection of civilians is an important bright-line, contemporary dilution of the inviolability of the civilian category allied with the emergence of new categories, such as 'active participation in hostilities', have created a certain fuzziness about who constitutes a civilian, and thus when an act of terrorism is instigated as a result of targeting individuals whose legal status may be unclear. It is also useful to point out that while state and non-governmental targets of terrorism have been widespread, democratic communities (and their civilian populations) are particularly vulnerable to terrorism by virtue of their open societies, a fact cogently demonstrated by attacks in Paris, Brussels and Nice in 2015 and 2016.

The 2004 Report of the Secretary-General's High-level Panel on Threats, Challenges and Change focused on the challenges posed to the UN from terrorism and has recommended that any definition of terrorism should contain the following elements; a restatement that acts under the 12 suppression conventions are terrorism; reference to the definitions contained in the 1999 International Convention for the Suppression of the Financing of Terrorism, and Security Council resolution 1566 (2004); and a description of terrorism as 'any action … that is intended to cause death or serious bodily harm to civilians or non-combatants, when the purpose of such an act, by its nature or context, is to intimidate a population, or to compel a Government or an international organization

[21] *See e.g.*, UN General Assembly, resolution 49, 'Measures to eliminate international terrorism', Art. 3, 9 December 1994, A/RES/49/60, http://www.un.org/documents/ga/res/49/a49r060.htm. The Security Council adopted a working definition in resolution 1566 (2004): '[c]riminal acts, including against civilians, committed with the intent to cause death or serious bodily injury, or taking of hostages, with the purpose to provoke a state of terror in the general public or in a group of persons or particular persons, intimidate a population or compel a Government or an international organization to do or to abstain from doing any act', 'Threats to international peace and security caused by terrorist acts', S/RES/1566(2004), para. 3, 8 October 2004, http://www.un.org/en/ga/search/view_doc.asp?symbol=S/RES/1566(2004), accessed 10 October 2017.

[22] Security Council resolution 1566 (2004), para. 17.

to do or to abstain from doing any act'.[23] The UN Global Counter-Terrorism Strategy adopted in 2006 established that all UN Member States agree on a coordinated and comprehensive response to terrorism. Notably that strategy identified the following elements as conducive to the spread of terrorism: 'prolonged unresolved conflicts, dehumanization of victims of terrorism in all its forms and manifestations, lack of the rule of law and violations of human rights, ethnic, national and religious discrimination, political exclusion, socio-economic marginalization and lack of good governance'.[24] The Strategy also identified the need to 'strength[en] and make best possible use of the capacities of the United Nations in areas such as conflict prevention, negotiation, mediation, conciliation, judicial settlement, rule of law, peacekeeping and peace-building'. The General Assembly reaffirmed this strategy on 8 September 2010, and urged states to make greater and consistent efforts to implement it.[25] In tandem, the Security Council has created a highly regulated sanctions regime,[26] and has taken measures to suppress the financing of terrorist organizations.[27] More recently, international and national action

---

[23] Report of the Secretary-General's High-Level Panel on Threats (2004), 'Challenges and change: A more secure world, our shared responsibility', para. 164, December, Sales No. E.05.I.5, http://www.un.org/en/peacebuilding/pdf/historical/hlp_more_secure_world.pdf, accessed 10 October 2017.

[24] United Nations General Assembly (2006), 'The United Nations Global Counter-Terrorism Strategy', 20 September, UN Doc. A/RES/60/288.

[25] UN General Assembly (2010), 'The United Nations Global Counterterrorism Strategy', Draft resolution 64, 8 September 2010, UN Doc.A/64/PV.117, http://www.un.org/en/ga/search/view_doc.asp?symbol=A/64/PV.117, accessed 10 October 2017.

[26] *See* Security Council resolution 1988 (2011) (levelling a new sanctions regime against the Taliban and establishing an 'Afghanistan Sanctions Committee' to oversee implementation); Security Council resolution 1989 (2011) (condemning Al-Qaida and levelling new sanctions against the organization); Security Council resolution 2082 (2012) (establishing further detailed criteria for determining individuals and entities associated with the Taliban); Security Council resolution 2160 (2014) (extending sanctions against the Taliban); Security Council resolution 2170 (2014) (condemning the 'gross, systematic and widespread' human rights abuses of ISIL and setting restrictions on specific individuals involved in ISIL. Also calling on states to take national measures to prevent people from traveling to aid ISIS and refrain from supplying the state with arms or financial aid; Security Council, resolution 2253 (2015) (expanding and strengthening its sanctions against Al-Qaida to include sanctions against ISIL).

[27] Security Council resolution 2133 (2014); Security Council resolution 2195 (2014); Security Council resolution 2199 (2015).

on terrorism has resulted in attempts to address 'violent extremism'. While the term 'violent extremism' lacks an agreed definition, in 2014 the UN Secretary-General noted the broad threat posed by violent extremism to the protection of human rights.[28] In 2015, the Secretary-General presented his Plan of Action to Prevent Violent Extremism.[29] The Secretary-General described violent extremism as a diverse phenomenon 'without clear definition', which is neither new nor exclusive to any region, nationality or system of belief.[30] Notably this plan articulates the position that a comprehensive approach to security-based counter-terrorism measures necessitates systematic preventative steps to address the underlying conditions that drive individuals to radicalize and join violent extremist groups.[31]

Terrorism has not only been a phenomenon associated with the actions of non-state actors, but there is also some acceptance (in some but not all state quarters) that states themselves have used terrorist methods to achieve dubious political ends. Notably some states have domestically endeavored to proscribe a specific crime of terrorism based on some of these commonly assumed characteristics. Others have chosen not to do so, but rather have used existing definitions of common crimes, such as murder, by adding terrorist intention or variant consequences in punishment.[32] Finally, when international law(s) characterize 'an act or situation as one of terrorism [this] cannot in itself serve as a basis for defining the international legal obligations of states. Rather each act or situation must be evaluated on its own facts … '. Inherent in this characterization is the view that the methods and means by which states respond to acts of terrorism are not unlimited.[33]

---

[28] Security Council (2014), Statement by the President of the Security Council, S/PRST/2014/23, 28 October, http://www.un.org/en/ga/search/view_doc.asp?symbol=S/PRST/2014/23, accessed 10 October 2017.

[29] UN General Assembly, Report of the Secretary General (2015), 'Plan of Action to Prevent Violent Extremism', 24 December, UN Doc. A/70/674.

[30] Ibid., at para. 2.

[31] The Plan sets out 70 recommendations to Member States and the UN system to prevent the further spread of violent extremism.

[32] For example, in Canada a prosecutor is required to prove beyond a reasonable doubt that the terrorist activity was committed 'in whole or in part for a political, religious or ideological purpose, objective or cause'. Anti-Terrorism Act, S.C., c. 41, s 80.01(1)(b)(i)(A), (2001) (Can.). For the problems that result from this attempt to criminalize motive, *see* Kent Roach (2003), *September 11 Consequences for Canada* (Montreal: McGill-Queen's University Press), pp. 25–29.

[33] Anti-Terrorism Act, ibid., para. 16; Roach, ibid., at 16.

The post-9/11 context has given new impetus to addressing violent, transnational, non-state actors including but not limited to Al-Qaeda and Islamic State in Iraq and Syria (ISIS). A new international security regime is the bulwark of these states' normative actions. It was ushered in by UNSCR 1373 (2001) and the creation of the UN Counter Terrorism Committee, in conjunction with the EU's 'regulations on combating terrorism'. Both the EU and the UN approaches had antecedents dating from the previous patchwork of multilateral anti-terrorism conventions and resolutions assembled over several decades, but their scope, content, and institutional power have increased considerably in the world we inhabit after 9/11. This cacophony of institutional action serves to obscure how little normative work has been undertaken to address the conditions conducive to the creation and consolidation of terrorism actions, actors, causes, situations, and armed conflicts around the globe. As the tide of terrorist atrocity rises, and the calls for action bellow ever more loudly, the space for considered attention to the causes of terrorism narrows. One observable feature of anti-terrorism regulation is the well-identified ratchet effect of terrorist acts on political actors,[34] and the ways in which atrocity crimes create ever-greater pressure to deepen security measures. Thus, as we reflect on why states and international institutional actors have spent so little time and energy on addressing conditions conducive, we should understand that as new and highly visible terrorist groups have emerged (ISIL, Al Nusra front), as large scale atrocities on soft-targets have become a feature of contemporary life (Pakistan, Paris, California), and as terrorist organizations not infrequently control territory imposing strict and abnegating codes of personal and communal behavior, the pressure to crack down and deliver security responses overwhelm other tactics. Subjective assessments of imminence, threat, and preparedness tighten timelines and create perceptible barriers to long-term strategizing, thereby discouraging a focus on the 'why' of violence as opposed to instant response. Moreover, a meaningful engagement with the 'why' of terrorism implicates not merely the readily apparent causes of radicalism (hyper-nationalism mobilizing individual ideologues, individual alienation, direct individual discrimination leading to political anomie, mental illness and dysfunction) but implicates structural causes of violence including economic exclusion, religious

[34] Fionnuala Ní Aoláin and Oren Gross (2014), 'The rhetoric of war: Words, conflict and categorization post 9/11', *Cornell Journal of Law and Public Policy*, **24** (2), Paper No. 14-47.

radicalization, cultural precariousness, elite dominance in political systems, race-based political benefits (and beneficiaries), poverty, and the relationship between existent and well-established power systems and the marginalization of political, economic and cultural outsiders. Risk-aversion is also propagated in such security-conscious environments, discouraging alliances with the major social, economic and political re-adjustments that are precisely required to address many of the conditions conducive to the production of terrorism.

2. WHAT ARE THE CONDITIONS CONDUCIVE?

The concept of conditions conducive speaks to the notion that causalities for terrorist violence can be disaggregated in meaningful ways. Broadly, disaggregation is carried out at a macro level, identifying wide-ranging arenas where particular conditions may give rise to politically motivated violence targeting civilians and civilian objects. Conditions-conducive analysis also requires micro and granular analysis in local contexts. The precise alignment of historical, social, cultural, economic, and political factors is infinitely variable across societies that have experienced sustained, politically motivated violence. Understanding local variance in conditions conducive analysis is also conceptually and practically important. Policy solutions to politically motivated violence will clearly be less effective if they fail to take into account local conditions and local specificities.

Multiple and scalar macro-causes of terrorism have been identified by scholars and policy makers. They include: structural violence; socio-economic exclusions;[35] poverty; sustained discrimination;[36] the

---

[35] Raul Caruso and Friedrich Schneider (2011), 'The socio-economic determinants of terrorism and political violence in Western Europe (1994–2007)', *European Journal of Political Economy*, **27** (1), 37–49. The article's objective is to empirically investigate the socioeconomic causes of terrorism and political violence in a sample of 12 countries in Western Europe. The findings conclude that in Western European countries the classical economic argument of opportunity cost can be confirmed – the larger the set of economic opportunities for an individual, the lower the likelihood or the willingness for him to be involved in a terrorist activity.

[36] *See* James A. Piazza (2011), 'Poverty, minority economic discrimination and domestic terrorism', *Journal of Peace Research*, **48** (3), 339–53. (Using data from the Minorities at Risk project, the author determines that countries featuring minority group economic discrimination are significantly more likely to experience domestic terrorist attacks, whereas countries lacking minority groups or

systematic denial of civil and political rights; counter terrorism strategies;[37] the lack of meaningful participation in governance systems for groups and minorities; and persistent armed conflict. The Global Counter-Terrorism Strategy recognizes the following conditions conducive to enabling the spread of terrorism: 'prolonged unresolved conflicts, dehumanization of victims of terrorism in all its forms and manifestations, lack of rule of law and violations of human rights, ethnic, national and religious discrimination, political exclusion, socio-economic marginalization, and lack of good governance'.[38] It bears reminding that the impetus to address these wide-ranging human rights violations have an existence independent of post 9/11 security regimes, and are being attended to via a variety of UN and regional mechanisms including 17 ambitious Sustainable Development Goals (SDG's).[39] A challenging question in this context is the extent to which the intermingling of development goals and activities (eradicating poverty and hunger, achieving universal primary education, reducing infant mortality, combatting HIV/Aids, ensuring environmental sustainability) are instrumentalized and commodified by bonding their advancement with the attainment of better global security outcomes for states. In real terms, despite concerns about the overlay of security interests with development priorities, human rights advocates have a Hobson's choice in this arena. To refuse to engage with major policy developments in the security field, inter alia addressing the structural causes of violence, is to risk being banished to the policy and political sidelines. Nonetheless, to ignore the potential manipulation and deployment of major human rights initiatives to address global socio-economic rights disparities would be naive. In short, the game may be in part to continually exercise judgment over the points of

---

whose minorities do not face discrimination are significantly less likely to experience terrorism. He also finds minority economic discrimination to be a strong and substantive predictor of domestic terrorism vis-á-vis the general level of economic development.)

[37] *See* UN Human Rights Council (2007), 'Promotion and protection of all human rights, civil, political, economic, social and cultural rights, including the rights to development', 21 November, UN Doc. A/HRC/6/17, https://documents-dds-ny.un.org/doc/UNDOC/GEN/G07/149/48/PDF/G0714948.pdf?OpenElement, accessed 10 October 2017. In this report the Special Rapporteur notes that terrorism and measures adopted to combat terrorist acts are both influenced by and have an impact upon economic, social, and cultural rights.

[38] UN General Assembly, 'Global Counter-Terrorism Strategy' (n 24).

[39] UN, 'Sustainable Development Goals: 17 goals to transform our world', http://www.un.org/sustainabledevelopment/sustainable-development-goals/, accessed 10 October 2017.

overlap and to be prepared to 'call out' the zealous use of security rationale (or limitations) as the ethical, moral or legal basis for addressing structural issues of poverty, disenfranchisement, and exclusion.

At the individual level, studies of terrorist mobilization have separately identified a range of factors that shape a person's unique response to external conditions of instability, discrimination, deprivation, and violent radicalization that triggers individuals to join violent groups or engage in terrorist acts. Each of the macro causes constitutes a unique eco-system in its own right, shaped by intersectional factors, including the political, social, and cultural environment in which the external harm of deprivation, exclusion, or violence is experienced. It would be naive to provide a linear explanation of terrorism in any country setting. It is precisely the pernicious variable geometry of causes factoring in the precise relationship between poverty and political representation that might explain why in one setting the intersection of rights deprivations functions as a condition conducive to terrorist acts, whereas a slightly different vector of the same causes in another country setting does not have the same effect. There is also a danger that a focus on identifying simple causes translates into a 'cookie cutter' approach that flattens out the real differences in mobilization to political violence.

Distinctions have been drawn between different types of macro conditions. These include: (1) structural causes such as demographic imbalances, a subjective sense of deprivation, a sense of injustice, and more generally, consequences of globalization; (2) facilitating causes, such as the existence of failed states, access to weapons and explosives, the development of mass media and the internet; (3) motivational causes, including conflicts and deep-rooted injustices of a historical nature; and (4) so-called triggering causes, which are events that ultimately push an individual to carry out a terrorist act.[40] The value of these distinctions is that not only do they focus attention on different kinds of triggers, but they allow us to conceptualize the interaction between structural, facilitating, motivational, and triggering causes in ways that lend themselves to very different political, legal, and policy solutions. This intersectional approach to addressing the causes conducive is an important first step to

---

[40] Counter-Terrorism Implementation Task Force (2008), 'First Report of the Working Group on radicalization and extremism that lead to terrorism: Inventory of state programmes', 18 February, http://data.unhcr.org/syrianrefugees/download.php?id=10129, accessed 10 October 2017. The Working Group invited all Member States to provide information on their policies and initiatives designed to address radicalization and violent extremism that lead to terrorism: 34 states responded.

providing granular and nuanced site-specific analysis of the motivators and conditions that enable politically and ideologically motivated violence.

These fine-tuned distinctions between causalities are not fully mapped in the UN's Global Counter-Terrorism Strategy.[41] Rather, there is some identification of macro causes and linkage to specific UN agencies that might have responsibility for advancing preventative strategies. These are outlined in Pillar 1, which has been to some extent neglected in the implementation of the Counter-Terrorism Strategy. Thus, in Pillar 1 of the Global Strategy entitled 'Measures to address the conditions conducive to the spread of terrorism', eight key elements are outlined, six of which specify the role of the UN or its specialized agencies in dampening the spread of terrorism.[42] Two elements – namely the augmentation of international law to legally prohibit incitement to commit a terrorist act and prevent such conduct, as well as reinforcing social inclusion agendas to address youth unemployment, marginalization, and victimization thereby propelling extremism and recruitment – have national rather than international anchors. This national thread was followed through in the establishment of the Working Group on Radicalization and Extremism that Lead to Terrorism, which has identified a range of state practices addressing radicalism in national settings, including but not limited to engaging and working with civil society, prison programs, education, tackling economic and social inequalities, internet use and monitoring, rehabilitation programs and, legislative reform.[43] In this realm, state level

---

[41] Nor is it clear if such clarity if found in the work of the Counter-Terrorism Implementation Task Force (CTITF), which is the main body coordinating implementation of the UN's Global Counter Strategy. The Task Force is comprised of thirty-eight entities.

[42] *See, e.g.*, '(1) To continue to strengthen and make best possible use of the capacities of the United Nations in areas such as conflict prevention, negotiation, mediation, conciliation, judicial settlement, rule of law, peacekeeping and peacebuilding; … (2) To continue to arrange under the auspices of the United Nations initiatives and programmes to promote dialogue, tolerance and understanding among civilizations, cultures, peoples and religions, and to promote mutual respect for and prevent the defamation of religions, religious values, beliefs and cultures; … (5) To reiterate our determination to ensure the timely and full realization of the development goals and objectives agreed at the major United Nations conferences and summits, including the Millennium Development Goals.'

[43] CTITF (2006), 'First Report of the Working Group on Radicalisation', http://data.unhcr.org/syrianrefugees/download.php?id-10129, accessed 10 October 2017. This Working Group is one of nine Working Groups established to

knowledge already shows us that radicalization processes are multi-faceted and follow very different dynamics at the local level, confirmation of the variant conditions that produce terrorism. The Working Group is distinguished by an approach that values the importance of preventative and long-term measures in fighting terrorism, a strategy frequently at odds with suppressive and coercive measures that seek (and promise) immediate results in the counter-terrorism sphere. It has also mapped the programs identified by states as contributing to the prevention of terrorism and extremism.[44] There is both positive and negative interaction between prevention and coercion, with accumulating data on the radicalizing effects of ill-conceived, discriminate, or badly implemented counter-terrorism approaches.[45]

Another lens to take on disaggregating the conditions conducive to the production of terrorist violence is from the perspective of the political economy of terrorism. Recent work by Bueno de Mesquita provides an overview of political economy literature on terrorism and offers useful insights into causality from an inverse perspective.[46] This work identifies four factors namely; (a) terror and the economy; (2) internal politics of terrorist organizations; (3) counterterrorism; and (4) government-terrorist negotiations to better understand the underlying relationship of causality and positioning. Even here, the limits are clear, specifically that we '[l]ack a thorough understanding of the relationship between a variety of structural and strategic features of the political economic environment

---

carry forward key elements of the Global Strategy. The Working Group is described as 'a vehicle for the Task Force to take up several of the Strategy's cross-cutting themes as well as a number of specific initiatives of the Strategy's Action Plan, in particular those addressing conditions conducive to the spread of terrorism.' Ibid., at para. 2.

[44] The practices of 34 countries are identified and reported on by the Working Group. 'In the 34 responses from Member States, the Working Group identified eleven key strategic issues (or types of programmes), around which the report is organised. These are: 1) engaging and working with civil society; 2) prison programmes; 3) education; 4) promoting alliance of civilizations and inter-cultural dialogue; 5) tackling economic and social inequalities; 6) global programmes to counter radicalisation; 6) the internet; 7) legislation reforms; 8) rehabilitation programmes; 9) developing and disseminating information; 9) and training and qualifying agencies involved in implementing counter-radicalisation policies'. Id., at para. 9.

[45] See Office of the High Commissioner on Human Rights (2008), 'Human Rights, Terrorism and Counter-Terrorism Fact Sheet 32' (July).

[46] Ethan Bueno de Mesquita (2008), 'The political economy of terrorism: A selective overview of recent work', *The Political Economist*, **10** (1), 1–12.

(e.g., the economy, democracy, political freedom, counterterrorism) and terrorism'.[47] Moreover, empirically there is a grave challenge that 'everything seems to cause everything else'.[48] Terrorism may cause and be caused by economic change or economic deprivation. Counter-terrorism may cause and be caused by terrorism, and counter-terrorism may cause economic suffering by destroying infrastructure, but also may stimulate other economies such as the security sector. Counter-terror crackdowns may diminish political freedom, causing an increase in terrorism, which results in more counter-terrorism, thereby damaging the economy and diminishing political freedom in a seemingly never-ending chain. The political economy analysis underscores the lack of systematic data on the nature, structure, and organization of terrorist organizations, long-term assessments on the patterns of violence, good models on the dampening (or enabling) effect of law on terrorism and counter-terrorism, as well as the ways in which causalities may shift over time as tactics and operatives change.

Complementing the UN Global Strategy is the UN Secretary-General's Plan of Action to Prevent Violent Extremism.[49] The Secretary-General confirms that violent extremism is a diverse phenomenon that is neither new nor specific to any region, nationality or belief system. Importantly he notes that:

> Nothing can justify violent extremism but we must also acknowledge that it does not arise in a vacuum. Narratives of grievance, actual or perceived injustice, promised empowerment and sweeping change become attractive where human rights are being violated, good governance is being ignored and aspirations are being crushed.[50]

The Secretary-General's Plan was partly produced as a result of the failure to implement those elements of the Global Strategy tackling prevention and causalities of terrorism. The Secretary-General's proposals affirm the importance of paying attention to the 'push' and 'pull' elements that enable terrorism to flourish. 'Push' factors are defined as structures creating conditions conducive, while 'pull' factors are individual motivations and processes 'which play a key role in transforming

---

[47] Ibid., 12.

[48] Ibid.

[49] Report of the Secretary General, 'Plan of Action to Prevent Violent Extremism' (n 29). Notably the 'Plan of Action' has a dedicated section on gender equality and women's empowerment, with mainstreamed language on the importance of a human rights and gender approach.

[50] Ibid., para. 3.

ideas and grievances into violent extremist action'.[51] As my analysis below peruses, there is a substantial and sizeable relationship between 'push' and 'pull' factors to the extent that one would be mistaken to carve out the individual's social situatedness as distinct from other structural elements. I claim both are intermeshed in ways that are important to understand and practically make the challenges of addressing conditions conducive a more complex task. In terms of the Secretary-General's identified schema, the Plan pays considerable attention to sustainable development (charting a relationship between poor implementation of the millennium development goals, poverty and political violence),[52] human rights, governance and rule of law (affirming the relationship between impunity, repression, insecurity and political/ideologically motivated violence),[53] social and economic instability (highlighting youth unemployment),[54] marginalization and unemployment (with a focus on majority groups acting in monopolistically ways that politically and economically exclude other groups),[55] protracted and unresolved conflict (where poor governance combined with unaddressed grievances create fertile ground for recruitment and violence);[56] and radicalization in prisons (showing harsh, corrupt, lax and insecure prison settings create conditions for the spread of extremist ideologies).[57] The Plan goes on to recommend concrete measures to take action, including national and regional action plans and the mobilization of resources to prioritize prevention. In sum, the Secretary-General's plan is notable for the dexterity and breadth of its capture and its willingness to name obvious and non-obvious factors that enable terrorism to thrive and spread. There is a positive vision in joining up various parts of the UN's institutional capacity (e.g. links to sustainable development goals) as well as to pinpoint the local responsibility for access to justice, delivery of services, professionalism of military and police, and reform of penitentiary systems. The challenge of course lies not in the message to states but in the translation of that message to action. All of the Secretary-General's recommendations point to unequivocal root and branch reform of legal, economic and political infrastructure within fragile, repressive, dysfunctional and weak states. The political will to do so is tepid in all these contexts. In parallel,

---

51 Id., para. 23.
52 Id., paras. 16 and 17.
53 Id., paras. 19, 20 and 27.
54 Id., para. 25.
55 Id., para. 26.
56 Id., para. 30.
57 Id., para. 31.

coercive counter-terrorism approaches reward systems that show external strength and military prowess, affirm 'tough' measures, and create disincentives to undo the power of existing political elites.[58] Without definitive acknowledgment of the direct tension between these two competing strands of terrorism management, plus prioritization of prevention with the corollary that reordering priorities will change the shape and content of coercive responses, there is little real potential for addressing conditions conducive in a meaningful way. Moreover, scholars and practitioners should be wary of the co-mingling that follows from addressing conditions conducive with military- and force-led counter-terrorism management. In this context, there are grave risks that the commodification and instrumentalization of broadly based goals for economic justice and equality (many already required by the treaty obligations of states) will be shoehorned into terrorism discourse in ways that impoverish and hollow out their meaning.

This tension alluded to above has a direct impact on understanding the context of protecting human rights in an age of terrorism. There is increased international institutional recognition that combatting terrorism must be done in a way that affirms the enjoyment of human rights and secures rather than undermines both derogable and non-derogable rights. Some international and regional institutions recognize (implicitly if not explicitly) that sustained deprivations of fundamental human rights norms may have significant implications for enabling terrorist violence. For example, the Council of the EU's Revised EU Strategy for Combating Radicalization and Recruitment to Terrorism affirms that preventative measures are critical and more effective than de-radicalization.[59] In this context this strategy confirms the need to 'promote security, justice and equal opportunity for all'.[60] The mantra of compliance by national legislation, policies and strategies combatting terrorism being grounded in a respect for human rights and the rule of law is getting strong play.[61] The rhetoric is not unimportant but it continues to perform in the

[58] Even in the context of the UN, we see an increasing emphasis on 'tough' language in the terrorism context. Thus, UN shifts in language from measures to prevent terrorism to measures to eliminate terrorism illustrate the premium on masculinity in the language of the response itself.

[59] Council of the European Union (2014), 'Revised EU Strategy for Combating Radicalisation and Recruitment to Terrorism', 19 May, http://register.consilium.europa.eu/doc/srv?l=EN&f=ST%209956%202014%20INIT, accessed 10 October 2017.

[60] Ibid., at para. 14.

[61] Report of the Secretary General, 'Plan of Action' (n 29), para. 50(a).

shadows of coercive measures addressing terrorism. Without serious engagement to the tension points, we remain in a situation where states think they can have it all; namely, 'business as usual' on the counter-terrorism front, soft measures on the prevention front, and without having to move beyond lofty rhetoric to practice.

3. THE MASCULINITY OF CAUSALITY

Stating the obvious, a sustained and systematic feminist engagement with terrorism, counter-terrorism, and the causalities and effects of both is long overdue. It is notable that terrorism and counter-terrorism have long been of only marginal interest to mainstream feminist legal theorizing, with some very important caveats.[62] A number of commentators have evidenced scholarly and policy interest in the category of female combatants. There are multiple studies of women in non-state actor groupings from European left leaning groups (IRA/Cumann na mBan/Baader Meinhoff Gang),[63] to post-colonial national liberation organizations (PLO, ANC, Tamil Tigers).[64] Female terrorists – particularly those associated with the violent politics of extremist jihadist groupings – have also recently elicited attention. Thus, for example, female suicide bombers in Chechnya, Israel-Palestine, and more recently in Nigeria as deployed by Boko Haram, have become the object of extraordinary attention. The preoccupation with the violent (and generally presumed aberrational) female is, in itself, the product of an essentialist discourse that requires a critical eye. Nevertheless, men remain the primary and visible actors in terrorist acts and counter-terrorism responses. In the legal field, a concentration on male actors has dominated national security conversations and as a result the 'causes' of terrorism are often coded male with little reflection on the gendered contexts, practices and intersectionalities that give profound insight into the conditions that produce and sustain terrorism. Exposing gender dynamics sustains a deeper policy encounter with how gender distinctions underpin many of the identified causalities of politically motivated violence including poverty, political exclusion,

---

62 Fionnuala Ní Aoláin (2013), 'Situating women in counterterrorism discourses: Undulating masculinities and luminal femininities', *Boston University Law Review*, **93** (3), 1085–1122.

63 Miranda Alison (2004), 'Women as agents of political violence: Gendering security', *Security Dialogue*, **35** (4), 447–63.

64 Miranda Alison (2009), *Women and Political Violence: Female Combatants in Ethno-National Conflict* (Abingdon: Routledge).

and social inequality. In this sense, human rights answers to the questions of causality also suffer from the deficiency of failing to engage the gender dynamics of human rights violations, naming how precisely it is that men and women are differently situated in respect of their engagement in politically motivated violence, the experience of violence and the harms that follow the infliction of violence, whether by terrorism or counter-terrorism methods.

There is some contemporary international institutional interest in the intersection of gender and terrorism, evidenced in the passage of UN Security Council resolution 2242 (2015) and the Global Study on Women, Peace and Security.[65] The Secretary-General's 2015 Plan of Action to Prevent Violent Extremism affirms that gender equality matters in addressing terrorism, not least because 'it is also no coincidence that societies for which gender equality indicators are higher are less vulnerable to violent extremism'.[66] This recent attention to women in conflict sites and to the gender dimensions of violent extremism runs risks of agenda hijacking whereby a narrow emphasis on gender distracts attention from the wider structural realities that produce gender inequality, exclusion and violence. For example, the United States and United Kingdom have recently given sustained attention to mothering as a site which can be utilized to prevent violent extremism, relying heavily on highly gender stratified tropes of motherhood as peaceful, pro-state, and presuming that women are willing to risk their own inter-group security within highly patriarchal settings to prevent their sons from joining radical groups.[67] The micro attention given to mothers as regulators of male behavior entirely ignores the broader social and cultural contexts in

---

[65] Fionnuala Ní Aoláin (2016), 'The war on terror and extremism: Assessing the relevance of the women, peace and security agenda', *International Affairs*, **92** (2), 275–91; *see* Radhika Coomaraswamy (2015), *Preventing Conflict Transforming Justice Securing the Peace: A Global Study of the Implementation of United Nations Security Council Resolution 1325* (New York: UN Women), http://wps.unwomen.org/~/media/files/un%20women/wps/highlights/unw-global-study-1325-2015.pdf, accessed 10 October 2017.

[66] Report of the Secretary General, 'Plan of Action' (n 29), para. 53.

[67] US Department of State Bureau of Counterterrorism, 'Programs and Initiatives', http://www.state.gov/j/ct/programs/, accessed 10 October 2017. Here the language of 'countering violent extremism' (CVE) programming places particular emphasis on engaging women who are described as 'uniquely' positioned to advance CVE goals. Similar strategies are being advanced by the United Kingdom. *See* HM Government (2015), 'Counter-Extremism Strategy', October, https://www.gov.uk/government/uploads/system/uploads/attachment_data/file/470088/51859_Cm9148_Accessible.pdf, accessed 10 October 2017.

which women operate, the constraints that frame their power in the domestic sphere, and the risks that accrue to women particularly in non-Western settings who are seen to function as the tools of western imperialist powers.

Moreover, international policy and legal engagement rarely engages men as a gendered category, thus gender is typically coded female. Simply put there is little policy reflection on what elements of masculinity, male identity, male bonding, and male status are implicated in radicalization, extremism, and engagement in political violence. By way of illustration, the Secretary-General's Plan of Action and the Working Group on Radicalisation and Extremism appear to do gender work when, in reality, their primary mandate is to collect data on women's roles in violent extremism, include women in counter-terrorism prevention, build women's civil society capacity so that they can act as barriers to violent extremism, and set aside funds to empower women as a place holder for broader economic, social, and political reforms in marginal communities that are at risk of producing terrorists.[68]

I now turn my attention to those male actors and specifically address the masculinities that intersect with terrorism, and the implications (such as can be traced) for human rights advancement.[69] Masculinity analysis rarely intersects with human rights theory and practice. My cue for this analysis comes partly from Paul Farmer's critical question, '[b]y what mechanisms, precisely, do social forces ranging from poverty to racism become embodied as human experience'.[70] Farmer and others scholars have identified how the biographies of perpetrators and victims of violence have followed from their gendered vulnerabilities.[71] As I noted above, the differences between 'push' and 'pull' factors in producing terrorism are less categorically defined when one appreciates that social forces and institutions structure the risk for violence and suffering in tandem. It is precisely the matrix of political violence, poverty, colonial and authoritarian legacies, and inherited gender orders that may pivot individuals and communities towards political violence. In this reading we better understand terrorist violence as a significant measure which is

[68] Ibid., para. 53(a)–(e).

[69] Jamie R. Abrams (2010), 'The collateral consequences of masculinizing violence' *William and Mary Journal of Women and the Law*, **16** (3), 703–52.

[70] Paul Farmer (2003), *Pathologies of Power: Health, Human Rights, and the New War on the Poor* (Los Angeles: University of California), p. 369.

[71] Kimberly Theidon (2013), *Intimate Enemies: Violence and Reconciliation in Peru* (Philadelphia: University of Pennsylvania).

both gendered and structured as opposed to an act encapsulated within the contours of a single incident.

While masculinity studies have evinced scholarly and policy interest in some domestic settings,[72] it is only relatively recently that masculinity practices have been opened up to scrutiny in the context of conflict and repression.[73] There has been a noticeable absence of any reflection on the relationship between violent masculinities, thwarted masculinities, and terrorism. Generally, masculinity theorists have identified an organic link between patriarchy, its contemporary outworkings, and various forms of masculinity as they arise within societies and institutions. A preponderance of literature across disciplines has deepened our understanding of how masculinities are constructed and differentiated.[74] Applying this understanding to the context of terrorism may provide important insights into mobilization as well as the gender overlay of conditions conducive to the production of terrorist violence.

Of particular interest to my analysis is the lens of 'hyper' masculinity. In my emphasis on hypermasculinity I draw on Angela Harris' definition of 'a masculinity in which the strictures against femininity and homosexuality are especially intense and in which physical strength and aggressiveness are paramount'.[75] I frame my analysis by affirming that other kinds of

---

72 R.W. Connell (2005), *Masculinities* (Berkeley: University of California Press); Nancy E. Dowd (2010), *The Man Question: Male Subordination and Privilege* (New York: New York University Press); David D. Gilmore (1990), *Manhood in the Making: Cultural Concepts of Masculinity* (New Haven, CT: Yale University Press); Michael S. Kimmel (2012), *Manhood in America: A Cultural History* (New York: Oxford University Press).

73 Joshua S. Goldstein (2001), *War and Gender: How Gender Shapes the War System and Vice Versa* (Cambridge: Cambridge University Press); Gary Barker and Christine Ricardo (2005), *Young Men and the Construction of Masculinity in Sub-Saharan Africa: Implications for HIV/AIDS, Conflict, and Violence* (Washington, DC: World Bank Working Paper Series, Conflict Prevention & Reconstruction), http://documents.worldbank.org/curated/en/481401468101357773/pdf/327120rev0PAPER0AFR0young0men0WP26.pdf, accessed 10 October 2017; Kimberly Theidon (2009), 'Reconstructing masculinities: The disarmament, demobilization, and reintegration of former combatants in Colombia', *Human Rights Quarterly*, **31** (1), 1–34.

74 Nancy J. Chodorow (1994), *Femininities, Masculinities, Sexualities: Freud and Beyond* (Lexington, KY: University Press of KY); R.W. Connell (1987), *Gender and Power: Society, the Person and Sexual Politics* (Stanford, CA: Stanford University Press).

75 Angela P. Harris (2000), 'Gender, violence, race and criminal justice', *Stan. L. Rev.*, **52**, 777, at 793.

masculinities co-exist with hypermasculinity. Notably, however, in situations of conflict, social deprivation, and endemic violence, hypermasculinity plays an enlarged and elevated role. Its social traction is intensified when violence is pervasive, and other social strictures are slackened. The unloosening of these patterns and hierarchies is particularly fraught in societies (or sub-communities) where peacefully gained social status may be subverted by violent stature gained by the use of the gun, ideology, and exploiting civilian vulnerability.

We would want to better understand why factors associated with hegemonic masculinity strongly correlate towards radicalization and the capacity for violent mobilization.[76] Hegemonic masculinity ideals originate through a combination of cultural expectations and social realities. They include the expectation that men are family patriarchs, and that men are defined in comparison to other men whom they seek to surpass in status, wealth, piety, number of children and social standing.[77] Hegemonic masculinity also includes strong incentives towards masculine performance, including the acceptance and use of violence. In the context of terrorism, radicalism and extremism it is critical to recognize the ways in which these sites enable men to authenticate their masculinity through the performance of and rewards for violence. For human rights practitioners, this exposes the focal point of understanding how gender intersects with the conditions conducive to the production of violence. Namely, that a strong emphasis on non-discrimination, including the absence of gender-based discrimination which serves as a fundamental tenet of human rights equality, unpicks the core masculinity compact in many societies which enables and supports male gender hierarchies, and reward men as men for their cultural, political, and economic performance of masculinity. The point is that addressing the conditions conducive to violence through an equality prism has both the long-term capacity to undo the privileges of patriarchy but also may operate to further entrench masculinity and create backlash to women's rights in the short term. One of the reasons there has been such a tepid response to addressing gender in a holistic way in counter-terrorism is that to do so comprehensively required undoing male privilege, and this task has in a multitude of realms proven to be highly fraught for human rights practitioners over many decades.

---

[76] Maleeha Aslam (2012), *Gender-Based Explosions: The Nexus between Muslim Masculinities, Jihadist Islamism and Terrorism* (New York: United Nations University Press).

[77] Maleeha Aslam (2014), 'Islamism and masculinity: Case study Pakistan', *Historical Social Research*, **39** (3), 135, 146.

However, to advance the practice of engaging in gender analysis and application, one starts by asking the 'man' question, interrogating where and how men are situated in relation to the creation, perpetration, and institutionalization of politically motivated violence. In what ways does hegemonic masculinity work in these contexts, and how do masculinities operate to benefit even those men who are at the margins of masculinity norms and practice in the context of terrorist actions? Somewhat ironically, even within the hierarchies of masculinity, subordinated masculinities can benefit from the social construction of male privilege, and value and terrorism may provide a defined outlet for masculinities that would otherwise be subordinated and devalued by society. Thus, men who cannot meet traditional expectations of masculinity – such as breadwinner, respect and honor, wealth, access to sexual partners of choice – may precisely find that radical or extremist political mobilization offers a compelling substitute for regular masculinity authentication. It is therefore not accidental that terrorist/violent extremist groups manipulate gender stereotypes to recruit men and women. ISIS notably employs hyper-masculine images to portray its fighters, as well as promised access to sexual gratification, marriage and guaranteed income as a reward for the glory of fighting. These motifs have proven indisputably alluring to marginalized men whose capacity to access any similar social capital or status in their own communities will be extremely limited.

One clear parallel for communities in which terrorist actors and actions are validated and supported is to analogize the emergence of hyper-masculinity with the role of the military in multiple cultures and societies. The military is closely tied with manhood, and, indeed, militaristic actions are supported by an ideology of male toughness.[78] In many fragile or weakened states, non-state actor groups and groups who use violent means to subvert or replace the state may perform the same kinds of affirmative manhood that the military does in many other state contexts. Self-evidently, men dominate most national and international militaries. In many societies, men who act militarily and the (generally) male political elite (including paramilitary elites) are deeply enmeshed in this cultural vision of manhood. As former combatants in Colombia explained to anthropologist Kimberly Theidon, for example, joining a paramilitary group allowed the men 'to "feel like a big man in the streets of their barrios", to "go out with the prettiest young women", and to

---

78 Goldstein (n 73), at 5 and 6; Kimberly Theidon (2007), 'Transitional subjects: The disarmament, demobilization and reintegration of former combatants in Colombia', *Int'l. J. Transitional Justice*, **1** (1), 76.

"dress well", privileges they insist would not have been possible if they weren't carrying a gun'.[79] I suggest that the prevalence of this kind of masculinity which has clear cross-over to male status within terrorist groups poses complex issues for understanding and undoing violence, and for addressing the ways in which other social conditions of diminishment intersect with masculine identity. When masculine identity is co-mingled with political violence and ideologies that perform masculine roles in ritualistically violent ways (beheading, systematic rape, sexual slavery, failure to distinguish civilians from combatants), undoing the pattern is a highly complex endeavor of not simply stopping the action but also hollowing out the act of symbolic male capital.

It is also vital to contextualize the reality of economic fragility faced in many states experiencing politically and ideologically motivated violence. As masculinity scholars have noted, a loss of economic and social status, and lack of access to the exercise of socio-economic rights (work, property, education, health) can have an outsized effect on the forms of masculinity that emerge in resource poor environments.[80] Fragile and materially dysfunctional states have proven to be an ample recruiting ground for terrorist groups.[81] Many such states have the highest number of refugee populations (who are predominantly female with child dependents) and internally displaced persons.[82] In this context, when one domain of status and economic subsistence is closed off (the functioning of a regular and ordered economy) such societies enable the dysfunctional economy of armed conflict and sustained violence to replace a

---

[79] Theidon, ibid., at 76.

[80] Judith Gardner and Judy El-Bushra (2016), 'The impact of war on Somali men and its effects on the family, women, and children', February, http://www.politicalsettlements.org/files/2016/02/The-impact-of-war-on-Somali-men-and-its-effects-on-the-family-women-and-children-by-Judith-Gardner-and-Judy-El-Bushra-RVI-Rift-Valley-Forum-Briefing-Paper-2016-1.pdf, accessed 10 October 2017.

[81] *E.g.*, As of 2016, there were over 16 million refugees and internally displaced persons (IDPs) from the five countries with the highest levels of terrorism in 2014. This includes Syria, which has over seven million IDPs. Approximately 70 percent of the UN Refugee Agency's total population of concern came from the 20 countries with the highest number of terrorism-related fatalities. See Institute for Economics and Peace (2015), 'Global Terrorism Index 2015', http://economicsandpeace.org/wp-content/uploads/2015/11/Global-Terrorism-Index-2015.pdf, p. 59 *et seq.*, accessed 10 October 2017.

[82] As of January 2009, Rwanda had 55 062 refugees; Somalia had 1842 refugees and 1 277 200 IDPs; Burundi had 21 093 refugees and 100 000 IDPs; and Columbia had 170 refugees and 3 000 000 IDPs. *See* UN Refugee Agency (UNHCR), http://www.refworld.org/, accessed 10 October 2017.

functional liberal economy of provision. The tools for men to survive and thrive in these societies are identity (frequently coded ideologically extremist) violence, and integration into collectives, here paramilitary and terrorist groupings. Men and young boys who are under or uneducated are at a considerable and material disadvantage and often (though not always necessarily) ripe for mobilization and radicalization. In this space of economic struggle, Gary Barker and Christine Ricardo illustrate the rise in the parallel economics of criminality and 'normal' violence, which allow certain forms of masculinity to endure and provide both status and material needs.[83] They note the particular difficulties of confronting violent masculinities in social settings that have operated to seal off men spatially from women and children. This is further compounded in societies that have deeply stratified gender roles, leaving little room for the expression of positive masculinities in either the public or private sphere.[84] The effects of such stratification are also intensified when one accounts for inter-generational transmission of violent norms, as well as in societies where age stratification is intense, creating forceful competition for economic and sexual resources and opportunities.[85] Notably, in the countering violent extremism context there is emerging analysis affirming gender and human rights compliant re-integration of former jihadists as a valuable element of rehabilitation.[86] This is not per se recognition of the relationship between performative and violent masculinities and the production of terrorism. However, it cedes some understanding of gender codes, gender equality, and gender identity in constructing systems of rehabilitation. Ultimately, the next step would integrate similar understanding into the terrain of prevention.

---

[83] *See* Barker and Ricardo (n 73), at 31 and 32.

[84] Here, the adoption of Security Council Resolution 2250 (2015) marks an important shift in the way the Security Council understands the role of youth in promoting and maintaining international peace. Understanding youth education, integration and social status as an important preventative ground for politically motivated violence as well as creating positive role models for young men as an aspect of prevention based on human rights principles of non-discrimination and equality between the sexes.

[85] The limits on access to land in sub-Saharan Africa are pivotal for the transmission of social status, marriage opportunity, and independence for young men. *See* Barker and Ricardo (n 73), at 12.

[86] Report of the Secretary General, 'Plan of Action' (n 29), para. 29.

The causes of violence and conflict in a range of societies are far too complex to comprehensively explore here.[87] But a number of cluster causalities are useful to identify: first, economic and social insecurity; second, a lack of legal and political status, particularly associated with group or ethnic identity; and third, the lack of opportunity for meaningful self-determination (whether external or internal) within the state. In multiple contexts, engaging in violence is a rational choice for men when few other opportunities may be provided to gain economic security (albeit that participation in violence provides a highly tenuous economic existence or longevity), social status and value within their communities, and security (again albeit tenuous and fragile) for their families and communities. As conflict literature has confirmed and the application to terrorism explores here, there is a strong overlap between all these causal categories and the emergence of certain forms of masculinity in situations that are ripe for terrorist violence. Without addressing the causalities outlined above within a framework that integrates masculinities, we may also fail to address the ongoing realities of how masculinities closely interconnect with terrorist actors and actions.

4. CONCLUSIONS

There are unequivocal advantages in countering terrorism while fully respecting human rights. States have recognized this rhetorically by affirming that effective counter-terrorism measures and human rights protections are complementary and mutually reinforcing goals.[88] It remains true that while human rights are important in their own right, they also serve as important political, symbolic, and legitimacy place-holders for states. As a more nuanced understanding of the range and interplay between limitations on human rights and terrorist actors, actions, causes, situations and armed conflicts emerges, we may be better prepared to address the production of terrorism and, like contagion, limit its spread.

Reducing terrorism violence is an admirable long-term goal for states and human rights' activists alike. In so far as there is increasing recognition that effective counter-terrorism strategies are likely to fail or

---

87 *See* Christian P. Scherrer (2002), *Genocide and Crisis in Central Africa: Conflict Roots, Mass Violence, and Regional War* (Westport, CT: Praeger Publishers).

88 United Nations General Assembly, 'The United Nations Global Counter-Terrorism Strategy' (n 24).

be ineffective without greater attention to the causes that produce terrorism, we see the emergence of shards of global policy language affirming the necessity to address the conditions conducive as canny, strategic, and effective counter-terrorism policy. Here utilitarian motives can lead to better human rights enforcement. However, categorically grappling with the scope and complexity of the conditions conducive is an extraordinarily complex task for states and international institutions. The macro lists (poverty, systematic discrimination, sustained political exclusion) are not 'easy fix' sites. The scale of the task in any one of these arenas may also explain why states have been reluctant to engage wholeheartedly with the macro causes of terrorism. Addressing any one of these structural causes inevitably engages redistribution of resources, identification of beneficiaries and the potential loss of financial benefits to societal elites who have much to lose politically and economically in any fundamental reordering. The status quo in many countries not only exists because of inherently resource-constrained environments, but precisely because they are married to nepotism, corruption, elite bargaining to personal advantage, and dynamics of group power that are gerrymandered to benefit some political groups over others. We might produce the perfect diagnosis for the causes conducive to the production of terrorism but their undoing is an inherently political project, one that threatens established political elites. It remains to be seen whether the incentives that follow from recognizing the costs of terrorism to lives, infrastructure, security, and peace have sufficient traction with political elites to force movement on the chess board. Moreover, there is ongoing tension between the coercive security mode of response to terrorism (fed by ongoing atrocity, insecurity and fear across the globe) and the long-term engagement with causalities that require root and branch reform of political, economic, social and gender systems. These tension points are consistently demonstrated by the lesser attention and status given to addressing the causes conducive to terrorism over the short-term gains of increasingly militarized national security responses.

5. One step forward, two steps back: The Security Council, 'foreign terrorist fighters', and human rights

Lisa Ginsborg

1. INTRODUCTION

On 24 September 2014, at a high level summit chaired by United States President Barack Obama, opened by UN Secretary-General Ban Ki-moon and addressed by scores of national leaders,[1] the UN Security Council met for the sixth time in 70 years at such a level,[2] and adopted by consensus resolution 2178 on 'Foreign Terrorist Fighters',[3] based on a draft text circulated by the United States.[4] Resolution 2178 was adopted almost exactly 13 years after the adoption of resolution 1373,[5] the first 'legislative type' resolution by the Security Council,[6] by which for the first time the Security Council had imposed a number of wide-ranging legal obligations on all UN Member States, under Chapter VII of the UN Charter, and which has been widely criticized for its 'rule of law' deficiencies. Resolution 2178 is reflective both of the problems and of the 'progress' made in the last decade in the field of counter-terrorism. In its failure to define terrorism while imposing broad counter-terrorism measures, and in its introduction of a legally problematic definition of

[1] UN Security Council (2014), 'Security Council unanimously adopts resolution condemning violent extremism, underscoring need to prevent travel, support for foreign terrorist fighters', press release, 24 September, UN Doc. SC/11580.

[2] Statement by President Barack Obama, ibid.

[3] UN Security Council resolution 2178, 24 September 2014.

[4] See http://un-report.blogspot.be/2014/09/updated-un-security-council-draft.html?spref=tw, accessed 7 June 2017.

[5] UN Security Council resolution 1373, 28 September 2001.

[6] Paul C. Szasz (2002), 'The Security Council starts legislating', *American Journal of International Law*, **96** (4), 901–905.

'foreign terrorist fighters' it repeats some familiar mistakes of the post-9/11 Security Council action, while also introducing some new ones. However, it also shows some signs that the Security Council may have learnt, at least in part, from its mistakes or from the 13 years after 9/11, that the complete disregard of human rights is not always helpful from a security perspective.

The explicit recognition that the respect for human rights, fundamental freedoms and the rule of law is 'an essential part of a successful counter-terrorism effort' and that the failure to comply with international obligations is 'one of the factors contributing to increased radicalization',[7] is evidence that the Security Council has made some ground since the adoption of resolution 1373, when human rights standards were seen as falling squarely outside the mandate of the Security Council's work on counter-terrorism.[8] Further the focus on countering violent extremism in order to prevent terrorism, on addressing the conditions conducive to the spread of violent extremism, on engaging relevant local communities and non-governmental actors in developing strategies to counter the violent extremist narrative and on promoting social inclusion and cohesion,[9] reflects the developments in the counter-terrorism approach by the UN and the counter-terrorism community more broadly, which should go hand in hand with the respect of human rights,[10] and which had often been invoked over the years but rarely put into practice by UN actors.[11]

The first signs of the effects of resolution 2178 are already visible, not only in the writing of legal scholars, and the work of the Security Council counter-terrorism committees, but also in domestic and regional counter-terrorist legislation. While the international community remains stranded on trying to reach consensus on an international definition of terrorism, a long path remains to avoid indeterminacy and the risks posed by the vague and sweeping language reintroduced by the Security Council, with new blind corners introduced by the notion of 'foreign terrorist fighters'. Yet the prominence of human rights and international law and the focus on countering violent extremism in order to prevent terrorism in a Chapter VII resolution give hope that a different agenda

---

[7] UN Security Council resolution 2178 (2014), preambular, para. 7.

[8] S/PV.4453 Security Council 4453rd meeting, http://www.un.org/Docs/pv4453e.pdf, accessed 16 October 2017.

[9] UN Security Council resolution 2178 (2014), OP 16.

[10] See General Assembly resolution 60/288, 20 September 2006, in particular Pillar I and Pillar IV.

[11] See 'Report of the Special Rapporteur on human rights while countering terrorism', UN Doc. A/65/258, para. 22.

may emerge out of the work of the Security Council and its counter-terrorism committees this time around. In its progressive side, resolution 2178 opens the door to new areas of activity by the Security Council committees, and other actors embracing the issue of prevention and countering violent extremism. The legal and political complexities arising out of resolution 2178 are multi-faceted and it would be impossible to address them all comprehensively in the current chapter. Yet in line with the theme of the present book and its reflection on the post-9/11 counter-terrorism decade, resolution 2178 seems to be as momentous as the Security Council's reaction to 9/11 through resolution 1373, which was criticized as counter-productive by many commentators. However, a more paused, principled and longer term vision may be materializing in the Security Council's action, emerging side by side with the familiar human rights risks of its post-9/11 action, while also opening the door to new areas of concern for the protection of human rights standards. Regular vigilance and increased attention to particular aspects of resolution 2178 are essential as the Security Council counter-terrorist agenda evolves, and once again opens the door for abuse by repressive governments.

2. FRAMING THE PROBLEM: FOREIGN FIGHTERS

The rise of the Islamic State in Iraq and the Levant (ISIL), and the brutality of its tactics took the international community by surprise in 2014.[12] Its expansion was found to be aided by the arrival of large numbers of foreign fighters, which are still considered to largely dominate its leadership structure.[13] These events gave particular impetus to some States to take measures to prevent further foreign fighters from joining their ranks, including through Security Council resolution 2178,[14] which expressed concern that foreign fighters are being recruited by and are joining entities such as ISIL, the Al-Nusrah Front (ANF) and other cells, affiliates, splinter groups or derivatives of Al-Qaida.[15] While the

---

[12] 'Report of the Independent International Commission of Inquiry on the Syrian Arab Republic, "Rule of terror: Living under ISIS in Syria"', UN Doc. A/HRC/27/CRP.3, 14 November 2014.

[13] Ibid., para. 13.

[14] 'Report of the United Nations High Commissioner for Human Rights on the protection of human rights and fundamental freedoms while countering terrorism', UN Doc. A/HRC/28/28, para. 32.

[15] UN Security Council resolution 2178 (2014), preambular, para. 12.

phenomenon of foreign fighters is not a new one, but one that has characterized conflicts for centuries, what is new and has become obvious to the international community over the past few years is the scale of the problem. As found by the Analytical Support and Al-Qaida Sanctions Monitoring Team, in May 2015:[16]

> The overall numbers have risen sharply, from a few thousand foreign terrorist fighters a decade ago to more than 25,000 today. The number of countries of origin has also significantly increased. During the 1990s, fighters came from a small group of countries. Today, however, they come from more than 100 Member States, including countries that have never experienced problems with groups associated with Al-Qaida.

Estimates of the figures vary, and the Monitoring Group considers that it may be impossible to reach an accurate global number, yet it had no doubt in May 2015 in recognizing the scale of the problem as an urgent global security matter,[17] while in October 2016 the Secretary-General stated that:

> the number of foreign terrorist fighters returning to their States of origin or residence and potentially intending to perpetrate attacks, along with the number of individuals being radicalized within those States, present a growing challenge to global security. The relative frequency of arrests of active ISIL cells around the globe (...) demonstrates this growing risk.[18]

The threat and the cost on human lives is extremely high for people living in the areas where terrorist groups operate, which may be at risk not only of terrorist attacks but other forms of brutality including rape and abuse of women.[19] Further, foreign fighters also pose a significant threat to their countries of origin or to third countries, as returnees may engage in terrorism related offences once they have left the conflict area, which may include raising funds, recruiting, training or radicalizing others.[20] Perhaps the greatest concern for Western States in fact has been

---

[16] 'Report of the Analytical Support and Sanctions Monitoring Team "Analysis and recommendations with regard to the global threat from foreign terrorist fighters"', UN Doc. S/2015/358, para. 10.

[17] Ibid., paras. 11 and 13.

[18] 'Third report of the Secretary-General on the threat posed by ISIL (Da'esh) to international peace and security and the range of United Nations efforts in support of Member States in countering the threat', UN Doc. S/2016/830, para. 10.

[19] Ibid.

[20] Id., paras. 17 and 18.

the fear of so-called *blowback*,[21] individuals returning home to carry out terrorist attacks, whether individually initiated or as part of an external plot.[22] Although some commentators have argued that the threat from returning jihadists has been exaggerated, and governments should focus on reintegrating at least some former fighters,[23] recent terrorist attacks in Europe have tragically confirmed that the threat is a real one.[24]

The phenomenon of foreign fighters remains understudied and limited by the scarcity and unreliability of data,[25] and still little is known about the personal journeys of foreign fighters.[26] Yet the Security Council has been unambiguous about its concern over the acute and growing threat posed by foreign terrorist fighters, which it considers to increase the intensity, duration and intractability of conflicts, and to also potentially pose a threat to their States of origin, the States they transit through and the States to which they travel, as well as States neighbouring zones of armed conflict.[27] The Security Council committees working on counter-terrorism, as well as their expert bodies, have since been active on this issue, producing reports and organizing meetings on the topic and related

---

[21] Mirko Sossai (2015), 'Foreign terrorist fighters: Una nozione ai confini del diritto internazionale', Federalismi.it, 25 September, http://www.federalismi.it/nv14/articolo-documento.cfm?Artid=30335, accessed 7 June 2017, at p. 6.

[22] Sandra Kraehenmann (2014), 'Foreign fighters under international law', Academy Briefing No. 7, Geneva Academy of International Humanitarian Law and Human Rights, October, at p. 13. See also 'Report of the Special Rapporteur on human rights and counter terrorism', UN Doc. A/HRC/29/51, para. 18.

[23] Daniel Byman and Jeremy Shapiro (2014), 'Homeward bound? Don't hype the threat of returning jihadists', *Foreign Affairs*, 30 September, http://www.foreignaffairs.com/articles/142025/daniel-byman-and-jeremy-shapiro/homeward-bound, accessed 7 June 2017.

[24] 'While investigations are ongoing, the information already available demonstrates that foreign terrorist fighters were involved in at least six terrorist attacks or plots in 2015: the terrorists had either directly travelled to conflict zones (e.g. Yemen, Syria) or were inspired or directed to commit acts of terror by other individuals currently in Syria'. Proposal for a Directive of the European Parliament and of the Council on combating terrorism and replacing Council Framework Decision 2002/475/JHA on combating terrorism, 2015/0281 (COD).

[25] Kraehenmann (n 22), at 5.

[26] Alastair Reed, Jeanine de Roy van Zuijdewijn and Edwin Bakker (2015), 'Pathways of foreign fighters: Policy options and their (un)intended consequences', International Centre for Counter-Terrorism (ICCT) Policy Brief, April, at p. 1.

[27] UN Security Council resolution 2178 (2014), preambular, paras. 8 and 10.

issues on regular basis.[28] Problems of definition, legal standards and implementation inevitably emerge as described below.

3. SECURITY COUNCIL RESOLUTION 2178 ON 'FOREIGN TERRORIST FIGHTERS'

As introduced above, through resolution 2178 the Security Council imposed a number of binding measures to be taken by all UN Member States to counter the threat of 'foreign terrorist fighters' and terrorism more generally. These included inter alia criminalizing and prosecuting travel or attempt to travel to a State other than their States of residence or nationality for the purpose of the perpetration of, planning, or participation in, terrorist acts, or the providing or receiving of terrorist training; the wilful provision or collection of funds with the intention that the funds should be used in order to finance such travel; as well as the wilful organization, or other facilitation, including acts of recruitment of such travel.[29] Further, Member States are to prevent entry or transit through their territories of any individual about whom that State has credible information that provides reasonable grounds to believe that he or she is seeking entry into or transit through their territory for the purpose of engaging in terrorist acts.[30] Other obligations resulting from the resolution included Member States requiring that airlines operating in their territories provide advance passenger information to the appropriate national authorities;[31] developing and implementing prosecution, rehabilitation and reintegration strategies for returning foreign terrorist fighters;[32] enhancing their efforts to counter violent extremism,[33] and to cooperate and consistently support each other's efforts in this area.[34]

The measures introduced are broad and far reaching and the notion of 'foreign terrorist fighters' is defined by the Security Council as, '[...] individuals who travel to a State other than their States of residence or nationality for the purpose of the perpetration, planning, or preparation of, or participation in, terrorist acts or the providing or receiving of

28 E.g., see CTC Resources page at http://www.un.org/en/sc/ctc/resources/index.html, accessed 16 October 2017.

29 UN Security Council resolution 2178 (2014), OP 6.

30 Id., OP 8.

31 Id., OP 9.

32 Id., OP 4.

33 Id., OP 15.

34 Id., OP 18.

terrorist training, including in connection with armed conflict'.[35] The resolution is to apply to all foreign terrorist fighters located anywhere in the world, as the measures are imposed on all States worldwide and are clearly delinked from a specific conflict situation, although the Security Council expresses particular concern that foreign terrorist fighters are being recruited by ISIL and ANF. While the definition of foreign terrorist fighters poses a number of problems, as will be further discussed below, the Security Council failed, once again, to define the notion of terrorism, while reaffirming that 'terrorism in all forms and manifestations constitutes one of the most serious threats to international peace and security'.[36]

Resolution 2178 clearly built upon The Hague-Marrakesh Memorandum on Good Practices by the Global Counterterrorism Forum (GCTF),[37] an informal, multilateral platform composed of 29 Member States and the EU,[38] whose work to assist interested States with the practical implementation of the UN counter-terrorism legal and policy framework. The Forum is explicitly recognized by the Security Council in resolution 2178, including its recent adoption of a comprehensive set of good practices to address the foreign terrorist fighter phenomenon.[39] While the Hague-Marrakesh Memorandum explicitly states that it does not intend 'to make and should not be interpreted as making any statement about the legal status of FTFs under national or international law, in particular, international humanitarian, international human rights, or refugee law',[40] resolution 2178 is swift in making the criminalization of 'foreign terrorist fighters' an international obligation, soon to be incorporated into regional and national laws.

The influence of the memorandum on resolution 2178 is reflected also in the more 'progressive' side of the resolution which focuses on

---

35 Id., preambular, para. 8.

36 Id., preambular, para. 1.

37 GCTF (2014), 'The Hague-Marrakech Memorandum on Good Practices for a More Effective Response to the FTF Phenomenon', September, https://www.thegctf.org/Portals/1/Documents/Framework%20Documents/A/GCTF-The-Hague-Marrakech-Memorandum-ENG.pdf?ver=2016-09-01-150615-977, accessed 26 October 2017. See also Kraehenmann (n 22), at 36, 42.

38 Specifically, its founding members are: Algeria, Australia, Canada, China, Colombia, Denmark, Egypt, the European Union, France, Germany, India, Indonesia, Italy, Japan, Jordan, Morocco, The Netherlands, New Zealand, Nigeria, Pakistan, Qatar, Russia, Saudi Arabia, South Africa, Spain, Switzerland, Turkey, the United Arab Emirates, the United Kingdom, and the United States.

39 UN Security Council resolution 2178 (2014), preambular, para. 18.

40 The Hague-Marrakech Memorandum on Good Practices (n 37).

countering violent extremism in order to prevent terrorism. In particular, the Security Council calls upon Member States to enhance efforts to counter violent extremism, including preventing radicalization, recruitment, and mobilization of individuals into terrorist groups;[41] and to:

> engage relevant local communities and non-governmental actors in developing strategies to counter the violent extremist narrative that can incite terrorist acts, address the conditions conducive to the spread of violent extremism, which can be conducive to terrorism, including by empowering youth, families, women, religious, cultural and education leaders, and all other concerned groups of civil society and adopt tailored approaches to countering recruitment to this kind of violent extremism and promoting social inclusion and cohesion.[42]

This was the first time the Security Council inserted this type of language into a counter-terrorism binding resolution under Chapter VII of the Charter.[43] Resolution 2178 thereby shows a certain evolution in the practice of the Security Council explicitly giving attention and weight to long-sighted preventive and human-rights friendly approaches to counter-terrorism. Yet the problems emerging from the resolution from an international law perspective are many.

4. LEGAL PROBLEMS RESULTING FROM THE SECURITY COUNCIL'S APPROACH TO FOREIGN TERRORIST FIGHTERS: THE FAILURE TO DEFINE TERRORISM IN A 'LEGISLATIVE' CHAPTER VII RESOLUTION

The first problem emerging from resolution 2178, immediately visible to any commentator who is familiar with the post-9/11 action by the Security Council and the literature on the topic,[44] is the lack of the

---

[41] UN Security Council resolution 2178 (2014), OP 15.

[42] Id., OP 16. This provision clearly mirrors The Hague-Marrakech Memorandum on Good Practices (n 37), #4.

[43] It had done so in UN Security Council resolution 1624 (2005), but not under Chapter VII.

[44] E.g., Martin Scheinin (2014), 'Back to post-9/11 panic? Security Council resolution on foreign terrorist fighters', Just Security, 23 September, https://www.justsecurity.org/15407/post-911-panic-security-council-resolution-foreign-terrorist-fighters-scheinin/, accessed 5 June 2017; Bibi van Ginkel (2014), 'The new Security Council Resolution 2178 on foreign terrorist fighters: A missed

definition of terrorism. As is well known, the international community has been stuck on trying to define terrorism for over 30 years, consistently failing to reach consensus on an international definition in different *fora* over time.[45] Although the Security Council has set out its own definition of terrorism in 2006 in resolution 1566,[46] it has consistently failed to refer to it when taking action against terrorism. Nowhere in resolution 2178 is terrorism defined, while the Security Council once again requires States to take legislative action against a series of terrorism-related offences.

Having failed to define terrorism when adopting resolution 1373, the Security Council had already promoted the swift adoption of anti-terrorism laws worldwide, while turning a blind eye, at least in the first few years after its adoption, to their human rights conformity.[47] Particular concerns emerged with regard to over vague and over broad definitions of terrorism, which often ended up being used well beyond the original intent of criminalizing terrorism on political opponents, dissenters, and members of minority communities.[48] How terrorism is defined in turn has the potential to endanger numerous other international human rights standards implicated in the criminalization of terrorism-related crimes and their application. In this regard resolution 2178, and the Security Council's failure to refer to resolution 1566, can be seen as 'adding salt to the wound'. In September 2015, Human Rights Watch published its findings that at least 33 countries have put in place laws or policies designed to counter 'foreign terrorist fighters' (FTFs), of which 24

---

opportunity for a holistic approach', ICCT, 4 November, http://icct.nl/publication/the-new-security-council-resolution-2178-on-foreign-terrorist-fighters-a-missed-opportunity-for-a-holistic-approach/, accessed 7 June 2017.

45 See Ben Saul (2006), *Defining Terrorism in International Law* (Oxford: Oxford University Press).

46 UN Security Council resolution 1566 (2004).

47 Nigel D. White (2011), 'The United Nations and counter-terrorism: Multilateral and executive law-making', in Ana Maria Salinas de Frías, Katja Samuel and Nigel D. White (eds), *Counter-terrorism: International Law and Practice* (Oxford: Oxford University Press), at 72.

48 Kieran Hardy and George Williams (2013), 'What is terrorism? Assessing domestic legal definitions', University of New South Wales Faculty of Law Research Series 2013, Working Paper 16 (February); Human Rights Watch (2012), Report: 'In the name of security: Counterterrorism laws worldwide since September 11', http://www.hrw.org/reports/2012/06/29/name-security-0, accessed 16 October 2017; Kim Lane Scheppele (2010), 'The international standardization of national security law', *Journal of National Security Law and Policy*, **4**, at 446.

following resolution 2178,[49] showing that the fears expressed by commentators at the time of adoption of resolution 2178,[50] may be becoming a reality. In particular it found that 'that overbroad language in these laws could target members of certain religious groups, stifle peaceful dissent, unduly curtail freedom of movement, or allow suspects to be held for long periods without charge'.[51] The current Special Rapporteur on human rights and counter-terrorism, Ben Emmerson, expressed concern at 'the broad nature of some of the provisions and the lack of definition of the terms "terrorism" or "extremism", which, on the basis of past experience, may lead some Governments to use the resolution to justify repressive measures against political dissenters with the apparent endorsement of the Security Council'.[52] The Counter-Terrorism Committee (CTC) too recognized that some States have adopted overbroad legislation in response to resolution 2178.[53] While the importance of the Security Council taking decisive action against terrorism is not under question, the Council does not appear to have learned its lessons. The former UN Special Rapporteur on human rights while countering terrorism, Martin

---

[49] Human Rights Watch (2015), 'US Summit: Revamp foreign terrorist fighter laws: Measures in 30 countries threaten rights', 28 September, https://www.hrw.org/news/2015/09/28/us-summit-revamp-foreign-terrorist-fighter-laws, accessed 16 October 2017. It lists the following countries: Austria, Australia, Belgium, Bosnia and Herzegovina, Canada, Cameroon, Chad, Denmark, Egypt, France, Germany, Italy, Ireland, Jordan, Kazakhstan, Kenya, Libya, Macedonia, Malaysia, Morocco, Netherlands, New Zealand, Norway, Pakistan, Russia, Saudi Arabia, Spain, Switzerland, Tajikistan, Tunisia, the United Arab Emirates, the United Kingdom, and Uzbekistan.

[50] E.g. Scheinin (n 44). Similarly, Kai Ambos raised the question as to whether it can be read as an 'infamous strategy on the part of these authoritarian states to have their repression of internal opposition rubber-stamped at the highest level of international law'. Kai Ambos (2014), 'Our terrorists, your terrorists?', EJIL Talk, 2 October, http://www.ejiltalk.org/our-terrorists-your-terrorists-the-united-nations-security-council-urges-states-to-combat-foreign-terrorist-fighters-but-does-not-define-terrorism/, accessed 7 June 2017.

[51] Ibid. For an overview of EU legislation passed in this area, see Piotr Bąkowski and Laura Puccio (2015), 'Foreign fighters': Member States' responses and EU action in an international context', European Parliamentary Research Service Briefing, February.

[52] 'Report of the Special Rapporteur on human rights and counter terrorism', UN Doc. A/HRC/29/51, para. 42.

[53] 'Preliminary analysis of the principal gaps in Member States' capacities to implement Security Council resolutions 1373 (2001) and 1624 (2005) that may hinder their abilities to stem the flow of foreign terrorist fighters pursuant to Security Council resolution 2178 (2014)', UN Doc. S/2014/807, at 4.

Scheinin, was blunt in his assessment: '[...] It wipes out the piecemeal progress made over 13 long years in introducing protections of human rights and the rule of law into the highly problematic manner in which the Security Council exercises its supranational powers'.[54]

Further the threat to international peace and security to which the Security Council is responding this time around is broader still: in resolution 2178 the Security Council determines that 'terrorism in all forms and manifestations constitutes one of the most serious threats to international peace and security and that any acts of terrorism are criminal and unjustifiable regardless of their motivations, whenever and by whomsoever committed',[55] giving broad scope to States to justify their potentially abusive counter-terrorist measures.[56] From an international institutional law perspective, and in particular from a UN law perspective, broad legislative action by the Security Council presents a number of problems, which are clearly replicated in resolution 2178. Applying general and permanent measures under Article 41 of the Charter of the United Nations, as was done in resolution 1373 and now 2178, coupled with the lack of a definition of terrorism, makes it impossible for the Council to assess the necessity of the measures imposed on a case-by-case basis.[57] One key difference exists however between the legislative action displayed by the Security Council in resolution 1373 and 2178. In fact, the majority of obligations contained in the operative part of resolution 1373 mirrored the obligations contained in the 1999 Convention for the Suppression of the Financing of Terrorism, albeit with the fundamental difference of leaving the key terms undefined.[58] Although the Convention had only been ratified by five States at the time, the obligations contained in resolution 1373 had

---

[54] Scheinin (n 44).

[55] UN Security Council resolution 2178 (2014), preambular, para. 1.

[56] Marko Milanovic (2014), 'UN Security Council adopts Resolution 2178 on foreign terrorist fighters', *EJIL: Talk!*, 24 September, http://www.ejiltalk.org/un-security-council-adopts-resolution-2178-on-foreign-terrorist-fighters/, accessed 16 October 2017.

[57] See Valeria Santori (2006), 'The UN Security Council's (broad) interpretation of the notion of the threat to peace in counter-terrorism', in Giuseppe Nesi (ed.), *International Cooperation in Counter-terrorism: The United Nations And Regional Organizations in the Fight Against Terrorism* (Aldershot: Ashgate), at 105; Matthew Happold (2003), 'Security Council Resolution 1373 and the Constitution of the United Nations', *Leiden Journal of International Law*, **16**, at 600; Björn Elberling (2005), 'The ultra vires character of legislative action by the Security Council', *International Organizations Law Review*, **2** (2), at 337–60.

[58] Happold, ibid.

already been 'legislated' by the General Assembly.[59] On the contrary the obligations contained in resolution 2178 are not part of the international legal framework. As summed up by Martin Scheinin: 'Resolution 2178 is worse –indeed, far worse – than Resolution 1373 from the perspective of the international rule of law'.[60]

Further, resolution 2178 was introduced as a series of binding rules on the international community on the basis of a memorandum produced by an informal group of States, namely the GCTF. Although the GCTF members are more numerous than the Security Council ones and include all the P-5 (five permanent members) sitting on the Security Council, such practice raises a number of questions from the point of view of legitimacy and rule of law. Although 'reliance on a technical body for the development of international standards is no novelty in international law',[61] if it can be considered as such, its international law and human rights implications have yet to be fully explored. The main problem emerging out of the memorandum and as a result in resolution 2178, is the definition of FTFs, which not only did not exist under international law, but some have argued is difficult to place within it.[62]

5. THE DEFINITION OF FOREIGN TERRORIST FIGHTERS

The definition of FTFs introduced by resolution 2178 displays several elements, a number of which have been considered problematic in the first commentaries written by legal scholars. Leaving aside the lack of definition of terrorism, several terms in the resolution lack in clarity and precision,[63] open the door for inconsistencies, potential abuses by actors applying it, and perhaps insurmountable problems from an international law perspective.

---

59 Martin Scheinin (2014), 'A comment on Security Council Res 2178 (foreign terrorist fighters) as a "form" of global governance', Just Security, 6 October, https://www.justsecurity.org/15989/comment-security-council-res-2178-foreign-fighters-form-global-governance/, accessed 10 May 2017.

60 Ibid.

61 Andrea Bianchi (2004), 'Enforcing international law norms against terrorism: Achievements and prospects', in Andrea Bianchi (ed.), *Enforcing International Law Norms Against Terrorism* (Oxford: Hart), at 529.

62 See Sossai (n 21).

63 See van Ginkel (n 44).

The definition of FTFs, which emerged clearly in distinction to mercenaries, because they are not gaining remuneration,[64] raises a number of problems in particular from the perspective of international humanitarian law (IHL), which have been outlined carefully by Sandra Kraehenmann.[65] The crux of the matter lies in the phrase 'including in connection with armed conflict'.[66] Of course determining what counts as an armed conflict, whether an international or a non-international armed conflict, is a complex question under IHL, and many controversies remain in relation to the US determination of being involved in a 'global war on terror'. However, the most complex legal questions arising out of resolution 2178 are to be found in the introduction of terrorist conduct in the context of an armed conflict, which appears somehow blind to the persistent difficulties in defining terrorism internationally. In fact, one of the most contentious areas in the negotiations over the draft comprehensive Convention on international terrorism,[67] remains the question of the scope of application of the Convention and the disputes in particular surrounding the application of the Convention to armed conflicts, armed forces and to 'foreign occupation', which point in the direction of a deadlock between the Organization of Islamic Conference (OIC) and the rest of the international community, with far wider political concerns tied up with the classification of insurgencies, acts of self-determination and State-sponsored terrorism.[68] The term 'Foreign Terrorist Fighter' itself was qualified by Ben Emmerson as 'the apex of the blurring of the concepts of terrorism and armed conflict'.[69]

Leaving aside for the current purpose the fact that ISIL has committed clear violations of IHL, given the potential scope of application of resolution 2178 to any armed conflict,[70] it appears that the characterization of foreign fighters as terrorists from an IHL perspective is not

---

[64] See David Malet (2013), *Foreign Fighters: Transnational Identity in Civil Conflicts* (Oxford: Oxford University Press), at 9.

[65] Kraehenmann (n 22).

[66] UN Security Council resolution 2178 (2014), preambular, para. 8.

[67] Surya P. Subedi (2002), 'The UN response to international terrorism in the aftermath of the terrorist attacks in America and the problem of the definition of terrorism in international law', *International Law Forum*, **4**, at 159.

[68] See also Gerhard Hafner (2006), 'The definition of the crime of terrorism' and Andrea Gioia (2006), 'The UN Conventions on the Prevention and Suppression of International Terrorism', in Nesi (n 57), at 16–20.

[69] 'Report of the Special Rapporteur on human rights and counter-terrorism', UN Doc. A/HRC/34/61, para. 48.

[70] See 'Report of the Office of the United Nations High Commissioner for Human Rights on the human rights situation in Iraq in the light of abuses

only irrelevant, but the definition is inconsistent with the rules of IHL.[71] This is reflected in the Security Council's own definition of terrorism contained in resolution 1566, which in referring to terrorism as criminal acts, 'which constitute offences within the scope of and as defined in the international conventions and protocols relating to terrorism'[72] adopts the approach of most international conventions against terrorism, which is to exclude armed conflicts.[73] As expressed by a number of commentators, resolution 2178 conflates the two legal regimes,[74] making it legally problematic for a number of reasons.

IHL explicitly prohibits acts that would be considered terrorism under the international conventions. First, it categorically prohibits the taking of hostages, which has been defined as terrorist behaviour in the International Convention on the Taking of Hostages, even in the context of armed conflict.[75] Second, it prohibits attacks on the civilian population with the primary aim of spreading terror,[76] which in the context of armed conflict could be a very broad determination, but has been clarified by the International Committee of the Red Cross (ICRC) as intending to prohibit: 'acts of violence or threats thereof the primary purpose of which is to spread terror among the civilian population without offering substantial military advantage'.[77] As reflected in Common Article 3 of the Geneva Conventions, IHL prohibits attacks against civilians who are not, or who are no longer, taking part in hostilities – acts which would generally be considered terrorist in nature outside the context of an

---

committed by the so-called Islamic State in Iraq and the Levant and associated groups', UN Doc. A/HRC/28/18.

[71] Kraehenmann (n 22), at 63.

[72] UN Security Council resolution 1566 (2004), OP 3.

[73] See also discussion of this in Martin Scheinin (2015), 'The Council of Europe's draft protocol on foreign terrorist fighters is fundamentally flawed', Just Security, 18 March, https://www.justsecurity.org/21207/council-europe-draft-protocol-foreign-terrorist-fighters-fundamentally-flawed/, accessed 7 June 2015.

[74] E.g., see Emilio De Capitani (2015), '"Foreign fighters" and EU implementation of the UNSC resolution 2178. Another case of "Legislate in haste, repent at leisure …"?', European Area of Freedom Security & Justice, 6 April, http://free-group.eu/2015/04/06/foreign-fighters-and-eu-implementation-of-the-unsc-resolution-2178-another-case-of-legislate-in-haste-repent-at-leisure-1/, accessed 16 October 2017.

[75] Adopted in New York 1979.

[76] Article 51(2) Additional Protocol I; Article 13(2) Additional Protocol II; and discussion in Kraehenmann (n 22), at 24.

[77] ICRC, Additional Protocols Commentary on Article 51(2), p. 618.

armed conflict.[78] This is intrinsically linked to the principle of distinction, which, put simply, determines that civilians should not be subject to attacks, and such acts would be classified as war crimes under IHL. However, significant problems emerge when it comes to acts which may not be forbidden under IHL, such as attacks on a military target. As noted also by the UN High Commissioner for Human Rights in relation to resolution 2178: 'The lack of an explicit exemption for acts that otherwise may be lawful under international humanitarian law is also a cause for concern'.[79] In line with this the ICRC has made it clear that with the exception of those offences which are classified as terrorist under IHL, 'the term "acts of terrorism" should be reserved for acts of violence committed outside of armed conflict'.[80] Further, the main UN counter-terrorism conventions generally contain exclusion clauses.[81] The reasons for this are complex but are mainly linked to the fundamental principle under IHL concerning belligerent equality. Further, labelling armed groups as 'terrorists' may hinder peace negotiations, as was evidenced when the Taliban were delinked from the Al-Qaida sanctions list in Security Council resolution 1988.[82]

Further, resolution 2178 raises serious concerns from an IHL perspective as it criminalizes the mere participation in an armed conflict with a specific group, which can neither be classified as terrorist activity nor as a war crime under IHL, but blurs the lines between different legal regimes and as noted by the ICRC would weaken the fundamental

---

[78] Kraehenmann (n 22), at 24.

[79] 'Report of the United Nations High Commissioner for Human Rights on the protection of human rights and fundamental freedoms while countering terrorism', UN Doc. A/HRC/28/28, para. 46.

[80] ICRC (2011), 'International humanitarian law and the challenges of contemporary armed conflicts', Official working document of the 31st International Conference of the Red Cross and Red Crescent, Geneva, 28 November to 1 December, at 51.

[81] This is true of the 1979 Hostages Convention (Article 12), the 1997 Terrorist Bombings Convention (Article 19: see Box 9), the 1999 Terrorist Financing Convention (Article 21), and the 2005 Nuclear Terrorism Convention (Article 4). As also noted by Kraehenmann, 'Counterterrorism treaties that cover acts that may occur during an armed conflict typically include provisions which exclude acts governed by IHL'. Kraehenmann (n 22), at 35.

[82] UN Security Council resolution 1988, 17 June 2011. See Kraehenmann (n 22), at 62.

principle under IHL concerning the equality of the parties. Further, as noted by Kraehenmann:

> the current approach imposes different legal consequences on those who join (or attempt to join) armed groups, depending on the group they join. This may generate inconsistencies of treatment where (as in Syria) alliances between numerous armed factions shift frequently, and foreign fighters can become attached to new groups unexpectedly or involuntarily as a result.[83]

The implications of the legal problems contained in resolution 2178 are likely to be reflected in its implementation at the national and regional level.[84] The most striking example has been the Additional Protocol to the Council of Europe Convention on the Prevention of Terrorism, adopted in May 2015.[85] The Protocol was adopted in response to resolution 2178, to supplement the Convention on the Prevention of Terrorism with a series of provisions aimed at implementing the criminal law aspects of resolution 2178.[86] However, differently from resolution 2178, the Protocol did not mention the notion of FTFs, nor armed conflict, while calling for the criminalization of 'travelling abroad for the purpose of terrorism', and related offences,[87] including the providing or receiving of training for terrorism in the territory of another State.[88] Further, the Protocol refers to the Council of Europe Convention for the definition of terrorism, which in turn is defined in relation to existing international conventions.[89] Taking into account that most of the conventions exclude armed conflict, the paradox emerges that the Protocol may be useless for violence in specific situations of armed conflict, which could include Syria and Iraq, as noted by Martin Scheinin in relation to its draft.[90] Its scope is perhaps only applicable to people travelling to

---

83 Kraehenmann (n 22), at 63.

84 E.g., see discussion of Italian draft law in Sossai (n 21).

85 Adopted by the Committee of Ministers at its 125th Session on 19 May 2015.

86 Nicola Piacente (2015), 'The contribution of the Council of Europe to the fight against foreign terrorist fighters', *eucrim*, 2015/1, https://eucrim.mpicc.de/archiv/eucrim_15-01.pdf, accessed 7 June 2017, at 12.

87 Additional Protocol to the Council of Europe Convention on the Prevention of Terrorism, Art. 4 *et seq.*

88 Id., Art. 3.

89 Council of Europe Convention on the Prevention of Terrorism, Warsaw, 16.V.2005, Art. 1.

90 Scheinin (n 73). He further noted, 'The current draft follows UNSC Res. 2178 in making the fundamental – but erroneous – assumption that foreign (including European) fighters joining the battle in countries of conflict, such as Syria or Iraq, would often be committing a terrorist offense simply by engaging

conflict-free zones, or to a foreign country to receive training in terrorism with a specific intention to return to Europe to commit acts of terrorism there.[91] But the remoteness of the crime would make the task of the prosecutor very complicated. Leaving aside the complexities with prosecuting crimes committed in another country under IHL, the problem is also evident from a domestic law perspective.

6. OTHER HUMAN RIGHTS CONCERNS EMERGING FROM RESOLUTION 2178

From a human rights angle the definition of FTF presents problems relating to preparatory offences and how remote they appear from the future ones to be committed in the name of terrorism.[92] As noted by the current UN Special Rapporteur on counter-terrorism, Ben Emmerson, 'the standard adopted for enforcement action, that is, credible information that the individual will engage in the acts set out in the resolution, arguably provides too much latitude to States and could result in arbitrary enforcement action being taken'.[93] This becomes increasingly so as the conduct to be criminalized in accordance with the Security Council resolution becomes more remote from the core criminal conduct, in particular in relation to the criminalization of travel to receive training to commit a terrorist offence. Or even worse in cases where:

> It is not addressing an act of terrorism (itself variously defined in international law), but rather, at the outermost, facilitating the travel of others (in a non-monetary and perhaps non-essential manner) to receive training that

---

in violence there. This assumption is wrong, or at least it is correct only in a small proportion of cases, the proper determination of which will be quite a challenging task of legal analysis'.

[91] Ibid.

[92] Sossai (n 21).

[93] 'Report of the Special Rapporteur on the promotion and protection of human rights and fundamental freedoms while countering terrorism', UN Doc. A/HRC/29/51, AEV, para. 42. See also on this matter Joint submission by Amnesty International and the International Commission of Jurists (2015), 'Preliminary public observations on the terms of reference to draft an additional protocol supplementing the Council of Europe Convention on the Prevention of Terrorism', March, https://www.amnesty.org/download/Documents/IOR6013932015ENGLISH.pdf, accessed 16 October 2017.

> could potentially used to commit an unspecified act of terrorism sometime in the future.[94]

This is reflected in the challenges faced by prosecutors across the world in the implementation of resolution 2178 in proving terrorist intent, and its links with travel and financing.[95] During a seminar organized on the topic in February 2015, the CTC found there had been few convictions related to foreign terrorist fighters in EU Member States, in part due to the challenges in generating admissible evidence, and converting intelligence to evidence.[96] The concluding observations of the report emphasized the 'need to find a balance between prosecution and prevention', and that prosecutors should take 'a strategic approach that ensured respect from human rights and the rule of law'.[97]

However, the increasing link between counter-terrorism and border controls, also give priority to intelligence driven and large-scale surveillance, which is seen by some to contribute to 'demoting traditional police and criminal justice responses to cross-border criminality, subject to the standard democratic rule of law and fundamental rights checks and balances'.[98] Further, as noted by Kai Ambos it is not clear how an official is to recognize inner terrorist intent, without incurring in offender-focused discrimination or de facto criminalization of any border crossing into States that border upon centres of terrorist activity, which would hardly stand up to human rights or constitutional review.[99] The dangers of profiling, both from a human rights law and a counter-terrorism effectiveness perspective, have already been discussed in much detail in the post-9/11 climate.[100] In the absence of conclusive evidence in relation to FTFs, 'preventive' measures such as blacklisting may be resorted to as less drastic steps than the criminalization of border crossing. During the adoption in December 2015 of Security Council resolution 2243 which

---

[94] Jens Iverson (2014), 'Notes of caution on the UNSC resolution obliging states to change domestic criminal law', *Leiden Law Blog*, 26 September, http://leidenlawblog.nl/articles/notes-of-caution-on-the-unsc-resolution-obliging-states-to-change-domestic, accessed 7 June 2017.

[95] Counter-Terrorism Committee (2015), 'Report on the sixth prosecutors' seminar on bringing terrorists to justice', UN Doc. S/2015/123.

[96] Ibid., paras. 23 and 24.

[97] Id., para. 44.

[98] Didier Bigo et al. (2015), 'The EU and its counter-terrorism policies after the Paris attacks', CEPS Paper in Liberty and Security, No. 84/November 2015.

[99] Ambos (n 50).

[100] E.g., see 'Report of the Special Rapporteur on human rights and counter-terrorism', UN Doc. A/HRC/4/26.

expanded its Al-Qaida sanctions framework to include a focus on ISIL/Da'esh, the United Kingdom reported that it had recommended for UN listing a list of British nationals who had travelled to Syria, and encouraged other countries to do the same.[101] While the UN has continued to emphasize the preventive nature of these listings, many have considered them to be criminal sanctions due to their severity especially in relation to the asset freeze.[102]

Aside from the numerous human rights principles implicated in the above considerations – often compounded by overbroad definitions of terrorism – including appropriate procedural standards, non-discrimination, the presumption of innocence and the principle of legality, implying non-retroactivity, precision, clarity and foreseeability, a number of specific human rights standards may be at risk in the implementation of resolution 2178, in particular related to its restrictions on travel and most directly linked to freedom of movement and to be protected against arbitrary deprivation of nationality.[103] Resolution 1373 had already called on States to prevent the movement of terrorists or terrorist groups by effective border controls and controls on issuance of identity papers and travel documents,[104] and many of the aspects prescribed by resolution 2178 are likely already criminal acts in a number of countries. However, resolution 2178 goes further in its focus on impeding travel, with clear risks which go beyond the conflict in Syria, and are linked directly to questions of freedom of movement, but in turn may affect a number of other rights, including the right to work, a family life and to health.[105] As in the immediate aftermath of resolution 1373, there has been a rush of new counter-terrorist legislation and the first problems from a human rights perspective are emerging. The High Commissioner for Human Rights noted: 'A number of States have taken measures to curtail the movement of foreign fighters. These include travel bans, the

---

[101] See UN (2015), 'Unanimously adopting Resolution 2253 (2015), Security Council expands sanctions framework to include Islamic State in Iraq and Levant', press release, 17 December, http://www.un.org/press/en/2015/sc12168.doc.htm, accessed 16 October 2017.

[102] Case T–85/09, *Yassin Abdullah Kadi v. Commission* (CJEU, 30 September 2010), para. 150.

[103] Article 12 International Covenant on Civil and Political Rights (ICCPR), see also 'Report of the United Nations High Commissioner for Human Rights on the protection of human rights and fundamental freedoms while countering terrorism', UN Doc. A/HRC/28/28, paras. 49 and 50.

[104] UN Security Council resolution 1373 (2001), OP 2(g).

[105] 'Report of the Special Rapporteur on human rights and counter-terrorism', UN Doc. A/HRC/29/51, AEV, para. 45.

withdrawal of passports and the denial of citizenship, all of which have an impact on the right to freedom of movement, as enshrined in article 12 of the International Covenant on Civil and Political Rights'.[106] While the right to freedom of movement is not absolute under international human rights law, in its General Comment No. 27, the Human Rights Committee emphasized that any restrictions on the right to freedom of movement must be based on clear legal grounds and meet the test of necessity and the requirements of proportionality.[107] Relevant procedural standards may also be at risk in the implementation of resolution 2178.[108]

Further, the arbitrary deprivation of nationality and the issue of statelessness raise particular concerns in the implementation of resolution 2178. The severe impact on individuals' lives resulting from statelessness makes it particularly problematic from a human rights perspective. The cases in which the deprivation of nationality resulting in statelessness can be recognized as serving a legitimate purpose are therefore strictly limited under international law.[109] Yet a number of States have already passed laws revoking citizenship, to be applied in the context of FTFs.[110] Moreover, as with resolution 1373, if States misuse the notion of terrorism to criminalize dissent, resolution 2178 could provide the avenue for political opposition groups that have been labelled as terrorists to be denied refugee

---

[106] 'Report of the United Nations High Commissioner for Human Rights on the protection of human rights and fundamental freedoms while countering terrorism', UN Doc. A/HRC/28/28, para. 50. By way of example, broader powers to revoke travel documents of citizens and residents have been provided in France, Australia and Malaysia, while the UK has adopted temporary exclusion orders. See 'Status of foreign fighters under international and national law', International Society for Military Law and the Law of War paper, http://www.ismllw.org/congres/2015_04_14_Prague_textes%20des%20orateurs/2015-04-15%20KRAEHENMANN.pdf, accessed 7 June 2017.

[107] Human Rights Committee (HRC) (1999), 'General Comment No. 27', UN Doc. CCPR/C/21/Rev.1/Add.9, para. 16.

[108] Report of the United Nations High Commissioner for Human Rights on the protection of human rights and fundamental freedoms while countering terrorism, UN Doc. A/HRC/28/28, para. 50. In particular, 'Measures such as travel bans, the revocation of passports and the denial of citizenship also raise important due process concerns, where decisions are taken following secretive proceedings, in absentia or on the basis of vaguely defined criteria without adequate safeguards to prevent statelessness'.

[109] Ibid. See also HRC resolution 10/13, 26 March 2009.

[110] Examples include Switzerland, Canada, United Kingdom, Australia; for an overview see Kraehenmann (n 22).

status.[111] This in turn would open the door to an exception to *non-refoulment* and the possibility of return to persecution.[112]

Finally, the call on Member States to 'employ evidence-based traveller risk assessment and screening procedures including collection and analysis of travel data',[113] and to 'require all airlines operating in their territories to provide advance passenger information to the appropriate national authorities',[114] call for additional caution as regards not only the right not to be subject to discrimination, but also the right to privacy. These are well recited arguments in the post-9/11 climate, in which racial profiling has been a common practice,[115] and although resolution 2178 warns against resorting to stereotypes founded on grounds of discrimination,[116] no mention is made of privacy rights. This is particularly surprising given the sensitivity of the issue of indiscriminate bulk data collection and data retention within the EU,[117] as well as the debates over the use of passenger name records.[118]

---

[111] See also Monette Zard (2002) who makes this argument in 'Exclusion, terrorism and the Refugee Convention', *F.M.R.*, **13**, 32; Rene Bruin and Kees Wouters (2003), 'Terrorism and the non-derogability of *non refoulment*', *International Journal of Refugee Law*, **15** (1), 5–29; J.C. Simeon (2010), 'Complicity and culpability and the exclusion of terrorists from convention refugee status post-9/11', *Refugee Survey Quarterly*, **29** (4), 104–37.

[112] Jean Allain (2001), 'The *jus cogens* nature of *non-refoulement*', *International Journal of Refugee Law*, **13** (4), 533–58, at 556. Given the *jus cogens* nature of the principle of *non-refoulment*, he argues that 'a proper reading of paragraph 3(g) of Resolution 1373, which calls upon States to act "in conformity with international law", would preclude the return of individuals to a State where their life or liberty would be threatened even if they had committed so-called terrorist acts', at 547.

[113] UN Security Council resolution 2178 (2014), OP 2.

[114] Id., OP 9.

[115] 'Report of the Special Rapporteur on human rights and counter-terrorism', UN Doc. A/HRC/4/26, at para. 60.

[116] UN Security Council resolution 2178 (2014), OP 2.

[117] Joined Cases C-293/12 and C-594/12, *Digital Rights Ireland and Seitlinger and Other* (CJEU, 8 April 2014); and discussion of its implications in Franziska Boehm and Mark D. Cole (2014), 'Data retention after the judgement of the Court of Justice of the European Union', June, https://www.janalbrecht.eu/fileadmin/material/Dokumente/Boehm_Cole_-_Data_Retention_Study_-_June_2014.pdf, accessed 7 June 2017.

[118] E.g., see statement by Giovanni Buttarelli (2015), 'Counter-terrorism, de-radicalisation and foreign fighters', Joint debate of the LIBE Committee, 27 January, https://edps.europa.eu/sites/edp/files/publication/15-01-27_libe_speech_gb_en.pdf, accessed 7 June 2017.

7. COUNTERING VIOLENT EXTREMISM IN ORDER TO PREVENT TERRORISM

As introduced above, resolution 2178 combines a more traditional repressive counter-terrorist agenda, with a more preventive, long-term approach of countering violent extremism in cooperation with civil society actors and communities. The 'progressive side' of resolution is innovative for the Security Council and to date has received little attention from legal scholars, although it has already stimulated some action in the context of the work of the CTC.[119] Some commentators have argued that the departure from resolution 1373 is in fact notable, not only in its stronger human rights language, but in its emphasis on efforts to prevent radicalization and recruitment as an 'essential element' in addressing the threat posed by foreign fighters.[120] It is unquestionable that the resolution presents a more holistic approach, which after recognizing, in line with Security Council resolution 1963,[121] 'that terrorism will not be defeated by military force, law enforcement measures, and intelligence operations alone',[122] presents a number of novel elements under the title 'Countering Violent Extremism in Order to Prevent Terrorism'. Also clearly inspired by the Hague-Marrakech Memorandum, it underscores inter alia that countering violent extremism is an essential element to countering the threat posed by FTFs,[123] the importance of engaging local communities and civil society in strategies to counter the violent extremist narrative,[124] and the role education can play in countering terrorist narratives,[125] as well as urging States to act cooperatively when taking national measures to prevent terrorists from exploiting technology, communications and resources, while respecting human rights.[126]

---

119 See reports S/2014/807; S/2015/338; S/2015/377; S/2015/683.

120 Naureen Chowdhury Fink (2014), 'Countering terrorism and violent extremism: The role of the United Nations today and the impact of Security Council Resolution 2178', Global Center on Cooperative Security, November, http://www.globalcenter.org/publications/countering-terrorism-and-violent-extremism-the-role-of-the-united-nations-today-and-the-impact-of-security-council-resolution-2178/, accessed 7 June 2017.

121 UN Security Council resolution 1963, 20 December 2010.

122 van Ginkel (n 44).

123 UN Security Council resolution 1963 (2010), OP 15.

124 Id., OP 16.

125 Id., OP 19.

126 Id., OP 17.

If these may be tall orders and ambitious goals, the language of the resolution reflects the shift in the counter-terrorism field and the increasing attention over the last ten years to the notion and policy practice of countering violent extremism, also referred to as 'CVE'. In line with the growing awareness by counter-terrorism experts and policymakers that law enforcement and military responses alone are not always sufficient and can at time exacerbate existing threats,[127] it recognizes the preventive side of CVE and the conditions conducive to terrorism. Although the 2006 UN Global Strategy had not explicitly mentioned the notion of 'countering violent extremism', in its focus on the preventive, comprehensive approach to countering terrorism, including the conditions conducive to terrorism, it anticipated many of the themes emerging from the CVE field.[128] Since then, CVE has evolved 'from a rhetorical commitment to an increasingly prominent subfield of counterterrorism policy and practice',[129] not only in the UN Security Council but in a wide variety of policy-making *fora*. In February 2015, over 60 country representatives gathered for the White House Summit on Countering Violent Extremism, and in January 2016 the UN Secretary-General released the UN Global Plan of Action to Prevent Violent Extremism to the General Assembly,[130] which 'calls for a comprehensive approach encompassing not only essential security-based counter-terrorism measures but also systematic preventive steps to address the underlying conditions that drive individuals to radicalize and join violent extremist groups'.[131] Although the budgets for CVE are reported to remain

---

[127] Global Center on Cooperative Security (2015), 'Strengthening rule of law responses to counter violent extremism: What role for civil society in South Asia?', May, http://www.globalcenter.org/wp-content/uploads/2015/05/May-2015_Strengthening-Rule-of-Law-Responses-to-Counter-Violent-Extremism3.pdf, accessed 17 October 2017.

[128] See also Global Center on Cooperative Security (2015), 'The next decade: Strengthening multilateral efforts for preventing and countering terrorism and violent extremism', May, http://www.globalcenter.org/wp-content/uploads/2015/07/Global-Center_The-Next-Decade_UN-and-CT-CVE_Project-Description.pdf, accessed 17 October 2017.

[129] Peter Romaniuk (2015), 'Does CVE work?: Lessons learned from the global effort to counter violent extremism', Global Center on Cooperative Security, September, http://www.globalcenter.org/wp-content/uploads/2015/09/Does-CVE-Work_2015.pdf, accessed 17 October 2017, at p. 2.

[130] UN Doc. A/70/675.

[131] UN Secretary-General (2015), 'At G7 Summit, Secretary-General previews counterterrorism action plan', press Release, 8 June.

relatively small when compared to traditional counter-terrorist activities,[132] and there is a general lack of clarity about what CVE precisely means and entails,[133] to the point of becoming a catch-all category,[134] in terms of 'flurry of activity', it may well be the 'most significant development in counterterrorism in the last decade',[135] and its endorsement by the Security Council in a legislative-type resolution is in line with this. Further, the central role of human rights protection, at least in certain areas such as socio-economic marginalization, as an aid to counter-terrorism emerges clearly in some areas of this field. Finally, its role in stimulating reflection about counter-terrorism policy itself, and the fact that at times counter-terrorism activity may be counter-productive and part of the problem, sits clearly in line with the topic of this book. As noted by the Secretary-General 'Many years of experience have proven that short-sighted policies, failed leadership, heavy-handed approaches, a single-minded focus only on security measures and an utter disregard for human rights have often made things worse'.[136]

In discussing resolution 2178, the High Commissioner for Human Rights emphasized the importance of addressing the conditions conducive to terrorism and CVE, in accordance with human rights, and going beyond the security approach by promoting dialogue and enhancing social cohesion as a new and important area of work by the Security Council.[137] Further, in October 2015 the Human Rights Council adopted the first ever resolution on 'Human rights and preventing and countering violent extremism', showing the counter-terrorism and human rights communities may have started to see eye to eye. The resolution recognizes inter alia that the objectives of CVE and countering terrorism and

---

132 Romaniuk (n 129), at 39.

133 'Report of the Special Rapporteur on human rights and counter terrorism', UN Doc. A/HRC/31/65, paras. 11–17 and 20–21.

134 Steven Heydemann (2014), 'Countering violent extremism as a field of practice', United States Institute of Peace, https://www.usip.org/sites/default/files/Insights-Spring-2014.pdf, accessed 17 October 2017.

135 Romaniuk (n 129), at 2. Several research centres in the area of CVE have been established, including the GCTF and Hedayah, in Abu Dhabi; for an overview, see Chowdhury Fink (n 120), at 3. Also for examples of CVE State programming, see UN Doc. S/2015/683, para. 102 *et seq.*

136 UN Secretary-General (2015), 'UN Secretary-General's remarks at General Assembly presentation of the plan of action to prevent violent extremism', http://www.un.org/sg/statements/index.asp?nid=9388, accessed 17 October 2017.

137 'Report of the United Nations High Commissioner for Human Rights on the protection of human rights and fundamental freedoms while countering terrorism', UN Doc. A/HRC/28/28, para. 39.

of the protection and promotion of human rights, fundamental freedoms and the rule of law are mutually reinforcing,[138] and calls on States to take a number of measures almost mirroring the language of resolution 2178, including to 'engage with local communities and non-governmental actors through a whole-of-society approach in developing strategies that respect human rights and fundamental freedoms to counter narratives that incite acts of violent extremism and terrorism'.[139]

If the human rights and counter-terrorism communities may be coming together, there are signs that significant reasons for concern from a human rights perspective remain. By way of example, a group of States expressed their concern after the adoption of the Human Rights Council resolution about a number of changes to the draft by oral revision just prior to action. In particular, the insertion of the limitation 'in accordance with national strategies' to the freedom of civil society to act was not considered to 'respect the important role of an independent, diverse and pluralistic civil society in addressing human rights issues'.[140] Further operative paragraph seven regarding communications technology, including the internet, was not considered to sufficiently reflect the language of the Human Rights Council about respecting human rights online and offline. As a result of these and other issues, the group of States did not regard all the language of the resolution 'as adopted as a precedent for the future'.[141] Similarly, others termed the outcome text as disappointing as it raises a number of problems from a human rights perspective, including 'unclear language that might undermine freedom of expression, in particular online; inappropriate limitations on the scope for a free and independent civil society; and a failure to account for the ways in which 'international cooperation' on CVE has effectively been used as justification for looking the other way when those "partner" governments violate human rights within their own borders'.[142] This controversy at the Human Rights Council may give a sense of the sensitivity of some of the issues at stake. There is no doubt that preventive responses to violent

---

138 UN Human Rights Council resolution 30/15 (2015), preambular, para. 4.

139 Id., OP 5.

140 'General Comment after the vote regarding draft resolution HRC30/L.25/Rev 1: Human rights and preventing and countering violent extremism: Ireland on behalf of a group of States', 2 October 2015.

141 Ibid.

142 International Service for Human Rights (2015), 'Resolutions adopted by the Human Rights Council at its 30th session', http://www.ishr.ch/news/resolutions-adopted-human-rights-council-its-30th-session#sthash.AUkXyNJW.dpuf, accessed 17 October 2017.

extremism may be seen as less repressive and reactionary, but may well have their human rights weak spots, and may even turn out to be more intrusive and subject to abuse than traditional criminal justice responses.[143]

The notion of CVE is very broad and may encompass a range of different policy responses, of different scopes, ranging from the macro-level to the micro one, of different activities to be undertaken, ranging from capacity building to education training or more traditional internet monitoring, and of different media or implementing agents, which may be community actors, civil society or public-private partnerships.[144] While the question of the effectiveness of CVE activities to date is beyond the scope of this chapter, the Security Council has been criticized for not spelling out sufficiently the measures to be taken by States in this part of the resolution resulting in an 'unbalanced strategy' and 'a missed opportunity to further the development and implementation of more genuine preventive measures'.[145] There is no doubt that the language of the resolution is very broad and lacking in specificity and concrete formulations. Nonetheless, the resolution adopted under Chapter VII of the Charter, still represents an important step towards a more preventive approach to counter-terrorism, and if implemented in a human-rights friendly manner subject to regular monitoring and capacity building under the guises of the CTC/Counter-Terrorism Committee Executive Directorate (CTED), together with other UN actors, has the potential to bring about significant change. The CTC is given a significant role in the resolution, including in the facilitation of technical assistance through the development of 'comprehensive counter-terrorism strategies that encompass countering violent radicalization and the flow of foreign terrorist fighters'.[146] And it is clear that since the adoption of the resolution the

---

[143] Bibi van Ginkel (2014), 'Addressing the foreign terrorist fighters phenomenon from a European Union perspective', Global Center on Cooperative Security, December, http://www.globalcenter.org/wp-content/uploads/2014/12/Dec2014_EU-FTFS_GCCS_HSC_ICCT.pdf, accessed 17 October 2017, at p. 15. See also 'Report of the Special Rapporteur on human rights and counter-terrorism', UN Doc. A/HRC/31/65, para. 54.

[144] Romaniuk (n 129), at 10.

[145] van Ginkel (n 44).

[146] UN Security Council resolution 2178 (2014), OP 24. Security Council resolution 2129 (2013), OP19, had already tasked CTED to further engage and enhance its partnerships with international, regional and sub-regional organizations, civil society, academia and other entities in conducting research and information-gathering, and identifying good practices in the context of a comprehensive approach to preventing the spread of terrorism and violent extremism.

CTC has taken the implementation of resolution 2178 on as one of its core areas of focus. If more preventive approaches start to form a part of the CTED ongoing assessment processes, in cooperation with key human rights actors, there is hope significant momentum will be given to a more long-sighted human-rights friendly approach to counter-terrorism, also through proactive engagement with civil society organizations.[147] Further, if the broad language of resolution 2178 is coupled with more concrete recommendations emerging in part from the UN Secretary-General strategy and from sharing practices which have been shown to work to prevent further radicalization and recruitment, there is hope that human rights will form a central part of such approaches. However, if the Security Council, and the Secretary-General are serious about the human-rights centred approach to counter-terrorism, grounded in good governance, the rule of law, political participation, quality education and decent jobs,[148] the preventive approach of CVE will have to go well beyond the counter-terrorism community. For the current purpose, a number of core elements may be identified which emerge clearly from the CVE part of resolution 2178, and relate to human rights standards in different ways, some positive, some negative.

First, from a human rights perspective, in the context of overbroad definitions of terrorism, there is no guarantee that the notion of extremism may prove more precise and better at avoiding arbitrary or sweeping measures in the name of CVE, which is at times inter-changed with counter-radicalization.[149] In fact, the term CVE may also be considered worse, in being more vague and providing even more of a *carte blanche* to justify repressive measures in its name.[150] As noted in the opening paragraphs of the Secretary-General strategy 'violent extremism is a diverse phenomenon, without clear definition'.[151] While new laws are introduced in this context,[152] the notion of extremism may prove even more open to abuse than the 'terrorism' classification, and may more

---

147 Chowdhury Fink (n 150), at 8.

148 Key priority areas in the Secretary-General strategy.

149 Owen Frazer and Christian Nünlist (2015), 'The concept of countering violent extremism', *CSS Analyses in Security Policy*, **183** (December), http://www.css.ethz.ch/content/dam/ethz/special-interest/gess/cis/center-for-securities-studies/pdfs/CSSAnalyse183-EN.pdf, accessed 7 June 2017.

150 E.g., David Sharia (2015), at The Threat of Foreign Terrorist Fighters and UN Security Council Resolution 2178 conference, International Institute for Counter-Terrorism (ICT), 10 September.

151 UN Doc. A/70/674, para. 2.

152 Sharia, (n 150). See also discussion of the Russian Federation laws on extremism in section 10.

easily escape the rule of law in cases where repressive action is taken in the name of purely preventive strategies. A better definition of what CVE is, and what it is not, would go a long way towards supporting the human rights promotion advocated by the Security Council and the Secretary General.[153]

8. COMMUNITY ENGAGEMENT AND CIVIL SOCIETY INVOLVEMENT IN CVE

Community engagement has been identified as an essential component of any CVE exercise, as the drivers of extremism are complex and context dependent, and the involvement of local communities is essential to any such approach.[154] This is recognized also by resolution 2178 which explicitly notes the importance of more localized prevention efforts, in particular through engaging local communities. Although with less specificity and less prominence given to prevention, the resolution mirrors the Hague-Marrakech Memorandum, which emphasized the importance of 'investing in the long-term cultivation of trusted relationships with communities susceptible to recruitment, considering the broader set of issues affecting the community'.[155] The Memorandum explicitly noted that community engagement in CVE has emerged as an extremely sensitive topic, and experience has shown to be at great risk of being counter-productive. Today there is in fact broad agreement that through simplistic assumptions and one-size-fits-all approaches to the radicalization process it may bring about negative unintended consequences.[156] It is therefore essential, the Memorandum notes in good practice number five, that CVE programmes 'avoid and seek to prevent the identification of the FTFs or violent extremism with any religion, culture, ethnic group nationality, or race',[157] which may well alienate communities and end up hampering counter-terrorism efforts at best and fuelling further radicalization at worst. As already expressed by the Special Rapporteur on

153 See also 'Report of the Special Rapporteur on human rights and counter-terrorism', UN Doc. A/HRC/31/65, paras. 21 and 35.

154 Eelco Kessels et al. (2015), 'Countering violent extremism and promoting community resilience in the Greater Horn of Africa', Global Center on Co-operative Security, May, http://www.globalcenter.org/wp-content/uploads/2015/05/HoA_Action_Agenda_Low_Res.pdf, accessed 17 October 2017, at p. 6.

155 The Hague-Marrakech Memorandum on Good Practices (n 37), at 2.

156 Romaniuk (n 129), at 15.

157 The Hague-Marrakech Memorandum on Good Practices (n 37), at 3.

human rights while countering terrorism in 2007: 'the victimization and alienation of certain ethnic and religious groups may have significant negative implications for law-enforcement efforts, as it involves a deep mistrust of the police. The lack of trust between the police and communities may be especially disastrous in the counter-terrorism context';[158] and a decade of CVE efforts have shown this to be the case. Tied to the key notion of non-discrimination which should guide any counter-terrorism policy, the dangers of profiling based on ethnicity, national origin and religion, which may not only be counter-productive from a counter-terrorism perspective, but have a number of serious human rights implications.[159] A number of studies have found that discriminatory measures which target groups and communities based on their religious, regional or ethnic belonging can lead to their stigmatization and consequently decrease community cohesion and end up increasing recruitment to the 'terrorist cause'.[160] While community-oriented policing methods are openly encouraged by the Secretary-General Global Plan of Action,[161] they can also have the counter-effect of limiting the authorities' ability to cooperate with and collect information from communities. The inherent dangers of mixing surveillance and rehabilitation work is visible in this context,[162] in which information gathered in 'CVE and community outreach settings' may be fed into ongoing surveillance and monitoring practices, while enhanced monitoring of a particular community may also have the effect of 'aggravating existing prejudices and reinforcing intolerance'.[163] Long-term approaches to community engagement and community policing in which each local community is not

---

[158] 'Report of the Special Rapporteur on human rights and counter-terrorism', UN Doc. A/HRC/4/26, paras. 55–58.

[159] Id., para. 62.

[160] E.g. see Christopher Baker-Beall, Charlotte Heath-Kelly and Lee Jarvis (eds) (2015), *Counter-Radicalisation: Critical perspectives* (Abingdon: Routledge); Adrian Cherney and Jason Hartley (2015), 'Community engagement to tackle terrorism and violent extremism: Challenges, tensions and pitfalls', *Policing and Society: An International Journal of Research and Policy*, **277**, 750–63; see also 'Special Rapporteur on human rights and counter-terrorism', UN Doc. A/HRC/31/65, para. 47.

[161] UN Doc. A/70/674, para. 51.

[162] Bigo et al. (n 98).

[163] Letter by civil society organizations, 'Re: Federal Support for Countering Violent Extremism Programs', 18 December 2014, https://www.aclu.org/files/assets/141218_cve_coalition_letter_2.pdf, accessed 17 October 2017.

targeted for security reasons but is engaged for its own benefit are essential in this respect.[164]

On the other hand, there appears to be broad recognition that if shaped and implemented without civil society participation and civic agency, counter-terrorism measures are likely to make the threat of violent extremism worse.[165] It is argued that to succeed, CVE requires 'integrative, broadly based state-civil society relationships',[166] given their key role in understanding local context and grievances. And it is hard to deny that many civil society organizations working in a range of areas from development to conflict transformation to human rights are more or less directly contributing to addressing the conditions conducive to the spread of terrorism.[167]

The role of civil society, also mentioned in resolution 2178, in turn raises a number of questions which go beyond questions of effectiveness, into the realm of protection of key human rights actors. While the CVE approach to counter-terrorism places importance on development and human rights non-governmental organizations (NGOs),[168] as we have seen from the Human Rights Council resolution civil society is a double-edged sword in this context, in which it may be a key actor in CVE activities, yet it also remains one of the prime targets at risk from the misuse of counter-terrorism laws and policies. Through direct experience in communities including in conflict zones, civil society may have knowledge and speak with authority about the grievances that give rise to violent extremism and their solutions,[169] and many NGOs now include these aspects in their work.[170] They may engage in deradicalization, rehabilitation and reintegration efforts,[171] while they may also provide

---

164 GCTF, 'Good practice on community engagement and community oriented policing as tools to counter violent extremism', https://www.thegctf.org/documents/10162/159885/13Aug09_EN_Good+Practices+on+Community+Engagement+and+Community-Oriented+Policing.pdf, accessed 17 October 2017.

165 David Cortright et al. (2012), 'Friend not foe: The role of civil society in preventing violent extremism', *Notre Dame Journal of International and Comparative Law*, **2** (2), Article 3, http://scholarship.law.nd.edu/ndjicl/vol2/iss2/3, accessed 7 June 2017.

166 Romaniuk (n 129), at 15.

167 Bibi van Ginkel (2012), 'Engaging civil society in countering violent extremism', ICCT, August, https://www.icct.nl/download/file/ICCT-Van-Ginkel-Civil-Society-in-CVE-August-2012.pdf, accessed 17 October 2017, at p. 8.

168 Cortright et al. (n 165), at 6.

169 Id., at 24.

170 UN Doc. A/70/371, para. 8.

171 Global Center on Cooperative Security (n 127), at 8.

alternative outlets for addressing grievances to those otherwise tempted by extremism.[172] As put by some 'In the global struggle against violent extremism civil society groups should be welcomed as friends, not hounded as foes'.[173]

However, there is increasing concern about the 'closing space' in which civil society has to operate in a number of repressive States, often under the rhetoric of counter-terrorism, which is in part related to the above discussion about the lack of the definition of terrorism.[174] These risks are also somewhat visible in UN resolutions, not only in the controversy discussed above in relation to the Human Rights Council resolution, but also in the endorsement by the Security Council and its committees of the work of the Financial Action Task Force (FATF). In particular its recommendation VIII stating that non-profit organizations are particularly vulnerable to abuse for terrorist financing,[175] has proved to be a 'useful tool for a number of States as a means of reducing civil society space and suppressing political opposition'.[176] In this context counter terrorist-financing measures have hindered the work of foundations and charitable agencies, while deep concerns have been raised in the development community as a result of the 'securitization of aid', also in the context of CVE initiatives.[177] On the whole, it is essential that in their implementation of resolution 2178 States bear in mind the risks, and do not manipulate the vulnerable role of civil society, by facilitating an 'open, inclusive space where different actors can work together toward a

---

[172] UN Doc. A/70/371, para. 8.

[173] Cortright et al. (n 165), at 7.

[174] E.g., see Opening Statement by UN High Commissioner for Human Rights Zeid Ra'ad Al Hussein at the 30th session of the Human Rights Council, http://www.ohchr.org/EN/NewsEvents/Pages/DisplayNews.aspx?NewsID=16414&LangID=E#sthash.dY0tfBQ8.dpuf, accessed 7 May 2017.

[175] FATF Special Recommendations 2003.

[176] See UN Doc. A/70/371, para. 33 – despite recognition by the Task Force of the importance of the role of civil society and its insistence that the measures adopted should not disrupt or discourage legitimate charitable activities. Also, for instance, in a study of the 'powerful yet unaccountable global standard–setting body' which is FATF, Hayes found that it is 'helping repressive civil society regulations to spread and flourish across the globe'. Ben Hayes (2013), 'From countering financial crime to criminalizing civil society: How the FATF overstepped the mark', Open Society Foundations, http://www.opensocietyfoundations.org/voices/countering-financial-crime-criminalizing-civil-society-how-fatf-overstepped-mark, accessed 17 October 2017.

[177] Cortright et al. (n 165), at 17.

solution'.[178] Overall, although community engagement may be an important approach to understand local grievances, there is concern that in light of the limited vague language of resolution 2178 and little detail of how this may be done in practice, it could also serve as a means for repressive governments to enhance their control over community organizations and civil society.[179]

9. HUMAN RIGHTS PROMOTION AS A COMPONENT OF CVE

From a human rights perspective, the comprehensive approach of resolution 2178 and its focus on the conditions conducive to the spread of violent extremism, on promoting social inclusion and cohesion,[180] and on the role education can play in countering terrorist narratives,[181] are signs of the Security Council embracing, at least in part, an approach to CVE which is grounded in human rights in line with the UN Global Counter-terrorism Strategy and the Secretary-General Global Plan of Action. There appears to be growing consensus today that, among the 'triggers' of terrorism, violations of human rights can play a role, including the denial of political rights, poverty or social and economic marginalization.[182] Further, the growing evidence of links between violent extremism and economic deprivation, bad governance and conflict has led to increasingly comprehensive approaches to counter-terrorism policies, in which human rights and development play a central part.[183] The former UN Special Rapporteur on counter-terrorism, Martin Scheinin, had already advocated the promotion of economic, social and cultural rights as a cornerstone in sustainable long-term strategies for the prevention of

---

178 van Ginkel (n 167), at 8.

179 Chowdhury Fink (n 120).

180 UN Security Council resolution 2178 (2014), OP 16.

181 Id., OP 19.

182 E.g., see Chris Bordeleau, Jeff J. Chalifoux and Karina Sangha (2015), 'The global fight against terror: An evaluation of counter-terrorism governance', Canadian Network for Research on terrorism, security and Society, Working Paper Series, no. 15-01, January, http://tsas.ca/wp-content/uploads/2015/01/TSASWP15-01_Bordeleau-Chalifoux-Sangha1.pdf, accessed 17 October 2017, at p. 18.

183 Ivan Briscoe and Bibi van Ginkel (2013), 'The nexus between development and security: Searching for common ground in countering terrorism', ICCT Policy Brief, March.

terrorism,[184] and during his mandate had warned against the negative effects of a number of measures that not only undermined human rights but were also at risk of providing a 'fertile soil for recruitment to movements that promise a prospect for change but resort to the unacceptable means of acts of terrorism'.[185] Amongst them, the social and economic marginalization of and discrimination against vulnerable groups, such as minorities, indigenous peoples or underprivileged households of women and children,[186] restrictions of cultural and linguistic rights, or the demolition of housing or destruction of other private property.[187] By way of example, in the context of his mission to Turkey in 2006, the Special Rapporteur argued in favour of furthering economic, social and cultural rights as a means of preventing terrorism and found that:[188]

> in the long run, full respect for economic, social and cultural rights helped to eliminate the risk of individuals making the morally inexcusable decision to resort to acts of terrorism, and recommended that persons belonging to different cultural and linguistic groups, including the Kurdish population, should enjoy protection of their cultural, linguistic and religious rights, including the possibility to freely use their language in public and private.

This included the view that improvements in respect of equality between women and men can also serve to prevent terrorism,[189] while protection of the right to education, as well as securing the effective enjoyment by women of economic, social and cultural rights were both cornerstones in sustainable long-term strategies for the prevention of terrorism.[190] The focus of the newly released Secretary-General's Global Plan of Action not only on, inter alia, education, skill development and employment facilitation, gender equality and empowering women – but also on

---

[184] 'Report of the Special Rapporteur on human rights and counter-terrorism', UN Doc. A/HRC/6/17, para. 64: 'While there is no scientific evidence of a causal connection between economic and social grievances and acts of terrorism, patterns of correlation can be demonstrated that suggest that societies characterized by such grievances and educational exclusion are often breeding or recruitment grounds for terrorists'.

[185] Id., para. 70.

[186] Ibid.

[187] 'Report of the Special Rapporteur on human rights and counter-terrorism', UN Doc. A/HRC/6/17/Add.4, para. 61.

[188] 'Report of the Special Rapporteur on human rights and counter-terrorism', UN Doc. A/HRC/4/26/Add.2, para. 59 *et seq.*

[189] Id., para. 88.

[190] Id., para. 62.

strengthening good governance, human rights and the rule of law as key priority areas, which places non-discrimination, development as well as the accountability of security services, law enforcement agencies and justice institutions in a central position – outlines a clear path to the promotion of human rights for the purposes of CVE.[191] In its explicit mention of the importance of 'empowering youth, families, women, religious, cultural and education leaders',[192] as well as 'the role education can play in countering terrorist narratives',[193] the Security Council too appears to be embracing at least in part this approach. Although CVE remains a complex field, and not all forms of promotion of tolerance, pluralism and the rule of law can be strictly defined as CVE,[194] by addressing the conditions conducive to terrorism and increasingly acknowledging that human rights and counter-terrorism are mutually reinforcing, the Security Council shows an increasing potential to address in its counter-terrorist practice some of the grievances often associated with violent extremism, such as underdevelopment, inequality and socio-political marginalization, as has been learned by the counter-terrorism community in the long decade after 9/11.[195]

10. CVE ONLINE

Finally, in the context of CVE, resolution 2178 raises another sensitive area of counter-terrorism protection with a number of human rights implications, namely terrorist prevention through countering violent extremism in communication technologies and in particular through the internet. As summed up by Walker and Conway:

> The UN has achieved almost no impact in the field of online laws against violent extremism, a position in part attributable to the US and other Western reluctance to invite and sanctify restrictions by undemocratic states on

---

[191] See UN Doc. A/70/675.

[192] UN Security Council resolution 2178 (2014), OP 16.

[193] Id., OP 19.

[194] Kessels et al. (n 154), at 13.

[195] See Naureen Chowdhury Fink, Peter Romaniuk and Rafia Barakat (2013), 'Evaluating countering violent extremism programming: Practices and progress', Center on Global Counterterrorism Cooperation, September, http://globalcenter.org/wp-content/uploads/2013/07/Fink_Romaniuk_Barakat_EVALUATING-CVE-PROGRAMMING_20132.pdf, accessed 17 October 2017.

freedom of expression on the web. However, the UN has occasionally called for specific action against online terrorism, such as via UNSCR 2178.[196]

This is evident in operative paragraph 17, in which, in the context of CVE, the Security Council urges States to 'act cooperatively when taking national measures to prevent terrorists from exploiting technology, communications and resources, including audio and video, to incite support for terrorist acts', although the respect of human rights and fundamental freedoms is recalled by the Security Council here too.[197] Terrorist recruitment or support through information and 'communication technologies, such as the internet and social media', are also mentioned previously in the resolution in the context of grounds for terrorist listing.[198] The importance, complexity and sensitivity of this area of activity for CVE and freedom of expression already emerges from the second report by the CTC on Member States implementation of resolution 2178, as well as in the reservations at the Human Rights Council discussed above.

Debate remains over the extent to which future terrorists may be radicalized through the internet or social media alone, without other external influences or direct contact.[199] Recent studies have found that although the internet provides increased opportunities for radicalization, there is little evidence of its role in 'self-radicalization' without any physical contact.[200] However, there is no doubt that many activities of extremist organizations are taking place online,[201] that the internet provides new avenues for propaganda and engagement with potential supporters, and that 'IS and its online supporters have proven themselves to be perhaps the most adept and prolific producers and disseminators of online content'.[202]

It is therefore unquestioned that countering violent extremism online, including through social media, is a very important and growing field of

196 Clive Walker and Maura Conway (2015), 'Online terrorism and online laws', *Dynamics of Asymmetric Conflict*, **8** (2), at 167.

197 UN Security Council resolution 2178 (2014), OP 17.

198 Id., OP 7.

199 UN Doc. S/2015/683, para. 9.

200 Bibi van Ginkel (2015), 'Responding to cyber jihad: Towards an effective counter narrative', ICCT, March, https://www.icct.nl/download/file/ICCT-van-Ginkel-Responding-To-Cyber-Jihad-Towards-An-Effective-Counter-Narrative-March2015.pdf, accessed 17 October 2017, at p. 2, referring to 2013 study by RAND Corporation.

201 Ibid.

202 Walker and Conway (n 196), at 158.

activity in the field of countering terrorism and violent extremism. This includes both monitoring and 'repressive' measures such as blocking, filtering and content take-down, as well as more positive or 'soft' measures involving the use of strategic communication and 'engaging in the battle of ideas'.[203] The latter may include public information campaigns, and the construction of 'alternative narratives' or 'counter-narratives', to challenge and counter the extremist narratives which are promoted on the web.[204] Repressive measures, which are focused directly on terrorist incitement and recruitment, by restricting access or removing content relating to violent extremism online, represent a central area of terrorism prevention and CVE online, as exemplified by the CTC's thematic focus of its second report on the implementation of resolution 2178. They also constitute a minefield from the point of view of international law and human rights standards, in which different jurisdictions and actors, including more or less global internet service providers (ISPs) and other intermediaries have also taken on the role of counter-terrorist enforcement actors. A brief excursus on the rights affected and challenges involved – which can be introduced but not fully addressed here – is essential to understand some of the key human rights risks of resolution 2178.

First, criticisms are increasingly arising about the emergence of a disproportionate blanket 'surveillance society'.[205] A number of studies have noted that, while electronic mass surveillance has been found to fail, a more targeted and rational approach to surveillance that improves the balance between fundamental rights and surveillance may be necessary also in a counter-terrorism context.[206] In particular, the requirements of necessity, proportionality, legitimate aim and legal basis, in order for limitations to certain human rights to be lawful, are essential in the context of online restrictions on the right to privacy but also a range of other rights, including freedom of expression.[207] As noted by the current Special Rapporteur on human rights while countering terrorism, 'the very existence of mass surveillance programmes constitutes a potentially

[203] Ibid.

[204] For an overview, see van Ginkel (n 200).

[205] Walker and Conway (n 196).

[206] E.g., see https://surveille.eui.eu/about-surveille/, accessed 17 October 2017.

[207] (2015), 'Assessing surveillance technologies', briefing note of Surveillance: Ethical Issues, Legal Limitation and Efficiency, https://surveille.eui.eu/wp-content/uploads/sites/19/2015/07/SURVEILLE-Policy-Brief.pdf, accessed 17 October 2017.

disproportionate interference with the right to privacy. […] The very essence of the right to the privacy of communication is that infringements must be exceptional, and justified on a case-by-case basis'.[208] In this context concerns are raised by behavioural profiling of open source data from online social networking activity by law enforcement and intelligence agencies: 'Profiling which implements predictive modelling techniques based on the collation of data from social network sites risks infringing an individual's right to privacy'.[209] Further the Special Rapporteur on freedom of expression has recently emphasized that States should not impose blanket prohibitions on encryption and anonymity, which would fail to be necessary and proportionate.[210] Encryption technology and tools that allow anonymity online, which are often restricted as quick reactions to terrorism, should also meet the standards of necessity and proportionality, as they constitute restrictions not only on the right to privacy but may also restrict the rights to freedom of opinion and expression, in particular with respect to journalists and human rights defenders.[211] The CTC also recognizes the human rights risks involved in the mass surveillance of private digital communications, and highlights that the surveillance of digital communications for purposes of CVE and preventing the recruitment of terrorists should be 'lawful and targeted (as opposed to broad-based)'.[212] There is a risk that resolution 2178, also in the context of CVE activities, may further justify surveillance activities at the expense of human rights. As noted by Cian Murphy,[213] implementation of the provisions of resolution 2178, 'may involve the enactment of criminal law offences but is more likely to involve systems of surveillance and administrative reporting that represent disciplinary rather than juridical power'.

Second, the importance of criminalizing incitement to terrorism in a not overbroad fashion, and not using vague terms such as 'glorifying' or

---

208 UN Doc. A/69/397, para. 18.

209 Jonathan Andrew (2013), 'SURVEILLE Deliverable 4.2: Paper on legal issues related to the use of surveillance data for profiling', European University Institute, at p. 42.

210 'Report of the Special Rapporteur on the promotion and protection of the right to freedom of opinion and expression', UN Doc. A/HRC/29/32, para. 60.

211 Id., para. 59.

212 UN Doc. S/2015/683, para. 20, quoting UN Doc. A/HRC/27/37, para. 24.

213 Cian C. Murphy (2015), 'Transnational counter-terrorism law: Law, Power and legitimacy in the "Wars on Terror"', Transnational Legal Theory King's College London Law School Research Paper No. 2015-14, at 13.

'promoting' terrorism,[214] is especially pressing in the context of countering violent extremism online. Further, beyond the problems resulting from the persistent lack of the definition of terrorism which have been discussed above and extend to this area too, as we have seen there is no guarantee that the use of the term 'extremism' is any better. The Russian Federation is just one example of a State in which broad and imprecise laws on 'extremism' may lead to disproportionate anti-extremist measures, also in the context spreading extremist materials through a mass media, including the internet.[215] The language of CVE and radicalization, which allows for widely differing interpretations and political action in the context of online activities, may lead inter alia to undue restrictions of freedom of expression and a chilling effect on journalists and political opponents. Further, identifying incitement to commit terrorist acts, while preserving freedom of expression, and differentiating it from other forms of political propaganda, is a complex task for law enforcement agencies, let alone for internet intermediaries.[216] As noted by the CTC: 'Law enforcement agencies must sift through vast amounts of data and differentiate between individuals who are merely expressing opinions and those who are likely to join a terrorist organization, travel or commit an act of terrorism in their own State, and take action to do so'.[217] Nonetheless internet intermediaries are increasingly called in to regulate internet content, which raises a number of delicate legal questions including about the liability of internet intermediaries. In particular the requirement by most States that ISPs immediately, upon obtaining knowledge or awareness of illegality of online content, remove or disable access to it, raises questions about when ISPs can be considered to have sufficient knowledge of the illegal nature of specific content or activity, especially in relation to more complex assessments such as incitement to terrorism. Meanwhile the Al-Qaeda monitoring team in June 2015, recommended that the Sanctions Committee 'invite relevant Internet and social media companies to brief the Committee on their efforts to respond to the exploitation of their services by Al-Qaida and associates, including the Islamic State in Iraq and the Levant, in 2015'.[218] On the contrary, Frank La Rue, has argued that using the internet as a positive

---

[214] 'Report of the Special Rapporteur on human rights and counter-terrorism', UN Doc. A/HRC/16/51.
[215] See Venice Commission CDL-AD(2012)016, at 19.
[216] UN Doc. S/2015/683, para. 16.
[217] Id., para. 15.
[218] UN Doc. S/2015/441, para. 41.

means of countering incitement to terrorism may constitute a more effective strategy.[219]

Most recently Security Council resolution 2354 on countering terrorist narratives welcomed the 'Comprehensive International Framework to Counter Terrorist Narratives' presented by the Counter-Terrorism Committee in April 2017.[220] Although not adopted under Chapter VII and hidden under the language of 'countering terrorist narratives', significant risks remain in the Security Council's vague endorsement of legal and law enforcement measures and public-private partnerships to counter incitement to commit acts of terrorism.[221] While recalling the importance of freedom of expression, and that all measures taken by Member States must comply with their human rights obligations,[222] and while recognizing that 'the line between unlawful and lawful communications can be difficult to discern',[223] problems remain in the Security Council's lack of definition of key terms, including not only 'terrorism' but also 'narratives',[224] and in the framework's focus on private partners as counter terrorism enforcers.[225] By way of example Microsoft's amendment of its terms of use to specifically prohibit the posting of terrorist content by, or in support of, organizations included on the Consolidated United Nations Security Council Sanctions List,[226] because 'there is no universally accepted definition of terrorist content', and because the 'U.N. Sanctions

---

219 'Report of the Special Rapporteur on the promotion and protection of the right to freedom of opinion and expression', UN Doc. A/66/290.

220 UN Security Council resolution 2354 (2017), OP 16.

221 Comprehensive International framework to counter terrorist narratives, in UN Doc. S/2017/375, Annex.

222 UN Security Council resolution 2354 (2017), preambular para. 11 and OP 2(e).

223 Comprehensive International framework to counter terrorist narratives UN Doc. S/2017/375, Annex para. 4.

224 As noted Dimitris Christopoulos, FIDH President, 'narratives' is "a vague concept which actually remains to be legally defined"', FIDH press release 24 May 2017, 'Countering terrorist narratives at the expense of human rights? The UN Security Council sets the alarming tone', https://www.fidh.org/en/international-advocacy/united-nations/security-council/countering-terrorist-narratives-at-the-expense-of-human-rights-the-un, accessed 15 November 2017.

225 E.g., see 'Counter-terrorism was never meant to be Silicon Valley's job. Is that why it's failing?', 29 June 2017, https://www.theguardian.com/technology/2017/jun/29/silicon-valley-counter-terrorism-facebook-twitter-youtube-google, accessed 15 November 2017.

226 Counter-Terrorism Committee webpage, https://www.un.org/sc/ctc/focus-areas/information-and-communication-technologies/, accessed 15 November 2017.

List includes a list of groups that the U.N. Security Council considers to be terrorist organizations',[227] raises particular concerns in light of the sanctions' declared preventative nature.[228]

Finally, general and specific legislation regulating measures of blocking, filtering and removal of internet content, raise considerable questions from a human rights perspective.[229] In general, restrictions to internet content should apply only when the national legal system provides for sufficient safeguards for freedom of expression, whether online or offline, and should satisfy the criteria of legality, legitimacy and proportionality under international human rights law. In particular, the legal framework authorizing restrictive measures should be foreseeable, accessible, precise and clear with regard to the application of restrictive measures, afford sufficient protection against arbitrary interferences by public authorities; it should provide for a determination of the scope of restrictive measures by a judicial authority or an independent body, and provide for an effective judicial review of the proportionality of restrictive measures, including an assessment whether the restrictive measure is the least far-reaching measure to achieve the legitimate aim.[230] This new area of regulation of online content is essential for terrorism prevention, while presenting numerous possibilities for abuse by repressive governments. Further the question of procedural guarantees regulating blocking, filtering and take down of internet content and whether the administrative blocking of websites in cases of terrorist incitement is appropriate under international human rights law is hotly debated.[231] While States introduce new laws regulating this aspect online, likely also under the impulse of

---

[227] 'Microsoft's approach to terrorist content online', 20 May 2016, https://blogs.microsoft.com/on-the-issues/2016/05/20/microsofts-approach-terrorist-content-online/, accessed 15 November 2017.

[228] By way of example see Third report of the Analytical Support and Sanctions Monitoring Team appointed pursuant to resolution 1526 (2004) concerning Al-Qaida and the Taliban and associated individuals and entities, 9 September 2005, UN Doc. S/2005/572, paras. 39-43.

[229] 'Report of the Special Rapporteur on human rights and counter-terrorism', UN Doc. A/HRC/31/65, paras. 38–40.

[230] See also (2015), 'State of democracy, human rights and the rule of law in Europe', Report by the Secretary General of the Council of Europe, https://edoc.coe.int/en/index.php?controller=get-file&freeid=6455, accessed 17 October 2017.

[231] E.g., see OHCHR (2016), 'UN rights experts urge France to protect fundamental freedoms while countering terrorism', 19 January, http://www.ohchr.org/EN/NewsEvents/Pages/DisplayNews.aspx?NewsID=16966&LangID=E#sthash.bCaO9ncL.dpuf, accessed 17 October 2017.

resolution 2178, it is essential that any restriction on internet content follows clear human rights safeguards including appropriate transparency, due process and appeals procedures in the terms of service of internet intermediaries. Finally, the problems of conflicting jurisdictions and differing domestic laws and practices, poses problems both for international cooperation and from a human rights perspective.[232] Leaving aside questions of effectiveness,[233] CVE online under the authorization of the Security Council calls for caution as it is at risk of providing easy abuse by repressive governments, while States continue to revise their legislations in response also to this aspect of resolution 2178.

11. CONCLUSIONS

In the aftermath of 9/11 the Security Council adopted for the first time in its history a legislative type resolution with a number of human rights consequences. Despite the push back and human rights reaction in the decade that followed, in 2014 the Security Council once again adopted a legislative resolution which was broad, wide ranging and enjoyed significant consensus.[234] The resolution raises significant problems from a human rights perspective. As long as the international community fails to adopt a definition of terrorism and the Security Council fails to make proper use of its own definition, any counter-terrorism resolution will be open to abuse. Resolution 2178 also introduces some new human rights risks, while the counter-terrorism field enters more forcefully into the regulation of border crossing, and introduces the legally controversial notion of 'foreign terrorist fighter'. However, resolution 2178 is also significantly new in its focus on CVE under the guises of Security Council Chapter VII action. While risks remain in the implementation of the resolution related to the abuse of the notion of extremism, discriminatory practices in community engagement, civil society repression through CVE engagement, the right to privacy and freedom of expression online, resolution 2178 reflects the hope that a more preventive long-term approach may also be entering the Security Council agenda and through its committees will form a part of global counter-terrorism, in which human rights protection is also a vehicle to prevent and counter terrorism.

232 UN Doc. S/2015/683, paras. 16–18.
233 E.g., see Romaniuk (n 129), at 32 and 33.
234 Sharia (n 150).

6. Acting ethically in the shadows: Intelligence gathering and human rights

Richard Barrett and Tom Parker

At the outset, it is important to make a clear distinction between domestic and foreign intelligence collection. The techniques practiced in both disciplines are essentially the same, but there are nevertheless important, indeed critical, differences. In democratic societies, domestic intelligence collection is typically a well-regulated activity that takes place within the same broad legal framework as more traditional law enforcement activities. By contrast, foreign intelligence collection is often conducted with deliberate disregard for foreign laws, espionage is after all an inherently illegal activity, but it is not conducted in an entirely lawless manner. In democracies, externally-focused intelligence agencies operate in accordance with the domestic laws of their parent country, even when breaking other nations' laws overseas. International human rights law is every bit an obligation for the intelligence community as it is for any other field of government, although international law does recognize the legitimate sensitivities that surround issues relating to national security.

While recognizing the need for intelligence gathering and acknowledging that gathering such intelligence may require the adoption of extraordinary measures and approaches,[1] international human rights law ascribes limits to how such extraordinary measures can be used. First and foremost, intelligence collection, by its very nature, is likely to infringe aspects of the right to privacy that all individuals enjoy under international human rights law. However, there are six accepted grounds in international law under which it may be acceptable to interfere with an individual's or group's privacy: National security, public safety, the

[1] For example, see 'Report of the UN High Commissioner for Human Rights on the protection of human rights and fundamental freedoms while countering terrorism', UN Doc. A/HRC/16/50.

economic wellbeing of the country, the prevention of disorder or crime, protection of public health or morals, and the protection of the rights and freedoms of others. All but public health and morals fall squarely within an intelligence service's purview. While there is a growing body of jurisprudence on the use of so-called Special Investigation Techniques by law enforcement and domestic security agencies – for instance, telephone intercepts, eavesdropping devices, surveillance tools, undercover operations and human source recruitment – there is far less jurisprudence that touches upon the collection of foreign intelligence although perhaps some basic principles can be inferred from court rulings, as well as other international bodies, particularly regarding mass data collection.

The UN's Human Rights Committee has noted that any law authorizing interference with an individual's right to privacy must itself comply with the provisions, aims and objectives of the International Covenant on Civil and Political Rights (ICCPR).[2] The Human Rights Committee also added that the reference in Article 17 to 'arbitrary interference' had been introduced intentionally 'to guarantee that even interference provided for by law should be in accordance with the provisions, aims and objectives of the Covenant and should be, in any event, reasonable in the particular circumstances'.[3] In the case of *Toonen v. Australia*, the Committee has further interpreted the concept of reasonableness in this context to indicate 'any interference with privacy must be proportional to the end sought and be necessary in the circumstances of any given case'.[4] The UN Office of the High Commissioner for Human Rights has further emphasized that States have an obligation to protect against the arbitrary exercise of Special Investigation Techniques.[5]

In *Klass v. Germany* (1978) the European Court of Human Rights stated that any system of secret surveillance conducted by the State must be accompanied by adequate and effective guarantees against abuse.[6] More recently in *Szabó and Vissy v. Hungary* (2016) the Court ruled that the 2011 National Security Act introduced by the Hungarian government

---

[2] UN Human Rights Committee (1994), 'General Comment 16', UN Doc. HRI/GEN/1/Rev.1 at 21, para. 3.

[3] Ibid., para. 4.

[4] Human Rights Committee (1994), *Toonen v. Australia*, Communication No. 488/1992, UN Doc. CCPR/C/50/D/488/1992, para. 8.3.

[5] Office of the High Commissioner for Human Rights (2008), *Human Rights, Terrorism and Counter-terrorism, Fact Sheet No. 32* (July 2008), at 45.

[6] *Klass v. Germany*, App. no. 5029/71 (ECtHR, 6 September 1978), para. 50.

conferred powers on State agents so overly broad and ill-defined that they could target 'virtually anyone',[7] commenting further: 'A measure of secret surveillance can be found as being in compliance with the Convention only if it is strictly necessary, as a general consideration, for the safeguarding of democratic institutions and, moreover, if it is strictly necessary, as a particular consideration, for the obtaining of vital intelligence in an individual operation'.[8] The use of 'strict' and 'vital' clearly signals the Court's intention to set a very high threshold.

But, it should be noted, the cases cited above all refer to domestic intelligence gathering and so the extent to which they also impact foreign intelligence operations is still open to considerable debate. Perhaps the most that can be said is that foreign intelligence operations must be necessary, proportional, and precisely targeted in their effect; intelligence activities should be regulated by domestic law; they cannot abuse an individual's fundamental human rights; and a criminal act committed for intelligence purposes is still a criminal act, and any country possessing sufficient jurisdiction is well within its rights to bring the perpetrator to justice. The latter point is the principle reason why so many intelligence officers serve overseas under diplomatic cover – should an operation go wrong, as in the case of the alleged Central Intelligence Agency (CIA) officer Ryan Fogle detained in Moscow in May 2013,[9] the diplomatic immunity afforded by their cover position is the only thing that keeps them out of jail.

It follows therefore that governments assume and accept that both their own foreign intelligence services – and those of other States – will act illegally in the interest of national security in that they will try to gain information to which they have no legal right of access. But this should not set a different standard between domestic and foreign intelligence services when it comes to international obligations under human rights law. It is a legal curiosity that whereas the US Constitution and a large body of US law protects US citizens from intrusive or abusive action by their own government, wherever they are in the world, it does not afford the same protections to the citizens of other countries. For example, a US launched drone strike on a US citizen abroad reportedly requires a higher

---

[7] *Szabó and Vissy v. Hungary*, App. no. 37138/14 (ECtHR, 12 January 2016) para. 89.

[8] Ibid., para. 73.

[9] Fogle was arrested while allegedly attempting to recruit a Russian counter-terrorism official and subsequently declared persona non grata.

standard of justification and a higher level of clearance than an attack on a non-US citizen. Similarly, although the CIA interpreted its authority to counter the al Qaeda threat following the attacks of 9/11 to include kidnap, illegal detention and 'enhanced interrogation techniques' that were later considered torture, it took care to conduct these operations abroad and against non-US citizens. Not only are these double standards ethically wrong, but the actions themselves remain, prima facie illegal under international human rights law.

Leaving these egregious examples aside, while intelligence officers operating overseas do sometimes break foreign law in pursuit of their country's national interest, it does not automatically follow that all intelligence officers are scofflaws who will stop at nothing to secure their objective. The other side of the coin is that intelligence officers also work in a highly controlled environment. To obtain and maintain a security clearance requires a certain amount of moral rectitude and a lifetime of law abiding behavior. As in the military sphere, legal advisers often play a critical role in the planning of intelligence operations. Effective parliamentary oversight, where it exists, ensures an element of accountability. The modern intelligence officer is painfully aware that he longer works entirely in the shadows.

Nonetheless, in the context of the post-9/11 conflict against Al Qaeda and its affiliates and successors, intelligence personnel have come under more pressure than ever to achieve results and this has led some western intelligence officers to commit well-documented human rights abuses. To be crystal clear, this is both illegal and indefensible, and when such incidents occur States have an obligation to investigate them and bring the perpetrators to justice. But to borrow a well-worn aphorism, it is also worse than a crime, it is a blunder. As we will seek to demonstrate below, it is also clearly possible to collect intelligence on potential terrorism threats both at home and abroad entirely within the boundaries of existing human rights law. While history offers plenty of examples of intelligence agencies around the world that have exceeded these boundaries, it is also replete with evidence that such activity was both unproductive and unnecessary.

1. HUMAN SOURCES AND INTERNATIONAL HUMAN RIGHTS LAW

A human intelligence asset can be the most valuable of all intelligence sources, and it is the threat that terrorist organizations tend to fear the most.[10] The Brazilian revolutionary Carlos Marighella took care to warn readers of his *Minimanual of the Urban Guerrilla* that 'the worst enemy of the urban guerrilla and the major danger we run is infiltration into our organization by a spy or informer'.[11] The reason for this concern is pretty self-evident – unlike more passive intelligence collection methods, a human source is dynamic, responsive to direction, and, above all, sentient. Such a source can offer insights other intelligence assets cannot, and, as Marighella noted, they come in two basic varieties – informants, private individuals already associated with the target, and spies, agents of the State who successfully manage to infiltrate a target group or operation. While infiltrating a trained agent or an undercover officer into an organization can be both more dangerous and more difficult than recruiting an informant who is already inside or close to it, the advantage of manoeuvring a directed source or a professional officer into such a position is that they tend to be substantially more reliable assets in the field and to have a great deal more credibility in court.

There is nothing in international human rights law to prevent State agencies from using either informants or spies, indeed it is actively encouraged by international institutions. The United Nations Convention against Transnational Organized Crime (UNTOC) encourages State parties to make use of participating informants in the investigation of organized crime groups, and the same logic can be applied to terrorist groups.[12] However, human intelligence operations are governed by the same human rights obligations as any other special investigation technique – recruiters cannot commit human rights violations, criminal acts, blackmail or threaten suspects to gain their cooperation. In addition, acting as an informant on or inside a terrorist group is inherently dangerous and the State has an obligation under human rights law to protect the life and security of its asset.

---

[10] It is worth noting that structured terrorist organizations almost invariably create a counter-intelligence department early on as part of their central directorate.

[11] Carlos Marighella (1970), *Minimanual of the Urban Guerrilla* (Havana: Tricontinental).

[12] Article 26 of the UN Convention against Transnational Organized Crime (UNTOC). See UN Office on Drugs and Crime (UNODC), Terrorism Prevention Branch (2014), 'Counter-Terrorism Legal Training Curriculum: Module 4 Human Rights and Criminal Justice Responses to Terrorism', https://www.unodc.org/documents/terrorism/Publications/Module_on_Human_Rights/Module_HR_and_CJ_responses_to_terrorism_ebook.pdf, accessed 11 October 2017, p. 91.

It is not uncommon for an informant operating in a criminal milieu to be put in a position where he or she may be expected by criminal confederates to commit a criminal act or risk exposure. States may therefore promise an informant immunity from prosecution should they be asked to participate in certain acts. The UNODC Model Legislative Provisions against Organized Crime, which are intended to assist States in implementing UNTOC, offer some guidance on the type of activities that an informant (or for that matter an undercover officer) infiltrated into a criminal group might reasonably undertake without being held criminally responsible, such as making available 'legal and financial means, transport, storage, housing and communications needed for the perpetration of those offences'.[13]

However, there is a limit to which a human intelligence asset can lawfully transgress laws in the public interest. International human rights law also places important restrictions on the activities of an informant acting under the direction of the State or its representatives – even when an informant is working for the authorities it is completely impermissible for him or her to participate in the abuse of fundamental human rights, such as acts involving killing, enforced disappearance or torture and ill-treatment, since the 'prohibition on torture and the arbitrary deprivation of life are absolute and cannot be justified, even by reference to important law enforcement goals such as the investigation of terrorism'.[14] Immunity must not lead to impunity where serious human rights violations are at stake.[15] It should also be stressed that the practice of the various international criminal tribunals has established the general principle under international criminal law that no one can be granted immunity from prosecution for involvement in war crimes, crimes against humanity, genocide or acts of torture.

There is no shortage of modern examples of law enforcement and intelligence agencies recruiting or turning members of terrorist groups and putting them back to work in the service of the State. British intelligence enjoyed considerable success in penetrating the Provisional

---

[13] 'Counter-Terrorism Legal Training Curriculum', ibid., at 93. See also UNODC (2012), Model Legislative Provisions against Organized Crime, https://www.unodc.org/documents/organized-crime/Publications/Model_Legislative_Provisions_UNTOC_Ebook.pdf, accessed 11 October 2017, at Article 15, paragraph 3.

[14] 'Counter-Terrorism Legal Training Curriculum' (n 12), at 93.

[15] Organization for Security and Cooperation in Europe (2007), *Countering Terrorism, Protecting Human Rights: A Manual* (Warsaw: OSCE/ODIHR), p. 144.

IRA despite the close-knit world of Irish republicanism. In the mid 1980s British military intelligence officers recruited a former Provisional IRA Quartermaster called Frank Hegarty who was aggrieved about his dismissal from his clandestine post by the local IRA commander in Londonderry, Martin McGuinness. The surprisingly moralistic McGuinness disapproved of Hegarty leaving his wife for his mistress. After Hegarty was able to worm his way back into the IRA's good graces he provided crucial intelligence on a major arms shipment sent to the Provisional IRA by Libya's Colonel Gaddafi.[16] Perhaps one of Britain's most significant successes was the recruitment of Denis Donaldson, a former Provisional IRA gunman who had taken part in the 1970 Short Strand gun battle between republicans and loyalists, and had been incarcerated in Long Kesh prison for terrorism-related offences. He also acted as one of the Provisional IRA's go-betweens with terrorist groups in Lebanon, including Hezbollah. In the 1990s he became a prominent figure in Sinn Fein and in 2000 was appointed the administrator for the party's bloc in the Northern Irish Assembly. He was well placed to pass crucial insights on republican positions to the British government as it negotiated the Good Friday Agreement that helped bring the conflict in Northern Ireland to an end. Donaldson publicly confessed to his role as an informer in December 2005, and was murdered by the Real IRA four months later.

British intelligence has also reportedly enjoyed some success infiltrating Al Qaeda. One apparent case that has received considerable publicity is that of Aimen Dean, a young Saudi who fought in Bosnia as a mujahedin volunteer alongside Bosnian government forces before being drawn into the orbit of Al Qaeda where he became a religious counselor working with the organization's new recruits. By his account, Dean began to question the legitimacy of Al Qaeda's use of terrorist violence in the aftermath of the 1998 attacks on the US embassies in Nairobi and Dar-es-Salaam, which killed many innocent local citizens in addition to US embassy staff. Seeking guidance from Al Qaeda's senior religious adviser, Abu Abdullah al-Muhajir, he found the arguments used to justify the collateral injury to innocent civilians, grounded as they were in a thirteenth-century fatwa written in response to Mongol incursions into Muslim lands, completely unconvincing and began to turn away from the organization. He left to the Gulf for medical treatment at the end of 1998 privately determined to leave Al Qaeda and while he was there, he says

---

[16] Stephen Grey (2015), *The New Spymasters: Inside Espionage from the Cold War to Global Terror* (New York: St Martin's Press), pp. 76 and 77.

he was approached by the Secret Intelligence Service (SIS) and ultimately recruited. After a number of months being debriefed by British intelligence officers he was asked if he would be prepared to go back to Al Qaeda and act as an informer. Dean says he agreed to the plan and remained an active intelligence source for many years. In an interview with the BBC conducted in 2015 Dean was asked if he had had any moral qualms about betraying his former comrades:

> Whatever moral misgivings I had, I have my ex-comrades to thank for driving those moral misgivings away because the more I saw what they were planning – for example, I was there basically when al-Qaeda was constructing their first workable chemical device and talking about this with such glee and such deep psychopathic satisfaction ... that is when you say to yourself, 'Why do I have any moral misgivings about spying on you guys?' Whatever they are doing is justifying whatever you are doing.[17]

Morten Storm, also known as Murad Storm Al-Denmarki, is another interesting case. After a troubled childhood, Storm joined the Bandidos motorcycle gang. He also became interested in Islam after coming across a biography of the Prophet Mohammed in his local library. He was arrested in 1997, befriended a Danish convert to Islam in prison and began to become more serious about his faith, which led him into extremist circles in both Denmark and the UK. Over time he also became friendly with Anwar al-Awlaki, the US-born religious scholar who would become the spiritual adviser to Al Qaeda in the Arabian Peninsula. In this period he says he was approached by several western intelligence agencies but rebuffed them all. But after he found his path to joining the Islamic Courts Union in Somalia blocked by Ethiopian troops gaining control of Mogadishu airport he began to question God's purpose for him. Storm eventually began to reject the extremist narrative promoted by his friends: 'Now I thought of the twin towers, Bali, Madrid in 2004, London in 2005 ... If they were part of Allah's preordained plan, I now wanted no part of it ... My loss of faith was as frightening as it was sudden ... I was the convert unconverted'.[18] Storm sought out the Danish Security and Intelligence Service (PET) and offered to spy on his former comrades for them – in doing so, Storm became a distinct type of human intelligence asset known in the jargon of espionage as 'a volunteer'.

---

[17] Peter Marshall (2015), 'The spy who came in from al-Qaeda', BBC News Magazine, 3 March, http://www.bbc.com/news/magazine-31700894, accessed 21 October 2015.

[18] Morten Storm (2014), *Agent Storm: My Life Inside Al Qaeda and the CIA* (New York: Atlantic Monthly Press), pp. 118 and 122.

According to Storm, the Danes were delighted to take him up on his offer, and introduced him to British and American intelligence officers. Storm claims that it was his information that enabled the US to establish the whereabouts of al-Awlaki in Yemen.

Having an asset in place who holds the trust of terrorist group members opens up further possibilities beyond the simple acquisition of intelligence, it can allow law enforcement and security agencies to disrupt terrorist plots before they escalate to the point at which the public is put at risk. A tactic often favored by the authorities is the sting operation, in which aspiring terrorists are unwittingly given the space by a person they trust to incriminate themselves in tightly controlled circumstances, such as an arms deal or a planned attack. When the British Security Service (MI5) learned in 2001 that the Real IRA was looking for a 'rogue State' to sponsor its operations,[19] MI5 officers posing as representatives of the Iraqi Intelligence Service met with members of the Real IRA in Dublin, Slovakia, Austria and Budapest before triggering an arms sting in Piest'any, Slovakia, that resulted in the arrest and subsequent conviction of three of the organization's members: Fintan O'Farrell, Declan Rafferty and Michael McDonald. Operation Samnite was the first MI5 operation in which evidence was gathered entirely overseas and it still stands out today as an exemplar of the power of international cooperation.[20]

In undercover operations and sting operations any individual acting under the direction of the authorities – law enforcement officers, intelligence officials, police informants or intelligence assets – must be careful to avoid any situation in which they become the instigator or agent provocateur behind a crime – such action on the part of the authorities is entrapment. Entrapment occurs when a person who would not otherwise be predisposed to commit an offence is encouraged to do so by a government official who then instigates prosecution against the same individual. On 26 November 2010, accompanied by an undercover FBI Special Agent, Mohamed Osman Mohamud, a Somali-American student at Oregon State University, tried to detonate a car bomb near a public Christmas tree lighting ceremony in Portland's Pioneer Courthouse Square attended by thousands of families. The bomb had been constructed with the FBI's help from inert material and did not explode. However, Mohamud did not know this and made a triggering call from

---

[19] Jason Bennetto (2002), 'Irish terrorists captured in MI5 sting plead guilty', *The Independent*, 3 May.

[20] Richard Norton-Taylor (2002), '30 years in jail for Real IRA trio', *The Guardian*, 8 May.

his cellphone to the bomb's detonator. He was then arrested. Mohamud had first come to notice because he had made contact with a suspected Al Qaeda recruiter in the Middle East, and because he had written an article on physical fitness for an English-language publication called *Jihad Recollections*. An undercover FBI Special Agent made contact with Mohamud in June 2010 posing as a terrorist. In early November 2010, undercover FBI agents traveled to a remote location with Mohamud for a trial run of the bombing in which Mohamud actually detonated a functional backpack bomb.

In a pre-emptive strategy in the Pioneer Courthouse Square case, to rebut allegations of entrapment the FBI agents deliberately offered Mohamud multiple less violent alternatives to take action in support of Al Qaeda's cause, including prayer, but Mohamud insisted he wanted to play an 'operational' role. In an affidavit, the FBI stated that Mohamud chose the venue for the attack and also shrugged off attempts to derail the plot when it was under way. US Attorney General Eric Holder told reporters: 'There were a number of opportunities the defendant was given to retreat and to take a different path and he chose at every step to continue'.[21] Mohamud was reportedly told several times that his planned bomb could kill women and children but he told agents: 'Since I was 15 I thought about all this ... It's gonna be a fireworks show ... a spectacular show'.[22]

The European Court of Human Rights has explored the question of entrapment in some detail. Two cases in particular, both relating to drug purchases, illustrate the basic principle at work quite clearly: *Francisco Teixeira de Castro v. Portugal* and *Grigoriy Arkadyevich Vanyan v. Russia.* In the Portuguese case a textile worker was offered money by two plainclothes police officers to supply them with heroin. Although he had no previous criminal record, Mr Teixeira de Castro did have the necessary contacts to obtain the drug.[23] Tempted by the money, the applicant accepted the officers' request and was subsequently charged and convicted of a drug offence. In reviewing the case the Court concluded that the officers 'did not confine themselves to investigating Mr. Teixeira de Castro's criminal activity in an essentially passive manner, but exercised an influence such as to incite the commission of

21 Dina Temple-Raston (2010), 'Alleged Portland bomber to claim entrapment', National Public Radio, 30 November, http://www.npr.org/2010/11/30/131704930/alleged-portland-bomber-to-claim-entrapment, accessed 7 June 2017.

22 Liz Robbins and Edward Wyatt (2010), 'Somali-born teenager held in Oregon bomb sting', *New York Times*, 27 November.

23 *Teixeira de Castro v. Portugal*, App. no. 44/1997/828/1034 (ECtHR, 9 June 1998).

the offence'.[24] The Russian case is very similar except that in this instance it was a police informant, rather than a police officer, who encouraged the suspect to make a drug purchase.[25] The 'passivity' standard set by the European Court essentially prohibits the authorities from playing any kind of active role in the commission of a criminal act as a pretext to making an arrest. Any evidence obtained as a result of police incitement must be excluded from trial.[26]

One final tactic often used in human intelligence operations is disruption – a concept as simple as it is efficient. Disruptions are non-judicial interventions designed simply to upset a terrorist group's plans. A disruption might be as simple as increasing the security presence around a target or releasing advance warning of an attack to the media, so that a terrorist cell is panicked into aborting its operation. On occasion, the authorities might even approach the suspect directly and warn him or her that the State is aware of their plans knowing that this leaves them with little choice but to abandon them. After the bombing of the Khobar Towers housing facility in Dhahran, Saudi Arabia, by a Saudi offshoot of Hezbollah, which killed 19 Americans in June 1996, the Clinton White House debated many military and non-military responses against Iran. One response that was implemented consisted of a large-scale covert operation that 'outed' Iranian agents around the world, putting them on notice that their affiliation was known to US intelligence, in order to deter Tehran from threatening US facilities. Among the participants was then-CIA station chief to Saudi Arabia John Brennan, who reportedly knocked on the car window of an Iranian intelligence officer, and announced: 'Hello, I'm from the U.S. embassy, and I've got something to tell you'.[27] The Iranian was left knowing his cover was blown, and wondering just how much the US knew about his activities and how badly his operational security had been compromised. For an operative in the field such uncertainty can be paralyzing.

---

24 Ibid., paras. 37 and 38.

25 *Vanyan v. Russia*, App. no. 53203/99 (ECtHR, 15 March 2006), paras. 45–50.

26 *Ramanauskas v. Lithuania*, App. no. 74420/01 (ECtHR, 5 February 2008), para. 60.

27 George Tenet (2009), *At the Center of the Storm* (New York: HarperCollins).

2. INTELLIGENCE AGENCIES AND TORTURE

The use of torture, or cruel, inhuman or degrading treatment, to compel suspects in custody to divulge information is not an approach most intelligence officers in the western world would consider to have any place in their profession. However, it is also an incontrovertible fact that some western intelligence and security agencies, just like some western military and police organizations, have made the mistake of experimenting with such tactics in their struggle with terrorist groups of one sort or another. They have gained little intelligence and lost much credibility by doing so, as the sordid story of the CIA's 'enhanced interrogation' program following the attacks of 9/11 demonstrates only too clearly.[28]

Proponents of torture often contend that it gets results that cannot be obtained using lawful techniques. The counterfactual is of course impossible to prove one way or another in any individual case, but while undoubtedly some people may cooperate under duress, the historical record also clearly shows that others do not. Professor Darius Rejali noted in an extensive study of the Gestapo's use of torture that this most brutal of organizations failed to break senior leaders of French, Danish, Polish and German resistance,[29] and that, compared to the information generated from public cooperation and informers, the leads gained from torture were, to quote an internal Gestapo report, 'pathetic'.[30] There are many other well-documented examples of members of armed groups resisting coercive interrogation.

The use of torture during the Battle of Algiers in 1957, fought between the French military and the indigenous Algerian independence movement led by the *Front de Libération Nationale* (FLN), is often held up as an example of torture being used to good effect to counter terrorism, but the historical record is rather more complicated than its advocates would

---

[28] The CIA use of 'enhanced interrogation techniques' was examined in detail by the US Senate Select Committee on Intelligence (SSCI), 'Committee Study of the Central Intelligence Agency's Detention and Interrogation Program', released on 9 December 2014, available at http://www.intelligence.senate.gov/study2014/sscistudy1.pdf, accessed 8 May 2017. See also UN Human Rights Council (2010),'Joint study on global practices in relation to secret detention in the context of countering terrorism of the Special Rapporteur on the promotion and protection of human rights and fundamental freedoms while countering terrorism', UN Doc. A/HRC/13/42.

[29] Darius Rejali (2007), *Torture and Democracy* (Princeton: Princeton University Press), p. 496.

[30] Darius Rejali (2007), '5 myths about torture and truth', *The Washington Post*, 16 December. See also Rejali (n 29).

have one believe. To be sure, some individuals tortured in French custody undoubtedly provided some useful information. However, as one French interrogator acknowledged, it was still difficult to separate the wheat from the chaff: 'Just as the interrogation starts they speak abundantly, cite the names of the dead or militants on the lam, indicate the placement of an old arms cache in which we will find only a couple of documents without interest'.[31] Furthermore, the FLN hierarchy knew that the men under its command faced torture if captured and moved to exploit the situation by instructing its fighters to give up the names and locations of their more moderate rivals in the *Mouvement National Algérien* (MNA).[32] The French were thus goaded into torturing MNA members, which only served to push their colleagues into the embrace of the FLN.[33]

In 2001 the former French intelligence officer Paul Aussaresses provoked an outcry in France by publishing a memoir, entitled *Services Spéciaux*, in which he described the harsh treatment he had meted out to the FLN operatives unlucky enough to fall into his hands: 'Beatings, electric shocks, and, in particular, water torture, which was the most dangerous technique for the prisoner'.[34] Aussaresses recalled one instance in which a prisoner died while being waterboarded without revealing anything of value with a chilling lack of remorse: 'I had no regrets over his death – if I had any regrets, it was because he did not talk'.[35] It wasn't the only time he failed to make someone talk – he admitted somewhat grudgingly in his memoir that his victims 'would talk either quickly or never'.[36] There wasn't much that Aussaresses was not prepared to do to someone unlucky enough to be placed in his custody, so we can take it from a very accomplished torturer that a willingness to torture does not guarantee results. Indeed, one of those apprehended by Aussaresses and his men was the editor of the pro-independence communist newspaper *Alger Républicain*, Henri Alleg. Despite being subjected to electric shocks and water torture, burned, beaten, and drugged with sodium pentothal, Alleg famously did not give up the name of the

---

31 Rejali (n 29), at 481.

32 National Algerian Movement.

33 Rejali (n 29), at 481 and 482.

34 Paul Aussaresses (2002), *The Battle of the Casbah: Terrorism and Counterterrorism in Algeria 1955–1957* (New York: Enigma Books), p. 128. *The original French title was Services Spéciaux: Algérie 1955–57.*

35 Adam Shatz (2001), 'The Battle of Algiers', *The Nation*, 18 June, http://www.thenation.com/article/battle-algiers-0/, accessed 30 December 2015.

36 Aussaresses (n 34), at 128.

individual who had hidden him from the authorities.[37] Henri Alleg's account of his treatment in French custody, *La Question*, published in 1958, became an international sensation.[38]

Despite the FLN's sly tactics and the bravery of individual captives, torture may have helped briefly to tip the balance in France's favor during the Battle of Algiers, but it is important to note that it did so at a profound strategic cost. The use of torture further radicalized Algerian Arabs, it alienated the French public, it contributed to the political collapse of the Fourth Republic, and it eroded good order and discipline within the French army to the point that disgruntled military personnel led two abortive coup attempts in 1958 and 1961. French military veterans also established the nativist terrorist group, the *Organisation de l'Armée Secrète* (OAS), and later the *Conseil National de la Résistance* (CNR)[39] which attempted to assassinate French President Charles de Gaulle on several occasions.[40] Algeria gained its independence in 1962, following a referendum in which 99.72 percent of those taking part (most European settlers had already left for France) voted in favor.

The *ne plus ultra* of the utilitarian argument in favor of torture is the ticking bomb thought-experiment.[41] Paul Aussaresses summarized the argument in *Services Spéciaux*: 'Just think for a moment that you are personally opposed to torture as a matter of principle and that you have arrested a suspect who is clearly involved in preparing a violent attack. The suspect refuses to talk. You choose not to insist. Then the attack takes place and it's extremely bloody. What explanation will you give to the victim's parents, the parents of a child, for instance, whose body was torn to pieces by the bomb, to justify the fact that you didn't use every method available to force the suspect into talking'.[42] As a thought-experiment the ticking bomb scenario dispenses with all the complications that make the real world so difficult to navigate, and as such it may provoke an interesting philosophical discussion but it has little value

---

37 See Henri Alleg (1958), *The Question* (New York: George Braziller Inc.).

38 Available at http://www.tandfonline.com/doi/abs/10.1080/095465507014 76141?journalCode=ftpv20, accessed 11 October 2017.

39 National Council of Resistance.

40 Paul Henissart (1970), *Wolves in the City: The Death of French Algeria* (New York: Simon and Schuster), pp. 475 and 476.

41 Rod Morgan and Tom Williamson (2009), 'A critical analysis of the utilitarian case for torture and the situational factors that lead some people to become torturers', in Tom Williamson et al., *International Developments in Investigative Interviewing* (Abingdon: Routledge), p. 131.

42 Aussaresses (n 34), at p. 41 of ebook.

as a tool for analyzing public policy. In the fantasy constructed by Aussaresses and his fellow enthusiasts you always have the right suspect in custody, the bomb is always real, the suspect always has the information you need, the suspect always talks when tortured, and the information the suspect then provides is always sufficiently accurate and detailed to avert the looming catastrophe. However, as Bob Brecher points out in *Torture and the Ticking Bomb*, in the real world none of these variables is quite so assured.[43]

Torture is a very blunt tool. Interviewers rarely have all the facts at their disposal when conducting interviews and a discursive, rapport-based interview technique is much more likely to assist the interviewer successfully navigate complex narratives of which he often has limited prior knowledge because it allows the subject to introduce new information into the conversation, and correct misapprehensions and flawed intelligence. Physical abuse creates a very different dynamic. The torturer sets the boundaries of the interview and it is driven forward by the knowledge he or she already possesses, and the assumptions he or she has made. The torturer is mostly reduced to asking closed questions, which further confines and restricts his or her exchange with the prisoner. French paratroopers were able to use torture with some initial intelligence-gathering success in the Battle of Algiers because they were seeking very specific information – a name or a location – and closed questions can at least adequately support this objective if the information the interrogator has at the outset of the interrogation is accurate. As one French veteran of Algeria admitted: 'A profound knowledge of the [terrorist] organization is required. It is useless to ask a funds collector about caches of weapons or bombs'.[44]

In addition, the attraction to acts of wanton cruelty that lurks inside some human beings is another important consideration. The patina of legitimacy imparted by superior orders often liberates dark impulses – the social psychologist Philip Zimbardo famously dubbed this phenomenon the 'Lucifer Effect'.[45] The reality is that much of the abuse that takes place in the interview room is driven by the frustration of the interrogators themselves – or in the immediate aftermath of an incident by anger at the perpetrators – rather than by any genuine calculation that

---

43 See Bob Brecher (2007), *Torture and the Ticking Bomb* (Oxford: Blackwell Publishing).

44 Roger Trinquier (1964), *Modern Warfare: A French View of Counterinsurgency* (London: Pall Mall Press), p. 23.

45 See Philip Zimbardo (2007), *The Lucifer Effect: Understanding How Good People Turn Evil* (New York: Random House).

abuse will result in getting the suspect in front of them to share the information they need.

For all these reasons and more, the utilitarian debate about torture is not a simple equation in which one guilty man's pain is the price paid to protect the wider population, as the Georgetown Professor of Law and Philosophy David Luban has cogently observed, 'it is the debate between the certainty of anguish and the mere possibility of learning something vital and saving lives'.[46] The celebrated French author Albert Camus, who was born and raised in Algeria and was deeply affected by the brutal conflict between the FLN and French settlers, further noted that an act of torture does not occur in a vacuum: 'Torture has perhaps saved some, at the expense of honor, by uncovering thirty bombs, but at the same time it arouses fifty new terrorists who, operating in some other way and in some other place, will cause the death of even more innocent people'.[47] This is no mere literary flight of fancy.

It is now a relatively uncontroversial observation that the US adoption of so-called 'enhanced interrogation techniques' proved to be a profound misstep that generated little intelligence and provided Al Qaeda with a propaganda windfall – the US treatment of prisoners was mentioned 32 times in Al Qaeda propaganda messages between 2003 and 2010, and by affiliate groups 26 times.[48] The first issue of the online magazine *Inspire*, published by Al Qaeda in the Arabian Peninsula in the summer of 2010, featured an essay by Osama bin Laden in which he specifically referenced 'the crimes at Abu Ghraib and Guantanamo, those ugly crimes which shook the conscience of humanity'.[49] US General David Petraeus, former Director of the CIA and commander of US forces in both Iraq and Afghanistan, had presciently observed in an interview earlier the same year: 'Abu Ghraib and other situations like that are non-biodegradable. They don't go away. The enemy continues to beat you with them like a stick'.[50] Mark Fallon, a US Naval Criminal Investigative Service (NCIS)

---

[46] David Luban (2006), 'Liberalism, torture and the ticking bomb', in Karen Greenberg (ed.), *The Torture Debate in America* (New York: Cambridge University Press), pp. 46 and 47.

[47] Albert Camus (1963), 'Preface to Algerian Reports', in Albert Camus, *Resistance, Rebellion and Death* (New York: Modern Library), p. 84.

[48] James Gordon Meek (2010), 'Gitmo fades as "recruiting tool for Al Qaeda"', *New York Daily News*, 25 January.

[49] Thérèse Postel (2013), 'How Guantanamo Bay's existence helps Al-Qaeda recruit more terrorists', *The Atlantic*, 12 April.

[50] Joseph Berger (2010), 'U.S. Commander describes Marja Battle as first salvo in campaign', *New York Times*, 21 February.

special agent who led the task force investigating the 2000 bombing of USS Cole and was a close colleague of the FBI agent Ali Soufan, who demonstrated that harsh treatment in that case added nothing to prior knowledge,[51] put it even more starkly, writing in 2014: 'It enabled – and, in fact, is still enabling – al Qaeda and its allies to attract more fighters, more sympathizers, and more money'.[52]

The use of torture and other forms of cruel, inhuman and degrading treatment by the US in this period also created significant ethical and legal dilemmas for some of its closest allies and European support for US counter-terrorism measures was drastically impacted by policies that clearly violated the European Convention on Human Rights.[53] Perhaps the most dramatic example of this was the *in absentia* conviction of 23 US agents in an Italian court for the role they played in the extraordinary rendition of radical Imam Hassan Mustafa Osama Nasr from Milan to Cairo in 2003.[54] Nine Italian officials, including two senior officers of the *Servizio per le Informazioni e la Sicurezza Militare* (SISMI),[55] also faced prosecution in the case. In 2012, Polish prosecutors charged the former head of Polish intelligence, Zbigniew Siemiatkowski, with 'unlawfully depriving prisoners of the their liberty' because of the alleged role he played in helping to establish a CIA black site in Stare Klejkuty, north-eastern Poland, in 2002–2003.[56] The Polish President at the time, Aleksander Kwasniewski, later ruefully admitted: 'We had concerns, but they did not include that the Americans would break the law in a knowing and uncontrolled way'.[57] The possibility of being held legally

---

51 See Ali H. Soufan (2011), *The Black Banners* (New York: W.W. Norton & Company).

52 Mark Fallon (2014), 'Dick Cheney was lying about torture', *Politico Magazine*, 8 December, http://www.politico.com/magazine/story/2014/12/torture-report-dick-cheney-110306.html#.VbvcDpNVikp, accessed 8 January 2016.

53 Intelligence and Security Committee (2007), 'Rendition', July, https://www.gov.uk/government/uploads/system/uploads/attachment_data/file/224654/rendition.pdf, accessed 11 October 2017, at pp. 12 and 13.

54 See Steve Hendricks (2010), *A Kidnapping in Milan: The CIA on Trial* (New York: W.W. Norton & Company).

55 Military Intelligence and Security Service.

56 Joanna Berendt and Nicholas Kulish (2012), 'Polish ex-official charged with aiding CIA', *The New York Times*, 27 March.

57 The Economist (2014), 'Detention site blues: Poles are not happy about CIA torture, but they need America too much to start a row', 11 December, https://www.economist.com/news/europe/21635984-poles-are-not-happy-about-cia-torture-their-soil-they-still-need-america-detention-site-blue, accessed 11 October 2017.

liable for the criminal acts of an allied power has inevitably had a chilling effect on the predisposition of some US allies to work so closely with their American counterparts. The British authorities have been surprisingly open about the difficulties that policies such as rendition to torture and the operation of secret prisons have caused the transatlantic 'special relationship'. The then Director General of MI5 Dame Eliza Manningham-Buller acknowledged in testimony before the Parliamentary Intelligence and Security Committee (ISC) in 2007: 'We certainly now have inhibitions ... greater inhibitions than we once did'.[58] Sir John Scarlett, then Chief of SIS, similarly reported that his agency sought 'credible assurances' that any action taken by the US on the basis of intelligence provided by UK agencies would be 'humane and lawful' and that when such assurances were lacking 'we cannot provide the information'.[59]

Darius Rejali has noted that there are essentially only three reasons for a State to employ torture: 'to intimidate, to coerce false confessions, and to gather accurate security information'.[60] Torturers may, through the exercise of brutality, successfully achieve the first two of these goals, but the record shows that as a means for collecting accurate information torture is unreliable, and its use comes at great personal, reputational and moral costs that can have a profoundly detrimental impact on counter-terrorism efforts by undermining popular support for the State, antagonizing key constituencies, and alienating much needed allies. This was certainly the experience of the US, which paid a high price for what comprehensive investigation has since established was an almost entirely unproductive policy.[61] When President Obama came into office in January 2009 one of his first actions was to issue Executive Order 13491 to improve the effectiveness of human intelligence gathering and to promote the safe, lawful, and humane treatment of individuals in US custody.[62] This executive order put a formal end to the use of so-called enhanced interrogation techniques and restricted the intelligence community to methods authorized and listed by the US Army Field Manual on Human Intelligence Collector Operations. Speaking at Fordham University in March 2010, Michael Sulick, then head of the CIA's

---

58 Intelligence and Security Committee (n 53), at 47.

59 Ibid.

60 Rejali (n 29), at 23.

61 See, inter alia, SSCI (n 28).

62 Barack Obama (2009), Executive Order 13491 – Ensuring Lawful Interrogations, The White House, 22 January, https://www.whitehouse.gov/the_press_office/EnsuringLawfulInterrogations, accessed 9 January 2016.

National Clandestine Service, told his audience 'I don't think we've suffered at all from an intelligence standpoint' because of this decision.[63]

3. HUMAN RIGHTS ISSUES SURROUNDING THE DISSEMINATION AND USE OF INTELLIGENCE

Regardless of the method of its acquisition, the use of intelligence can also give rise to human rights considerations. If intelligence is not used, it has no value. This may seem obvious, but the collector of intelligence is often far more concerned about the method of collection and the importance of protecting the source, than about the potential impact of the intelligence if disseminated. The most secure option will be to prevent all dissemination, and if the value of the information appears marginal and without immediate relevance, a decision to store the information without dissemination may be the most sensible course of action. Even when the information may have immediate value and relevance, if any action taken as a result could lead to the exposure of the source, then again the right decision may be to hold onto it until some collateral can be developed or to disseminate it but with restrictions on its use.

A famous example of this in the popular imagination occurred in World War II when the British government, through its successful penetration of the Enigma coding machine used by the German High Command, was thought to have known that the Luftwaffe intended to bomb the city of Coventry in November 1940. It was widely believed that the then Prime Minister, Winston Churchill, decided to suppress the information so as not to risk exposing the most significant intelligence breakthrough since the start of the war, and one that was likely to have a major impact on its outcome, so saving many more lives. In fact, although the code breakers had become aware that a massive bombing raid was in preparation, the target was not clear, with most believing it would be London or the South East of the country. But the myth persists, and usefully illustrates the tensions that can arise between the desire to collect more intelligence and the argument for using what has been collected already, even if it exposes the source.

A similar but real incident that had a major affect on the use of terrorist-related intelligence occurred in December 1988 around the

---

[63] Jeff Stein (2010), 'CIA's top spy: No losses from waterboarding ban', *Washington Post* Partner blog, 1 April, http://voices.washingtonpost.com/spy-talk/2010/04/cias_top_spy_no_losses_from_wa.html, accessed 8 January 2016.

bombing of Pan American flight 103 over Lockerbie in Scotland, which caused the death of 270 people. It was found that the US Embassy in Helsinki had received an anonymous tip that such an attack might occur on a Pan Am flight from Frankfurt to New York just two weeks beforehand. The Federal Aviation Administration issued a bulletin that the State Department distributed to numerous embassies abroad, but although the Moscow Embassy did make the bulletin available to the entire American community in Moscow (in error), there was a widespread impression in the public mind that the government had only warned its own personnel.

The subsequent enquiry into the attack looked at the issue of public notification at length, and concluded that 'either the information remains closely held by those with a legitimate need to know, or it must be made public'.[64] In other words, there should be no double standard. The Commission acknowledged the importance of credibility and specificity in deciding when to pass on threat intelligence to the public, but was clear in its recommendation that 'The U.S. Government should, as a matter of course and policy, consciously consider the question of notification and carefully review the factors outlined'.[65] As a result, the US government now makes public all terrorist threats to civilian targets that it regards as potentially credible, though it may still withhold specific detail if to release it might jeopardize the source. This reflects the general and common sense principle that all intelligence collection on terrorism has the ultimate objective of saving lives, and that the right to life is a right shared equally by all.

4. HUMAN RIGHTS ISSUES SURROUNDING THE SETTING OF INTELLIGENCE REQUIREMENTS

The decision to disseminate or to withhold intelligence, or to allow its onward use or to forbid it, is always influenced by the reason for collecting it in the first place. In terms of best practice, intelligence requirements are not set by intelligence collectors, but by those policy makers or government agencies that are the potential customers. They must bid for the intelligence resources by arguing the importance of getting the information that they seek. In all western countries, there will

[64] President's Commission on Aviation Security and Terrorism (1990), 'Report of the President's Commission on Aviation Security and Terrorism', 15 May, https://archive.org/details/PCASTreport, accessed 11 October 2017, Ch. 6.

[65] Ibid.

be many more requirements than there are resources available to fill them. 'Nice to know' does not make the cut in counter-terrorism, and nor should it. Human assets are not deployed lightly; it is unreasonable to have them risk their liberty or even their lives to collect information of low value. The intelligence requirement must also demonstrate within reason that the information cannot be obtained by overt means.

The intelligence requirement may be for action as well as information, such as the disruption operations mentioned above. But it must also be endorsed by all concerned as within the law, or, if outside the law, of sufficient value to merit an exemption to be provided by a designated official when the opportunity to achieve the objective arises or the planning gets to a point that offers a reasonable chance of success. In the UK this is a government minister or for more routine matters a senior official. In the US requirements are set by the Director of National Intelligence through an inter-agency process known as the National Intelligence Priorities Framework. Other ad hoc requirements emerge from the National Security Staff through a principals committee. At times the president himself will authorize an operation if its consequences may be particularly sensitive or controversial. Congress retains oversight by having control of the necessary budget. But however elaborate the process may be for setting the requirements, the agencies are generally left to decide on their own how best to meet them.

The collectors of intelligence, or those who take the approved counter-terrorist action, are not the only ones required to make a decision about the morality of the means, or the ethical and legal implications of the result. This should be a collective decision by government, as represented by the person signing off the submission or, in the case of the US, the finding. As such the decision becomes the collective decision of the society in whose name the government acts. The proper observance of the fundamental principles of human rights in intelligence requirement setting, intelligence collection and the dissemination of the product, is therefore of wider importance than merely as a way to control abuses by the individual intelligence officer or his customer. Terrorists are by definition people who object to how things are done by the governments they target; and although they aim to challenge public support for government policy by undemocratic means, largely through intimidation, it is important that in responding to the threat of terrorism the government does not reinforce the terrorist narrative that it acts against the public interest. Policies can change, but principles do not.

Terrorism, however, is an area where governments can all too easily abuse and debase the value of their intelligence services and operatives by seeing them as instruments of national politics rather than national security. Terrorism is too loosely defined in some jurisdictions to ensure that the capacity of the State to act in secret does not lead to abuses of human rights, even to the extent of the extra-judicial killing or incarceration of people in opposition who would not fit the more commonly accepted definitions of terrorism. Here the individual duty of all parties; the politicians, the intelligence services and the consumers of intelligence, must be to uphold international norms and conventions, even though this may require significant acts of individual courage, both moral and physical, in societies, of which there are many, where the organs of State are merely tools that the ruler uses to perpetuate his control.

5. THE SPECIAL ALLURE OF CLASSIFIED INFORMATION

It is reasonable for the customers of intelligence to expect it to tell them something new, important and interesting. This can lead to undue trust being placed in information that is classified because of the method of its acquisition, but not necessarily graded according to its reliability. Rightly or wrongly, something that is acquired at great effort and risk, and stamped secret in large red letters, is likely to have more weight than an analyst's report based on open source information. Unlike the analyst's report, however, an agent who is highly placed within a terrorist organization is likely to produce single source reports that cannot be corroborated by sources elsewhere because his access is unique. His reports may have serious impact on the rights of others; they may result in arrests and detentions, or in serious invasions of privacy, but they may nonetheless be wrong, whether deliberately misconstrued or innocently misreported. The nature of such source reporting makes it very unlikely that there is any meaningful opportunity to cross-examine its originator or even for a willing source to go back and check that what he reported was correct. The briefing, debriefing and examination of the motivation of sources is therefore not just a matter of good agent handling in the context of terrorism, but also of crucial importance in ensuring that human rights abuses do not result from misreported facts or erroneous assessments. In an area where information is always going to be in short supply, open to varying interpretations and often demanding immediate action, the risks of getting it wrong are considerable, as of course are the risks of doing nothing.

The issue of classification is accordingly one that has occupied intelligence services over the ages. A State will classify information according to the damage likely to arise from its unauthorized disclosure.

The damage may be commercial; it may be related to the security of the State; or it may be related to the effectiveness of policy, or the instruments of policy. An intelligence service will take a different approach, classifying its product according to the nature and sensitivity of the source. It may not be terribly important to know what a terrorist leader had for breakfast, but if only his cook has the answer, then the information is by definition highly classified. A third method is to classify information according to the reporting record of the source. Intelligence services and their customers have tried to combine all three criteria by grading sources according to the potential damage to the State, damage to the operation and reliability of the source, the first two referring to the need for protection of the information, the third related to its use.

6. ISSUES ARISING FROM INTELLIGENCE SHARING AND 'ACTION ON'

Not all intelligence that provides identifying particulars of a member of a terrorist group is problem free when it comes to the proper observance of human rights, especially when that intelligence also reveals the person's location. From a human rights point of view, handling this sort of intelligence can be highly problematic in the age of rendition and extra judicial killing. Domestic laws in most countries may be clear on such issues but they are not always in conformity with the laws of other countries. In some jurisdictions, such as currently in the US as a result of the powers conferred upon him by the Authorization for Use of Military Force adopted by Congress in September 2001, the president may order the killing of an individual 'in order to prevent any future acts of international terrorism against the United States',[66] where there is no

[66] See Public Law 107–40, 107th Congress, 18 September 2001, https://www.gpo.gov/fdsys/pkg/PLAW-107publ40/pdf/PLAW-107publ40.pdf, accessed 11 October 2017. The Authorization for the Use of Military Force adopted by Congress on 14 September 2001 and signed into law four days later was directed against the planners and perpetrators of the attacks of 9/11. This has governed all subsequent military action against terrorist groups, despite their increasingly tenuous connection with 9/11. In 2015, in order to cover the subsequent and additional threat posed by the so-called Islamic State, the White House proposed that Congress further authorize the limited use of the US armed forces against the Islamic State of Iraq and the Levant. Congress declined to do so.

reasonable prospect of arrest or other means of disruption.[67] This has led to the controversial use of armed drones in third countries, most notably Afghanistan, Pakistan, Somalia and Yemen, whether or not with the agreement of the relevant government.

A problem quickly arises where intelligence gathered by an agency that operates in a jurisdiction where such killing is not legal is passed to an agency that operates in one where it is, potentially exposing the originator to a significant legal liability. Limiting the right to take 'action on' without reference to the originator becomes extremely difficult, especially if the receiving agency believes that the information relates more to its own national security than to the originator's. In the worst case, the originating agency may face a difficult choice of withholding the information at the risk of failing to warn an ally of an impending attack so as to avoid complicity in possible action that might be against domestic law or international human rights law, or risking that transgression in the broader interest of preventing greater harm. Inevitably, by the very nature of intelligence on terrorists and terrorism, it is rare that a piece of information about the location of an individual is also clear about his immediate intentions.

These questions of the moral and legal dilemmas that arise from the ownership and control of intelligence and the right of a subsequent recipient to take 'action on' based on what it reveals have been debated at length, both between and within agencies. Some of the issues have been made public, for example in the report on rendition by the Intelligence Services Committee of the Houses of Parliament in the UK discussed earlier.[68] Realistically, it is not reasonable for any intelligence service providing information to another to have complete confidence that it will only be used in accordance with strictures laid down and assurances given at the time of exchange, especially in matters of life and death. But even where an intelligence service may notify another that one of its nationals is, for example, returning home from fighting with an extremist group abroad, so resulting in his arrest and incarceration under that country's law, if the extremist group is not proscribed by a Security Council resolution adopted under Chapter VII of the UN Charter, there may be disagreement whether such arrest is justified without more process to examine what activities the individual may have been involved in. If however the originating agency does not pass on the information,

---

67 A White House note of 23 May 2013 sets out the procedures and standards for drone use.

68 Intelligence and Security Committee (n 53), at 13.

the country of residence of the returning fighter may justifiably complain that the refusal is not in accordance with other Security Council resolutions, such as Security Council resolution 2253 (2015).[69]

Although the international community, including at the level of the Security Council, is increasingly insistent that intelligence on terrorism be shared, leaving aside any operational reasons for not doing so, for example, the risk that the source may be exposed by action taken as a result, there are often very real ethical or even legal issues to take into account as well. No rules can cover all eventualities, and enforcement of whatever rules are agreed will always be subject to the exigencies, interpretations and imperatives of the moment. Moral dilemmas litter the intelligence world, and are not made simpler by the environment in which it spins. Laws governing the collection of intelligence do not generally touch on its use, and for good reason, so leaving crucial questions up to the source, the source handler, their own house rules, and the requirements of the customer. What should be done, for example, if a highly placed source in an active terrorist group is able to provide evidence that would prove beyond doubt the innocence of a man convicted of terrorist acts, but only by exposing himself as an agent of the State, and so losing access to current attack planning and possibly risking his own life and liberty? And who should decide the right course of action in such cases? It may sound hypothetical, but such circumstances are not far-fetched.

7. ISSUES ARISING FROM TECHNICAL INTELLIGENCE OPERATIONS AND THE ROLE OF THE PRIVATE SECTOR

These issues also arise in those forms of intelligence collection that do not involve a human source. Although the revelations in 2013 and subsequently by Edward Snowden, a former US government contractor and employee of the CIA, went far beyond the National Security Agency's (NSA) domestic collection efforts, nonetheless he did initiate a useful debate on the way that the fear of terrorism had led to unauthorized intelligence collection activity that impinged on the individual rights to privacy of US citizens. The bulk collection of data on the basis that it

[69] Security Council resolution 2253 (2015), preliminary para. 29, http://www.un.org/en/ga/search/view_doc.asp?symbol=S/RES/2253(2015), accessed 11 October 2017.

might be useful in a subsequent investigation would seem not just reasonable but sensible from the point of view of an intelligence agent. The NSA was not acting to undermine the US, but rather to protect it. Nonetheless, the criticism of the NSA and the re-emphasis on its need to act within the law, and, if that seemed insufficient, argue for the law to be changed, were useful reminders that however well motivated and well intentioned any intelligence official may be, in a democracy he is not the one to decide that the interests of the State are better served by contravention rather than observance of the law.

A further debate concerning the interception of communications in the interest of preventing terrorism arises over the issue of encryption. During the latter half of 2015, new features developed for smart phones included a level of peer-to-peer encryption that even major government agencies like NSA could not easily break. The Director of the FBI urged commercial telecommunications companies to ensure that the government was provided a back door into their encryption software, while the tech companies responded that this would give a commercial edge to their non-US rivals and that the government should not demand they take such action voluntarily. It is hard to argue with the tech companies on this score. Highly secure peer-to-peer encryption of communications is now a fact of life, it cannot be uninvented and will presumably become more and more sophisticated as time goes by. Even if the vast majority of users of encryption only seek privacy, rather than to escape the scrutiny of the State, all other things being equal, they would be unlikely to choose a service that allowed the State access to their communications over one that did not. If the US government insists that the communications companies that operate in the US provide a back door to their encryption services, then the US government should introduce legislation that obliges them to do so. This of course would still not solve the problem that bad actors might choose alternative, foreign sources of encryption.

In the aftermath of the attacks in the US of September 2001, the intelligence services of most western countries could tap into a widespread sense of sympathy and obligation among the management of commercial companies that operated within their country's jurisdiction. They could ask informally for help with tracing communication links between suspects, and even revealing information about their clients and the content of their calls. This was true also in the financial world, where intelligence operatives could readily find officials willing to help in support of national counter-terrorism efforts to suppress or investigate the financing of terrorism. The intelligence officials were merely doing their job: recruiting sources with access to the information they required; but the assumption developed among government officials that anyone who could help should help. This was an extension of the 'either you are with us, or you are with the terrorists' doctrine promulgated by President Bush in his address to a joint Session of Congress on 20 September 2001.[70]

This attitude led to the outsourcing to the private sector of many of the moral and ethical – if not legal – decisions about privacy and proportionality in counter terrorism. But the private sector operates according to commercial decisions, and will maximize its profits insofar as the law allows. Asking a multi-national tech company to provide information voluntarily in one jurisdiction, begs the question as to what it should do with the same request in another, where the authorities may set the 'terrorism' bar considerably lower. In all cases, private companies that are privy to client information that merits protection under specific contract law and by more general rights to privacy, should not be asked to provide intelligence where a refusal to do so might lead to commercial disadvantage. If the government believes that such requests should be met then it should introduce appropriate laws. This then gives the option to both the company and its clients to decide whether or not they wish to do business in such an environment.

8. CONCLUSION

International law recognizes that States may need to recruit informants, conduct sting operations, intercept communications, and deploy electronic surveillance measures. Navi Pillay, the former UN High Commissioner for Human Rights, has acknowledged the vital role that intelligence collection plays in the prevention of terrorist violence: 'The use of accurate intelligence is indispensible to preventing terrorist acts and bringing individuals suspected of terrorist activity to justice'.[71] The Council of Europe's Committee of Experts on Special Investigation Techniques in relation to Acts of Terrorism similarly noted in a report published in 2005: 'The objective of the European Convention on Human Rights is not to disarm the authorities responsible for prevention or prosecution in criminal matters. The Convention sets out criteria in order

[70] See http://georgewbush-whitehouse.archives.gov/news/releases/2001/09/20010920-8.html, accessed 11 October 2017.

[71] Report of the United Nations High Commissioner for Human Rights on the protection of human rights and fundamental freedoms while countering terrorism, A/HRC/16/50, para. 33.

that the authorities' activities should constantly be guided by the rule of law and the pursuit of the democratic ideal'.[72]

Not every terrorist attack or national security threat can be prevented, and not every pivotal event can be foreseen. The harsh reality is that when opportunities to prevent attacks are missed, or some game-changing development catches the intelligence community by surprise, this typically reflects a failure of competency, imagination, or capacity on the part of the authorities, rather than any malign restriction or check placed on the intelligence services by the law. Clues that might have enabled the US authorities to disrupt the planning of the September 11 attacks on Washington and New York – most notably the presence of future hijackers Khalid al Mihdhar and Nawaf al Hazmi in the US – were not acted upon in large part because of the stovepiping that characterized the American intelligence community at the time.[73] The chance sightings of the London Transport bombers Mohammed Siddique Khan and Shazad Tanweer in the company of known Islamic extremists were not followed up because MI5 was overwhelmed by what seemed at the time to be more important investigative leads.[74] More intrusive powers would not have prevented either attack and would likely have just generated additional intelligence clutter further obscuring the needle represented by Al Qaeda's activities in a giant haystack of irrelevant data.[75] In the intelligence business less is often more, intelligence driven investigation is efficient; data driven investigation for the most part is not.

The tests set by international human rights law for the use of Special Investigative Techniques go to the heart of the dilemma that faces all intelligence agencies operating within democratic systems – how does one protect the public while also protecting the rights and freedoms they enjoy. There is little point adopting policies that ultimately undermine the institutions they are supposed to protect. As a bumper sticker popular in the US declaims: 'Freedom isn't free'. Some risk is inevitably involved

---

[72] Council of Europe (2005), *Terrorism: Special Investigation Techniques* (Strasbourg: COE), at p. 27.

[73] National Commission on Terrorist Attacks Upon the United States (2004), *The 9/11 Commission Report: Final Report of the National Commission on Terrorist Attacks Upon the United States*, Authorized Edition (New York: W.W. Norton and Company), at pp. 266–72.

[74] Intelligence and Security Committee (2009), 'Could 7/7 have been prevented? Review of the intelligence on the London terrorist attacks on 7 July 2005', HM Stationery Office, May, paras. 47 and 68–70.

[75] Rosa Brooks (2015), 'The Threat is Already Inside: And nine other truths about terrorism nobody wants to hear', *Foreign Policy*, 20 November.

living in a free society. The challenge is to get the balance right, to ensure, in the words of the current Director General of MI5, Andrew Parker, that being on the authorities' radar is not the same as being under their microscope.[76] Intelligence officers are a country's first line of defense and international human rights law provides an effective framework within which to operate. An intelligence service that loses touch with that reality may ultimately pose a bigger threat to the society it is seeking to protect, than any terrorist group or foreign power.

[76] Address by the Director General of the Security Service, Andrew Parker, to the Royal United Services Institute (RUSI), Whitehall, 8 October 2013.

7. The preventive criminal justice strategy against terrorism and its human rights implications

Ulrich Garms*

1. INTRODUCTION – THE PREVENTIVE CRIMINAL JUSTICE RESPONSE TO TERRORISM

In 2010, Ahmed Ghailani was on trial before a Federal Court in New York accused of playing a key role in organizing the 1998 Al Qaida bombings of the US Embassies in Kenya and Tanzania, which killed 224 people. Ghailani had been captured in Pakistan in 2004 and detained at a secret detention facility of the US Central Intelligence Agency (a so-called 'black site') and at the naval base in Guantánamo for five years before being put on trial in a civilian court. Key evidence against Ghailani was found as a result of statements he made – under torture, according to the defence – during his detention at the black site. The Federal judge ruled that evidence inadmissible on constitutional grounds.[1] As a result, the jury acquitted Ghailani on 284 out of 285 charges, including on the 224 counts of murder, and found him guilty on

* Programme Officer, Terrorism Prevention Branch, UN Office on Drugs and Crime. The views expressed in this chapter are the author's alone, and do not necessarily represent those of the UN.

1 In the ruling declaring inadmissible the evidence derived from Ghailani's collaboration with his interrogators at the black site, the judge stated: 'The Court has not reached this conclusion lightly. It is acutely aware of the perilous nature of the world in which we live. But the Constitution is the rock upon which our nation rests. We must follow it not only when it is convenient, but when fear and danger beckon in a different direction. To do less would diminish us and undermine the foundation upon which we stand'. US District Court Southern District of New York, *United States of America v. Ahmed Khalfan Ghailani*, Case no. S10 98 Crim. 1023(LAK), 12 July 2010.

only one charge: conspiracy to blow up US government buildings. The judge nonetheless imposed a sentence of life without parole.

The reaction to the outcome of this case showed that it was not only Ghailani who was on trial in the New York Federal Court, but also the idea that major terrorism cases can be tried before civilian courts, with defendants enjoying the full protection of constitutional rights and fair trial principles. US Attorney General Eric Holder concluded that '[t]oday's sentencing of Ahmed Ghailani shows yet again the strength of the American justice system in holding terrorists accountable for their actions'.[2] Human Rights Watch concurred: 'Trying Ghailani in US federal court rather than before a flawed, ad hoc military commission was the smart as well as the lawful thing to do'.[3]

An opinion piece in the *New York Post*, and many others in the United States, reached diametrically opposed conclusions:

> Is there any better proof that Team Obama's preferred approach to fighting terror – through civilian courts – is dangerously misguided than yesterday's acquittal of one of the 1998 US embassy bombers on all but one of 285 charges? … That obscene verdict – and the tortured, civilian-court process that led to it – should put an end, once and for all, to any thought of trying other terrorists in similar fashion. … President Obama and Attorney General Eric Holder need to learn from this horrific case. No more civilian trials for terrorists.[4]

The present chapter is based on the conviction that civilian courts can effectively and fairly try persons accused of having planned and carried out heinous acts of terrorism. Respect for human rights from the early stages of the investigation is often a precondition for fair and successful trials. The UN Office on Drugs and Crime (UNODC) Terrorism Prevention Branch, where I work, is mandated by the UN Global Counter-Terrorism Strategy to provide States technical assistance 'in developing

---

[2] David Ariosto (2011), 'Guantanamo detainee sentenced to life for Africa bombings', CNN, 25 January, http://edition.cnn.com/2011/CRIME/01/25/new.york.guantanamo.sentencing/, accessed 7 June 2017.

[3] Human Rights Watch (2010), 'US: Ghailani trial shows federal courts up to the task', 17 November, https://www.hrw.org/news/2010/11/17/us-ghailani-trial-shows-federal-courts-task, accessed 7 June 2017.

[4] New York Post (2010), 'Terror-trial travesty', 18 November, http://nypost.com/2010/11/18/terror-trial-travesty/, accessed 12 October 2017.

and maintaining … effective and rule of law-based criminal justice systems'[5] to bring terrorists to justice.

What, however, is an effective and rule of law-based criminal justice response to terrorism? In a 'Working Paper' published in 2006, UNODC argues that the protection of human rights, starting with the right to life, requires States to use their criminal justice systems not only to identify and punish perpetrators of terrorist attacks, but also to 'interrupt and interdict preparations for terrorist violence'.[6] What is required is a preventive criminal justice strategy against terrorism.

That criminal justice should contribute to the prevention of crime is of course nothing new. Next to retribution on the one side and reformation and social rehabilitation of the offender on the other, prevention of crime is a well-established objective of criminal justice in several regards: prevention by 'neutralizing' the offender through imprisonment, prevention by deterring recidivism, prevention by reforming the offender into a law abiding citizen, and by deterrence of others who might be minded to commit the same or similar offences.[7]

---

[5] UN General Assembly (2006), The United Nations Global Counter-Terrorism Strategy, A/RES/60/288.

[6] UN (2006), 'Preventing terrorist acts: A criminal justice strategy integrating rule of law standards in implementation of United Nations anti-terrorism Instruments, Technical Assistance Working Paper', http://www.unodc.org/documents/terrorism/Publications/Preventing_Terrorist_Acts/English.pdf, accessed 12 October 2017, para. 1.

[7] In the case of terrorism, however, doubts have been expressed whether these preventive functions of criminal justice and punishment work. A review of academic literature reaches the conclusion that 'most authors reject the idea of deterrence as an effective measure against terrorism'. See Bibi van Ginkel (2015), 'The (in-)effectiveness of "deterrence" as an instrument', Clingendael Netherlands Institute of International Relations, 30 March, https://www.clingendael.nl/publication/effectiveness-deterrence-instrument-against-jihadist-terrorist-threats, accessed 7 June 2017. The reasons for the alleged ineffectiveness of deterrence are to be found in the aim to cause maximum damage and spread fear and terror, in the ideological or religious motivation of terrorist offenders, in the purported absence of rational cost-benefit calculation, in the search for publicity to draw attention to the cause, and finally in the attractions of martyrdom. Interestingly, however, a study of the motives of potential foreign terrorist fighters from the Netherlands published by two colleagues of Van Ginkel at the International Council on Clean Transportation (ICCT) three months after her literature review, indicates that fear of arrest during attempted travel to Syria is one of the reasons why men and women considering travelling from the Netherlands for Syria to join ISIL or the al-Nusra Front desist. See Edwin Bakker and Peter Grol (2015), 'Motives and considerations of potential

The claim made by the proponents of a preventive criminal justice strategy against terrorism, however, is that the criminal justice response must contribute to terrorism prevention in a way that goes far beyond this, that the criminal justice response must no longer be reactive (to terrorist attacks that have taken place), but proactive, 'forward-leaning'. According to former US Deputy Attorney General Paul McNulty:

> Awaiting an attack is not an option. That is why the Department of Justice is doing everything in its power to identify risks to our Nation's security at the earliest stage possible and to respond with forward-leaning – preventative – prosecutions.[8]

The EU Counter-Terrorism Coordinator, Gilles de Kerchove, equally advocates in favour of a preventive criminal justice strategy against terrorism:

> One counter-argument used against the criminal justice response is that it cannot prevent attacks but it only serves to convict the perpetrators after an attack has been committed. This is not true; in the EU and Council of Europe context, a number of preparatory offenses have been created, which criminalize inherently dangerous behavior before an attack is committed, such as public provocation to commit a terrorist attack, membership in a terrorist organization, etc. … If a criminal justice response is advocated, the legal framework and therefore also the material crimes have to provide the necessary tools to allow the disruption of attacks and convictions before an attack is committed.[9]

---

foreign fighters from the Netherlands', ICCT Policy Brief, July, https://icct.nl/wp-content/uploads/2015/07/ICCT-Bakker-Grol-Motives-and-Considerations-of-Potential-Foreign-Fighters-from-the-Netherlands-July2015.pdf, accessed 12 October 2017, p. 13.

[8] Quoted in Jerome P. Bjelopera (2013), 'The Federal Bureau of Investigation and Terrorism Investigations, Congressional Research Service Report for Congress', https://www.fas.org/sgp/crs/terror/R41780.pdf, accessed 12 October 2017.

[9] Gilles De Kerchove and Christiane Höhn (2013), 'Counter-terrorism and international law since 9/11, including in the EU-US context', in T.D. Gill et al. (eds), *Yearbook of International Humanitarian Law 2013*, Vol. 16, December, pp. 267–95, https://www.cambridge.org/core/journals/yearbook-of-international-humanitarian-law/article/chapter-10-counterterrorism-and-international-law-since-911-including-in-the-euus-context/64C7E5838F9F4992F0F62026DA97E834, accessed 7 June 2017, p. 273. The EU Counter-Terrorism Coordinator and his senior advisor adduce a number of 'strategic reasons for the criminal justice approach' to terrorism (ibid., at 269, 271, 279), arguing that it is more effective than 'long-term military detention for terrorist suspects' (id., at 279).

The EU Counter-Terrorism Coordinator also acknowledges, however, that some have human rights-based misgivings about this approach: 'some human rights advocates argue that the terrorist crimes now go too far and kick in too early by not requiring an attack to have happened'.[10]

In section 2 of this chapter, I will examine the concern that States may have gone too far, from a human rights perspective, in establishing new offences purported to be necessary for the preventive criminal justice response to terrorism. More specifically, 'going too far' means disproportionate limitations of fundamental freedoms of expression and association, violations of the principle whereby criminal laws must be written in a way that gives reasonable legal certainty, is foreseeable and accessible, and alleged violations of the presumption of innocence. I will primarily look at two types of offences: preparatory acts offences and those related to the foreign fighters phenomenon.

A forward-looking, preventive criminal justice strategy against terrorist violence requires not only 'a comprehensive system of substantive offences',[11] but equally important 'investigative powers and techniques, evidentiary rules, and inter-State cooperation mechanisms.'[12] These investigative powers, including expanded surveillance powers and use of undercover agents, and procedural rules, such as those loosening the permissibility of anonymous witness testimony or the use of 'secret evidence', will be addressed in section 3, in particular with respect to their impact on the right to a fair trial.

The chapter will end with section 4 drawing some conclusions.

2. OFFENCES FOR A PREVENTIVE CRIMINAL JUSTICE RESPONSE TO TERRORISM

2.1 Criminalization Requirements of a Preventive Criminal Justice Strategy

A preventive criminal justice strategy against terrorism requires the State to criminalize offences such as conspiracy to commit acts of terrorism, financing of terrorism, incitement of terrorism, recruitment to terrorism,

---

[10] Ibid. De Kerchove and Höhn reject these concerns by pointing out that offences criminalizing 'inherently dangerous behaviour' exist also in other areas of law.

[11] UNODC, 'Preventing terrorist acts' (n 6), at para. 2.

[12] Ibid.

or training for terrorism. I will call these offences that are typical of the preventive criminal justice strategy 'advanced criminalisation offences'.[13] They are to be distinguished from what I will refer to as 'principal offences', i.e. offences that constitute (or may constitute if accompanied by a terrorist intent) terrorist attacks against life, physical integrity, and public security, such as aircraft hijacking, hostage taking, or exploding a bomb in a public place.

Two aspects of these advanced criminalization offences are particularly important: first, the conduct they criminalize precedes the threshold of a punishable attempt to commit the principal offence.[14] In other words, their effectiveness for preventive purposes lies also in that they allow investigating and prosecuting authorities to investigate, deploy surveillance measures such as phone intercepts, carry out arrests, and eventually prosecute even though no attempt to commit a principal offence has (yet) been committed.

Second, the conduct criminalized by the 'advanced criminalization offences' is punishable even if no principal offence is committed, attempted or even specifically planned. This is explicitly spelled out in article 2(3) of the 1999 International Convention for the Suppression of the Financing of Terrorism: 'for an act to constitute an offence [of financing of terrorism] it shall not be necessary that the funds were actually used to carry out an offence'. In most legal systems it is not necessary that the person providing funds knew which specific planned terrorist attack or other activity would be supported with her contribution. Similarly, the offence of 'receiving training for terrorism' in article 3 of the Additional Protocol to the 2005 Council of Europe Convention on the Prevention of Terrorism, criminalizes receiving training irrespective of the subsequent perpetration of a principal terrorist offence, and would not appear to require that the trainer or the trainee made specific plans to use

---

[13] A concept very close to the concept of 'advanced criminalization offences' I propose is the *Vorfeldtatbestand* in German criminal law doctrine. Note that there is some overlap but no identity between the category of offences I propose to call 'advanced criminalization offences' and the concept of inchoate offences.

[14] The threshold of what conduct amounts to a punishable depends of course on national law. Under the English Criminal Attempts Act 1981 (CAA 1981), section 1(1), e.g., a person is guilty of attempting to commit an offence under the 'a person does an act which is more than merely preparatory to the commission of the offence'. As discussed below, clear delimitation between (not criminalized) preparatory acts and criminal attempt is considered an important safeguard in a rule of law based criminal justice system.

the skills being transmitted.[15] Indeed, the effectiveness of the offence for prevention purposes would be seriously undermined if the law or the courts were to require prosecutors to prove existence of a specific plan to make use of the funds or the training, and the funder's or trainee's knowledge of the plan.

In resolution 2178 (2014), the Security Council requires all UN Member States to make punishable in their legal systems certain advanced criminalization offences related to the foreign terrorist fighters phenomenon: travel (including attempted travel) to participate in training or the commission of acts of terrorism, financing of such travel, and organizing such travel. Previously, in resolution 1373 (2001), the Security Council had demanded that all States establish financing of terrorism as an offence, as well as recruitment to terrorism and, according to a possible interpretation, also 'preparation' of terrorist acts.[16] In resolution 1624 (2005) the Security Council calls upon all States to adopt the necessary measures to '[p]rohibit by law incitement to commit a terrorist act or acts'. In the same spirit, the 'Rabat Memorandum' of the Global Counter-Terrorism Forum (GCTF)[17] proposes as 'Good Practice 13: Criminalize Conspiracies, Solicitation and other Preparatory Acts of Terrorism'.

---

15 Nicola Piacente (2015), 'The contribution of the Council of Europe to the fight against foreign terrorist fighters', *eucrim*, 2015/1, https://eucrim.mpicc.de/archiv/eucrim_15-01.pdf, accessed 7 June 2017, p. 13.

16 UN, 'Preventing terrorist acts' (n 6), at para. 34.

17 The GCTF is 'an informal, multilateral counterterrorism (CT) platform focusing on identifying critical civilian CT needs, mobilizing the necessary expertise and resources to address such needs, and enhancing global cooperation' (GCTF (2015), 'Global Counterterrorism Forum Co-Chairs' Fact Sheet: About the GCTF', 27 September, https://2009-2017.state.gov/r/pa/prs/ps/2015/09/247369.htm, accessed 12 October 2017). The GCTF was launched by the United States of America in 2011 and has 30 members (29 States and the European Union). It 'regularly convenes key CT policymakers and practitioners from nations around the world, as well as experts from the United Nations and other multilateral bodies' (ibid.). Among the products of the GCTF are numerous documents, often called 'memoranda', 'designed to serve as practical guides for rule of law-based CT and CVE capacity-building activities and implementing CT good practices' (ibid.), including the 'Rabat Memorandum on Good Practices for Effective Counterterrorism Practice in the Criminal Justice Sector', https://www.thegctf.org/Portals/1/Documents/Framework%20Documents/A/GCTF-Rabat-Memorandum-ENG.pdf, accessed 12 October 2017. The GCTF has considerable financial resources to organize numerous capacity building activities in many of the countries most affected by terrorism, promoting the practices set forth in the memoranda.

In recent terrorism legislation, offences such as conspiracy or criminal association for terrorism purposes, incitement, encouragement, recruitment, training for terrorism and many others play a very prominent role. Kenya's Prevention of Terrorism Act 2012[18] exemplifies a preventive criminal justice approach: it defines 'terrorist act' in section 2, makes the commission of a 'terrorist act' an offence in section 4, and then dedicates subsequent sections to various offences mostly concerning conduct in preparation of terrorist attacks, such as training or recruiting. The list of advanced criminalization offences was further expanded in 2014, when new counter-terrorism legislation,[19] passed following a wave of particularly gruesome attacks, added numerous additional offences, including 'radicalization', 'possession of an article in connection with an offence', and travelling to a country designated as a 'terrorist training country', some of which were declared unconstitutional by the High Court.[20] This approach is taken even further in Nigeria's Terrorism Prevention Act,[21] which provides the death penalty for whoever 'knowingly … directly or indirectly willingly … commits an act preparatory to or in furtherance of an act of terrorism'.

In light of all this, it is remarkable that, while the global conventions and protocols against terrorism (i.e. treaties such as the 1997 Convention for the Suppression of Terrorist Bombings) require States to criminalize a broad array of forms of participation in the completed or attempted offence (planning, directing, aiding and abetting, being part of a joint criminal enterprise), they make no mention of conspiracy, incitement, recruitment, training, preparatory acts, etc. One notable exception is, of course, the 1999 Financing of Terrorism Convention. A second exception is the very recent 2010 Convention for the Suppression of Unlawful Acts Relating to International Civil Aviation which is the first global counter-terrorism treaty to require States to establish a conspiracy-type offence (article 5(a)). With these two exceptions, the global conventions and protocols do not require States to criminalize the advanced criminalization offences.[22]

---

18 The Prevention of Terrorism Act No. 30 of 2012.

19 Security Laws (Amendment) Act 2014.

20 *Coalition for Reform and Democracy (CORD) & 2 Others v. Republic of Kenya & 10 Others* [2015] eKLR, available at http://kenyalaw.org/caselaw/cases/view/106083/, accessed 12 October 2017.

21 The provisions referred to below are contained in the Terrorism Prevention (Amendment) Act, 2013, amending the Terrorism Prevention Act, 2011.

22 The UN Transnational Organized Crime Convention, on the other hand, obliges States to establish either a conspiracy-type or a criminal association

I would suggest that the concerns advanced criminalization offences raise from the point of view of the rule of law and human rights, particularly when combined with the risks of vague or overly broad definitions of terrorism and political abuse of terrorism charges, are a main reason for this conspicuous omission in the universal counter-terrorism treaties.

This is not the place to review the freedom of expression and other human rights considerations regarding the definition of offences such as incitement to terrorism, encouragement of terrorism, glorification or justification of terrorism.[23] I will also not review some of the human rights problems that arise with respect to financing of terrorism offences, both from a criminal justice point of view (legal certainty, accessibility and foreseeability of the offence) and from the perspective of the impact on civil society organizations and humanitarian action.[24] Instead, I would like to illustrate, on the basis of some case studies, the debate surrounding the human rights and rule of law implications of two types of advanced criminalization offences that appear to be at the centre of many governments' current or recent attention, firstly, 'preparatory acts', particularly in connection with the threat of so-called 'lone wolf' terrorists and, secondly, travel by foreign terrorist fighters.

2.2 Preparatory Acts

Consider the following scenario: X lives in a European country; he has researched on the internet writings justifying attacks against the 'unbelievers', particularly against police and military; he has also used Google Earth to study the surroundings of several police stations in his town. It is reasonable to assume that he might be a serious threat, including to the life of policemen in his home town. We would want X to be somehow stopped in his (presumable) tracks before he carries out an attack. If X had been plotting with others to identify vulnerable targets in town, in

---

(*association de malfaiteurs*)-type of offence to capture participation in organized crime groups or plots. See also article 27-1 of the UN Convention Against Corruption.

[23] For one summary of the substantial body of national and international case law, analysis and recommendations from human rights bodies, see UNODC (2014), *Human Rights and the Criminal Justice Response to Terrorism*, Ch. 2.3, available at https://www.unodc.org/documents/terrorism/Publications/Module_on_Human_Rights/Module_HR_and_CJ_responses_to_terrorism_ebook.pdf, accessed 12 October 2017. See also Chapters 2 and 3 of this book.

[24] See Ben Emmerson (2015), 'Special Rapporteur on human rights and counter-terrorism', UN Doc. A/70/371, and Chapters 1 and 3 of this book.

many countries criminal association or conspiracy offences might criminalize his conduct already at this very early stage. X, however, seems to be acting on his own, or in any event he has not left any traces of his conspiring with others. To protect lives and public safety, we might want to push the preventive criminal justice approach against terrorism to the point of making already X's conduct sketched above punishable as a terrorism related offence, 'preparatory acts'. This would give our criminal law great preventive reach and effect. It would also allow the police to obtain warrants for surveillance measures against X.

On the other hand, many would feel ill at ease if the two elements above in X's case (reading extremist material and spending hours surfing on Google Earth) were, on their own or in combination, sufficient to constitute an offence. We would want to see additional elements: maybe X undertook something towards procuring weaponry, or he should have entered into an agreement with others to prepare for an attack, or he should have attempted to recruit others to this effect. Or we would want the prosecution to prove that X was firmly resolved to carry out an attack on a police station.

Having an offence in our criminal code that is completed by X's conduct so far would clash against two fundamental principles of criminal law in liberal, rule of law based societies: First, criminal law should punish harmful conduct, not bad thoughts (no 'thoughtcrime'). Second, individuals are presumed to be law abiding until they engage in conduct that is unambiguously prohibited. These principles are not as such enshrined in human rights treaties. They are, however, to some extent reflected in the presumption of innocence and in the principle that criminal law provisions must be accessible and foreseeable, which is a key requirement of the *nullum crimen sine lege* principle in article 15 International Covenant on Civil and Political Rights (ICCPR) and article 7 European Convention on Human Rights (ECHR).[25]

A leading Austrian criminal law manual takes a very critical view towards the criminalization of preparatory acts: 'In criminal law systems based on the rule of law, which limit themselves to punishing conduct that is (actually) harmful for society and not bad intentions, preparatory acts are not punishable. Totalitarian systems [on the other hand] tend to extend the criminalisation of the attempted offence to cover preparatory acts (for instance, in the former German Democratic Republic, the possession of an inflatable dinghy was punishable as attempt to leave the

[25] See UNODC, *Human Rights and the Criminal Justice Response to Terrorism* (n 23), Ch. 2.1. See also Chapters 1 and 2 of this book.

Republic's territory). Clearly delimiting preparatory acts from the attempted offence is therefore particularly important'.[26]

Tunisia's 2015 counter-terrorism law is at the other end of the spectrum. There the legislator has chosen a formulation that goes very far in the direction of criminalizing bad intentions. Article 5(3) provides that 'whoever has resolved to commit a terrorist offence [under the present law] has committed that offence and shall be punished by half of the penalty provided for the offence, as long as the resolve is accompanied by any act preparatory to its execution'.[27] Case law will show whether this would constitute a sufficient basis to prosecute X in the scenario above. A key question might be whether the judges consider that the internet research of extremist material and the Google Earth surfing prove a resolve to commit a terrorist offence.

2.2.1 The German case law regarding the preparatory acts offence

In Germany, the legislator introduced in 2009 a new offence criminalizing 'preparation of grave acts of violence threatening the State' as article 89a of the German Penal Code (StGB). It carries a penalty of six months to ten years' imprisonment. Article 89a defines grave acts of violence threatening the State as offences against life or personal liberty (as defined in certain other provisions of the penal code) when the circumstances of the offence are such that it threatens the existence or security of a State or international organization or the fundamental constitutional principles of Germany. Sub-paragraph 2 of article 89a limits the application of the provision to those cases in which the offence is prepared either by providing or receiving training in the use of weapons or explosives, or the production, acquisition or storage of weapons, explosives or materials suited for that purpose. In 2015, a further subparagraph was added (subparagraph 2a), criminalizing the preparation of a grave act of violence threatening the State by travelling from Germany to another State to receive training as defined in subparagraph 2.

[26] Helmut Fuchs (2012), *Strafrecht Allgemeiner Teil I*, 8th edn (Vienna: Springer), pp. 243 and 244, my translation from German.

[27] Loi organique no. 2015-26 du 7 août 2015, relative à la lutte contre les infractions terroristes et la répression du blanchiment d'argent. Section 12D of the Kenya Prevention of Terrorism Act (offence of 'radicalization') would equally appear to go rather far in the direction of criminalizing bad thoughts: 'A person who adopts or promotes an extreme belief system for the purpose of facilitating ideologically based violence to advance political, religious or social change commits an offence and is liable on conviction, to imprisonment for a term not exceeding thirty years'.

Although the German legislator was very careful to limit the criminalization of preparatory acts, this provision has been at the centre of a lively debate.[28] The German Supreme Court (*Bundesgerichtshof*) has issued several judgments affirming the compatibility of article 89a with the Constitution while showing its concern to ensure that the application remains compatible with the fundamental principles of German criminal law. A closer look at one of these cases illustrates the complexities of the application of a preventive criminal justice strategy against terrorism that strives to comply with human rights and rule of law standards.

In this case,[29] a young man who had undergone a process of radicalization downloaded from the web approximately 10 000 pages of violent extremist jihadist material, including several issues of an Al Qaida online publication. One issue of this publication contained instructions for the production of a homemade explosive device sufficient to kill at least ten persons ('Make a bomb in the kitchen of your Mom'). The young man rented a room and started collecting components, including by scraping off the heads of between 7–8000 matches. One afternoon, in shredding parts of firecrackers in a kitchen blender, the young man set off an explosion which caused burns to his face and arms and major damage to the room he had rented.

The first instance court in Frankfurt found him guilty of the preparation offence in article 89a StGB. In the appeals judgment, the Supreme Court noted that the criminalization of 'preparations' did not violate the principle of legal certainty because subparagraph 2 of article 89 provided a closed list of conducts that could amount to preparations. The Supreme Court also noted that potentially vague terms such as 'threatening the fundamental constitutional principles of Germany' had been given a fairly specific meaning in previous court decisions which the legislator had referred to in the travaux preparatoires to article 89a.[30] The judges further noted that the legislator's aim in enacting article 89a was to take into account the growing decentralization of terrorist organizations and the threat posed by persons acting on their own to carry out terrorist attacks. Prior to the enactment of article 89a preparations for terrorist

---

[28] See, e.g., Henning Radtke and Mark Steinsiek, *Bekämpfung des internationalen Terrorismus durch Kriminalisierung von Vorbeireitungshandlungen? – Zum Entwurf eines Gesetzes zur Verfolgung der Vorbereitung von schweren Gewalttaten (Referentenentwurf des BMJ vom 21.4.2008)*, Zeitschrift für internationale Strafrechtsdogmatik (ZIS) 9/2008, available at www.zis-online.com, accessed 12 October 2017.

[29] *Bundesgerichtshof*, judgment of 8 May 2014, 3 StR 243/13.

[30] Ibid., at 11 and 12.

attacks were punishable only if they involved an organization or agreements between several persons.

The German Supreme Court warned, however, that article 89a criminalized conduct that was far removed from an attack against the ultimate goods to be protected, such as life and liberty. This is particularly the case with the criminalization of acquisition and storage of components of explosive devices, which amounts to criminalizing the preparations of the preparations.[31] The Supreme Court considered that its application will only be compliant with constitutional principles if there is proof beyond reasonable doubt of a 'manifested, unconditional resolve of the perpetrator to carry out the planned grave act of violence threatening the State, even if the plans have not yet matured beyond a rough outline'.[32] In the specific case before it, the Supreme Court found that while the plans regarding the way the attack would have been carried out had sufficiently matured to justify a guilty finding, the first instance court's findings regarding the accused's resolve to execute those plans were unclear and inconsistent and did not establish with sufficient clarity that the accused was 'firmly resolved' to carry out his plans. The Supreme Court vacated the guilty finding and asked the first instance court to retry and redecide this aspect of the case.

The approach could be summarized as follows: to counterbalance the criminalization of preparatory acts, which it considers highly suspicious, the Supreme Court sets a high legal and evidential threshold for the *mens rea*. In my view, this creates a double difficulty. First, heavy reliance on *mens rea* to justify the criminalization of conduct that is not unequivocally criminal, is a step in the direction of criminalizing bad thoughts rather than bad acts. Second, gathering strong evidence proving the intentions and the 'firm resolve' behind the conduct of a suspected lone wolf terrorist (who may not have planned any attacks in detail yet), or the intentions behind a person's conduct during her stay in Syria, might be very difficult. This evidentiary difficulty risks undermining the preventive efficacy of the article 89a offence. One way of overcoming this evidentiary challenge would be for the courts to accept elements of the *actus reus* as evidence for the *mens rea* as well: why would anyone scrape off the heads of 7000 matchsticks if he was not firmly resolved to use the powder to produce a device for a terrorist attack? That approach, however, by fusing evidence of *actus reus* and *mens rea*, would undermine the safeguard intended by the Supreme Court in reading such a high

[31] Id., at 44.
[32] Id., at 45 (my translation from German).

mens rea threshold into the offence. It would in the end be up to the suspect to prove that, while he may have been contemplating doing something evil with the improvised explosive device (IED) components he was acquiring and producing, he had not made up his mind yet. I will come back to the question of the burden of proof – and of the presumption of innocence – regarding preparatory acts offences in discussing the Australian 'declared areas' offence against foreign terrorist fighters.

2.2.2 The French legislation criminalizing 'individual terrorist enterprises'

The intricate problem of giving the criminal justice system the tools for an effective preventive criminal justice response to the threat posed by lone wolf terrorists and foreign terrorist fighters (FTFs), while upholding fundamental principles of criminal law, also emerged in a very instructive way in France in 2014. On 9 July 2014, the French government submitted to the legislature a draft law to strengthen counter-terrorism measures. The draft law aimed to respond to the threat of persons leaving France to join terrorist organizations, particularly in Syria. Its article 5 created the offence of 'individual terrorist enterprise' in reaction to alarm about 'lone wolf' terrorists following the attack against the Jewish Museum in Brussels in May 2014 and, before that, the murders committed by Mohammed Merah in Toulouse and Montauban in March 2012. The conduct criminalized by the draft article would have consisted of 'looking for, obtaining or making objects or substances creating a danger for others for the purpose of preparing the commission' of certain terrorist offences, in connection with an 'individual enterprise aiming to seriously undermine public order by intimidation or terror'. The government's intention was to provide an offence that would criminalize preparations for a terrorist attack also in the absence of an agreement between two or more persons.[33]

The legislation committee of the National Assembly reviewing the draft law decided that the *actus reus* of the offence had to be made more robust. It would be completed only if a person cumulated two elements of preparatory conduct: in addition to the act of 'looking for, obtaining or making objects or substances creating a danger for others for the purpose of preparing the commission' of a terrorist offence, there would be a second *actus reus* leg, consisting of either having engaged in scoping or

[33] Projet de loi renforçant les dispositions relatives à la lutte contre le terrorisme, Exposé des motifs, p. 7.

surveillance of a potential target, or having undergone weapons or explosives training, or having been a habitual visitor of internet sites inciting to terrorism. The offence would be complete only if a suspect's conduct fulfilled both elements.

In spite of the amendments introduced by the parliamentary committee in first reading of the draft law, the National Consultative Commission on Human Rights (CNCDH) in its advisory opinion on the draft law raised fundamental concerns.[34] It recalled that in French law, in principle, preparatory acts are not punishable and the attempt to commit an offence is punishable only when there is a 'beginning of execution' (*commencement d'execution*). The CNCDH conceded that there were already other offences making preparatory acts punishable independent of whether the offence is subsequently committed. It nonetheless expressed the concern that such offences interfere (*portent atteinte*) with the principle of legality and the presumption of innocence. It argued that by punishing conduct that is far removed from the offence to be prevented, the criminalization of preparatory acts necessarily relies on *actus reus* and *mens rea* elements that remain ambiguous.[35] The CNCDH expressed particular alarm about the criminalization of the act of 'looking for' dangerous objects or substances, which it considered to be conduct even preceding preparatory acts, 'very imprecise', raising grave problems of foreseeability and therefore open to 'dangerously subjective' evaluation.[36] The CNCDH's advisory opinion warned that an offence criminalizing the 'preparation of the preparation' would be incompatible with the principle of legality, in particular requirements of clarity and foreseeability of the offence. The CNCDH even expressed its fear of a 'disquieting resurgence of the doctrine of the "criminal law of the enemy"; this would amount to a "victory of fear", the victory of a security-dominated criminal law over the classical criminal law strictly governed by the principle of legality'.[37]

In November 2014, the French Parliament adopted the law, including the 'individual terrorist enterprise' offence in a version very close to the

---

34 Commission nationale consultative des droits de l'homme, *Avis sur le projet de loi renforçant les dispositions relatives à la lutte contre le terrorisme*, 25 September 2014. The CNCDH is a governmental human rights body providing, among other functions, human rights advice on draft legislation. The CNCDH also expressed grave concerns about the urgent – or rushed – procedure by which provisions raising fundamental rule of law and human rights concerns were being introduced.

35 Ibid., para. 14.

36 Id., para. 15.

37 Id., para. 16.

one adopted in first reading by the committee (i.e. it was not moved by the alarm bells rung by the human rights advisory committee). Interestingly, it added a fourth preparatory act to the second leg catalogue introduced at the committee stage: having been abroad in the theatre of operations of a terrorist group. From a different angle: the French legislator chose to comply with the Security Council imposed requirement to criminalize terrorism-related foreign travel not by creating an autonomous offence, but rather by making FTF travel a possible element of the 'individual terrorist enterprise' offence.

2.3 FTF-related Offences in Council of Europe Protocol and Australia

Security Council resolution 2178 of 24 September 2014 deals with the threat posed by 'foreign terrorist fighters'. The resolution was adopted under Chapter VII of the UN Charter and is therefore binding on all UN Member States. The resolution's operative paragraph (OP) 6 requires all UN Member States to ensure that their criminal law allows the prosecution and punishment as serious offences of: (a) travel or attempted travel from their territory of individuals 'for the purpose of the perpetration, planning, or preparation of, or participation in, terrorist acts, or the providing or receiving of terrorist training'; (b) wilful provision or collection of funds to be used for the conduct described under (a); and (c) 'wilful organization, or other facilitation' of travel as described under (a).[38]

2.3.1 The Additional Protocol to the 2005 Council of Europe Convention on the Prevention of Terrorism

In 2005, the Council of Europe (CoE) adopted a Convention on the Prevention of Terrorism which requires Member States to establish, in their domestic law, three advanced criminalization offences: recruitment, public provocation and providing training for terrorism.[39] Following the adoption of Security Council resolution 2178, the CoE Committee of

---

[38] My intention here is to focus on the question of how States are taking into consideration prevention aims, on the one hand, and human rights considerations, on the other, in incorporating the requirements of OP6 into domestic law.

[39] Council of Europe Convention on the Prevention of Terrorism, CETS No. 196, entered into force on 1 June 2007. As discussed above, these are advanced criminalization offences that are not required by the universal conventions and protocols against terrorism, but could be seen to be required by Security Council resolutions 1373 (2001) and 1624 (2005).

Experts on Terrorism (CODEXTER) immediately set to work on a Protocol additional to the 2005 Convention regarding the FTF-related offences in OP 6 of the Security Council resolution.[40]

In article 1, the Protocol stresses the link between a preventive criminal justice approach to terrorism and the protection of human rights: 'The purpose of this Protocol is to supplement the provisions of the Council of Europe Convention on the Prevention of Terrorism [...], thereby enhancing the efforts of Parties in preventing terrorism and its negative effects on the full enjoyment of human rights, in particular the right to life'. Articles 2 to 6 of the Protocol require States to establish five advanced criminalization offences in their criminal law: participating in an association or group for purposes of terrorism (article 2), receiving training for terrorism (article 3), travelling abroad for the purpose of terrorism (article 4), funding travelling abroad for the purpose of terrorism (article 5) and organizing or otherwise facilitating travelling abroad for the purpose of terrorism (article 6).[41]

In the public consultation process during the elaboration of the Protocol, Amnesty International (AI) and the International Commission of Jurists (ICJ) made submissions highly critical of the draft Protocol (they also lamented that the 'speed of the process, and the very short period during which the draft will have been publicly available prior to its finalization and agreement, do not allow for an appropriate degree of consultation and debate on this complex topic'[42]). I will consider three of their concerns which highlight the potential for tension between the preventive criminal justice approach to terrorism and human rights values.

First, AI and ICJ warn that problems arising from 'the wide and uncertain definition of "terrorist offence"' are 'compounded by the fact that offences ancillary to the principal offence ("terrorist offence"), such as those which are the focus of the draft Protocol, criminalize conduct which to varying extents is distant from the principal offence, and is

---

[40] Additional Protocol to the Council of Europe Convention on the Prevention of Terrorism, CETS No. 217, not in force at the time of writing. On the drafting process, see Piacente (n 15).

[41] Many CoE Member States will of course have criminalized some or all of the conduct covered by the Protocol, as our discussion of French and German criminal law above shows.

[42] *Submission of Amnesty International and the International Commission of Jurists to the Committee on Foreign Fighters and Related Issues (COD-CTE)* of 19 March 2015, https://www.amnesty.org/en/documents/ior60/1281/2015/en/, accessed 12 October 2017, p. 1.

therefore more difficult to identify with certainty. This raises serious concerns as to compliance with the principle of legality, a core general principle of law, enshrined, *inter alia*, in Article 7 ECHR and Article 15 ICCPR, which requires laws to be clear and accessible and for their application in practice to be sufficiently foreseeable.'[43]

Second, with regard to the offence of receiving training for terrorism (article 3), the two human rights non-governmental organizations (NGOs) warn that 'it is essential that offences of "receiving training for terrorism" must be subject to the establishment of specific intent of carrying out, or contributing to the commission of the principal offence as a result of the training. In the absence of such intent, conduct risks being criminalized without a sufficient proximate causal link with the principal criminal offence.'[44]

Third, the joint AI and ICJ submission criticizes the offence of travelling abroad for the purpose of terrorism (article 4) on the ground that it 'covers conduct that is several stages removed, and therefore lacks a proximate causal link, to any principal offence which may take place'. They add that these concerns are further exacerbated by article 4.3, criminalizing the attempt to travel. Their recommendation is that 'the draft Protocol should lay down a prerequisite of a sufficiently direct connection with a principal criminal act and stipulate that a clear and unequivocal intent has to be established'.[45]

The gist of the second and third point of criticism appears to be that unless offences such as receiving training or travelling abroad for the purpose of terrorism require proof of a link between the travel or the training and a specific plot to carry out a terrorist attack, they remain impermissibly vague. Requiring proof of a link between the travel to or training in Syria, Iraq or Libya and specific plans to carry out acts of terrorism in a CoE Member State, however, would greatly diminish the scope for prosecutions based on these offences: first, because those who travel or train may have no knowledge of how their recruiters will ask them to put their skills at work in the future; second, because even if specific plans are communicated to a trainee while undergoing training in Syria, gathering evidence on this point may present insurmountable obstacles.

---

[43] Id., at 1 and 2.
[44] Id., at 5.
[45] Id., at 6.

These challenges were stressed by UNODC in a recent paper submitted to the UN's Commission on Crime Prevention and Criminal Justice, where UNODC remarks with regard to the prosecution of FTFs that:

> 55. … Building a solid criminal case requires overcoming major operational or legal challenges. Those include the difficulty … in proving the intentional element of the crime or offence committed, …
>
> 57. Criminal justice practitioners face serious difficulties in proving the intentional element, i.e., the intention to join a terrorist group and/or to participate directly or indirectly in terrorist operations. The collection of the required legal standard of evidence in court may also be very challenging given the great difficulty of obtaining evidence from the conflict zones.[46]

These evidentiary difficulties regarding the purpose of travel to conflict zones where terrorist groups are active and of training persons receive in such conflict zones have prompted the Australian legislature to take a very different approach from the one urged by ICJ and AI in their submissions to CODEXTER.

2.3.2 Australia's Foreign Fighters Bill

In September 2014, the federal government of Australia introduced into Parliament a Bill to fill gaps in the country's counter-terrorism legislation, particularly with regard to the threat purportedly posed by returning foreign (terrorist) fighters.[47] In presenting the draft legislation to Parliament, the Attorney General explained that '[t]hose that travel to a declared area without a sole legitimate purpose *might* engage in a hostile activity with a listed terrorist organisation. These people *may* return from a declared area with enhanced capabilities which *may* be employed to facilitate terrorist or other acts in Australia'[48] (emphasis added).

The Bill provided for a new offence, section 119.2, of entering or remaining in a 'declared area' in which a 'listed terrorist organisation is engaging in hostile activity' (as of 10 May 2016, in application of this

[46] UNODC (2016), 'Discussion guide for the thematic discussion on criminal justice responses to prevent and counter terrorism in all its forms and manifestations, including the financing of terrorism, and technical assistance in support of the implementation of relevant international conventions and protocols', UN Doc. E/CN.15/2016/6, April, paras. 55–58.

[47] Counter-Terrorism Legislation Amendment (Foreign Fighters) Bill.

[48] Explanatory Memorandum to the Counter-Terrorism Legislation Amendment (Foreign Fighters) Bill, 2014, para. 225, https://www.attorneygeneral.gov.au/Mediareleases/Documents/140923-EMCTForeignFightersBill2014.pdf, accessed 9 May 2016.

provision, the Australian government had declared the Raqqa province in Syria and Mosul district, the Ninewa province, in Iraq as 'declared areas' for the purposes of this offence). Contrary to the offence in article 4 of the CoE Convention Additional Protocol or of article 89a(3) of the German penal code, the Australian law does not require the prosecution to show that the individual travelled to the declared area for the 'purpose of terrorism'. Rather, it provides that an individual accused of having entered a 'declared area' can rely on a defence consisting of showing that he had a legitimate purpose for entering the area. That legitimate purpose must be the sole purpose for entering the declared area. The Bill lists (subsection 119.2(3)) conduct that can constitute a 'legitimate purpose', such as providing humanitarian aid, performing an official duty for the UN or a government, 'making a bona fide visit to a family member' or making a news report.

In several ways, section 119.2 exemplifies the potential of a strategy aiming to use criminal law and prosecutions to prevent acts of terrorism from occurring rather than limiting criminal justice to reacting to offences once they have been committed. On the one hand, the three degrees of 'may' and 'might' used by the Explanatory Memorandum to the Bill to explain the causal link between travel to a 'designated area' and an eventual terrorist attack in Australia highlight that there are several steps between the conduct criminalized and the causation of actual harm in Australia. On the other hand, the preventive potential lies precisely in the promise of providing a tool to the authorities for nipping in the bud the transformation of a marginalized youth into a hardened killer. By placing the evidential burden of showing the existence of a 'sole legitimate purpose' justifying the travel, the law (at least initially) relieves the prosecution of the sometimes difficult burden of proving that a person's travel to Raqqa was for purposes of putting himself at the service of Daesh or receiving training for terrorism. Moreover, this offence will allow the authorities to obtain warrants to place a person (and thereby necessarily also his circle of family, friends, acquaintances and community relations) under surveillance on the sole suspicion that he or she may be attempting travel to a 'designated area'.

The report of the Parliamentary Committee on Intelligence and Security, which held a public inquiry to hear views on the draft law, provides a very vivid account of the debate for and against this preventative use of criminal justice against terrorism. 'Many inquiry participants expressed strong in-principle concerns about the impact of the proposed "declared area" offense … For example, Professor Ben Saul [argued that the] offence relating to a "declared area" would criminalize conduct which is not in itself demonstrably harmful, violent or terrorist […] It is also a misuse and over-extension of the criminal law in view of existing, extensive offences of foreign incursion and terrorism'.[49] The Islamic Council of Victoria submitted that the proposed offence would be discriminatory against the Muslim community. The Law Council of Australia warned that the offence would have a particular impact on certain segments of the population with family connections or trading engagements in declared areas. It argued that '[t]his impact (when combined with the breadth of the offence and the evidential burden on the accused) risks marginalising precisely those segments of the Australian community whose cooperation and goodwill is most essential to curb the terrorist threat.'[50]

A speaker in favour of the proposed offence, on the other hand, argued that it would be an effective way to overcome the 'enormous problems with prosecutions under the [the existing legislation that could be used to prosecute foreign fighters], because the evidence thresholds were set far too high'. He added that the government should have the ability 'to proscribe areas and say Australians should not go there – because the only reason you would go there basically would be to undertake quite serious crimes, potentially even war crimes'.[51]

Of particular interest to this chapter is the argument surrounding the shift in the burden of proof. The Attorney-General's Explanatory Memorandum recalls that:

> article 14 ICCPR provides that, as a key aspect of the right to a fair trial, everyone charged with a criminal offence shall have the right to be presumed innocent until proved guilty according to law. The burden is on the prosecution to prove a criminal charge beyond reasonable doubt.[52]

The Explanatory Memorandum goes on to assert that:

> The new offence under section 119.2 does not reverse the onus of proof or limit the presumption of innocence. To the extent that there is a limitation on Article 14 of the ICCPR, those limitations are reasonable, necessary and proportionate to countering the threat posed to Australia and its national security interests by foreign fighters returning to Australia from areas where

---

[49] The Parliament of the Commonwealth of Australia (2014), 'Advisory report on the Counter-Terrorism Legislation Amendment (Foreign Fighters) Bill 2014', October, at 2.347.

[50] Ibid., at 2.348 and 2.349.

[51] Id., at 2.351.

[52] Explanatory Memorandum to the Counter-Terrorism Legislation Amendment (Foreign Fighters) Bill, 2014, para. 226.

> the Foreign Affairs Minister is satisfied that a listed terrorist organisation is engaging in a hostile activity.[53]

Several inquiry participants, however, expressed strong concerns regarding the presumption of innocence and fair trial. They argued that, while the provision may not technically reverse the onus of proof, because the prosecution would still have to prove entering or remaining in the declared area, 'it is the accused who will bear the burden of demonstrating an innocent intent, rather than requiring the prosecution to demonstrate a nefarious intent'.[54] Another participant argued that 'it is highly likely that the accused would be convicted if he exercised his right to silence and did not give evidence. Therefore it is a reversal of onus and presumption of guilt'.[55]

The participant speaking for the Australian Human Rights Commission had some suggestions for improving the provision but defended the allocation of the burden of proof. She argued that the approach of placing a preliminary element of evidence onto the defendant was 'not unreasonable' and was consistent with other areas of criminal law: People travelling to a declared area 'have taken the risk and they are in the best position to provide at least a first level of evidence before the persuasive burden is reactivated in terms of the crown'.[56]

The Australian Parliament was in the end apparently convinced by the arguments made in favour of the declared area offence and adopted the provision as proposed by the government.[57]

---

[53] Id., para. 229.

[54] 'Advisory report' (n 29), at 2.358.

[55] 'Advisory report' (n 29), at 2.359.

[56] 'Advisory report' (n 29), at 2.362.

[57] Very soon thereafter, also the Kenyan Parliament passed its version of a 'declared area' offence. The new section 30C(1) of the Prevention of Terrorism Act reads: 'A person who travels to a country designated by the Cabinet Secretary to a be a terrorist training country without passing through designated immigration entry or exit points shall be presumed to have travelled to that country to receive training in terrorism'. The provision does not mention any legitimate reasons for travelling to a designated country, but the second paragraph of the section exempts any 'person who ordinarily resides in Kenya within an area bordering a designated country' from its application.

3. THE INVESTIGATIVE POWERS AND CRIMINAL PROCEDURE RULES REQUIRED BY THE PREVENTIVE CRIMINAL JUSTICE STRATEGY

The prevention of terrorism requires the detection of secretive agreements, planning, and preparations to commit terrorist attacks. This is mainly the work of intelligence agencies or of agencies having a dual – intelligence and criminal investigation – mandate.

The preventive criminal justice strategy against terrorism, on the other hand, requires evidence admissible in court proving these secretive agreements, planning, and preparations. Evidence has to be collected without alerting the suspect and the persons he associates with, whether co-conspirator or innocent, to the investigation. This will often require the use of so-called 'special investigation techniques'[58] (SITs) by the criminal investigators, such as the use of undercover agents and informers, placing listening devices in buildings and cars, phone-tapping, obtaining call record data and metadata of e-mail communications.[59] A second related potential source of evidence for a preventive criminal justice strategy is increasing the flow of information between intelligence actors and the criminal justice system and lowering the obstacles to the conversion of intelligence material into evidence admissible in a criminal trial.[60]

The counter-terrorism conventions and protocols and Security Council resolutions do not refer to the use of special investigation techniques.

---

[58] The CoE has defined SITs as follows: '"Special investigation techniques" means techniques applied by the competent authorities in the context of criminal investigations for the purpose of detecting and investigating serious crimes and suspects, aiming at gathering information in such a way as not to alert the target persons' (Recommendation Rec(2005)10 of the Committee of Ministers to member states on 'special investigation techniques' in relation to serious crimes including acts of terrorism, Adopted by the Committee of Ministers on 20 April 2005).

On human rights aspects of the use of SITs in terrorism investigations, see UNODC, *Human Rights and the Criminal Justice Response to Terrorism* (n 23), at p. 88.

[59] Also see Chapter 6 of this book.

[60] On the role intelligence information can serve in terrorism investigations and prosecutions, see the GCTF, 'Recommendations for Using and Protecting Intelligence Information in Rule of Law-Based, Criminal Justice Sector-Led Investigations and Prosecutions', https://www.thegctf.org/documents/10162/159887/14sept19_gctf+rabat+gp+6+recommendations.pdf, accessed 12 October 2017.

However, the UN Convention against Corruption calls on State Parties 'to allow for the appropriate use by its competent authorities of ... special investigative techniques, such as electronic or other forms of surveillance and undercover operations, ... and to allow for the admissibility in court of evidence derived therefrom'.[61] The UN Convention against Transnational Organized Crime equally encourages States to make use of SITs.

It is the threat of terrorism, however, and the needs of terrorism-related investigations that are pushing many countries to amend existing laws, to broaden investigatory powers and to broaden the way in which intelligence information can be used in criminal proceedings. Many countries which did not previously have a legal framework for the use of SITs in criminal investigations, such as Kenya,[62] Niger,[63] Nigeria,[64] and Tunisia,[65] have recently equipped themselves with provisions on the use of covert investigation techniques as part of new counter-terrorism legislation. In these four countries, as well as in many others, my colleagues at UNODC and I work with national criminal justice institutions to provide training and develop training materials on the human-rights compliant use of SITs in the investigation, prosecution and trial of terrorism cases.

The impact of expanded surveillance powers on human rights, including the right to privacy and fundamental freedoms of religion, expression and association are explored in other chapters of this book.[66] Here, I will limit myself to two aspects related to the use of material generated by SITs in prosecutions: first, the role of undercover agents and informants; second, limitations to the defendant's right to examine and challenge evidence against it in the interest of protecting information on intelligence sources and covert investigation techniques.

Before turning to these questions, two preliminary observations should be considered. First, as argued above, the early detection of terrorist plots – and thus the protection of the population against terrorist attacks – is not possible without covert surveillance techniques. If criminal justice is

---

[61] UN Convention Against Corruption (UNCAC), art. 50(1); see also the UN Convention against Transnational Organized Crime (UNTOC), arts. 20(1) and 26.

[62] Prevention of Terrorism Act, 2012, section 36.

[63] Ordonnance n. 2011-13 du 27 janvier 2011, modifiant et complétant la loi n. 61-33 du 14 aout 1961 portant institution du Code de procédure pénale, 605.4.

[64] Terrorism Prevention (Amendment) Act, 2013, sections 29 and 33.

[65] Loi organique no. 2015-26 du 7 août 2015, relative à la lutte contre les infractions terroristes et la répression du blanchiment d'argent, art. 54-65.

[66] See Chapters 2, 3 and 5.

to have a role in prevention, then criminal justice actors must use SITs. Second, the expansion of the use of SITs in criminal proceedings should allow investigators and prosecutors to reduce their reliance on witness statements and particularly on confessions. Reduced need to build investigations and prosecutions on confessions should mean lesser incentives to resort to torture or other coercive means. Even where criminal justice is still guided by the maxim 'la confession est la reine de la preuve', the ability to confront suspects with incriminating communication intercepts, phone record data or GPS records will increase the likelihood of investigators and prosecutors being able to pressure suspects to collaborate without recourse to prohibited means of pressure. Moreover, the availability of such 'objective' evidence should reduce the likelihood of miscarriages of justice. From this perspective, the expansion of the use of special investigation techniques will have an eminently positive impact on respect for human rights in criminal proceedings.

3.1 Agent Provocateur Cases

The use of informants and undercover agents can be a key tool in the investigation of terrorist offences, particularly in a preventive criminal justice approach, where the aim is to save lives and protect the public by placing under surveillance, stopping and bringing to justice persons (secretly) planning and preparing the commission of acts of violence.

In the United States of America, the involvement of informants and undercover agents has been the predominant feature of the prosecution of so-called 'homegrown' terrorists since the 9/11 attacks. The Federal Bureau of Investigation (FBI) has said that of all the terrorist plots disrupted between 9/11 and September 2009, only two plotters were 'prepared to move ahead with their plots without the benefit or knowledge of government informants or U.S. officials'.[67] In line with this claim, a July 2014 report by Human Rights Watch and Columbia Law School, based on the examination of 27 post-9/11 terrorism cases in the United States, finds that '[a]ll of the high-profile domestic terrorism plots of the last decade, with four exceptions, were actually FBI sting operation – plots conducted with the direct involvement of law enforcement informants or agents, including plots that were proposed or led by informants'.[68]

---

[67] Quoted with further references in Bjelopera (n 8), at 21.

[68] Human Rights Watch (HRW) and Columbia Law School (2014), 'Illusion of justice: Human rights abuses in US terrorism prosecutions', 21 July,

The two statements agree that there were hardly any US homegrown terrorist plots without the FBI's knowledge, but their interpretation of this is very different. According to an observer sympathetic to the FBI's 'proactive, forward-leaning posture' to terrorism investigations and prosecutions:

> Agent provocateur cases – sting operations – rely on expert determination by law enforcement that a specific individual or group is likely to move beyond radicalized talk and engage in violence or terrorist plotting. The ultimate goal is to catch a suspect committing an overt criminal act such as pulling the proverbial trigger but on a dud weapon. By engaging in such strategy, investigators hope to obtain ironclad evidence against suspects.[69]

According to Human Rights Watch, on the other hand:

> in some cases the Federal Bureau of Investigation may have created terrorists out of law-abiding individuals by conducting sting operations that facilitated or invented the target's willingness to act. ... In such instances, the government's purpose appears to have been preventive: to root out and prosecute individuals it believes might eventually plan and carry out terrorism.[70]

The question of where the line runs between the use of an agent or informer as a legitimate means of gathering information or evidence and impermissible inducement to commit crime is at the heart of the decision of the Supreme Court of British Columbia in *R. v. Nuttall.*[71] In this case, two Canadians (a couple, Mr Nuttall and Ms Korody, two rather marginalized individuals who had recently converted to Islam) conspired to plant explosives on the grounds of the British Columbia legislature. Undercover police played a decisive role in hatching the plan and in the logistics for the attack: the main undercover officer had acted as the couple's 'spiritual guide', while other officers had impersonated members of a foreign terrorist group that threatened the couple if they were to back off from the attack plans. The jury convicted Nuttall and Korody of several terrorism offences. The defendants applied to the Supreme Court, arguing that the police's 'failure to respect the boundaries of permissible

---

https://www.hrw.org/report/2014/07/21/illusion-justice/human-rights-abuses-us-terrorism-prosecutions, accessed 12 October 2017, p. 21.

69 Bjelopera (n 8), at 21. Note that Bjelopera appears to use the term 'agent provocateur case' synonymous with 'sting operation', without a negative connotation, while to many other writers the term 'agent provocateur' will already imply an impermissible inducement to commit an offence.

70 HRW (n 68), at 2.

71 *R. v. Nuttall*, 2016 BCSC 1404, 29 July 2016.

police conduct resulted in a police generated crime',[72] and that the proceedings should be stayed on grounds of entrapment and abuse of process by the police.

The British Columbia Supreme Court stayed the proceedings on both grounds advanced by the defendants. With regard to the defence of entrapment, the judge found that '[t]he police took two people who held terrorist beliefs but no apparent capacity or means to plan, act on or carry through with their religiously motivated objectives and they counselled, directed, urged, instructed and moulded them into people who could, with significant and continuous supervision and direction by the police, play a small role in a terrorist offence'.[73] The judge further concluded that 'to permit the defendants' conviction to stand in the face of this kind of police misconduct would be offensive and would cause irreparable damage to the integrity of the justice system'.[74] This was 'one of the rare cases where a stay of proceedings is warranted due to an abuse of process'.[75]

The facts of the *Nuttall* case are fairly extreme in terms of the police's overzealous conduct. However, the Human Rights Watch report on US terrorism prosecutions argues that also in many of the cases they examined 'the informants and agents often … chose targets [i.e. terrorism suspects] who were particularly vulnerable – whether because of mental disability, or because they were indigent and needed money that the government offered them. In some cases – which have been particularly troubling for American Muslim communities – targets were seeking spiritual guidance, and the government informants or agents guided them towards violence'.[76] The sting operation cases examined in the Human Rights Watch report raise serious questions as to whether the defendants would have planned and advanced preparations for an attack without the involvement of the informants or agents. In none of the US cases, however, was the defence of entrapment successfully raised.

Former FBI Director Mueller and Attorney General Holder have described the use of sting operations as 'essential' to terrorism prevention.[77] It is indeed difficult to imagine an effective preventive criminal justice strategy against terrorism without the use of informants and undercover agents. To ensure that these investigation techniques do not

[72] Ibid., at para. 2.
[73] Id., at para. 775.
[74] Id., at para. 835.
[75] Id., at para. 837.
[76] HRW (n 68), at 22 and 23.
[77] Bjelopera (n 8), at 22.

violate human rights, strict guidelines for the conduct of sting operations, robust internal control mechanisms, and in-depth training of officers involved are required.[78]

Moreover, as demonstrated by the *Nuttall* case, the role of judges is essential in subjecting the police conduct to scrutiny whenever the defence raises a plausible claim of impermissible instigation or inducement by undercover agents. In the *Ramanauskas* case (a case dealing with police inducement to accept bribes), the ECtHR stated that, where an accused alleges that evidence has been obtained by entrapment, 'the criminal courts must carry out a careful examination of the material in the file, since for the trial to be fair … all evidence obtained as a result of police incitement must be excluded'.[79]

3.2 Protection of Evidence from Intelligence Sources and from Covert Investigation Methods

As stated in the GCTF's Rabat Memorandum, '[i]n order to safeguard the lives of victims and informants, protect sources and methods, and maintain the usefulness of sensitive investigative techniques, governments must be able to protect certain types of information and techniques from public disclosure, even in the course of public criminal justice proceedings'.[80] In terrorism cases, the need to protect certain types of information and techniques may go beyond preventing public disclosure and include preventing disclosure to the defendant.[81] I will discuss the implications of two measures used to achieve these objectives: anonymous witnesses and giving lawyers access to information that is kept from their clients.

One of the basic principles of a fair hearing is that the individual charged with a criminal offence be informed of the evidence that

---

[78] GCTF, 'Rabat Memorandum' (n 17), Good Practice 3: Provide a Legal Framework and Practical Measures for Undercover Investigations of Terrorist Suspects or Organizations.

[79] *Ramanauskas v. Lithuania*, App. no. 74420/01 (ECtHR, 5 February 2008), para. 60. Canadian law on entrapment is analysed in depth in *Nuttall* (n 71), at para. 537 ff.

[80] GCTF, 'Rabat Memorandum' (n 17), Good Practice 6: Enact Measures to Protect Sensitive Law Enforcement and Intelligence Information in Terrorism Cases.

[81] See, e.g., GCTF, 'Hague Memorandum on Good Practices for the Judiciary in Adjudicating Terrorism Offenses', Good Practice 6, available at https://www.thegctf.org/documents/10162/140201/14Sept19_GCTF+The+Hague+Memorandum.pdf, accessed 12 October 2017.

supports the allegations against him or her. Closely connected to this principle is the requirement that a defendant must have adequate time to prepare to challenge the prosecution evidence, and to do so with the support of legal counsel. Thirdly, there is the right to 'examine, or have examined, the witnesses against him'.[82]

These safeguards are separate from, and additional to, the right to a public hearing. Limitations to the public nature of court hearings are explicitly permitted by the major human rights treaties. Under article 14 ICCPR, the press and the public may be excluded from all or part of a trial where this serves a legitimate aim, which includes national security and the interests of justice. There is no provision in the ICCPR, the ECHR, or other human rights treaties governing limitation of the defendant's right to know the evidence against him. Still, international human bodies (particularly the ECtHR) and national courts have developed criteria regarding permissible limitations to this safeguard, too.

Reconciling the needs of investigations and prosecutions in terrorism cases, particularly where intelligence methods and sources are involved, with the safeguards protecting the right to a fair trial requires considerable resources and a sophisticated legal framework. The criminal justice system has to be equipped with a finely granulated spectrum of methods to protect classified or sensitive law enforcement information, from the use of pseudonyms, to holding hearings closed to the public, to court room infrastructure enabling witnesses to enter, testify and leave without being seen by the public, or – if appropriate – by the defendant, to video link technology allowing the scrambling of the witnesses' image and voice distortion. Disclosure rules should permit delayed or redacted disclosure of witness statements and sensitive documents, and enable the judge to receive *ex parte* motions and hold *ex parte* hearings to review the intelligence or other information to determine whether it should be disclosed. Court registries must be equipped with secure paper and electronic filing systems enabling them to handle in parallel redacted and unredacted versions of documents.

Recent practice in Kenya and Nigeria shows how challenging the introduction of such a system of protective measures is, if it is to be effective and at the same time respectful of defence rights.

In Kenya, legislation in 2014 introduced a provision allowing the prosecution to withhold evidence otherwise subject to disclosure to the

---

[82] ICCPR, article 14(3), letters (b) and (e).

defence 'until immediately before the hearing'.[83] The circumstances in which the public interest would justify delaying disclosure of evidence included that the evidence 'touches on matters of national security', 'touches on the identity of an informant' or 'discloses some unusual form of surveillance or method of detecting crime'. It is recognized in other jurisdictions, including international criminal tribunals, that delayed disclosure can be a legitimate means to reduce the risk of intimidation of witnesses without denying the defendant the right to know the identity of the witness altogether. While the objective pursued by the new provision was legitimate, it was probably drafted in an overly broad way.

The High Court of Kenya struck the new provision down on the ground that it would impermissibly limit the right to a fair trial, and specifically article 50(2)(j) of the Constitution requiring that an accused person is 'to be informed in advance of the evidence the prosecution intends to rely on, and to have reasonable access to that evidence'.[84] The judges recalled that under Kenya's Constitution the right to a fair trial in article 50 is absolute. They maintained that the new section would lead to 'trials by ambush which both the Constitution as well as international law frown upon'.[85]

Nigeria equally introduced provisions to protect the identity of informants and other witness who may be at risk as part of counter-terrorism legislation.[86] The difficulty in the application of these provisions, however, lies in a lack of clarity regarding the distinction between protection against disclosure to the public and complete witness anonymity, i.e. non-disclosure of the witness's identity to the defendant. This has resulted in unpredictable judicial rulings on protective measures, which creates risks to witnesses and to the viability of the prosecution case.[87]

The use of anonymous witnesses, i.e. witnesses whose identity is at no stage disclosed to the defence, is particularly delicate. Witness anonymity

---

[83] Section 16 of the Security Laws Amendment Act introducing a new Section 42A in the Kenya Criminal Procedure Code.

[84] *Coalition for Reform and Democracy (CORD) & 2 Others v. Republic of Kenya & 10 Others* (n 20).

[85] Ibid., at 348. The High Court also criticized that the new provision did not require the prosecution to obtain leave of the court in advance (id., at 333 and 334).

[86] Sections 33 and 34 of the Terrorism Prevention (Amendment) Act, 2013.

[87] See ISS Africa (2015), 'Fighting Boko Haram: why Nigeria needs a cohesive witness protection programme', *OasesNews*, 5 May, http://oasesnews.com/newsmakers/item/3444-fighting-boko-haram-why-nigeria-needs-a-cohesive-witness-protection-programme, accessed 12 October 2017.

can substantially limit the ability of the defendant to challenge prosecution witness testimony, as it precludes defence investigations into a witness's background, and limits the ability to identify and draw attention to factors putting into question the credibility of the witness.

Nonetheless, there are very limited circumstances in which refusing to disclose the identity of a witness to the defence may be justified. The Rules of Procedure and Evidence of the Special Tribunal for Lebanon, the first UN tribunal established to try a terrorism case, contain detailed procedures and safeguards to allow the use of anonymous witnesses under certain circumstances. Rule 93 contemplates that the judge may question the witness in the absence of the parties on the ground of a risk to the life of the witness that cannot be prevented by lesser witness protection measures, or where 'imperative national security interests' are at risk.

In terrorism cases, witness anonymity vis-à-vis the defence might often be sought to protect the identity of intelligence officers and undercover agents. In this regard, the ECtHR has held that the use of anonymous police witnesses gives rise to particular difficulties since they owe a general duty of obedience to the State's executive authorities and usually have links with the prosecution.[88] In *Nuttall*, the judge made a very damaging assessment of the credibility of some the police officers involved in the undercover operation ('[i]t was quite apparent that he had a personal stake in the outcome of the investigation and was not objective').[89] This highlights the importance of scrupulously exploring less drastic protection measures, as well as of the key role a proactive judge has to play if anonymity is granted. The ECtHR also stressed that an accused should not be convicted 'solely or decisively' on the basis of evidence furnished by anonymous witnesses.

Some legal systems seek to mitigate the impact of the limitations placed on national security grounds on the accused person's ability to examine the evidence in his case by granting security-vetted defence counsel greater access than to the defendant. This can be achieved by security clearance and access to sensitive documents being granted to the accused's counsel, or by the government appointing 'special advocates' to act on the suspect's behalf, as in England. These 'special advocates' will be given access to the 'closed material', which the government refuses to disclose to the detainees on grounds of national security, and will make

---

88 *Van Mechelen and Others v. The Netherlands*, 55/1996/674/861-864 (ECtHR, 23 April 1997), para. 56.

89 *Nuttall* (n 71), at para. 14.

arguments on their clients' behalf to challenge the closed material. In both procedures, defence counsel is strictly prohibited from discussing the protected material with their client.[90]

According to defence counsel who have been involved in such procedures, these measures fall far short from compensating the disadvantage created to the defendant by refusing it access to the protected material. A lawyer who defended clients in terrorism trials in the United States observes that the procedures protecting classified information 'present [for the defence lawyer] a daunting array of professional, moral, and ethical dilemmas'.[91] Defence counsel's effectiveness is severely hampered by the inability to discuss the protected material with their client, who would generally be in a much better position to identify potentially exculpatory elements. The secrecy surrounding the material will also be an obstacle in the way of potential defence lines of investigation resulting from leads in the protected material. Moreover, as the English Court of Appeal has observed, 'the relationship between a lawyer in the know and his client is bound to be damaged because, in addition to preventing frankness and fettering the free flow of information between lawyer and client, the order is likely to nurture in the client a belief that his lawyers are putting other interests, possibly including those of the prosecution, above his own'.[92]

In the case *A. and Others*,[93] which dealt with administrative detention and not criminal procedure, the ECtHR therefore was sceptical of the UK's 'special advocates' scheme. The Court found that the 'special advocates' could be a way of mitigating the disadvantage suffered by the detainees. According to the Court, however, the more important question remained whether the 'open material' accessible to the detainees provided them sufficient information to be able to challenge the allegations against them.

Moreover, giving defence counsel access to material which their clients may not see presupposes that the lawyers are safe from intimidation and threats from their clients and their clients' associates. In many countries, however, defence counsel would be at great risk of intimidation from their clients if they had access to protected government information.

---

[90] See Chapters 1 and 2 of this book.

[91] Joshua L. Dratel (2003), 'Ethical issues in defending a terrorism case: How secrecy and security impair the defence of a terrorism case', *Cardozo Public Law, Policy & Ethics Journal*, **2**, 81.

[92] *R v. G and another* [2003] UKHL 50, [2004] 1 AC 1034.

[93] *A. and Others v. the United Kingdom*, App. no. 3455/05 (ECtHR, 19 February 2009), paras. 203 and 204.

In conclusion, the use of evidence generated from intelligence sources and covert investigation techniques generates complex challenges for all parties to the case. Intelligence agencies, criminal investigators and prosecutors will have to bear disclosure and fair trial aspects in mind from the start of an investigation, and involvement of the prosecutors in the police investigation from early on becomes all the more imperative. All actors, investigators, prosecutors, judges, other court officers, defence counsel, will have to be trained to navigate these complexities.

4. CONCLUSIONS

The preventive criminal justice strategy against terrorism, combining advanced criminalization offences, investigative powers and criminal procedure rules, seeks to marry effective protection of societies against acts of terrorism with respect for the rights and due process safeguards that are the hallmark of the administration of criminal justice in democratic societies.

In this chapter I have argued that such a preventive criminal justice strategy against terrorism does not come without side effects that are undesirable from a human rights perspective. I have drawn attention to the tension between what I have called 'advanced criminalization' and the requirements of strict legality and foreseeability of criminal law, and the principle whereby in democratic societies criminal justice should be a last resort to suppress conduct that is unambiguously harmful to others. I have further highlighted respects in which the use of intelligence sources and SITs, both of them essential to an effective preventive criminal justice strategy against terrorism, inevitably require the limitation of some fair trial safeguards.

In these concluding remarks, I would like to draw attention to three broader ambiguities inherent in the innovations that the preventive criminal justice approach against terrorism is bringing to criminal justice systems around the world.

First, so far I have argued that the use of SITs is necessary to gather evidence to prove the elements of advanced criminalization offences. Interception of communications between conspirers is necessary to prove the existence of plans being plotted in secret. Undercover agents or informers need to approach youth on a trajectory of radicalization towards violent extremism to detect, stop and prove the attacks they might be plotting before these come dangerously close to fruition. However, the relationship also runs in the other direction: advanced criminalization offences, such as preparatory acts or travelling for purposes of terrorist training, broaden the scope of what may plausibly constitute a terrorist offence from the actual perpetration of serious violence to actions that are suspect only because they are (or might be) related to terrorist intentions. As a result, police will be able to lawfully obtain a warrant for surveillance of communications not only for X, who is reasonably suspected to have participated in a terrorist bombing, but also for Y, who is reasonably suspected to have attempted to obtain an item that could be used to build an explosive device, and maybe even Z, whose worldview suggests he might at some point make such an attempt. The field of persons that can lawfully be put under surveillance grows exponentially. Possibly, indeed, the main preventive effect of advanced criminalization offences is not in enabling prosecutions for conduct preparatory to a terrorist attack (which might be unattractive to prosecutors because of difficulties in proving the *mens rea*). Rather, the preventive effect might lie primarily in this broadening of the circle of persons who can be lawfully placed under surveillance. In other words, not the investigative powers in the service of proving offences, but the offences in the service of enabling investigative powers. Conversely, the risk to human rights of these offences might not so much lie in prosecutions for conduct that would never have led to a terrorist attack, but rather in excessive loosening of the criteria to obtain surveillance measures.

Second, many countries have introduced new or broadened existing surveillance powers of the law enforcement agencies to counter terrorism. In some countries, these powers are reserved to the investigation of terrorism-related offences. This can be seen positively as self-restraint by the State, or – on the opposite – as the highly suspect creation of an exceptional legal regime for one category of offences. More often, the new legislation will extend the additional surveillance and investigation powers not only to terrorism offences, but also more broadly to organized crime and an array of other serious (or even not so serious) offences. This can be welcomed as counter-terrorism offering the opportunity to give law enforcement long overdue powers necessary to effectively combat groups trafficking in drugs, weapons and human beings. It can also, however, be viewed as the dangerous abuse of the social alarm created by the threat of terrorism to grant police wide ranging surveillance powers beyond the exceptional exigencies of preventing acts of terrorism.

Third, throughout this chapter I have dealt with the consequences of the measures necessary to implement a preventive criminal justice strategy against terrorism in the context of democratic societies and of governments engaged in a genuine, good faith counter-terrorism effort. We cannot disregard, however, that advanced criminalization offences and expanded surveillance powers can equally be adopted by undemocratic governments' intent to use counter-terrorism as a pretext to oppress, violate human rights and fundamental freedoms and suppress peaceful opposition. Such regimes will not fail to use the rhetoric of the preventive criminal justice approach to terrorism for their own ends. This is not an argument to reject the concept of the preventive criminal justice approach to terrorism. I do not see an equally valid alternative. It is imperative, however, to see the unintended human rights consequences of this approach, to be better able to look for ways to mitigate them.

8. Questions of accountability in countering terrorism

Lisa N. Oldring*

In December 2014, the US Senate Select Committee on Intelligence published in redacted form the summary findings and conclusions of its 6700-page study of the programme of detention and interrogation operated by the Central Intelligence Agency (CIA) between 2002–2009. According to the summary, the Senate Committee study detailed a 'program of indefinite secret detention and the use of brutal interrogation techniques in violation of US law, treaty obligations and [...] values' which was initiated 'by CIA personnel, aided by two outside contractors'.[1] Although treatment by the CIA of high-profile detainees in particular had already been exposed, the Senate Committee study outlined disturbing new details of serious abuse including instances of mock executions, forced rectal feeding, and widespread use of forced sleep deprivation and solitary confinement, as well as suggesting a pattern of gross incompetence on the part of those hired to design and carry out interrogations.[2] The report also revealed that personnel rarely were reprimanded or held to account by the CIA for serious and significant violations, raising critical questions of oversight.

* The views expressed herein are those of the author and do not necessarily reflect the views of the UN.

[1] US Senate Select Committee on Intelligence (SSCI) (2014), 'Committee Study of the Central Intelligence Agency's Detention and Interrogation Program', released on 9 December 2014, available at http://www.intelligence.senate.gov/study2014/sscistudy1.pdf, accessed 8 May 2017.

[2] In July 2006, the UN Committee Against Torture expressed concern over the apparent impunity of US personnel involved in acts of torture or cruel, inhuman and degrading treatment or punishment, and called on the State to promptly, impartially and thoroughly investigate all such allegations. UN Committee Against Torture (2006), 'UN Committee against Torture: Conclusions and Recommendations, United States of America', UN Doc. CAT/C/USA/CO/2, 25 July.

Nearly three years after the release of the summary findings and recommendations, the full 6700-page Senate Committee study has not been made public, in spite of repeated calls for its release.[3] Efforts to secure individual accountability for serious violations committed under the umbrella of the CIA detention and interrogation programme, and to obtain redress for victims have largely been frustrated,[4] although legal action against two individual contractors for their role in its design and implementation eventually resulted in a legal settlement against them.[5]

---

[3] On 10 February 2017, the Department of Justice provided the Federal District Court for the District of Columbia with a copy of this report for preservation and safekeeping. See Carol Rosenberg (2017), 'Trump Justice Department delivers CIA "Torture Report" to federal court', *Miami Herald*, 10 February, http://www.miamiherald.com/news/nation-world/world/americas/guantanamo/article132126204.html accessed 9 June 2017.

[4] In August 2009, 'information pertaining to alleged mistreatment of detainees' prompted the US Attorney General to initiate a preliminary review into 'whether federal laws were violated in connection with the interrogation of specific detainees at overseas locations'. The review, which was restricted to 'unauthorized' interrogation methods applied by agents of the CIA, led to criminal investigations in just two cases out of 101 instances of alleged abuse of individual detainees. Even these two investigations were closed without prosecution since 'the admissible evidence would not be sufficient to obtain and sustain convictions beyond a reasonable doubt', according to the Department of Justice. In response to the report of the SSCI, the US Department of Justice announced that it would not reopen any investigation into allegations of torture as its investigators 'did not find any new information that they had not previously considered in reaching their [earlier] determination'. See (2009), 'Attorney General Eric Holder regarding a preliminary review into the interrogation of certain detainees', Justice News, 24 August, http://www.justice.gov/opa/speech/attorney-general-eric-holder-regarding-preliminary-review-interrogation-certain-detainees, accessed 13 October 2017; (2012), 'Statement of Attorney General Eric Holder on closure of investigation into the interrogation of certain detainees', Justice News, 30 August, http://www.justice.gov/opa/pr/statement-attorney-general-eric-holder-closure-investigation-interrogation-certain-detainees, accessed 13 October 2017. See also Advocates for US Torture Prosecutions (2014), 'Shadow Report to the United Nations Committee Against Torture on the Review of the Periodic Report of the United States of America', 29 September, http://hrp.law.harvard.edu/wp-content/uploads/2014/10/CAT-Shadow-Report-Advocates-for-US-Torture-Prosecutions.pdf, accessed 13 October 2017.

[5] On 13 October 2015, the American Civil Liberties Union filed a lawsuit against James Mitchell and Bruce Jessen, two individuals reportedly contracted by the CIA to design, implement and oversee the 'enhanced interrogation' programme. The lawsuit was filed under the Alien Tort Statute on behalf of three of the individual victims of the programme. A settlement agreement was reached in August 2017 before the case reached a jury trial. See (2017), 'Salim v.

In light of the details that are known about the treatment of individuals under the CIA detention and interrogation programme, the lack of accountability for serious human rights violations committed under the CIA programme is especially disturbing. Counter-terror measures adopted by many governments, however, have resulted in violation of human rights and challenged fundamental rule of law principles. In response to real or perceived security threats, governments have adopted emergency or other exceptional legislation, at times bypassing democratic legislative processes and falling foul of the principle of legality. Criminal justice rules, practices and policies have been modified, ostensibly in response to security imperatives.[6] Far-reaching surveillance practices have been introduced and maintained, in many instances without procedural safeguards or effective oversight. Practices including abductions, extra-legal transfers, secret or prolonged administrative detention, and torture have been exposed, and repudiated.

Many of the violations taking place in the counter-terrorism context have been exposed as both illegal and, from a counter-terrorism perspective, ineffective, yet the exposure and condemnation of such practices has not resulted in systematic investigation, accountability or justice for victims.[7] Some governments have maintained that certain invasive measures are necessary and proportionate against an ongoing and extraordinary threat of terrorism, insisted that such practices are consistent

---

Mitchell – Lawsuit against psychologists behind CIA torture program', ACLU, 17 August, https://www.aclu.org/cases/salim-v-mitchell-lawsuit-against-psychologists-behind-cia-torture-program, accessed 13 October 2017. On 22 February 2017, the Department of Justice indicated it would invoke the State secrets privilege to prevent the deposition of Gina Hapsel, appointed as Deputy CIA Director, to discuss her role in overseeing the alleged torture of two terrorism suspects and the destruction of videotapes documenting their torture in a secret prison in Thailand. Spencer Ackerman (2017), 'DoJ moves to prevent CIA official from detailing role in Bush-era torture', *The Guardian*, 22 February, https://www.theguardian.com/us-news/2017/feb/22/cia-torture-gina-haspel-court-deposition-trump?CMP=Share_AndroidApp_Gmail, accessed 13 October 2017.

[6] H. Duffy (2015), *The War on Terror and the Framework of International Law*, 2nd edn (Cambridge: Cambridge University Press), Ch. 4. See also Report of the UN High Commissioner for Human Rights (2010), 'Report on the promotion and protection of human rights while countering terrorism', UN Doc. A/HRC/16/50, 15 December.

[7] See, for example, the Senate Committee's first two findings and conclusions, which state that: 'The CIA's use of its enhanced interrogation techniques was not an effective means of acquiring intelligence or gaining cooperation from detainees' and 'The CIA's justification for the use of its enhanced interrogation techniques rested on inaccurate claims of their effectiveness'. According to the

with domestic and international law, or evaded scrutiny by invoking State secrecy. In some States, a lack of political will has overridden initiatives towards criminal justice for serious violations; while in others, a stated commitment to combat impunity for human rights violations has not been carried out effectively in practice. Deviation from the universal human rights norms enshrined in international law also has undermined criminal justice where States have adopted measures, in the investigation and prosecution of individuals accused of terrorist activity, which fall short of international standards. The lack of accountability for violations of international law not only has prevented individual victims from accessing justice but also has undercut the ability of the State to claim to uphold the rule of law and to hold other countries to account for violations thereof.

This chapter considers, as a matter of moral effectiveness as well as legal duty, the obligation of States to respect human rights in the course of countering terrorism and ensure accountability, including individual criminal accountability for serious violations when they occur. Whilst the challenges contributing to a lack of accountability in the counter-terrorism context are numerous, this chapter focuses on three, namely: the definition of terrorism and legal framework applied by States in terrorism-related cases; the expansion of intelligence agencies' powers without effective oversight or safeguards against abuse; and the influence of national security considerations on criminal justice, notably through an expansive use of the State secrets' privilege. Where examples exist, measures taken by States to combat impunity, ensure transparency and justice for victims, and uphold the rule of law in the counter-terrorism context, are highlighted.

1. COUNTER-TERRORISM ACCOUNTABILITY

1.1 Obligations under International Law

As demonstrated in Chapter 7, many States have invested heavily, and justifiably, in holding individuals to account for terrorist-related offences. Less evident is a demonstrated commitment to ensure accountability for

Senate Committee report, even prior to 2001, from its own experience with coercive interrogations, the CIA had determined 'that such techniques 'do not produce intelligence', 'will probably result in false answers' and had historically proven to be ineffective'. SSCI (n 1), Foreword.

human rights violations committed by government agents in the counter-terrorism context. Such accountability is, nonetheless, no less an obligation under international law than is the duty to take measures to prevent terrorist violence, and to identify and punish perpetrators of terrorist attacks. Importantly, ensuring accountability for human rights violations also serves to enhance the moral and practical effectiveness of States' efforts to combat terrorism.

The obligation of States to try to prevent and repress terrorist acts, and to investigate and prosecute those responsible is enshrined in a host of multilateral and regional treaties or protocols, resolutions and declarations. This duty also stems from the due diligence obligation on States to take all appropriate and necessary steps to safeguard the right to life of those within their jurisdiction. States also must adopt preventive measures to protect anyone whose life is known or suspected to be at risk from the criminal acts of another individual.

Defining acts of terrorism in domestic criminal legislation in line with the principle of legality is one critical step to prevention, and to ensuring that those who commit such acts are brought to justice. States also must put in place effective criminal justice and law enforcement systems including measures to deter the commission of offences and investigate violations where they occur; ensure that those suspected of criminal acts are prosecuted; provide victims with effective remedies; and take other necessary steps to prevent a recurrence of violations.

These responsibilities are nested, however, within a broader web of commitments. States must ensure that any measure taken to counter terrorism adheres to their international and domestic legal obligations, including international human rights law. The duty to ensure compliance with, and prevent violations of international human rights law applies to counter-terrorism policies, legislation and practices, subject only to lawful derogation from, or limitation to, specific rights. It includes ensuring, for example, that guarantees of due process are respected when persons who are alleged to have committed terrorism-related offences are arrested, charged, detained and prosecuted. Such guarantees are essential to ensuring that the guilty are held to account, that justice is done and that victims have access to effective remedy. States also must ensure accountability for any gross or serious violations of international human rights law and international humanitarian law, including those that take place in the counter-terrorism context.

In other words, States have a dual obligation under international law to ensure accountability. This involves responding to threats and acts of terrorism through the criminalization, investigation and prosecution of terrorist offences, in line with international and domestic law. It also entails ensuring accountability for human rights violations, with specific duties required of all three branches of government.[8] From a public policy perspective, this involves ensuring that government agents assume responsibility for their actions and that they are held to account for their actions by explaining and justifying them to those affected, with some form of enforceable sanction if their conduct or explanation for it is found wanting. From a criminal law perspective, accountability is essential to ensuring justice and reparation for victims, while also serving as a deterrent to future violations.[9] The obligation to ensure accountability is undoubtedly one of the most important legal obligations arising from international human rights law.

Over the last decade, States have been explicit in their commitment to uphold these principles of accountability through counter-terrorism measures that are grounded in respect for human rights and the rule of law, with increasing appreciation of the importance of human rights to counter-terrorism efforts. Through the Global Counter-Terrorism Strategy – a comprehensive plan of action agreed to by all UN Member States in 2006 and reaffirmed repeatedly since then – governments committed to ensuring respect for human rights and the rule of law as the very basis of the fight against terrorism. They undertook also to 'make every effort to develop and maintain an effective and rule of law-based national criminal justice system that can ensure, in accordance with … obligations under international law, that any person who participates in the financing, planning, preparation or perpetration of terrorist acts or in support of terrorist acts is brought to justice, on the basis of the principle to

[8] The obligation to seek accountability is explicitly referred to in instruments of international human rights law and has been reinforced by interpretations of the law. The International Covenant on Civil and Political Rights (ICCPR), the Convention against Torture and Other Cruel, Inhuman or Degrading Treatment or Punishment, the International Convention for the Protection of All Persons from Enforced Disappearance, and the Optional Protocols to the Convention on the Rights of the Child on the involvement of children in armed conflict and on the sale of children, child prostitution and child pornography impose an obligation on all State parties to provide an effective remedy for violations of the rights and freedoms contained in these treaties, including a duty to investigate and punish those responsible.

[9] International Bar Association (IBA) (2011), *Terrorism and International Law: Accountability, Remedies and Reform*, A Report of the IBA Task Force on Terrorism (London: IBA), p. 165.

extradite or prosecute, with due respect for human rights and fundamental freedoms'.[10]

The UN Security Council on numerous occasions has reaffirmed that counter-terrorism measures taken by States must comply with all their obligations under international law, including human rights law, underscoring that 'effective counter-terrorism measures and respect for human rights, fundamental freedoms and the rule of law are complementary and mutually reinforcing, and are an essential part of a successful counter-terrorism effort'.[11] Thus, there is broad recognition that international human rights norms and standards are essential to effective counter-terrorism measures, while also providing legitimacy and clear, internationally accepted baselines for State conduct.[12]

1.2 Accountability, Good Governance and the Rule of Law

Ensuring respect for human rights in the counter-terror context also can contribute as a deterrent to prevent new violations, uphold the rule of law and secure public trust in the justice system, through investment in institutions and processes that are accountable, effective and legitimate. By the same token, accountability is the basis on which trust in public institutions, leaders and duty-bearers is fostered. Equally, however, a lack of rule of law accountability contributes to a climate of impunity and may facilitate repetition of violations, where perpetrators are free to commit them without fear of sanction.[13] It also undermines global counter-terrorism efforts, weakens the credibility of those same governments that oppose human rights abuses committed by other governments and is counter-productive. The UN Deputy High Commissioner for Human Rights has noted that in cases where counter-terrorism measures

---

[10] UN Global Counter-Terrorism Strategy, GA resolution 60/288, 8 September 2006, Pt IV, para. 4.

[11] Statement by the President of the Security Council, S/PRST/2013/1, 15 January 2013. See also UN Security Council (UNSC) resolution 1904 (15 December 2009) and UNSC resolution 1963 (20 December 2010), para. 10, encouraging the Counter-Terrorism Executive Directorate to 'ensure that all human rights issues relevant to the implementation of resolutions 1373 (2001) and 1624 (2005) are addressed consistently and even-handedly'.

[12] 'Report of the United Nations High Commissioner for Human Rights on the protection of human rights and fundamental freedoms while countering terrorism', 17 December 2012, UN Doc. A/HRC/22/26, para. 30.

[13] See, for example, Human Rights Watch (2009), 'Selling justice short: Why accountability matters for peace', 7 July, https://www.hrw.org/sites/default/files/reports/ij0709webwcover_1.pdf, accessed 9 June 2017.

have resulted in human rights violations, 'this injustice has been a rallying cry by violent extremist groups in recruitment of new supporters'.[14] More specifically, according to the findings of the Multi-National Counter-Terrorism Expert Network, '(e)mpirical evidence suggests [...] that torturing one can result in the radicalization of one hundred, not least because a government's use of indiscriminate repression seems to assist the flow of recruits to, and communal support or toleration for, terrorist groups' and that 'egregious and indiscriminate harsh overt repression by the state under the guise of tackling terrorism is likely to have counter-productive effects overall'.[15]

Human rights accountability in the counter-terrorism context thus requires adherence to internationally-recognized rule of law standards, including respect for the supremacy of law, equality before the law, accountability to the law, and fairness in the protection and vindication of rights. This requires the adoption of policies, laws and practices that are accessible, open to meaningful public scrutiny and subject to effective oversight, in order to ensure a system of balanced and effective checks and balances. Effective procedural safeguards and adequately resourced institutional arrangements must be in place, along with structures and processes that provide access to justice for victims where violations occur.[16] To be meaningful, it also requires a commitment to ensuring a separation of powers and a distribution of competencies across different structures in order to avoid undue concentration of power in any one

---

[14] Statement by the Deputy UN High Commissioner for Human Rights Deputy High Commissioner for Human Rights at the Panel discussion on the Human Rights Dimensions of Preventing and Countering Violent Extremism, 16 March 2016, http://www.ohchr.org/en/NewsEvents/Pages/DisplayNews.aspx?NewsID=17245&LangID=E, accessed 13 October 2017. See also Human Rights Watch (2015), 'No more excuses: A roadmap to justice for CIA torture', 1 December, https://www.hrw.org/report/2015/12/01/no-more-excuses/roadmap-justice-cia-torture, accessed 9 June 2017, at p. 4: 'Detainee abuse, including abuse of prisoners by the US military, has been used by terrorist groups to obtain new recruits and contributed to anti-US sentiment in many countries'.

[15] K. Samuel, N. White and A. Salinas de Frias (2012), 'Multi-national counter-terrorism expert network: Report of key findings and recommendations on the rule of law and counter-terrorism', Nottingham University, January, https://www.nottingham.ac.uk/hrlc/documents/projectsummaries/pdfs/wjp-project-report-on-counter-terrorism-feb-12-final2.pdf, accessed 13 October 2017, p. 123.

[16] See 'Report of the UN Special Rapporteur on the promotion and protection of human rights and fundamental freedoms while countering terrorism: Compilation of good practices on legal and institutional frameworks and measures that ensure respect for human rights by intelligence agencies while countering terrorism, including their oversight', 17 May 2010, UN Doc. A/HRC/14/46.

authority, as well as to procedural and legal transparency. Through adherence to these principles, the rule of law framework can have a power-restraining effect to prevent excesses and abuses.

1.3 Accountability for Serious Human Rights Violations and the Right of Victims to a Remedy

Where there is credible evidence to suggest there has been a serious violation of human rights, the State concerned must conduct a prompt, independent, impartial and thorough investigation, which is capable of leading to the identification and, where appropriate, the punishment of the perpetrator(s) and those on whose authority the violations were committed.[17] This duty stems from the general obligation of States to respect and ensure respect for human rights, and to fulfil the right to an effective remedy.[18] Moreover, according to the UN Human Rights

---

[17] Human Rights Committee (2004), 'General Comment 31', CCPR/C/21/Rev.1/Add.13, 26 May, para. 18; *El-Masri v. Macedonia*, App. no 39630/09 (ECtHR, 13 December 2012), para. 182; 'Joint study on global practices in relation to secret detention in the context of countering terrorism of the Special Rapporteur on the promotion and protection of human rights and fundamental freedoms while countering terrorism, Martin Scheinin; the Special Rapporteur on torture and other cruel, inhuman or degrading treatment or punishment, Manfred Nowak; the Working Group on Arbitrary Detention represented by its vice-chair, Shaheen Sardar Ali; and the Working Group on Enforced or Involuntary Disappearances represented by its chair, Jeremy Sarkin', 20 May 2010 UN Doc. A/HRC/13/42. These obligations are consistent with the principle of State responsibility, which holds that 'every internationally wrongful act of a State entails the international responsibility of that State', and further that 'the responsible State is under an obligation to make full reparation for the injury caused by the internationally wrongful act'. International Law Commission, Articles on Responsibility of States for International Wrongful Acts. The general principle also applies to violations of international humanitarian law in international armed conflict, according to the grave breaches provisions of the Geneva Conventions and, in non-international armed conflict, as a matter of customary law.

[18] Article 2 International Covenant on Civil and Political Rights; Human Rights Committee, 'General Comment 31' (n 17). The obligation to investigate and ensure accountability is reflected in various international and regional human rights treaties, as well as in soft law instruments such as the UN Basic Principles and Guidelines on the Right to a Remedy and Reparation for Gross Violations of International Human Rights Law and Serious Violations of International Humanitarian Law, the UN Basic Principles on the Use of Force and Firearms by Law Enforcement Officials, and the UN Principles on the Effective Prevention and Investigation of Extra-Legal, Arbitrary and Summary Executions.

Committee, a failure to investigate alleged violations of international human rights law may amount to a violation in its own right.[19] A State may also be responsible for lack of due diligence if it has failed to prevent or punish violations of international human rights or humanitarian law committed by State agents or private actors.[20] The right to an effective remedy for victims, which is reflected in virtually every human rights treaty and soft law instrument, is essential for the effective protection of all other human rights and must be complied with even during a state of emergency.[21]

Inter-dependent with this obligation is the right of victims to know the truth – that is, to seek and obtain information on the causes and conditions pertaining to gross violations of human rights law and to learn the truth in regard to these violations.[22] The European Court of Human Rights underscored the importance of the right to truth for victims in its judgment in 2012 against Macedonia for that country's role in the extraordinary rendition of Khalid El-Masri. Recognizing the extreme seriousness of the multiple violations of the European Convention on Human Rights including the prohibitions on torture, and against arbitrary detention, as well as a failure to investigate and to provide an effective remedy, the Court ordered that Macedonia pay 60 000 Euros to Mr El-Masri. The Court emphasized the importance of the case 'not only for the applicant and his family, but also for other victims of similar crimes and the general public, who had the right to know what had happened'.[23]

A finding of State responsibility for violations of international human rights law should lead to the adoption by the State of measures to repair the damage it may have caused and to prevent future violations.[24] This may involve measures ranging from payment of reparations to victims and their families, and cessation of any ongoing violation and assurance of non-repetition, as well as the adoption of legal mechanisms to prevent

---

[19] Human Rights Committee, 'General Comment 31' (n 17).

[20] Human Rights Committee, 'General Comment 31' (n 17), para. 8.

[21] Human Rights Committee 'General Comment 29', CCPR/C/21/Rev.1/Add.11, para. 14.

[22] UN Basic Principles and Guidelines on the Right to a Remedy and Reparation for Gross Violations of International Human Rights Law and Serious Violations of International Humanitarian Law, GA resolution 60/147, 16 December 2005, Annex, para. 24.

[23] *El-Masri v. The Former Yugoslav Republic of Macedonia*, App. no. 39630/09 (ECtHR, 13 December 2012), para. 191.

[24] GA resolution 60/147 (n 22), Annex.

future abuses.[25] The case of Maher Arar often is cited as noteworthy in this regard, in terms of remedy and reparation eventually received by Arar in Canada for that government's role in his detention and rendition to torture. A dual Canadian-Syrian national, in September 2002 Arar was detained at JFK airport in New York, denied meaningful access to counsel, and secretly rendered to Syria, on the basis of inaccurate information shared with US intelligence agents by Canadian law enforcement officials. In Syria, he was tortured and detained incommunicado in an underground cell for over ten months, though never charged with a crime. While a Commission of Inquiry established by the Canadian government in 2004 carried out its work, a lawsuit initiated by Arar that same year, including claims of negligence, defamation, false imprisonment, assault and battery, complicity to torture, conspiracy, and abuse of public office, eventually led to mediation between the parties. In settlement of this lawsuit, the then-Prime Minister formally apologized for the government's role in Arar's rendition and torture and offered $10 million in compensation to Arar and his family, in addition to costs for his legal fees. Significant settlements, including compensation and formal public apology, also have been reached more recently in Canada in the cases of Omar Khadr, and of Abdullah Almalki, Ahmad Abou-Elmaati and Muayyed Nureddin, although not without public controversy.[26]

---

[25] The UN General Assembly has urged States, 'while countering terrorism (…) [t]o ensure that (…) victims receive adequate, effective and prompt reparation, which should include, as appropriate, restitution, compensation, rehabilitation and guarantees of non-recurrence, including where the violation constitutes a crime under international or national law, to ensure accountability for those responsible for such violations'. UN Basic Principles and Guidelines on the Right to a Remedy and Reparation for Gross Violations of International Human Rights Law and Serious Violations of International Humanitarian Law, GA resolution 68/178, 28 January 2014, para. 6(p).

[26] 'Report of the Internal Inquiry into the Actions of Canadian Officials in Relation to Abdullah Almalki, Ahmad Abou-Elmaati and Muayyed Nureddin' (2008), http://epe.lac-bac.gc.ca/100/206/301/pco-bcp/commissions/internal_inquiry/2010-03-09/www.iacobucciinquiry.ca/pdfs/documents/final-report-copy-en.pdf, accessed 10 June 2017; 'Concluding Observations of the Committee against Torture', 25 June 2012, CAT/C/CAN/CO/6, para. 16. By contrast, similar efforts on behalf of victims seeking justice in the United States have largely been frustrated. See, for example, Beth Van Schaack, 'Not to be forgotten: The case of Maher Arar', *Just Security*, 19 December 2014, https://www.justsecurity.org/18526/forgotten-case-maher-arar/, accessed 10 June 2017.

For the victim, the right to an effective remedy entails a duty on the State to have this right 'determined by competent judicial, administrative or legislative authorities, or by any other competent authority provided for by the legal system of the State, and to develop the possibilities of judicial remedy'.[27] In this regard, it is important that individuals have access to credible oversight and complaint processes without fear of retaliation, as States have an obligation to remove all barriers that may impede their access to justice.[28] In terms of remedies, payment of compensation to those who have suffered violation of their rights may help to prevent the fostering of resentment amongst aggrieved individuals and their families as a result of illegal practices, although reparation need not be limited to financial compensation.[29] It can also serve as an investment in future stability, through recognition of State fault and provision of a concrete form of remedy, particularly where legal and/or institutional reform also is carried out in order to guarantee non-recurrence. Where a human rights violation rises to the level of a gross violation however, non-judicial remedies will be considered inadequate and criminal prosecution will be required.

2. CHALLENGES AND IMPEDIMENTS TO ACCOUNTABILITY

In spite of these obligations, instances of accountability for serious violations of international human rights law in the counter-terrorism context are relatively scarce, with individual criminal responsibility in a

---

27 Article 2, para. 3(b) ICCPR.

28 GA resolution 60/147 (n 22), Annex, Principles 2 and 11. See also 'Report of the United Nations High Commissioner for Human Rights on the protection of human rights and fundamental freedoms while countering terrorism', 17 December 2012, UN Doc. A/HRC/22/26.

29 The UN Basic Principles and Guidelines suggest that reparation may include restitution, compensation, rehabilitation, satisfaction and guarantees of non-repetition. Regional human rights courts have referred to international customary law rules on State responsibility to order the payment of compensation to victims of human rights abuse, for example where the Inter-American Court of Human Rights states: '[i]t is a principle of International Law that any violation of an international obligation which causes damage gives rise to a duty to make adequate reparations. The obligation to provide reparations is regulated in every aspect by International Law'. *Case of the Rochela Massacre v. Colombia* (IACHR, 11 May 2007), Series C, No. 163, para. 226.

handful of cases.[30] State practice has revealed a host of challenges and impediments to accountability which have contributed, in some measure, to perpetuating impunity for human rights violations in the counter-terrorism context. These include overly-broad or vague definitions in law of terrorist or national security-related offences, which has left open a risk of abuse; the expansion of the executive; and the influence of national security considerations in criminal justice processes.

2.1 National Legislation

Concepts related to national security and counter-terrorism are pervasive in national legislation around the globe, providing the basis for expansive executive, intelligence-gathering and law enforcement powers in many countries. National laws criminalize various acts associated with terrorism. They endow police with enhanced powers of investigation and arrest in regard to such offences; establish regimes for communications surveillance, as well as the targeted surveillance of individuals; provide for asset-freezing, and the imposition of travel bans on 'terrorists' and 'terrorist organisations', as well as trade sanctions against countries that reportedly harbour or support terrorists. In view of their wide-reaching potential consequences, the precise definition in national criminal law of terrorist-related crimes is therefore critical to ensure the effectiveness of such legislation to prevent and address activity which is truly 'terrorist' in nature. It is equally important to prevent human rights violations by agents of the State, as well as to ensure that perpetrators of any violations are held to account through a rule of law framework.

As outlined in detail in Chapter 7, in order to effectively address and counter terrorism through a criminal justice approach, a State must criminalize offences such as conspiracy to commit acts of terrorism, financing of terrorism, incitement of, and recruitment to terrorism, as well as terrorist acts, in accordance with international standards.[31] This requires clarity and precision in the legal definition of an activity as criminal, as a baseline for ensuring both the effectiveness of the law, as

---

30 For an overview of cases through 2011, see IBA (n 9).

31 A collection of declarations, resolutions, and multilateral and regional treaties set out the legal obligations of States to prevent and suppress terrorism. These instruments require States to enact national legislation to address specific terrorism-related acts, for example, to the financing of terrorism, to air safety, or to maritime navigation and platforms, and require States to criminalize and investigate those acts, to prosecute or extradite suspected perpetrators, to freeze the assets of suspected terrorists, among other duties.

well as the accountability of agents of the State that are responsible for enforcing it. If a law is vague or overly-broad, it provides neither fair notice to individuals of what conduct is prohibited or potential consequences for violation of that law, nor clear standards for those entrusted with law enforcement, thus leaving open the possibility of abuses. A fundamental requirement of the rule of law, this legal certainty serves to ensure that those subject to the law are protected against the arbitrary use of State power, whilst allowing for the effective function of criminal justice processes.

In Chapter 2 of this book, Professor Scheinin assesses the role played by the UN Security Council in the establishment of the post-9/11 counter-terrorism legislative framework.[32] For present purposes, the influence of Security Council resolution 1373 (2001) in terms of human rights accountability bears mention, as it included a far-reaching declaration by the Security Council of *any* act of terrorism as a threat to international peace and security. It also imposed a range of legislative obligations on all States, raising definitional issues in the process around what constitutes a 'terrorist act' or 'terrorism', and who counts as a 'terrorist' or a 'participant'. Although these terms were left undefined by the Security Council, the resolution triggered an obligation on States to criminalize the financing of terrorism; suppress terrorist groups; deny refugee status to terrorists; prevent the movement of terrorists; and bring terrorists to justice, among other measures. The resolution further required States to establish such terrorist acts as 'serious criminal offences in domestic laws and regulations', with punishment commensurate with the seriousness of the acts.

As the resolution did not include an explicit provision for ensuring that the measures it required States to adopt were compliant with international

---

[32] While each of the instruments referred to in footnote 31 includes a component definition of terrorist activity, none provides a comprehensive definition of terrorism. Multilateral efforts to enshrine a definition of terrorism in a binding international instrument have continued for over a decade, stalling, primarily, over a lack of agreement on the distinction between acts of terrorism and the 'legitimate struggle of peoples in the exercise of their right to self-determination or under foreign occupation'; whether 'State terrorism' should fall within its scope; and whether the activities of armed forces of a State in peacetime should be considered within the scope of the convention. See Draft Comprehensive Convention Against International Terrorism, A/59/894, and reports of the Ad Hoc Committee established by General Assembly resolution 51/210 of 17 December 1996, 13th and 15th sessions, UN Docs A/64/37 and A/66/37. See also Ben Saul (2006), *Defining Terrorism in International Law* (Oxford: Oxford University Press).

human rights law, the interpretive discretion was left to individual States, many of which responded by adopting criminal legislation reflecting amorphous definitions of terrorism that fell short of the principle of legal certainty. In the years to follow, many countries adopted legislation containing definitions of terrorism that lack the required precision and certainty, as such entrusting government officials, prosecutors and police with broad discretion and opening the door to abuses by law enforcement. With the international legitimacy conferred by the Security Council, some States made use of such laws as a basis for far-reaching measures resulting in violation of a range of human rights.[33]

In 2009, the Panel of Eminent Jurists convened by the International Commission of Jurists summarized the impact of counter-terrorism laws adopted in the years immediately following 9/11, and the lack of accountability that often resulted, in its findings following a study of global counter-terrorism policies and practices.[34] Following a process of consultation that included 16 national and sub-regional hearings, covering more than 40 countries, the Panel concluded that:

> [c]ounter-terrorism laws reduce safeguards; the lack of safeguards facilitates a range of human rights violations; and that limitations on remedies, most particularly judicial remedies, creates impunity for human rights violators. This impunity, particularly over time, can give cover for extra-legal practices, such as disappearances, secret detention and torture. A culture of lawlessness can take hold, and feeds and fuels the very conflict, and terrorism, that the legislation was intended to end.[35]

The Panel suggested further that counter-terrorist mechanisms often lacked the normal guarantees of oversight and accountability, leaving

---

[33] See 'Reports of the Special Rapporteur on the promotion and protection of human rights and fundamental freedoms while countering terrorism', 28 December 2005, UN Doc. E/CN/4/2006/98, and 22 December 2010, UN Doc. A/HRC/16/51.

[34] The Panel was mandated by the International Commission of Jurists to 'examine the compatibility of laws, policies and practices adopted to counter terrorism, with basic principles of the rule of law, international human rights law and, where applicable, with international humanitarian law' through a process of consultation over a two-year period. International Commission of Jurists (2009), 'Assessing damage, urging action: Report of the Eminent Jurist Panel on Terrorism, Counter-Terrorism and Human Rights', http://www.un.org/en/sc/ctc/specialmeetings/2011/docs/icj/icj-2009-ejp-report.pdf, accessed 11 May 2017, pp. 7 and 8.

[35] Ibid., p. 40.

those responsible for violations with impunity for their actions and victims no avenue for redress.[36]

Since 2005, UN Security Council resolutions have included standard clauses providing that measures taken to combat terrorism should comply with States' obligations under international law, including human rights law, and there are good practice examples of efforts by States to ensure compliance of national legislation with international human rights law.[37] Experience has proven, however, that 'counter-terrorism measures introduced in moments of crisis or extreme political stress and which are intended as short-term measures can readily become entrenched with the passage of time and invoked routinely by law enforcement authorities', and much of the emergency legislation enacted by States in the years immediately following the terrorist attacks of 9/11 remains in force.[38]

Experts have highlighted the ongoing risks inherent in vaguely-worded or overly-broad counter-terror legislation – including crimes for speech that is seen to encourage terrorism either directly or indirectly, for example – and to caution against the expansion of executive power through such laws without adequate checks and balances.[39] The Independent Reviewer of Terrorism Legislation in the United Kingdom, for example, noted that such laws 'are undesirable even if they are not misused' and are cause for concern even where authorities are seen

---

[36] Id., p. 10.

[37] See, for example, UN Counter-Terrorism Implementation Task Force CTITF Working Group on Protecting Human Rights while Countering Terrorism (2014), *Basic Human Rights Reference Guide: Conformity of National Counter-Terrorism Legislation with International Human Rights Law* (New York: UN).

[38] 'Report of the United Nations High Commissioner for Human Rights on the protection of human rights and fundamental freedoms while countering terrorism', 19 December 2014, UN Doc. A/HRC/28/28, para. 27. See also *In the Name of Security: Counterterrorism laws worldwide since September 11*, Human Rights Watch: 29 June 2012.

[39] 'Report on counter-terrorism measures and human rights adopted by the Venice Commission at its 83rd Plenary Session', Venice, 4 June 2010, para. 33. See also, for example, Office of the United Nations High Commissioner for Human Rights (OHCHR) (2014), 'UN experts urge Ethiopia to stop using anti-terrorism legislation to curb human rights', press release, 18 September; OHCHR (2014), 'Statement by the United Nations Special Rapporteur on the rights to freedom of peaceful assembly and of association at the conclusion of his visit to the Republic of Rwanda', press release, 27 January.

'generally … to exercise their discretions with great care'.[40] In Canada, sweeping new legislation introduced in 2015 conferred powers on the Canadian Security Intelligence Service to take 'measures' both within or outside Canada to disrupt 'threats to the security of Canada', broadly defined, and established a new criminal offence of knowingly 'advocating or promoting the commission of terrorist offences in general', without further definition or limitation. Critics of the legislation raised serious concerns over the vague and overly-broad nature of the new criminal law powers and offences, which they argue are 'vulnerable to constitutional challenge',[41] while questioning their necessity in view of pre-existing offences under domestic criminal law of directly inciting, threatening, counselling or conspiring to commit terrorist activities.[42] The lack of a sunset clause or provision for periodic review of the bill also provoked concern, along with overarching concerns over the lack of effective oversight and procedural safeguards in place to protect against abuses.[43] In 2017 the government introduced new national security legislation before Parliament, Bill C-59, ostensibly with a view to addressing these and other issues.

---

[40] While noting that the United Kingdom 'quite rightly has very tough laws against terrorism', the Independent Reviewer urged Parliament to review the overly-broad definition of terrorism to 'avoid the potential for abuse'. David Anderson (2014), 'UK Independent Reviewer of Terrorism Legislation criticises too-broad definition of terrorism', Brick Court Chambers, 22 July, https://terrorismlegislationreviewer.independent.gov.uk/wp-content/uploads/2014/07/22-July-2014-PRESS-RELEASE.pdf, accessed 13 October 2017.

[41] Canadian Bar Association, Submission on Bill C-51, Anti-terrorism Act, 2015. In July 2015, Canadian civil society organizations filed a challenge with the Ontario Superior Court on the grounds that sections of the bill violate the Canadian Charter of Rights and Freedoms in a manner that is not justified in a free and democratic society.

[42] Provisions in the bill which would allow for judicial warrants to be issued, following secret proceedings, to authorize constitutional breaches including violations of the Canadian Charter have been sharply criticized as amounting to 'a perversion of the rule of law and separation of powers'. See Canadian Bar Association, ibid. See also 'Report of the UN Special Rapporteur on the promotion and protection of human rights and fundamental freedoms while countering terrorism' (n 16), Practice 5: 'Intelligence services are explicitly prohibited from undertaking any action that contravenes the Constitution or international human rights law. These prohibitions extend not only to the conduct of intelligence services on their national territory but also to their activities abroad'.

[43] Study of Bill C-51 (Antiterrorism Act 2015), Submissions to the Senate Standing Committee, 2 April 2015, available at www.antiterrorlaw.ca, accessed

There are numerous other examples of new legislation or reform to existing legislation that have raised serious concern.[44] A series of laws adopted by Turkey in 2013 and 2014 which provided for greatly expanded surveillance power, threats to journalists who expose abuses by the national intelligence agency, and restrictions on the use of the internet prompted criticism by individuals and groups at national and international level.[45] Anti-terrorism legislation under consideration in Brazil in November 2015 was criticized as overly-broad, carrying with it the potential for abuse.[46] Concerns were raised in January 2016 in relation to the state of emergency in France and the law on surveillance of electronic communications as imposing 'excessive and disproportionate restrictions' to the legitimate exercise of the rights to freedom of expression, peaceful assembly and association, and privacy, and as lacking in clarity and precision.[47]

New issues continue to arise in relation to security legislation, as the complexity and changing nature of the threat of terrorism poses new challenges for governments. With these have come additional challenges to ensuring human rights accountability. As part of international efforts to stem the flow of foreign fighters, for example, the UN Security Council adopted resolution 2178 in September 2014. The resolution mandated States to prevent the 'recruiting, organizing, transporting or equipping of individuals who travel to a State other than their States of residence or

---

13 October 2017; Notice of application, Ontario Superior Court of Justice, https://ccla.org/cclanewsite/wp-content/uploads/2015/07/Notice-of-Application-Re-Bill-C-51-C1382903xA0E3A.pdf, accessed 13 October 2017.

[44] See also Report of the UN Secretary-General on Protecting Human Rights and Fundamental Freedoms while Countering Terrorism, A/72/316, 11 August 2017, paras. 26–33.

[45] (2014), 'Turkey's new law on Internet curbs draws concern from UN rights office', UN News Centre, 14 February; Human Rights Watch (2014), 'Turkey: Spy agency law opens door to abuse', 29 April.

[46] OHCHR (2015), 'Proposed anti-terrorism legislation currently being considered by Brazil's Congress is too broadly drafted and may unduly restrict fundamental freedoms', 15 November, www.ohchr.org/en/NewsEvents/Pages/DisplayNews.aspx?NewsID=16709&LangID=E#sthash.V6nWYYlv.dpuf, accessed 13 October 2017.

[47] OHCHR (2016), 'UN rights experts urge France to protect fundamental freedoms while countering terrorism', 19 January, www.ohchr.org/en/NewsEvents/Pages/DisplayNews.aspx?NewsID=16966&LangID=E#sthash.NSGkSF7m.dpuf, accessed 13 October 2017. See also 'Two UN rights experts urge France to bring its draft counter-terrorism law in compliance with its international human rights obligations', 27 September 2017, http://www.ohchr.org/EN/NewsEvents/Pages/DisplayNews.aspx?NewsID=22165&LangID=E, accessed 22 November 2017.

nationality for the purpose of the perpetration, planning of, or participation in terrorist acts'. Importantly, resolution 2178 reaffirmed the obligation of all Member States to comply with international human rights law when fighting terrorism, noting that a failure to comply with human rights and other international obligations has contributed to increased radicalization and fostered a sense of impunity. Nonetheless, reference in the text to 'extremism', to 'terrorists' as a category of individuals in addition to specific acts to be sanctioned, and to 'terrorism in all forms and manifestations' as one of the most serious threats to international peace and security, without qualification or further definition, has prompted concerns that the resolution could fuel the adoption of repressive measures at national level against otherwise lawful, non-violent activities of groups or individuals,[48] with further implications for the accountability of State agents.[49]

The recent focus by States on initiatives to counter or prevent violent extremism, including measures following on the adoption of resolution 2178, have prompted concerns over their human rights impact, particularly in light of the 'elasticity' of the term 'violent extremism'. These include administrative and policy measures that focus on preventing individuals from being drawn into terrorist activity, as well as legislative measures that criminalize preparatory offences to terrorism.

In a recent report to the UN Human Rights Council, the UN Special Rapporteur on the promotion and protection of human rights and fundamental freedoms while countering terrorism noted that measures that target specific individuals or groups based on a determination that they are particularly 'at risk' of violent extremism are concerning, in view of the potential for discriminatory impact on specific minority, ethnic, religious or indigenous groups. In stigmatizing specific groups and communities, he noted, such measures can undermine the support that governments need to successfully implement their programmes and have a counter-productive effect. Further:

> the creation of inchoate offences that are far removed from the commission of acts of violence can violate freedom of expression, thought, conscience, religion or belief, while freedom of assembly and association can be impacted by measures to curb 'extremist' NGOs. Measures that involve educational institutions can impact on the right to education and academic freedom.

---

48 'Report of the United Nations High Commissioner for Human Rights on the protection of human rights and fundamental freedoms while countering terrorism', 19 December 2014, UN Doc. A/HRC/28/28, para. 46.

49 Ibid., para. 47.

> Administrative measures taken on the basis of suspicion, or secret intelligence, raise very serious concerns about the right to the presumption of innocence, due process and a fair trial.[50]

In order to ensure both the effectiveness of counter-terror measures and accountability in terms of human rights, as the experiences of the years immediately post-9/11 have demonstrated, it is critical that national counter-terror legislation is limited to the countering of terrorism as clearly and precisely defined.[51] States must define the material and mental elements of terrorist offences in accordance with their general criminal law, while ensuring that any new provisions comply with their other obligations under international law. This includes adhering to the principle of legality, which prohibits the application of *ex post facto* laws and requires that the criminalized conduct be described in clear and unambiguous language that narrowly defines the punishable offence, and distinguishes it from conduct that is either not punishable or is punishable by other penalties. As the Special Rapporteur has suggested, it is equally important that States ensure that strategies and policies to counter violent extremism are firmly grounded in, and comply with international human rights law.[52]

2.2 Expansion of Executive Powers

As the global counter-terrorism agenda has grown, the scope of executive powers in many countries has become more prominent, most notably through the expanded reach of intelligence services. With the increased emphasis on the prevention of terrorism, the powers of intelligence agencies in many places have been broadened beyond traditional intelligence functions related to information-gathering, processing and analysis.[53] In some instances intelligence agencies have taken on law enforcement powers such as arrest, detention, search and seizure, and the

---

[50] 'Report of the Special Rapporteur on the promotion and protection of human rights and fundamental freedoms while countering terrorism', 22 February 2016, UN Doc. A/HRC/31/65, para. 37.

[51] UN Counter-Terrorism Implementation Task Force CTITF Working Group on Protecting Human Rights while Countering Terrorism (n 37).

[52] 'Report of the Special Rapporteur on the promotion and protection of human rights and fundamental freedoms while countering terrorism', 22 February 2016, UN Doc. A/HRC/31/65.

[53] On the role of intelligence services, see A. Wills (2010), *Guidebook: Understanding Intelligence Oversight* (Geneva: DCAF). The former UN Special Rapporteur on the promotion and protection of human rights and fundamental

use of force. Such expansion has not always been undertaken with sufficient consideration to the procedural safeguards and oversight necessary to protect against abuses and ensure accountability, where abuses occur.[54]

While intelligence services play a critical role in protecting national security and in countering terrorism, their very nature creates challenges in terms of accountability. A large degree of secrecy necessarily will accompany national security policy and operations, with certain deference to executive authority over legislative and judicial power.[55] Obtaining clarity in terms of the legal authority and structure of intelligence agencies can prove difficult or impossible, which adds to the difficulties in assessing the lawfulness or legitimacy of specific intelligence activities and ensuring accountability for any wrongdoing.[56] However, good practice experience suggests that the far-reaching information-gathering powers of intelligence agencies can be mitigated through precise and

---

freedoms while countering terrorism has suggested that the purpose of intelligence services should be limited to the collection, analysis and dissemination of information that assists policy-makers and other public entities in taking measures to protect national security. See Martin Scheinin (2010), 'Compilation of good practices on legal and institutional framework and measures that ensure respect for human rights by intelligence agencies while countering terrorism, including their oversight', 5 May, UN Doc. A/HRC/14/46, Principle 1.

[54] For detailed assessments, see 'Report on the democratic oversight of the security services adopted by the Venice Commission at its 71st Plenary Session', Venice, 1–2 June 2007 (CDL-AD(2007)016-e); 'Reports of the Special Rapporteur on the promotion and protection of human rights and fundamental freedoms while countering terrorism', UN Docs A/HRC/10/3 and A/HRC/14/46; Gerald Staberock (2012), 'Intelligence and counter-terrorism: Towards a human rights and accountability framework?', in A. Salinas de Frias, K. Samuel and N. White (eds), *Counter-Terrorism, International Law and Practice* (Oxford: Oxford University Press).

[55] In addition, the Venice Commission noted that 'security intelligence gathering is one of the main areas of national decision-making which a government is most unwilling to submit to national legislative scrutiny and judicial review and, *a fortiori*, to international supervision and control'. 'Report on the Democratic Oversight of the Security Services adopted by the Venice Commission at its 71st Plenary Session' (n 54), para. 81.

[56] Staberock (n 54), at 360. See also the report of the UN High Commissioner for Human Rights on the right to privacy in the digital age, where the High Commissioner noted 'the disturbing lack of governmental transparency associated with surveillance policies, laws and practices, which hinders any effort to assess their coherence with international human rights law and to ensure accountability'. Report of the High Commissioner for Human Rights (2014), 'The right to privacy in the digital age', UN Doc. A/HRC/27/37, para. 48.

narrowly-formulated competencies, defined under publicly-available laws and with effective oversight.[57] Where a political culture fosters a culture of openness and respect for human rights, intelligence services are more likely to operate within a framework of democratic accountability.[58]

This balance has been challenged in the post-9/11 era.[59] Intelligence services have been mandated with powers to make arrests without a warrant and to detain, without explicit human rights safeguards including guarantee of due process rights such as the right to counsel.[60] Surveillance powers have increased and, with technological advancements, communications technology has drastically enhanced the ability of intelligence services to conduct electronic surveillance, interception and data collection, raising questions around the extent to which such measures are consistent with international and domestic law.[61] International intelligence cooperation, which has become increasingly vital to counter terrorism, has brought with it additional risks to human rights where countries have enhanced their cooperation with intelligence services and States that may not respect international legal standards, without adequate legislation to regulate such information-sharing and beyond the supervision of any independent authority.[62]

---

[57] 'Compilation of good practices on legal and institutional framework and measures that ensure respect for human rights by intelligence agencies while countering terrorism, including their oversight' (n 53); Hans Born and Ian Leigh (2005), *Making Intelligence Accountable: Legal Standards and Best Practice for Oversight of Intelligence Agencies* (Oslo: Publishing House of the Parliament of Norway).

[58] Born and Leigh, ibid., at 15.

[59] Staberock (n 54), at 354.

[60] As one recent example, see O Francis (2015), 'South Sudan fires interior minister as security law implemented', Bloomberg, 14 April, http://www.bloomberg.com/news/articles/2015-04-14/south-sudan-fires-interior-minister-as-security-law-implemented, accessed 16 October 2017.

[61] Report of the High Commissioner for Human Rights (2014), 'The right to privacy in the digital age', UN Doc. A/HRC/27/37, para. 15. See also European Parliament, LIBE (2014), 'Report on the US NSA surveillance programme, surveillance bodies in various Member States and their impact on EU citizens' fundamental rights and on transatlantic cooperation in Justice and Home Affairs', 2013/2188(INI); PACE, Committee on Legal Affairs and Human Rights (2015), 'Mass surveillance', Rapporteur: Mr Pieter Omtzigt (April).

[62] Report of the High Commissioner for Human Rights (2014), 'The right to privacy in the digital age', UN Doc. A/HRC/27/37, para. 30 and 'Report of the Special Rapporteur on the promotion and protection of human rights and fundamental freedoms while countering terrorism to the General Assembly', 23 September 2014, UN Doc. A/69/397, para. 44. See also H. Born, I. Leigh and

Revelations in 2013 and 2014 (the 'Snowden revelations') of the scope of the transnational surveillance network, operating under the lead of the US NSA (National Security Agency) and UK GCHQ (Government Communications Headquarters), exposed human rights violations and triggered a flurry of legal action in various jurisdictions, with individuals and groups demanding greater accountability and reform, including effective oversight and procedural safeguards.[63] At regional level, this included decisions of the European Court of Human Rights which built upon the Court's earlier jurisprudence addressing surveillance practices that violate States' obligations under the European Convention on Human

---

A. Wills (2015), *Making International Intelligence Cooperation Accountable* (Geneva: DCAF), p. 40: 'Intelligence services in non-democratic states are more likely to have a number of characteristics that make cooperating with them high risk from a human rights point of view. First, these services are not normally subject to legal regulations that comply with international standards. For example, broad mandates may give services the scope to interfere in political processes and in legitimate exercise of rights and fundamental freedoms. Effective regulations on the collection of information are unlikely to exist and services may even be permitted to detain and interrogate for the purposes of intelligence gathering. Second, services in non-democratic states exist primarily to protect the security and interests of an incumbent regime or head of state/government. Consequently, they are often deployed against political opponents and critics of a regime exercising basic freedoms. Third, intelligence services in non-democratic states are rarely subject to independent oversight and/or judicial scrutiny. This means their activities are not subject to checks that can prevent and remedy human rights violations. Finally, such services are unlikely to have an institutional culture that promotes respect for human rights and the rule of law'.

[63] For example, Court of Justice of the European Union, judgment in Case C–362/14, *Maximillian Schrems v. Data Protection Commissioner* (CJEU, 6 October 2015) and judgment in Joined Cases C–293/12 and C–594/12, *Digital Rights Ireland and Seitlinger and Others* (CJEIU, 8 April 2014). In the European Court of Human Rights, *10 Human Rights Organizations and Others v. the United Kingdom*, App. no. 24960/15; *Big Brother Watch and Others v. United Kingdom*, App. no. 58170/13; *Bureau of Investigative Journalism and Alice Ross v. UK*, App. no. 62322/14. By one count, 13 independent complaints were filed in the European Court against France in relation to its new surveillance law in 2015 alone. See M. Ermert (2016), 'Europe: queue of complaints against snooping laws grows by the month', Internet Policy Review, 12 March, http://policyreview.info/articles/news/europe-queue-complaints-against-snooping-laws-grows-month/397, accessed 16 October 2017. Cases at national level, for example, include legal action in Germany initiated by two oversight bodies against the government for inhibiting the work of constitutional watchdogs, in relation to the complicity of the national intelligence service with the NSA.

Rights. Recognizing the challenges that individuals face in demonstrating that they have been a victim of a human rights violation in this context (and thus to have 'standing' in court), the Court relaxed the requirement for individuals to prove that they have been the subject of secret surveillance.[64] In *Roman Zakharov v. Russia* the Court found serious and systematic faults with the Russian legislative framework regulating the surveillance of mobile communications.[65] It concluded that legal provisions governing interception of communications did not provide for adequate and effective guarantees against arbitrariness and the risk of abuse which was inherent in any system of secret surveillance, and which was particularly high in a system such as in Russia where the secret services and the police had direct access, by technical means, to all mobile telephone communications.[66] In *Szabo and Vissy v. Hungary* the Court ruled that national security legislation introduced by the Hungarian government in 2011, which allowed for secret mass surveillance, amounted to a violation of Article 8 of the European Convention since it did not provide for sufficient safeguards against abuse. The Court commented on the scope of the surveillance measures, which could include 'virtually anyone', noting that the measures took place 'entirely within the realm of the executive and without an assessment of strict necessity'. In finding a violation of Article 8 of the Convention, the Court held further that 'new technologies enable the Government to intercept masses of data easily concerning even persons outside the original range of operation, and given the absence of any effective remedial measures, let alone judicial ones'.[67]

---

[64] For example, in *Szabo and Vissy v. Hungary*, App. no. 37138/14 (ECtHR, 12 January 2016) the Court accepted that '... in recognition of the particular features of secret surveillance measures and the importance of ensuring effective control and supervision of them [...] under certain circumstances, an individual may claim to be a victim on account of the mere existence of legislation permitting secret surveillance, even if he cannot point to any concrete measures specifically affecting him'.

[65] *Roman Zakharov v. Russia*, App. no. 47143/06 (ECtHR, 4 December 2015).

[66] Ibid.

[67] *Szabo and Vissy v. Hungary* (n 64).

The use of armed drones for targeted killings also has raised questions of accountability, alongside issues related to the efficacy of such measures from a counter-terrorism perspective.[68] In the United States, lethal drone operations have operated under separate, parallel programmes by the CIA and the military's Joint Special Operations Command, which have 'different authorities, policies, accountability mechanisms, and oversight', in spite of calls for such operations to be subsumed under military command to ensure greater transparency, oversight and accountability.[69] During a panel discussion at the UN Human Rights Council, experts reported on cases where individuals have sought accountability on behalf of civilian victims of drone strikes and their families and noted that legal action had been thwarted by the position taken by States that 'judicial inquiry into decisions regarding the use of drones [is] inappropriate'. They cited cases where requests for judicial review had been met with 'assertions of exclusive executive decision-making authority in matters of national security, immunity for officials, and the need for secrecy with regard to relevant government information'.[70] In the United Kingdom, concerns related to the policy of the government on the use of armed drones, including a lack of transparency, prompted the Parliamentary Joint Committee on Human Rights to initiate an inquiry in order to clarify 'what the policy is, what legal framework applies, how decisions

---

68 See, for example, Report of the Special Rapporteur on the promotion and protection of human rights and fundamental freedoms while countering terrorism, 28 February 2014, UN Doc. A/HRC/25/59; Council of Europe Parliamentary Assembly, Committee on Legal Affairs and Human Rights (2015), 'Drones and targeted killings: the need to uphold human rights and international law', 16 March, Doc. 13731; D. Cortright, R. Fairhurst and K. Wall (2015), *Drones and the Future of Armed Conflict: Ethical, Legal and Strategic Implications* (Chicago/London: University of Chicago Press).

69 M. Zenko (2013), 'Transferring CIA drone strikes to the Pentagon', Council on Foreign Relations Policy Innovation Memorandum, April, https://www.cfr.org/report/transferring-cia-drone-strikes-pentagon, accessed 11 June 2017. Zenko notes that as early as 2004, the 9/11 Commission had recommended that lead responsibility for directing and executing paramilitary operations shift to the Defense Department. See also E. Auner (2014), 'Congress resists Pentagon drone oversight as U.S. and partners continue targeted killings', *World Politics Review*, 21 January; and B. Bender (2015), 'Obama's plan to shift oversight to the Pentagon flagged in face of opposition in Congress', Politico, 23 April, www.politico.com/story/2015/04/drone-strikes-cia-pentagon-war-defense-117294, accessed 10 June 2017.

70 'Summary of the Human Rights Council interactive panel discussion of experts on the use of remotely piloted aircraft or armed drones in compliance with international law', UN Doc. A/HRC/28/38, para. 20.

are taken in practice and what accountability there is for such important decisions about the use of lethal force by the State'.[71] The UN Special Rapporteur on the promotion and protection of human rights and fundamental freedoms while countering terrorism has suggested that the lack of transparency by States regarding their use of drones, including details on civilian casualties, as the single greatest obstacle to an evaluation of the impact of armed drones on civilians, as it made it extremely difficult to assess the legality of their use and ensure accountability.[72]

These challenges highlight the importance of democratic intelligence oversight as a means to prevent human rights violations, ensure accountability and enhance the effectiveness of intelligence services.[73] Studies have suggested that ensuring that intelligence agencies are accountable also fosters 'public trust and confidence in the work of intelligence services' while guaranteeing that intelligence services operate with full respect for human rights and within the rule of law.[74] In the counter-terrorism context, where law enforcement or intelligence agencies adopt measures which either are arbitrary or discriminatory, such approaches may not only undermine public trust and confidence, they may contribute to fuel radicalization within particular communities. The establishment of an intelligence culture that is rooted in human rights and the rule of law, with an appreciation for cultural diversities and sensitivities, is thus critical from both a human rights and counter-terrorism perspective. The creation of regulatory and oversight frameworks to guarantee compliance

---

[71] Joint Select Committee (2015), 'UK policy on the use of drones for targeted killing inquiry', 29 October, http://www.parliament.uk/business/committees/committees-a-z/joint-select/human-rights-committee/news-parliament-2015/uk-drone-policy-evidence-15-16/, accessed 16 October 2017.

[72] 'Summary of the Human Rights Council interactive panel discussion of experts on the use of remotely piloted aircraft or armed drones in compliance with international law', A/HRC/28/38, para. 21. See also 'Report to the General Assembly of the Special Rapporteur on the promotion and protection of human rights and fundamental freedoms while countering terrorism', 18 September 2013, UN Doc. A/68/389.

[73] Born, Leigh and Wills describe the purpose of oversight as 'to hold intelligence services to account for their policies and actions in terms of legality, propriety, effectiveness, and efficiency', while its qualification as democratic is dependent 'on whether these activities are conducted by democratically elected individuals instead of appointed individuals, for example, an elected member of parliament or of the executive'. Born, Leigh and Wills (n 62), p. 7.

[74] 'Report of the Special Rapporteur on the promotion and protection of human rights and fundamental freedoms while countering terrorism', 17 May 2010, UN Doc. A/HRC/14/46, para. 13.

by intelligence services with international human rights law, both domestically and through their cooperation with other States, equally is important.

In his study of intelligence oversight practices, the UN Special Rapporteur concluded that the range of agencies, institutional structures and governments operating in different jurisdictions will preclude a 'one-size-fits-all' approach, and that there is no single model for effective intelligence oversight. Nevertheless, a number of elements of good practice that contribute to the respect for the rule of law and human rights by intelligence services can serve to guide the creation of institutional frameworks.[75] Reviews of intelligence services carried out in recent years at national level have produced a range of practical recommendations for enhancing intelligence accountability, many of which align with the Good Practice Principles developed by the Special Rapporteur in 2010.[76]

For instance, accountability processes are facilitated where the mandates of intelligence agencies are clear and precise, as oversight and review bodies are then better able to hold them to account for their performance of specific functions.[77] Where national legislation governing the functioning of intelligence services does not provide for adequate control and oversight, and where oversight institutions are not provided with an adequate mandate, expertise or resources, accountability gaps inevitably emerge.[78] Accountability gaps in relation to international intelligence cooperation also can be addressed, for example, through the extension of the mandate of external oversight bodies, the development of transnational standards and/or the provision in agreements for international intelligence cooperation that the parties' international legal obligations take priority over them.[79]

---

75 Ibid.

76 Commission of Inquiry into the Actions of Canadian Officials in Relation to Maher Arar (2006) (Arar Commission) Report of the Events Relating to Maher Arar Canada: Canadian Government Publishing Catalogue No. CP32-88/1-2006E + CP32-88/1-1-2006E. p. 1204 (3 volumes).

77 'Report of the Special Rapporteur on the promotion and protection of human rights and fundamental freedoms while countering terrorism', 17 May 2010, UN Doc. A/HRC/14/46, para. 10.

78 See, for example, Office of the Privacy Commissioner of Canada (2014), 'Special Report to Parliament', 28 January; (2015), 'Open letter to Parliament: Amend C-51 or kill it', *National Post*, 27 February, http://news.nationalpost.com/full-comment/open-letter-to-parliament-amend-c-51-or-kill-it, accessed 16 October 2017.

79 See 'Report of the Special Rapporteur on the promotion and protection of human rights and fundamental freedoms while countering terrorism', 17 May

Good practice experiences suggest that intelligence services also should be endowed with robust internal management and control mechanisms, while external processes of review should operate across executive, parliamentary and judiciary structures. External review should include at least one civilian body that is institutionally independent of the executive and the intelligence agency, adequately empowered and sufficiently resourced to carry out its functions.[80] Such a review body should have a mandate to audit, review and assess the legitimacy of the actions of the intelligence services, with real powers to review and investigate at its discretion, for example to 'compel and examine even secret information, respond (and propose resolutions) to public complaints, make public reports of its findings and conclusions, and have in place a means to protect and secure confidential information'.[81]

The importance of ensuring accountability through such oversight arrangements was recognized by the European Parliament in relation to ongoing efforts towards accountability for human rights violations committed in the context of the CIA rendition programme, where it called on Member States:

> in the light of the increased cooperation and exchange of information between their secret intelligence and security agencies, to ensure full democratic scrutiny of those agencies and their activities through appropriate internal, executive, judicial and independent parliamentary oversight, preferably through specialised parliamentary committees with extensive remits and powers, including the power to require information, and with sufficient investigative and research resources to be able to examine not only issues

---

2010, UN Doc. A/HRC/14/46, Practice 34; European Parliament Committee on Civil Liberties, Justice and Home Affairs (2014), 'National security and secret evidence in legislation and before the courts: exploring the challenges', September, http://www.europarl.europa.eu/RegData/etudes/STUD/2014/509991/IPOL_STU(2014)509991_EN.pdf, accessed 16 October 2017, p. 70; Born, Leigh and Wills (n 62), at 189.

80 'Report of the Special Rapporteur on the promotion and protection of human rights and fundamental freedoms while countering terrorism', 17 May 2010, UN Doc. A/HRC/14/46, Practice 6. See also Report of the UN High Commissioner for Human Rights (2014), 'The right to privacy in the digital age', UN Doc. A/HRC/27/37, para. 38.

81 C. Forcese, K. Roach and L. Sherriff (2015), 'Bill C-51 Backgrounder #5: Oversight and review: Turning accountability gaps into canyons?', National Security Law, 27 February, http://craigforcese.squarespace.com/national-security-law-blog/2015/2/27/bill-c-51-backgrounder-5-oversight-and-review-turning-accoun.html, accessed 16 October 2017.

such as policy, administration and finances, but also the operational work of the agencies.[82]

At national level, the approach of the Arar Inquiry initiated by the Canadian government and carried out under Justice O'Connor as investigating judge has been referred to as a model, insofar as that 'the judge was provided with all documentation, irrespective of the possible national security claims that arose; the Canadian government highlighted the passages it considered to be classified; the judge determined the claim on the merits; and his determination was potentially amenable to judicial review'.[83] O'Connor himself attributed the success of his inquiry, in terms of establishment of facts in the case, to the fact that he was empowered to compel the production of evidence and the attendance of witnesses, and to assess the competing interests of national security and public accountability for himself.[84]

Accountability is thus best served where intelligence agencies are overseen by a combination of internal, executive, parliamentary, judicial and expert institutions. Where oversight functions are spread across the three branches of government, this can serve to avoid concentration of power in intelligence collection, and to promote transparency and accountability among the authorities entrusted with the identification, collection and analysis of intelligence information. Civil society also can, and in many places does play a critically important role in monitoring the counter-terrorism activities of the executive branch, including public oversight of intelligence agencies, as well as raising human rights concerns and putting forward recommendations for enhanced human rights compliance and accountability, particularly in States where effective formal oversight and monitoring structures may not be functioning.

2.3 National Security Considerations in Criminal Justice Processes

With the increase in intelligence-led law enforcement, national security considerations also have permeated criminal justice processes, raising a

---

[82] European Parliament resolution of 11 September 2012 on alleged transportation and illegal detention of prisoners in European countries by the CIA: follow-up of the European Parliament TDIP Committee report (2012/2033(INI)).

[83] 'Report of the Special Rapporteur on the promotion and protection of human rights and fundamental freedoms while countering terrorism', 1 March 2013, UN Doc. A/HRC/22/52.

[84] Commission of Inquiry into the Actions of Canadian Officials in Relation to Maher Arar (n 76).

number of challenges in terms of accountability. The reliance on intelligence for criminal justice purposes, for example, has raised fair trial concerns related to differences in evidentiary standards, as intelligence-gathering procedures are subject generally to lower legal thresholds than those governing the collection of evidence for use in a criminal proceeding. A study of European Union Member States revealed an increasingly blurred distinction between 'information' and 'intelligence' which, in turn, has contributed to 'ambiguity in the nature and validity of secret materials when presented as "evidence" in court'.[85] At the same time the accused may be denied the right to review and challenge evidence when disclosure of intelligence submitted as evidence is suppressed.[86]

One expert summarized the tension that can play out in practice between intelligence and law enforcement in the prevention of terrorism, noting that 'there have been many growing pains in adjusting to the changed relation of intelligence and evidence, with intelligence agencies failing to satisfy evidentiary standards and police misinterpreting and mishandling intelligence'.[87] The complexities of transnational terrorism has added further challenges. The expansion of intelligence cooperation both domestically and internationally, while critical to the prevention of terrorism, has included more extensive sharing of raw data on individuals collected by internet or mobile devices, in particular, raising questions with regard to judicial accountability including difficulties in assessing the quality, lawfulness and accuracy of information.[88] The increase in the sharing of information between law enforcement and intelligence agencies in different jurisdictions also has raised risks that such information may have been obtained by illegal means.[89]

---

[85] European Parliament Committee on Civil Liberties, Justice and Home Affairs (n 79).

[86] 'Report of the UN High Commissioner for Human Rights on the promotion and protection of human rights while countering terrorism', 15 December 2010, UN Doc. A/HRC/16/50. See also 'Report on counter-terrorism measures and human rights adopted by the Venice Commission at its 83rd Plenary Session', Venice, 4 June 2010.

[87] Kent Roach (2011), *The 9/11 Effect. Comparative Counter-Terrorism* (Cambridge: Cambridge University Press), p. 448.

[88] See European Parliament Committee on Civil Liberties, Justice and Home Affairs (n 79), Section 2 and Annex I. See also Report of the UN High Commissioner for Human Rights (2014), 'The right to privacy in the digital age', UN Doc. A/HRC/27/37.

[89] See the concerns raised by the UN Special Rapporteur on torture and other cruel, inhuman or degrading treatment or punishment in his report to the Human Rights Council, UN Doc. A/HRC/25/60.

Additional challenges have arisen where judicial deference to the executive in cases related to national security, even where such cases may involve serious human rights violations, has undermined accountability. The invocation of 'public interest' or 'qualified' immunity for public officials and the application of the 'political question' doctrine (whereby a court determines that the issue before it is best resolved within the politically accountable branches of government) are two examples.[90] The broad use of a 'State secrets' privilege also has prevented accountability for human rights violations in a number of cases. Although conceived originally and legitimately to address cases where the need for secrecy may be necessary to exclude specific evidence, the exposure of which would necessarily harm national security, the use of 'State secrets' in some States has expanded from an evidentiary privilege to a 'justiciability doctrine' in order to exclude entire lawsuits against government officials or otherwise shield government activity from judicial scrutiny.[91]

The European Court of Human Rights addressed the issue of State secrecy in cases related to the accountability of European States for their role in the CIA secret detention and interrogation programme. The case of Khaled El-Masri, a German citizen, is a well-known example. El-Masri was detained in December 2003 in Skopje, held incommunicado for 23 days and abused by Macedonian authorities who had mistaken him for an al Qaida suspect. He was later handed over to the CIA, rendered incommunicado to Kabul where he was held in a secret

---

[90] International Commission of Jurists (n 34), at 85. For a review of jurisprudence in the US, see Stephen I. Vladeck (2012), 'The new national security Canon', *Am. U. L. Rev.*, 61, 1295, 1321–25, where the author addresses the evolution of various doctrines in US federal court jurisprudence that have figured prominently in national security civil suits to deny relief in cases implicating national security.

[91] See Parliamentary Assembly of the Council of Europe, Committee on Legal Affairs and Human Rights (Rapporteur: Mr Dick Marty) (2011), 'Abuse of state secrecy and national security: obstacles to parliamentary and judicial scrutiny of human rights violations', Doc. 11907, 16 September; 'Report of the UN High Commissioner for Human Rights on the promotion and protection of human rights while countering terrorism', 15 December 2010, UN Doc. A/HRC/16/50. The former UN Special Rapporteur on the promotion and protection of human rights and fundamental freedoms while countering terrorism also highlighted concerns over the use of State-secrecy provisions and public interest immunities by Germany, Italy, Poland, Romania, the former Yugoslav Republic of Macedonia, the United Kingdom or the United States 'to conceal illegal acts from oversight bodies or judicial authorities, or to protect itself from criticism, embarrassment and – most importantly – liability' (UN Doc. A/HRC/10/3, para. 59).

prison and subject to repeated interrogation, physical abuse and humiliation for more than four months. On accepting El-Masri's capture as a case of mistaken identity, in May 2004 the CIA flew him, blindfolded, earmuffed and chained to his seat, to Albania where he was left on a roadside without explanation. Legal action initiated on behalf of El Masri in the United States was dismissed on grounds that 'the very subject of the litigation is itself a state secret', with the government's interest in preserving State secrets outweighing the individual's right to seek and receive justice.[92]

Action was brought on behalf of El-Masri against Macedonia before the European Court of Human Rights which ruled, on 13 December 2012, that Macedonia had violated El-Masri's rights under the European Convention on Human Rights, finding that his treatment by the CIA at Skopje airport amounted to torture. The Court rejected attempts to rely on the State secrets privilege, noting that 'the concept of "State secrets" has often been invoked to obstruct the search for the truth. State secret privilege was also asserted by the US government in the applicant's case before the US courts'.[93] While recognizing the complexity of the circumstances, the Court considered further that 'an adequate response by the authorities in investigating allegations of serious human rights violations, as in the present case, may generally be regarded as essential in maintaining public confidence in their adherence to the rule of law and in preventing any appearance of collusion in or tolerance of unlawful acts', with a 'sufficient element of public scrutiny of the investigation or its results to secure accountability in practice as well as in theory'.[94]

The case of Usama Mostafa Hassan Nasr, known as Abu Omar, equally is noteworthy. Abu Omar was abducted in 2003 from Milan and taken to an air base in Germany before being transferred to Egypt, where he was detained for four years and tortured. In 2009, following a prosecution brought by Italy, 22 CIA operatives and one US air force commander were convicted *in absentia* for their role in aiding and abetting his kidnapping.[95] In February 2013, Italy's former chief of intelligence was

---

[92] A claim filed by the American Civil Liberties Union on behalf of El-Masri against the former CIA Director and unnamed CIA agents for their involvement in the case was dismissed, while the US Supreme Court declined to accept jurisdiction. *El-Masri v. U.S.*, 479 F.3d 296 (4th Cir. 2007).

[93] *El-Masri v. The Former Yugoslav Republic of Macedonia*, App. no. 39630/09 (ECtHR, 13 December 2012), para. 191.

[94] Ibid., para. 192.

[95] The court had rejected immunity for the US air force commander; however, he was later pardoned by the Italian president.

convicted on retrial and sentenced to up to ten years in prison, along with his deputy director and three other CIA agents. In February 2014, the Constitutional Court annulled the lower court's decision and the *Corte Suprema di Cassazione* later quashed the convictions of the five individuals, noting that 'penal action could not be continued due to the existence of the state secret'.[96] On 23 February 2016, the European Court of Human Rights ruled that the CIA's abduction and extrajudicial transfer to Egypt of Abu Omar violated the European Convention on Human Rights. The Court held that 'the legitimate principle of "State secrecy" had clearly been applied by the Italian executive in order to ensure that those responsible did not have to answer for their actions' and, further, that 'the investigation and trial had not led to the punishment of those responsible, who had therefore ultimately been granted impunity'.[97]

The efforts of Maher Arar to obtain justice through courts in the United States is another example. In *Arar v. Ashcroft*, Arar challenged his rendition to torture as a violation of his constitutional right to due process and the Torture Victim Prevention Act. In response, the US government claimed that even if the allegations were true Mr Arar had no judicial remedy and requested that the court dismiss the case on State secrecy grounds, notably that 'litigating [Arar's] complaint would necessitate disclosure of classified information'.[98] In 2006, the US District Court for the Eastern District of New York dismissed the lawsuit, stating that US officials could not be held liable owing to national security and foreign policy considerations, a ruling upheld by a panel of three judges of the Second Circuit Appeals Court. In November 2009, the full Court of Appeals dismissed the case, suggesting that in the case of extraordinary rendition, 'it is not the court's role to decide whether US officials can be held accountable because of foreign policy, national security and secrecy concerns'.[99]

---

96 Yasha Maccanico (2014), 'State secrets in the Abu Omar case: The transatlantic relationship undermines the rule of law in cases involving human rights abuses by intelligence services', Statewatch, August, http://www.statewatch.org/analyses/no-254-abu-omar-yasha.pdf, accessed 26 October 2017; and Reuters (2014), 'Italian former spy chief cleared in CIA rendition case', 24 February, http://www.reuters.com/article/us-italy-cia/italian-former-spy-chief-cleared-in-cia-rendition-case-idUSBREA1N1HY20140224, accessed 26 October 2017.

97 *Nasr and Ghali v. Italy*, App. no. 44883/09 (ECtHR, 23 February 2016).

98 *Arar v. Ashcroft et al.*, Notice of Filing, C.A. No. 04-CV-249-DGT-VVP, 18 January 2005.

99 The US Supreme Court rejected Arar's petition for *certiorari* on 14 June 2010. Soon after his release in October 2003, the Canadian government launched

The State secrets doctrine has been invoked in other cases, including as grounds for dismissal of legal proceedings in a case related to the alleged extraordinary rendition and torture of Binyam Mohamed and several other individuals.[100] In other recent cases, however, US courts have accepted a more constrained interpretation of executive privilege. In *Ibrahim v. Department of Homeland Security*, the US government invoked the State secrets privilege to seek dismissal of a suit by a Stanford University doctoral student who had been erroneously included on the government's no-fly list (a secondary list derived from the Terrorist Screening Database) and was denied re-entry into the United States following a trip to Malaysia.[101] In finding against the government, the Federal District Court judge made clear that the government had overreached in its invocation of the State secrets privilege, particularly as the information at issue had been available in the public domain and, in any event, was 'too stale to warrant protection from public view'.[102] In its ruling, the court found that procedures to correct errors on the government's no-fly list do not provide either adequate due process protections or effective remedy to the victim, and proceeded to order relief for the applicant.[103]

Case law in various jurisdictions and discussion in political fora both point to recognition of the need for reform to contain the over broad use

---

a public inquiry into the events surrounding his case. The inquiry found that the Royal Canadian Mounted Police (RCMP) had provided inaccurate intelligence to US authorities regarding Arar, and failed to ensure proper supervision and oversight in the handling of information; that Canadian consular officers had been under a 'working assumption' that he had been tortured, suggesting Canada's complicity in torture by Syrian officials; and that the RCMP had failed in its reporting to the government. In January 2007, the Canadian government declared Mr Arar to be innocent of any involvement in terrorism, issued him a public apology and awarded him financial compensation.

100 *Binyam Mohamed et al v. Jeppesen DataPlan, Inc*, United States Court of Appeals for the Ninth Circuit No. 08-15693, 8 September 2010.

101 *Ibrahim v. Department of Homeland Security et al.*, Case 3:06-cv-00545-WHA, 14 January 2014. See also S. Stellin (2013), 'Who is watching the watch lists?', *New York Times*, 30 November, http://www.nytimes.com/2013/12/01/sunday-review/who-is-watching-the-watch-lists.html?_r=0&pagewanted=all, accessed 16 October 2017.

102 *Ibrahim v. Department of Homeland Security et al*, ibid.

103 According to reports, the Government Accountability Office and other oversight agencies have raised concerns about how people are nominated to be on the terrorist watch list, the accuracy of information in the database and the effectiveness of procedures to remove or correct inaccurate records.

of executive privilege.[104] Even as early as 2002, the Inter-American Court of Human Rights stated, for example, that 'public bodies cannot shield themselves behind the protective cloak of official secrets to avoid or obstruct the investigation of illegal acts ascribed to members of its own bodies'.[105] In 2009, the US government adopted a policy on the use of State secrets in order to bolster public confidence and 'provide greater accountability and reliability in the invocation of the state secrets privilege in litigation', including more rigorous procedures for evaluating assertions of the State secrets privilege.[106] The European Parliament also has emphasized the need to 'review by limiting and restrictively defining the exceptions that flow from the notion of 'State secret' [...] to avoid abuses and deviations that [...] contradict human rights obligations' and 'establish specific mechanisms to allow for access to secret information by parliaments and judges, as well as for the release of the information after a certain period of time'.[107] The Parliamentary Assembly of the Council of Europe called for the elaboration of guidelines on human rights and the fight against impunity which would stress that 'state secrecy and immunities do not prevent effective, independent and impartial investigations into serious human rights violations [...] and that those responsible should be held to account', resulting in the adoption of Guidelines on eradicating impunity for serious human rights violations by the Committee of Ministers in March 2011.

A criminal justice response to terrorism that is grounded in respect for human rights and the rule of law can help to ensure that institutions at national, regional and international levels are accountable, effective and legitimate. It is also the best means for effectively countering terrorism, a notion recognized by Member States in their adoption and re-affirmation

---

104 'Report of the UN High Commissioner for Human Rights on the promotion and protection of human rights while countering terrorism', 15 December 2010, UN Doc. A/HRC/16/50.

105 Inter-American Court of Human Rights, *Myrna Mack Chang v. Guatemala*, judgment of 22 February 2002 (reparations and costs), (Ser.C) no. 91 (2002).

106 For an overview of the application of the state secrets privilege in US courts, see T. Garvey and E. Liu (2011), 'The state secrets privilege: Preventing the disclosure of sensitive national security information during civil litigation', Congressional Research Service Report for Congress, 16 August.

107 European Parliament resolution of 11 September 2012 on alleged transportation and illegal detention of prisoners in European countries by the CIA: follow-up of the European Parliament TDIP Committee report (2012/2033(INI)), 11 September 2012.

of the Global Counter-Terrorism Strategy.[108] Recent judgments at national and regional levels should prompt States to consider reviewing their current legislation, policies and practices to ensure that national security considerations do not compromise the effective functioning of criminal justice processes. With respect for the principle of accountability, judges should review every piece of evidence that the executive claims is subject to the State secrets privilege, with dismissal only as a last resort to be considered once this process is exhausted.[109] Further, where executive privilege is invoked, the executive should be required, where possible without harming national security, to introduce alternative forms of evidence. Courts also may consider appointing an external, independent expert to scrutinize the evidence for national security content. In any case, State secrecy must never be invoked in such a way as to prevent accountability or deny victims their right to effective remedy.

3. CLOSING THE ACCOUNTABILITY GAP

The reasons for the persistent lack of accountability for human rights violations committed in the context of States' counter-terrorism agendas in the years since 9/11 are numerous, varied and overlapping. They range from the host of accountability challenges created as a result of vague or overly broad counter-terror legislation; a lack of effective oversight and robust procedural safeguards in place at national level to protect against abuse of powers by the executive; an excessive deference to the executive on matters related to national security; as well as an overarching lack of political will and 'executive inertia motivated by a desire to "draw a line" under the past'.[110] Each has contributed in some measure to impunity for

---

[108] Global Counter-Terrorism Strategy (n 10), Plan of Action: Pillar IV, para. 5.

[109] 'Report of the Special Rapporteur on the promotion and protection of human rights and fundamental freedoms while countering terrorism', 1 March 2013, UN Doc. A/HRC/22/52, para. 38: 'the domestic judiciary are bound to subject executive claims of non-justiciability on national security grounds to the most penetrating scrutiny. Similar scrutiny must be directed to executive claims to exemption from normal rules of disclosure in legal proceedings' (footnotes omitted).

[110] 'Report of the Special Rapporteur on the promotion and protection of human rights and fundamental freedoms while countering terrorism', 1 March 2013, UN Doc. A/HRC/22/52, para. 37.

human rights violations in the counter-terrorism context, whilst also proving counter-productive from an anti-terrorism perspective.

Through their pledge to implement a global counter-terrorism agenda, all States have clearly asserted their commitment to uphold the rule of law and respect international law in the adoption and implementation of counter-terrorism measures. Recent case law suggests that courts at national and regional level are holding States to their obligations under international human rights law, while political bodies also have demonstrated their determination to combat impunity, as is evident in the recent decision by the European Parliament to resume its inquiry on 'alleged transportation and illegal detention of prisoners in European countries by the CIA'.[111] Whilst recognizing the challenges faced by States in meeting security imperatives and affording them a reasonable degree of discretion – acknowledging, for example, that the executive is best-placed to assess the extent and nature of national security threats – courts have remained steadfast in holding States to account under the rule of law, including respect for international human rights law.[112]

Looking forward, as impunity is a significant contributing element in the recurrence of violations, ensuring human rights accountability will be critical in order to prevent future violations and ensure that victims are afforded their right to the truth and to redress. Through investment in institutions and processes that are accountable, effective and legitimate, strengthening respect for human rights in the counter-terror context can contribute as a deterrent to prevent new violations, uphold the rule of law and secure public trust in the justice system. Increasingly, too, there is recognition that human rights accountability contributes to security objectives, since 'accountability develops trust, which builds security'.[113] Experiences since 9/11 have demonstrated that not only can legitimate

[111] European Parliament resolution of 11 February 2015 on the US Senate report on the use of torture by the CIA (2014/2997(RSP)120.).

[112] Multi-National Counter-Terrorism Expert Network (2012), *UN Reform, the Rule of Law and Counter-Terrorism: How can past lessons inform future responses?* (Nottingham: University of Nottingham); A.M. Salinas de Frias, K.L.H. Samuel and N.D. White, *Counter-Terrorism: International Law and Practice* (Oxford: Oxford University Press), p. 82.

[113] Government of Canada (2013), 'Building resilience against terrorism: Canada's counter-terrorism strategy', https://www.publicsafety.gc.ca/cnt/rsrcs/pblctns/rslnc-gnst-trrrsm/rslnc-gnst-trrrsm-eng.pdf, accessed 16 October 2017, p. 11.

security imperatives be accommodated within the rule of law and with full respect for international human rights law, they are most effective when anchored in these legal principles, norms and standards.[114]

[114] Multi-National Counter-Terrorism Expert Network (n 112); Salinas de Frias, Samuel and White (n 112).

Bibliography

Abrams, Jamie R. (2010), 'The collateral consequences of masculinizing violence', *William and Mary Journal of Women and the Law*, **16** (3), 703.

Alison, Miranda (2004), 'Women as agents of political violence: Gendering security,' *Security Dialogue*, **35** (4), 447–63.

Alison, Miranda (2009), *Women* and *Political Violence: Female Combatants in Ethno-National Conflict* (Abingdon: Routledge).

Allain, Jean (2001), 'The *jus cogens* nature of *non-refoulement*', *International Journal of Refugee Law*, **13** (4), 533–58.

Alleg, Henri (1958), *The Question* (New York: George Braziller Inc.).

Ambos, Kai (2014), 'Our terrorists, your terrorists?', EJIL: *Talk!*, 2 October, http://www.ejiltalk.org/our-terrorists-your-terrorists-the-united-nations-security-council-urges-states-to-combat-foreign-terrorist-fighters-but-does-not-define-terrorism/, accessed 7 June 2017.

American Civil Liberties Union (ACLU) (2016), 'Comments to the Privacy and Civil Liberties Oversight Board on its review of Executive Order 12333', 13 January, https://www.aclu.org/letter/aclu-comments-privacy-and-civil-liberties-oversight-board-its-review-executive-order-12333, accessed 11 May 2017.

Amnesty International (2015), 'Europe's gatekeeper: Unlawful detention and deportation of refugees from Turkey', 16 December, EUR 44/3022/2015.

Amnesty International (2016a), 'Turkey "safe country" sham revealed as dozens of Afghans forcibly returned hours after EU refugee deal', press release, 23 March.

Amnesty International (2016b), 'EU-Turkey deal: Greek decision highlights fundamental flaws', press release, 20 May.

Article 19 (2016), 'UNHRC 31: States must reject flawed resolution on "terrorism"', 22 March.

Aslam, Maleeha (2012), *Gender-Based Explosions: The Nexus between Muslim Masculinities, Jihadist Islamism and Terrorism* (New York: United Nations University Press).

Aslam, Maleeha (2014), 'Islamism and masculinity: Case study Pakistan', Historical Social Research 39, no. 3.

Aussaresses, Paul (2002), *The Battle of the Casbah: Terrorism and Counterterrorism in Algeria 1955–1957* (New York: Enigma Books).

Baker-Beall, Chris, Heath-Kelly, Charlotte and Jarvis, Lee (eds) (2015), *Counter-Radicalisation: Critical Perspectives* (Abingdon: Routledge).

Bakker, Edwin and Grol, Peter (2015), 'Motives and considerations of potential foreign fighters from the Netherlands', ICCT Policy Brief, July, http://icct.nl/wp-content/uploads/2015/07/ICCT-Bakker-Grol-Motives-and-Considerations-of-Potential-Foreign-Fighters-from-the-Netherlands-July2015.pdf, accessed 7 June 2017.

Bellal, Annyssa and Casey-Maslen, Stuart (2011), 'Rules of engagement: Protecting civilians through dialogue with non-state actors', Geneva Academy of International Humanitarian and Human Rights Law, https://nlbcdytz.preview.infomaniak.website/joomlatools-files/docman-files/Research%20documents/Rules-of-Engagement-EN.pdf, accessed 19 October 2017.

Bianchi, Andrea (2004), 'Enforcing international law norms against terrorism: Achievements and prospects', in A. Bianchi (ed.), *Enforcing International Law Norms Against Terrorism* (Oxford: Hart).

Bigo, Didier et al. (2015), 'The EU and its counter-terrorism policies after the Paris attacks', CEPS Paper in Liberty and Security, No. 84/November 2015.

Bordeleau, Chris, Chalifoux, Jeff J. and Sangha, Karina (2015), 'The global fight against terror: An evaluation of counter-terrorism governance', Canadian Network for Research on Terrorism, Security and Society, Working Paper Series, no. 15-01, January.

Born, Hans and Leigh, Ian (2005), *Making Intelligence Accountable: Legal Standards and Best Practice for Oversight of Intelligence Agencies* (Oslo: Publishing House of the Parliament of Norway).

Born, Hans, Leigh, Ian and Wills, Aidan (2015), *Making International Intelligence Cooperation Accountable* (Geneva: DCAF).

Brecher, Bob (2007), *Torture and the Ticking Bomb* (Oxford: Blackwell Publishing).

Briscoe, Ivan and Van Ginkel, Bibi (2013), 'The nexus between development and security: Searching for common ground in countering terrorism, ICCT Policy Brief, March.

Bruin, Rene and Wouters, Kees (2003), 'Terrorism and the non-derogability of *non-refoulement*', *International Journal of Refugee Law*, **15** (1), 5–29.

Bueno de Mesquita, Ethan (2008), 'The political economy of terrorism: A selective overview of recent work', *The Political Economist*, **10** (1), 1–12.

Burniske, Jessica with Modirzadeh, Naz and Lewis, Dustin (2014), 'Counter-terrorism laws and regulations: What aid agencies need to know', Humanitarian Practice Network at Overseas Development Institute, No. 79, November.

Camus, Albert (1963), 'Preface to Algerian Reports', in Albert Camus, *Resistance, Rebellion and Death* (New York: Modern Library).

Carothers, Thomas and Brechenmacher, Saskia (2014), 'Closing space: Democracy and human rights support under fire', Carnegie Endowment for International Peace, http://carnegieendowment.org/2014/02/20/closing-space-democracy-and-human-rights-support-under-fire-pub-54503, accessed 5 June 2017.

Caruso, Raul and Schneider, Friedrich (2011), 'The socio-economic determinants of terrorism and political violence in Western Europe (1994-2007)', *European Journal of Political Economy*, **27** (1), S37–S49.

Cherif Bassiouni, Mahmoud (1999), 'International terrorism,' in M. Cherif Bassiouni (ed.), *International Criminal Law* (Leiden, The Netherlands: Koninklijke Brill NV).

Chodorow, Nancy J. (1994), *Femininities, Masculinities, Sexualities: Freud and Beyond* (Lexington, KY: University Press of Kentucky).

Cockburn, Patrick (2013), *The Jihadis Return, ISIS and the New Sunni Uprising* (New York: OR Books).

Cohen, Neal, Hasty, Robert and Wonton, Ashley (2014), 'Implications of the USAID partner vetting system and state department risk analysis and management system under European Union and United Kingdom data protection and privacy law', Counterterrorism and Humanitarian Engagement Project, Research and Policy Paper, March.

Cole, David (2010), 'The sacrificial Yoo: Accounting for torture in the OPR Report', Georgetown Public Law and Legal Theory Research Paper No. 10-73, *J. Nat'l Security L. & Pol'y*, **4**, 455–64, at 457–60.

Cole, David (2016), 'Engines of liberty: How civil society helped restore constitutional rights in the aftermath of 9/11", Just Security, 28 March, https://www.justsecurity.org/30249/engines-liberty-civil-society-helped-restore-constitutional-rights-aftermath-911/, accessed 15 May 2017.

Coomaraswamy, Radhika (2015), *Preventing Conflict Transforming Justice Securing the Peace: A Global Study of the Implementation of United Nations Security Council Resolution 1325* (New York: UN Women), http://www.unwomen.org/~/media/files/un%20women/wps/highlights/unw-global-study-1325-2015.pdf, accessed 8 June 2016.

Cortright, David, Fairhurst, Rachel and Wall, Kristen (2015), *Drones and the Future of Armed Conflict: Ethical, Legal and Strategic Implications* (Chicago/London: University of Chicago Press).

Cortright, David, Millar, Alistair, Gerber-Stellingwerf, Linda and Lopez, George A. (2012), 'Friend not foe: The role of civil society in preventing violent extremism', *Notre Dame Journal of International and Comparative Law*, **2** (2), Article 3, http://scholarship.law.nd.edu/ndjicl/vol2/iss2/3, accessed 7 June 2017.

Crawford, Gordon (2008), 'EU human rights and democracy promotion in Central Asia: From lofty principles to lowly self-interests', *Perspectives on European Politics and Society*, **9** (2), 172–91.

Crenshaw, Martha (1981), 'The causes of terrorism', *Comparative Politics*, **13** (4), 379–99.

De Kerchove, Gilles and Höhn, Christiane (2013), 'Counter-terrorism and international law since 9/11, including in the EU-US context', in T.D. Gill et al. (eds), *Yearbook of International Humanitarian Law 2013*, Vol. 16 (The Hague: T.M.C. Asser Press), pp. 267–95, https://www.cambridge.org/core/journals/yearbook-of-international-humanitarian-law/article/chapter-10-counterterrorism-and-international-law-since-911-including-in-the-euus-context/64C7E5838F9F4992F0F62026DA97E834, accessed 7 June 2017.

Dratel, Joshua L. (2003), 'Ethical issues in defending a terrorism case: How secrecy and security impair the defence of a terrorism case', *Cardozo Public Law, Policy & Ethics Journal*, **2**, 81.

Duffy, Helen (2015), *The War on Terror and the Framework of International Law*, 2nd edn (Cambridge: Cambridge University Press).

Duffy Toft, Monica (2012), 'Self-determination, secession and civil war', *Terrorism and Political Violence*, **24** (4), 581–600.

Elberling, Björn (2005), 'The ultra vires character of legislative action by the Security Council', *International Organizations Law Review*, **2** (2), at 337–60.

Electronic Frontier Foundation (2014), 'A primer on Executive Order 12333: The mass surveillance starlet', 2 June, https://www.eff.org/deeplinks/2014/06/primer-executive-order-12333-mass-surveillance-starlet, accessed on 11 May 2017.

Farmer, Paul (2003), *Pathologies of Power: Health, Human Rights, and the New War on the Poor* (Los Angeles: University of California).

Fink, Naureen Chowdhury, Romaniuk, Peter and Rafia Barakat (2013), 'Evaluating countering violent extremism programming: Practices and progress', Center on Global Counterterrorism Cooperation, September.

Gaibulloev, Khusrav, Sandler, Todd and Sanifort, Charlinda (2011), 'Assessing the evolving threat of terrorism', *Global Policy*, **3** (2), 135–44.

Gallie, W.B. (1969), 'Essentially contested concepts', in M. Black (ed.), *The Importance of Language* (Ithaca: Cornell University Press), pp. 121–46.

Gasser, Hans-Peter (2002), 'Acts of terror, "terrorism" and international humanitarian law,' *International Review of the Red Cross*, **84** (847), 552–54.

Gioia, A. (2006), 'The UN Conventions on the Prevention and Suppression of International Terrorism', in G. Nesi, *International Cooperation in Counter-Terrorism* (Aldershot: Ashgate).

Grey, Stephen (2015), *The New Spymasters: Inside the Modern World of Espionage from the Cold War to Global Terror* (New York: St Martin's Press).

Gross, Oren and Ní Aoláin, Fionnuala (2006), *Law in Times of Crisis: Emergency Powers in Theory and Practice* (New York: Cambridge University Press).

Hafner, G. (2006), 'The definition of the crime of terrorism', in G. Nesi, *International Cooperation in Counter-Terrorism* (Aldershot: Ashgate).

Happold, Matthew (2003), 'Security Council Resolution 1373 and the Constitution of the United Nations', *Leiden Journal of International Law*, **16**, 593–610.

Hardy, Kieran and Williams, George (2013), 'What is terrorism? Assessing domestic legal definitions', *University of New South Wales Faculty of Law Research Series 2013*, Working Paper 16 (February).

Harvard Program on Humanitarian Policy and Conflict Research (2011), 'Humanitarian action under scrutiny: Criminalizing humanitarian engagement', HPCR Working Paper (February), http://c0186748.cdn1.cloudfiles.rackspacecloud.com/HPCR%20CHE%202011.pdf, accessed 17 May 2017.

Hayes, Ben (2012), 'Counter-terrorism, "policy laundering" and the FATF: Legalising surveillance, regulating civil society', Transnational Institute/Statewatch, https://www.tni.org/en/publication/counter-terrorism-policy-laundering-and-the-fatf, accessed 15 May 2017.

Hendricks, Steve (2010), *A Kidnapping in Milan: The CIA on Trial* (New York: W.W. Norton & Company).

Henissart, Paul (1970), *Wolves in the City: The Death of French Algeria* (New York: Simon and Schuster).

Hessbruegge, Jan Arno (2012), 'European Court of Human Rights protects migrants against "push back" operations on the high seas', *Insights*, **16** (14), 1.

Heyns, Christof et al. (2015), Evidence to the UK Joint Committee on Human Rights for the UK Parliamentary Inquiry into UK policy on the use of drones for targeted killings (DRO0024), http://data.parliament.uk/writtenevidence/committeeevidence.svc/evidencedocument/human-rights-committee/the-uk-governments-policy-on-the-use-of-drones-for-targeted-killing/written/25641.html, accessed 17 February 2016.

Hicks, Neil (2004), 'The impact of counter terror on the promotion and protection of human rights: A global perspective', Human Rights First Paper prepared for 'Human Rights in an Age of Terrorism' a conference at the University of Connecticut, 9–11 September.

Hualing, Fu (2012), 'Responses to terrorism in China', in V.V. Ramraj, M. Hor, K. Roach and G. Williams (eds), *Global Anti-Terrorism Law and Policy*, 2nd edn (Cambridge: Cambridge University Press), p. 347.

Human Rights Watch (2002), 'Human Rights Watch World Report 2002', http://pantheon.hrw.org/legacy/wr2k2/, accessed 11 May 2017.

Human Rights Watch (2009), 'Selling justice short: Why accountability matters for peace', 7 July 2009, https://www.hrw.org/sites/default/files/reports/ij0709webwcover_1.pdf, accessed 9 June 2017.

Human Rights Watch (2012), 'In the name of security, counterterrorism laws worldwide since September 11', 29 June, https://www.hrw.org/report/2012/06/29/name-security/counterterrorism-laws-worldwide-september-11, accessed 5 June 2017.

International Committee of the Red Cross (ICRC) (2007), 'International humanitarian law and the challenges of contemporary armed conflicts', *International Review of the Red Cross*, **89** (867), 724–25.

ICRC (2011a), 'International humanitarian law and terrorism: questions and answers', 1 January, https://www.icrc.org/eng/resources/documents/faq/terrorism-faq-050504.htm, accessed 11 May 2017.

ICRC (2011b), 'International humanitarian law and the challenges of contemporary armed conflicts', Official working document of the 31st International Conference of the Red Cross and Red Crescent, Geneva, 28 November to 1 December.

Institute for Economics and Peace (2016), 'Global Terrorism Index 2016', http://economicsandpeace.org/wp-content/uploads/2016/11/Global-Terrorism-Index-2016.2.pdf, accessed 11 May 2017, p. 51.

International Bar Association (IBA) (2011), *Terrorism and International Law: Accountability, Remedies and Reform*, A Report of the IBA Task Force on Terrorism (London: IBA), p. 165.

International Commission of Jurists (2009), 'Assessing damage, urging action: Report of the eminent jurist panel on terrorism, counter-terrorism and human rights', http://www.un.org/en/sc/ctc/specialmeetings/2011/docs/icj/icj-2009-ejp-report.pdf, accessed 11 May 2017.

International Human Rights and Conflict Resolution Clinic (Stanford Law School) and Global Justice Clinic (NYU School of Law) (2012), 'Living Under drones: Death, injury and trauma to civilians from US drone practices in Pakistan', September.

Iverson, Jens (2014), 'Notes of caution on the UNSC resolution obliging states to change domestic criminal law', *Leiden Law Blog*, 26 September, http://leidenlawblog.nl/articles/notes-of-caution-on-the-unsc-resolution-obliging-states-to-change-domestic, accessed 7 June 2017.

Jackson, Ashley and Aynte, Abdi (2013), 'Talking to the other side: Humanitarian negotiations with Al-Shabaab in Somalia', HPG Working

Paper, December, https://www.odi.org/sites/odi.org.uk/files/odi-assets/publications-opinion-files/8744.pdf, accessed 15 May 2017.

Koser, Khalid (2016), 'Migration, violent extremism and terrorism: Myths and realities', *World Bank Blog*, Migration and Violent Extremism in Contemporary Europe, 16 March, http://blogs.worldbank.org/peoplemove/migration-and-violent-extremism-contemporary-europe, accessed 12 June 2017.

Koser, Khalid and Cunningham, Amy E. (2015), 'Migration, violent extremism and terrorism: Myths and realities', in Institute for Economics and Peace, 'Global Terrorism Index 2015', https://www.files.ethz.ch/isn/194968/Global-Terrorism-Index-2015.pdf, accessed 12 June 2017, p. 83.

Koufa, Kalliopi (2006), 'The UN, human rights and counter-terrorism', in G. Nesi (ed.), *International Cooperation in Counter-terrorism: The United Nations and Regional Organizations in the Fight Against Terrorism* (Aldershot: Ashgate).

Kraehenmann, Sandra (2014), 'Foreign fighters under international law', Geneva Academy Briefing No. 7, October.

Kundnani, Arun (2009), 'Spooked! How not to prevent violent extremism', Institute of Race Relations, October.

Kundnani, Arun (2015), 'A decade lost: Rethinking extremism and radicalisation', Claystone, January.

Luban, David (2006), 'Liberalism, torture and the ticking bomb', in K. Greenberg (ed.), *The Torture Debate in America* (New York: Cambridge University Press).

Luban, David (2014), 'Just looking for loopholes', Just Security, 19 October, https://www.justsecurity.org/16540/just-loopholes/, accessed on 30 March 2016.

Mackintosh, Kate and Duplat, Patrick (2013), 'Study of the impact of donor counter-terrorism measures on principled humanitarian action', July, https://docs.unocha.org/sites/dms/documents/ct_study_full_report.pdf, accessed 15 May 2017.

Malet, David (2013), *Foreign Fighters: Transnational Identity in Civil Conflicts* (Oxford: Oxford University Press).

Marighella, Carlos (1970), *Minimanual of the Urban Guerrilla* (Havana: Tricontinental).

Melzer, Nils (2009), 'Interpretive guidance on the notion of direct participation in hostilities under international humanitarian law', ICRC, May.

Metcalfe-Hough, Victoria, Keatinge, Tom and Pantuliano, Sara (2015), 'UK humanitarian aid in the age of counter terrorism: Perceptions and reality', Humanitarian Policy Group, ODI, https://www.odi.org/sites/

odi.org.uk/files/odi-assets/publications-opinion-files/9479.pdf, accessed 15 May 2017.

Milanovic, Marko (2011), *Extraterritorial Application of Human Rights Treaties: Law, Principles and Policy* (Oxford: Oxford University Press).

Milanovic, Marko (2014), 'UN Security Council Adopts Resolution 2178 on foreign terrorist fighters', EJIL: *Talk!*, 24 September, http://www.ejiltalk.org/un-security-council-adopts-resolution-2178-on-foreign-terrorist-fighters/, accessed 7 June 2014.

Milanovic, Marko (2015), 'Human rights treaties and foreign surveillance: Privacy in the digital age', *Harvard Law Review*, **56** (1), 81–146.

Morgan, Rod and Williamson, Tom (2009), 'A critical analysis of the utilitarian case for torture and the situational factors that lead some people to become torturers', in T. Williamson et al., *International Developments in Investigative Interviewing* (Abingdon: Routledge).

Mueller, John and Stewart, Mark (2016), 'Conflating terrorism and insurgency', *Lawfare* (blog), 28 February, https://www.lawfareblog.com/conflating-terrorism-and-insurgency, accessed 7 June 2017.

Newland, Kathleen (2015), 'The US record shows refugees are not a threat', Migration Policy Institute, October, http://www.migrationpolicy.org/news/us-record-shows-refugees-are-not-threat, accessed 12 June 2017.

Ní Aoláin, Fionnuala (2013), 'Situating women in counterterrorism discourses: Undulating masculinities and luminal femininities', *Boston University Law Review*, **93** (3), 1085.

Ní Aoláin, Fionnuala (2016), 'The war on terror and extremism: Assessing the relevance of the women, peace and security agenda', *International Affairs*, **92** (2), 275–91.

Ní Aoláin, Fionnuala and Gross, Oren (2014), 'The rhetoric of war: Words, conflict and categorization post 9/11', *Cornell Journal of Law and Public Policy*, **24** (2), 241–89.

Nowak, Manfred (2005), *U.N. Covenant on Civil and Political Rights: CCPR Commentary*, 2nd rev. edn (Kehl: N.P. Engel).

Nowak, Manfred (2006), 'What practices constitute torture? US and UN Standards', *Human Rights Quarterly*, **28**, 809–41.

Nowak, Manfred and McArthur, Elizabeth (2008), *The International Convention Against Torture, A Commentary* (New York: Oxford University Press).

Open Society Justice Initiative (OSI) (2013), 'Globalizing torture: CIA secret detention and extraordinary Rendition', OSI, https://www.opensocietyfoundations.org/sites/default/files/globalizing-torture-20120205.pdf, accessed 13 May 2017.

Patel, Faiza (2011), 'Rethinking radicalization', Brennan Center for Justice at New York School of Law.

Patel, Faiza (2015), 'Bulk collection under section 215 has ended … What next?', Just Security, 30 November, https://www.justsecurity.org/27996/bulk-collection-ended-whats-next/, accessed 11 May 2017.

Pejic, Jelena (2011), 'The protective scope of common article 3: More than meets the eye', *International Review of the Red Cross*, **93** (881), 189–225.

Piacente, Nicola (2015), 'The contribution of the Council of Europe to the fight against foreign terrorist fighters', *eucrim*, 2015/1, https://eucrim.mpicc.de/archiv/eucrim_15-01.pdf, accessed 7 June 2017.

Piazza, James A. (2011), 'Poverty, minority economic discrimination and domestic terrorism', *Journal of Peace Research*, **48** (3), 319–38.

Price, Michael (2015), 'Community outreach or intelligence gathering? A closer look at "countering violent extremism" programs', Brennan Center for Justice at New York School of Law, January.

Ramraj, Victor (2012), 'The impossibility of global anti-terrorism law', in V.V. Ramraj, M. Hor, K. Roach and G. Williams (eds), *Global Anti-Terrorism Law and Policy*, 2nd edn (Cambridge: Cambridge University Press).

Reed, Alastair, de Roy van Zuijdewijn, Jeanine and Bakker, Edwin (2015), 'Pathways of foreign fighters: Policy options and their (un)intended consequences', International Centre for Counter-Terrorism Policy Brief, April.

Rejali, Darius (2007), *Torture and Democracy* (Princeton: Princeton University Press).

Richardson, Louise (2006), *What Terrorists Want* (London: John Murray).

Roach, Kent (2003), *September 11 Consequences for Canada* (Montreal: McGill-Queen's University Press).

Roach, Kent (2006), 'The post 9/11 migration of Britain's 2000 Terrorism Act', in S. Choudry (ed.), *The Migration of Constitutional Ideas* (Cambridge: Cambridge University Press).

Roach, Kent (2011), *The 9/11 Effect. Comparative Counter-Terrorism* (Cambridge: Cambridge University Press).

Romaniuk, Peter (2015), 'Does CVE work? Lessons Learned from the global effort to counter violent extremism', Global Center on Cooperative Security, September.

Samuel, Katja, White, Nigel, Salinas de Frias, Ana Maria (2012), 'Multi-national counter-terrorism expert network: Report of key findings and recommendations on the rule of law and counter-terrorism', Nottingham University, January.

Sandler, Todd (2014), 'The analytical study of terrorism: Taking stock', *Journal of Peace Research*, **51** (2), 257–71.

Santori, Valeria (2006), 'The UN Security Council's (broad) interpretation of the notion of the threat to peace in counter-terrorism', in G. Nesi (ed.), *International Cooperation in Counter-terrorism: The United Nations and Regional Organizations in the Fight Against Terrorism* (Aldershot: Ashgate).

Saul, Ben (2006a), *Defining Terrorism in International Law* (Oxford: Oxford University Press).

Saul, Ben (2006b), 'Defending "terrorism": Justification and excuses for terrorism in international criminal law', *Australian Yearbook of International Law*, **25**, 177–226.

Saul, Ben (2012), 'The special tribunal for Lebanon and terrorism as an international crime: Reflections on the judicial function', Legal Studies Research Paper No. 12/64, Sydney Law School, September.

Scheinin, Martin (2014a), 'Back to post-9/11 panic? Security Council resolution on foreign terrorist fighters', Just Security, 23 September, https://www.justsecurity.org/15407/post-911-panic-security-council-resolution-foreign-terrorist-fighters-scheinin/, accessed 5 June 2017.

Scheinin, Martin (2014b), 'A comment on Security Council Res 2178 (foreign terrorist fighters) as a "form" of global governance' Just Security, 6 October, https://www.justsecurity.org/15989/comment-security-council-res-2178-foreign-fighters-form-global-governance/, accessed 10 May 2017.

Scheinin, Martin (2015a), 'The Council of Europe's draft protocol on foreign terrorist fighters is fundamentally flawed', Just Security, 18 March, https://www.justsecurity.org/21207/council-europe-draft-protocol-foreign-terrorist-fighters-fundamentally-flawed/, accessed 7 June 2015.

Scheinin, Martin (2015b), 'The essence of privacy, and varying degrees of intrusion', *VerfBlog*, 7 October, http://www.verfassungsblog.de/en/the-essence-of-privacy-and-varying-degrees-of-intrusion/, accessed 5 June 2017.

Scheinin, Martin (2015c), 'Mass surveillance and the right to privacy: Adding nuance to the Schrems case', Just Security, 13 October, https://www.justsecurity.org/26781/adding-nuance-context-max-schrems-case-safe-harbor/, accessed 15 May 2017.

Scheinin, Martin and Ginsborg, Lisa (2011), 'You can't always get what you want: The Kadi II conundrum and the Security Council 1267 terrorist sanctions regime', *Essex Human Rights Review*, **8**, 7.

Scheinin, Martin and Vermeulen, Mathias (2010), 'Unilateral exceptions to international law: Systematic analysis and critique of doctrines that seek to deny or reduce the applicability of human rights norms in the fight against terrorism', European University Institute Working Papers, Law, 2010/08.

Scheppele, Kim Lane (2010), 'The international standardization of national security law', *Journal of National Security Law and Policy*, **4**, 437–53.

Simeon, James C. (2010), 'Complicity and culpability and the exclusion of terrorists from convention refugee status post-9/11', *Refugee Survey Quarterly*, **29** (4), 104–37.

Sossai, Mirko (2015), 'Foreign terrorist fighters: Una nozione ai confini del diritto internazionale', Federalismi.it, 25 September.

Soufan, Ali H. (2011), *The Black Banners* (New York: W.W. Norton & Company).

Staberock, Gerald (2012), 'Intelligence and counter-terrorism: Towards a human rights and accountability framework?', in A. Salinas de Frias, K. Samuel and N. White (eds), *Counter-Terrorism, International Law and Practice* (Oxford: Oxford University Press).

Stimson Centre (2015), 'Recommendations and report of the task force on US drone policy', 2nd edn, https://www.stimson.org/sites/default/files/fileattachments/recommendations_and_report_of_the_task_force_on_us_drone_policy_second_edition.pdf, accessed 22 January 2018.

Storm, Morten (2014), *Agent Storm: My Life Inside Al Qaeda and the CIA* (New York: Atlantic Monthly Press).

Subedi, Surya P. (2002), 'The UN response to international terrorism in the aftermath of the terrorist attacks in America and the problem of the definition of terrorism in international law', *International Law Forum*, **4**, 159–69.

Szasz, P.C. (2002), 'The Security Council starts legislating', *The American Journal of International Law*, **96** (4), 901–5.

Tenet, George (2009), *At the Center of the Storm* (New York: HarperCollins).

Theidon, Kimberly (2013), *Intimate Enemies: Violence and Reconciliation in Peru* (Philadelphia: University of Pennsylvania).

Trinquier, Roger (1964), *Modern Warfare: A French View of Counterinsurgency* (London: Pall Mall Press).

van der Does de Willebois, Emile (2010), 'Nonprofit organizations and the combatting of terrorism financing: A proportionate response', World Bank Working Paper No. 208, Ch. 3.

van Ginkel, Bibi (2014), 'The new Security Council Resolution 2178 on foreign terrorist fighters: A missed opportunity for a holistic approach', International Centre for Counter-Terrorism, 4 November, http://icct.nl/publication/the-new-security-council-resolution-2178-on-foreign-terrorist-fighters-a-missed-opportunity-for-a-holistic-approach/, accessed 7 June 2017.

van Ginkel, Bibi (2015), 'The (in-)effectiveness of "deterrence" as an instrument', Clingendael Netherlands Institute of International Relations, 30 March, https://www.clingendael.nl/publication/effectiveness-deterrence-instrument-against-jihadist-terrorist-threats, accessed 7 June 2017.

van Schaack, Beth (2014), 'Not to be forgotten: The case of Maher Arar', Just Security, 19 December, https://www.justsecurity.org/18526/forgotten-case-maher-arar/, accessed 10 June 2017.

Vladeck, Stephen I. (2012), 'The new national security canon', *Am. U. L. Rev.*, **61**, 1295, 1321–25.

Walker, Clive and Conway, Maura (2015), 'Online terrorism and online laws', *Dynamics of Asymmetric Conflict*, **8** (2), 156–75.

White, Nigel D. (2011), 'The United Nations and counter-terrorism: Multilateral and executive law-making', in A.M.S. de Frías, K. Samuel and N. White (eds), *Counter-terrorism: International Law and Practice* (Oxford: Oxford University Press).

Wills, Aidan (2010), *Guidebook: Understanding Intelligence Oversight* (Geneva: DCAF).

Zard, Monette, (2002), 'Exclusion, terrorism and the Refugee Convention', http://www.fmreview.org/sites/fmr/files/FMRdownloads/en/FMR pdfs/FMR13/fmr13.11.pdf, accessed 20 October 2017.

Zimbardo, Philip (2007), *The Lucifer Effect: Understanding How Good People Turn Evil* (New York: Random House).

Index

9/11 terrorist attacks
  counter-terrorism measures following 93–106
  global impact 12
  immediate aftermath 25, 93
  impact of post-9/11 counter-terrorism measures on all human rights 92–124
  national responses following 25
  United Nations response to terrorism prior to 13–17
  United Nations response to terrorism following 17–22

A. and Others v. the United Kingdom (2009)
  and administrative detention 62, 63, 64
  and counter-terrorism 88, 89, 114, 116
  and preventive criminal justice strategy 296
Abeid, Atef 19
Abou-Elmaati, Ahmad 310
Abu Ghraib, detention of people at 44, 251
Abu Omar *see* Nasr, Imam Hassan Mustafa Osama (Abu Omar)
access to courts 63, 115–16
accountability 300–37
  challenges and impediments 50, 311–35
    national legislation 312–19
  closing gap of 335–7
  counter-terrorism 303–11
    good governance and rule of law 306–308
    obligations under international law 303–306
  executive powers, expansion 319–28
  international humanitarian law of 132
  national security considerations 328–35
  new counter-terrorism measures 131–2
  rule of law 302, 303, 305–308, 312, 313, 316, 322, 325, 326, 331, 332, 334, 336, 337
  serious human rights violations/rights of victims to a remedy 308–11
ACLU v. Clapper (2015) 85, 86
acts of terrorism 17
  see also terrorism; 'war against terror'
  duty of States to prevent 60
  under IHL 38
  and war paradigm 28, 31, 35
  whether emerging international 'terrorism' paradigm 37
actus reus 59, 121, 277, 279
administrative detention 61–4, 68, 87
  on grounds of national security 64, 112–17
Afghanistan conflict (2002) 30, 126, 259
  see also Taliban, Afghanistan
agent provocateur cases 289–92
aircrafts (remotely piloted), use in counter-terrorism operations 126–32
  see also drone strikes
  applicable legal frameworks, determining 129
  contentious areas regarding applicability of IHL 129–31

human rights impact of drone strikes 31, 127–9
intensity of hostilities 130
legitimate targets in non-international armed conflict 131
non-state armed group, degree of organization 130
Algiers, Battle of (1957) 247–9, 250
Alleg, Henri 248–9
Almalki, Abdullah 310
Al-Nusra Front (ANF) 29, 197
Al-Qaida 1, 78, 197, 263
see also Islamic State in Iraq and the Levant (ISIL); Taliban, Afghanistan
bombings of US Embassies in Kenya and Tanzania (1998) 265
intelligence gathering 242–3
monitoring of 232
propaganda messages by 251
sanctions regime
compatibility with powers under Chapter VII of UN Charter 101
compliance with basic principles of due process 101–106
criminalization of material support for terrorism 146
establishment 100
key characteristics 100
key concerns 100–106
Sanctions Committee of the Security Council 103, 105
Sanctions List 100, 103, 104, 122, 209, 233, 234
and war paradigm 26, 28
Amnesty International (AI) 281, 282
Analytical Support and Al-Qaida Sanctions Monitoring Team 198
Antiterrorism, Crime and Security Act 2001, UK 87–8
Arar, Maher 310, 332
Arar v. Ashcroft (2005) 332
Arbour, Louise 61, 68
Ashcroft, John (US Attorney General) 20
asset freezing 104–105
Aussaresses, Paul 248, 249
Australia
Foreign Fighter Bill 283–6
Explanatory Memorandum of Attorney-General 284, 285–6
Human Rights Commission 286
Islamic Council of Victoria 285

Bagram Air Base, detention of people at 44
Ban Ki-moon (UN Secretary General) 195
Barker, Gary 192
Bin Laden, Osama 251
biometrics, collection of 118, 119
blowback 199
body scanners 118, 119
Boko Haram, Nigeria 29, 156
Brecher, Bob 250
Brennan, John 246
Bueno de Mesquita, Ethan 181
bulk personal datasets 86
bulk surveillance 47, 85–6, 133–5
burden of proof 278
Bush, George W. 26

Camus, Albert 251
Canada
Anti-terrorism, Crime and Security Act 2001 68
case law 55
Immigration and Refugee Protection Act 2001 68
Security Intelligence Service 316
State secrecy provisions 65–6
CAT Committee *see* Committee against Torture (CAT Committee)
causality, masculinity of 185–93
Central Asian States 21
Central Intelligence Agency (CIA) 44, 47, 265, 300
see also United States (US)
detention and interrogation programme 54, 239, 247, 300–302, 330
violations by 302, 327

chain-refoulement 53
Charter of the United Nations
  see also United Nations Security Council (UNSC); United Nations (UN)
  Article 41 205
  Article 103 93
  balance between powers of UN organs 94
  Chapter VII 93, 101, 105, 195, 202, 259
    failure to define terrorism in a 'legislative' resolution under 202–206
    see also resolution 1373 (Security Council); resolution 2178 (Security Council)
  principles and purpose 14
  State obligations under 97
Cheney, Dick 58
China 37
Churchill, Winston 254
CIA *see* Central Intelligence Agency (CIA)
civil society
  access to financial services 151
  foreign terrorist fighters, negative impact of measures concerning 141–52
  involvement in countering violent extremism 222–6
  regulation, through addressing financing of terrorism 69–72
  and resolution 2178 224
  restriction of operations 75
civilian courts, terrorism cases tried in 266
civilians
  casualties of terrorist attacks or war 126, 132
  as human shields 40
  use of military courts to try 29, 35–6
classified information, intelligence gathering 257–8
CNCDH (National Consultative Commission on Human Rights) 279
CNR (*Conseil National de la Résistance*) 249
CODEXTER *see* Committee of Experts on Terrorism (CODEXTER)
CoE *see* Council of Europe (CoE)
Colombia 37
Commission on Crime Prevention and Criminal Justice, UN 283
Committee against Torture (CAT Committee) 42, 45, 52, 55
  and diplomatic assurances 57, 58
Committee of Experts on Terrorism (CODEXTER), CoE 280–81, 283
conditions-conducive analysis 166–94
  causality 185–93
  defining conducive conditions 177–85
  Global Counter-Terrorism Strategy 174, 178, 180
  macro conditions 179–80
  masculinity 185–93
  'push' and 'pull' factors 182–83, 187
  rule of law 178, 184
  terminology/definitional clarity 167–77
conducive conditions *see* conditions-conducive analysis
control orders 88, 89
conventions
  see also European Convention on Human Rights (ECHR)
  Convention against Corruption 288
  Convention against Transnational Organized Crime (UNTOC) 240, 288
    Model Legislative Provisions against Organized Crime 241
  Convention for the Prevention and Punishment of Terrorism (1937) 170
  Convention for the Suppression of Unlawful Acts Relating to International Civil Aviation (2010) 272
  Geneva Conventions
    Additional Protocol 169

Common Article 3 208
International Convention for the Suppression of Acts of Nuclear Terrorism (2005) 15
International Convention for the Suppression of Terrorist Bombings (1997) 15
International Convention for the Suppression of the Financing of Terrorism (1999) 15, 18, 73, 95, 101, 146, 173, 205
preventive criminal justice strategy 270, 272
International Convention on the Taking of Hostages (1979) 208
Conway, Maura 228–9
Council of Europe (CoE)
Additional Protocol to CoE Convention on the Prevention of Terrorism (2005) 210, 270, 280–83
Committee of Experts on Special Investigation Techniques 262
Committee of Experts on Terrorism (CODEXTER) 280–81, 283
Parliamentary Assembly 334
responsibilities of 46–7
countering violent extremism (CVE) 161–4, 216–22
see also violent extremism
breadth of notion 220
budgets for 217–18
community engagement and civil society involvement in 222–6
human rights promotion as a component of 226–8
online 228–35
Plan of Action to Prevent Violent Extremism (Secretary-General) 76, 78, 161, 175, 182, 183, 187, 217, 223, 227
post-2014 UN agenda 25
counter-terrorism
accountability 303–11
good governance and rule of law 306–308
obligations under international law 303–306
civil society regulation 69–72
drone strikes affecting 128
emergency legislation 105, 106
financing of terrorism, addressing 69–72
global 20, 235, 272, 306, 314, 319, 336
and human rights *see* human rights and counter-terrorism
humanitarian assistance, impact of legislation on 73–6, 122–3
immigration law 67–9, 88
instrumentalization of various branches of national and international law to 66–76
and intelligence 59
international framework 96
legislation not complying with IHRL 19, 20
negative impact 92, 141–52
new measures 125–65
mass digital surveillance 133–8
remotely piloted aircrafts, use in counter-terrorism operations 126–32
post 9/11 measures 2
Al-Qaida sanctions regime 100–106
key human rights concerns 106–23
Security Council resolutions 1373 and 2178 *see* resolution 1373 (Security Council); resolution 2178 (Security Council)
problem of lack of definitional clarity 96–7, 166–7, 168, 170–73, 195, 281
rights-limiting measures 19
top-down approach to creation of framework 19
transparency and accountability 131–2
upholding human rights while countering terrorism 84–90

war paradigm, uses in context of 26–40
Counter-Terrorism Committee (CTC) 18, 19, 24, 231
approach to human rights 97–8
Comprehensive International Framework to Counter Terrorist Narratives' 233
mandate 98
on resolution 2178 204
set up by resolution 1373 93, 97, 176
Counter-Terrorism Committee Executive Directorate (CTED) 97–9, 220
Counter-Terrorism Implementation Task Force Working Group on Tackling the Financing of Terrorism, UN 23–4, 143, 180
Court of Justice of the European Union (CJEU) 85
covert investigation methods, protection of evidence from 292–7
crimes against humanity 38, 39, 40
criminalization
of acts of terrorism 17
advanced criminalization offences 270
asset freezing as a criminal charge 104–105
of individual terrorist enterprises (France) 278–80
of material support for terrorism 146–52
of preparatory acts 59, 121–2
preventive criminal justice strategy 269–73
'terrorist' criminal law framework distinguished from IHL 38
CTC *see* Counter-Terrorism Committee (CTC)
CTED *see* Counter-Terrorism Committee Executive Directorate (CTED)
CVE *see* countering violent extremism (CVE)
Da'esh *see* Islamic State in Iraq and the Levant (ISIL)
data mining algorithms 133
Data Protection Commissioner, EU 137
Dean, Aimen 242, 243
Al-Denmarki, Murad Storm 243–4
deportation 57, 83, 87, 89, 160
see also detention
and administrative detention 61, 62, 63
cases 62, 114, 116
impossibility of 68, 113
Detainee Treatment Act 2005, US 41, 55
detention
abuse of 62, 63
access to courts 115–16
administrative *see* administrative detention
arbitrary 47, 50, 110–11, 116, 309
executive authorities, increased powers for 109–10
of foreigners 113
illegal 336
lawfulness of 63, 69, 115, 116
national security, administrative detention on grounds of 112–17
and non-refoulement obligations 43–4
preventive 89
proxy 44–7
without review 68
Working Group on Arbitrary Detention 115
development, right to 74–6
diplomatic assurances 56–8
disruption 246
Donaldson, Denis 242
drone strikes
see also aircrafts (remotely piloted), use in counter-terrorism operations
counter-terrorism, affecting 128
human rights impact 31, 127–9
lawfulness of 129
lethal 29, 31, 129, 324

Recommendations and Report of the Stimson Task Force on US Drone Policy (2015) 128
uses of 126
due process 54, 63
compliance of Al-Qaida sanctions regime with basic principles of 101–106

ECHR *see* European Convention on Human Rights (ECHR)
ECtHR *see* European Court of Human Rights (ECtHR)
El-Masri, Khalid 309, 330–31
Eminent Jurist Panel (ICJ) 36, 53, 81
Emmerson, Ben (UN Special Rapporteur on human rights and counter-terrorism) 6–7, 67, 71, 163, 204, 207, 211, 273
encryption 261
enemy combatants 35, 43
enhanced interrogation techniques 25, 54, 253, 301, 302
see also interrogation
intelligence gathering 239, 247, 251–2
Enigma coding machine 254
entrapment 245–6
EU Charter of Fundamental Rights 137
European Convention on Human Rights (ECHR) 53, 87, 113
see also freedom of association; freedom of expression; freedom of movement; human rights; human rights and counter-terrorism
fair trial 64, 88
freedom of association 72
freedom of expression 50, 59, 119
freedom of movement 119
life, right to 132
nullum crimen sine lege principle 274
preventive criminal justice strategy 274, 282
privacy rights 137
violation 252, 322–3
European Court of Human Rights (ECtHR) 45–6, 63, 66, 114
and Al-Qaida sanctions regime 105–106
on entrapment 245–6
on intelligence services 116–17
'reasonable suspicion' concept, bulk interception 85–6
European Union (EU)
see also European Convention on Human Rights (ECHR); European Court of Human Rights (ECtHR)
Charter of Fundamental Rights 137
Counter-Terrorism Coordinator 269
EU-Turkey Statement (2016) 67
Revised EU Strategy for Combating Radicalization and Recruitment to Terrorism 184
ex parte motions and hearings 293
exceptionalism discourse 77
executive authorities, increased powers for
detention and interrogation 109–10
expansion of executive powers and accountability 319–28
intelligence cooperation 110–11
extradition 52, 59, 87, 96, 115, 128, 160
see also deportation; detention
and administrative detention 61, 63
impossibility of 68, 113
extraordinary renditions 44–7, 309
for purpose of torture 45, 252
extra-territorial actions 29
extraterritorial mass surveillance programmes 47–8, 49

FAFT *see* Financial Action Task Force (FATF)
fair trial 64, 88
Fallon, Mark 251–2
Farmer, Paul 187
Federal Bureau of Investigation (FBI) 289, 290
female terrorists 185

Financial Action Task Force (FATF) 69–70, 225
see also financing of terrorism, addressing
definition of role 69, 141
monitoring bodies 146
Recommendation 8 142–5
Interpretative Note 141
limitations of 144–5
revised Best Practices for the implementation of Recommendation 8 145–6
financing of terrorism, addressing 69–72
see also Financial Action Task Force (FATF)
foreign terrorist fighters, impact of provisions 141–6
International Convention for the Suppression of the Financing of Terrorism (1999) 15, 18, 73, 95, 101, 173, 205, 270, 272
and NGOs 147, 148–52
preventive criminal justice strategy 271
FLN (*Front de Libération Nationale*) 247, 249
Fogle, Ryan 238
Foreign Intelligence Surveillance Amendments Act 2017, US 47
foreign terrorist fighters (FTFs) 1, 195–235
Additional Protocol to CoE Convention on the Prevention of Terrorism (2005) 210, 280–283
Australian Foreign Fighter Bill 283–6
counter-terrorism, new measures 138–40
criminalization of material support for terrorism, impact 146–52
defining 196, 200–201, 206–11
financing of terrorism, impact of provisions on 141–6
FTF-related offences 280–86
migrants, measures concerning rights of 152–60
negative impact of measures against on civil society 141–52
phenomenon of foreign fighters 197–200
and resolution 2178 138, 140, 195, 200–202, 280
rights-limiting measures 118
rule of law 195, 196, 205, 206, 212, 219, 222, 228
terrorism, failure to define in a ‘legislative’ Chapter VII resolution 202–206
violent extremism, countering to prevent terrorism 161–4
France
Algiers, Battle of (1957) 247–9, 250
individual terrorist enterprises, legislation criminalizing 278–80
Paris terrorist attacks (2015), reactions to 25
surveillance of international communications 47
freedom of association 72
freedom of expression 50, 59, 119
freedom of movement 119
FTFs *see* foreign terrorist fighters (FTFs)
fundamentalists 57

Gaddafi, Colonel 242
Gaulle, Charles de 249
Gaza 126
GCTF *see* Global Counter-Terrorism Forum (GCTF)
General Assembly *see* United Nations General Assembly (UNGA)
General Court of the European Union 104–105
Germany
case law regarding preparatory acts offence 275–8
Constitution 276
Penal Code (SiGB) 275
Supreme Court 276, 277
Ghailani, Ahmed 265–6

Global Center on Cooperative Security 217, 220, 222, 224
global counter-terrorism 20, 235, 272, 306, 314, 319, 336
  see also UN Global Counter-Terrorism Strategy and Plan of Action (UN GCTS), 2006
Global Counter-Terrorism Forum (GCTF)
  The Hague-Marrakesh Memorandum on Good Practices 201–202, 216, 222
  'Rabat Memorandum' 271, 292
Global Study on Women, Peace and Security 186
global war against terror 30, 52
  see also 'war against terror'
Good Friday Agreement 242
Government Communications Headquarters (GCHQ), UK 322
Guantanamo Bay, persons detained in 40, 43, 44, 251

The Hague-Marrakesh Memorandum on Good Practices, Global Counter-Terrorism Forum (GCTF) 201–202, 216, 222
Hamdan v Rumsfeld (2006) 27
Harris, Angela 188
al Hazmi, Nawaf 263
Hegarty, Frank 242
Hezbollah 246
High Commissioner for Human Rights, UN 3, 56, 66, 98, 136
  and foreign terrorist fighters (FTFs) 213, 218
  on surveillance 48–9
High-level Panel on Threats, Challenges and Change (2004) 173
hijacking 14
human rights
  and counter-terrorism *see* human rights and counter-terrorism
  fair trial 64
  gross violations committed by terrorist groups 16
  intelligence information
    dissemination and use of 254–5
    setting of intelligence requirements 255–7
  international law *see* international human rights law (IHRL)
  promotion of as a component of CVE 226–8
  States with poor records 44, 50
  or terrorism, versus human rights and terrorism 77–9
  upholding while countering terrorism 84–90
  violations of 16, 76, 110, 209, 308–11
Human Rights Committee, UN 53, 57, 83
  accountability concerns 308–309
  and administrative detention 114, 117
  externalization of measures to limit applicability of IHRL 41–2
  foreign terrorist fighters (FTFs) 140
  and intelligence gathering 237
  surveillance 48, 49
Human Rights Council 16, 47, 318
  and violent extremism 218, 219, 224, 229
human rights and counter-terrorism 79–84
  see also rights-limiting measures
  administrative detention 61–4
    on grounds of national security 112–17
  breach of fundamental human rights by governments 21
  definition of terrorism and related offences 106–108
  drone strikes, human rights impact 31, 127–9
  executive authorities, increased powers for 109–23
  impact of counter-terrorism measures on humanitarian action 73–6, 122–3

key human rights concerns post-9/11 106–23
links between 4
preparatory offences, increased criminalization of 121–2
rights-limiting administrative measures 112–18
surveillance powers, increased 118–21
'terrorist listings and sanctions 112
Human Rights Watch (HRW) 19, 37, 203
preventive criminal justice strategy 266, 289, 290, 291
human shields, use of civilians as 40
humanitarian activities, impact of counter-terrorism measures on 73–6, 122–3
Hungary 237–8, 323
Hussein, Saddam 30

Ibraham v. Department of Homeland Security (2014) 333
ICCPR *see* International Covenant on Civil and Political Rights (ICCPR)
ICJ *see* International Commission of Jurists (ICJ)
ICRC *see* International Committee of the Red Cross (ICRC)
IHL *see* international humanitarian law (IHL)
IHRL *see* international human rights law (IHRL)
immigration law 67–9, 88
migrants, measures concerning rights of 152–60
Immigration and Refugee Protection Act 2001, Canada 68
improvised explosive device (IED) 278
inchoate offences 59
individual terrorist enterprises, French legislation criminalizing 278–80
Inspire (Al Qaeda online magazine) 251
Intelligence and Security Committee of Parliament (ISC), UK 253, 284
intelligence services
see also undercover activities
and accountability concerns 320–21
classified information 257–8
confidential information 59
counter-terrorism measures 59
democratic oversight, need for 325, 326
disruption 246
ECtHR on use of 116–17
entrapment 245–6
executive authorities, cooperation between 110–11
human rights issues
dissemination and use of intelligence information 254–5
setting of intelligence requirements 255–7
human sources and international human rights law 239–46
increased reliance on intelligence information 58–66, 329
information as a basis for rights-limiting measures 58–61
intelligence agencies and torture 247–54
intelligence gathering and human rights 236–64
intelligence sharing and 'action on' 258–60
international cooperation 49–51
lawfulness of 111, 320, 329
legal versus operational uses of information 50
National Intelligence Priorities Framework 256
Portland Pioneer Courthouse Square case 244–5
private sector, role 262
protection of evidence from intelligence sources/covert investigation methods 292–7

reliance without adequate consideration for due process safeguards 63
setting of intelligence requirements 255–7
sharing of information between States 50
Special Investigation Techniques *see* Special Investigation Techniques
state security provisions 65–6
technical operations 260–62
Inter-American Commission on Human Rights (IACHR) 42, 171–2, 173
Inter-American Court of Human Rights 334
International Commission of Jurists (ICJ) 281, 282, 314
International Committee of the Red Cross (ICRC) 30, 130, 131, 208
International Court of Justice (ICJ), Eminent Jurist Panel 36, 53, 81
International Covenant on Civil and Political Rights (ICCPR) 35, 53, 62, 113
court hearings 293
derogation or non-derogation from certain human rights provisions under 82, 83
foreign terrorist fighters (FTFs) 213–14
and intelligence gathering 237
international human rights law, limitation of applicability 41, 43, 45
legality principle 139
nullum crimen sine lege principle 274
preventive criminal justice strategy 282
privacy rights 135–7
International Criminal Tribunal for the former Yugoslavia (ICTY) 31–2
international human rights law (IHRL) 13
counter-terrorism legislation not complying with 19, 20
duty of States to prevent acts of terrorism 60
externalization of measures to limit applicability of 40–51
detentions abroad and non-refoulement obligations 43–4
extraordinary renditions and proxy detention 44–7
international intelligence cooperation 49–51
legal framework 41–2
surveillance 47–9
and human sources 239–46
intelligence gathering 236
legal framework 29, 30, 32, 33–4
restrictions to rights permitted and conditions imposed 81–2
and right to life 132
international humanitarian law (IHL)
see also accountability
of accountability 132
civilian versus military targets 38
contentious areas regarding applicability 129–31
determination of terrorist groups for purpose of 36
foreign terrorist fighters (FTFs) 207
legal framework 29, 30, 32, 33
rules 208
terrorist acts under 38
'terrorist' criminal law framework distinguished 38
violations 207–208
and 'war against terror' 27, 28
international law
see also international human rights law (IHRL); international humanitarian law (IHL)
accountability requirements 303–306
externalization of measures to limit applicability of
detentions abroad and non-refoulement obligations 43–4

extraordinary renditions and proxy detention 44–7
international intelligence cooperation 49–51
surveillance 47–9
instrumentalization of various branches of national and international law 303–306
new binding rules set up by resolution 1373 93–4
and resolution 2178 95
rule of law 95
internet service providers (ISPs) 230
interrogation 111, 117, 248, 250
by CIA 54, 247, 300–303
enhanced techniques 25, 54, 239, 247, 251–2, 253, 301, 302
executive authorities, interrogation powers of 109–10
harsh/coercive 44, 247
specific cases 65, 251–2, 330
investigative powers and criminal procedure rules
agent provocateur cases 289–92
preventive criminal justice strategy 287–97
protection of evidence from intelligence sources/covert investigation methods 292–7
Investigatory Powers Tribunal, UK 86
IRA (Irish Republican Army) 242
Iran 246
Iraq
drone strikes in 126
international armed conflict (2003) 30
ISIL in 29, 94
Irish Republican Army (IRA) 242
ISIS/ISIL *see* Islamic State in Iraq and the Levant (ISIL)
Islamic State in Iraq and the Levant (ISIL) 29, 94, 174, 176, 232
and Al-Qaida sanctions regime 100, 104, 212
brutality of 197
disguise of fighters 153
as foreign terrorist fighters (FTFs) 197, 198
hyper-masculine images used by 190
inclusion in Al-Qaida Sanctions List 104
in Iraq and Syria 29, 94–5
joining 138, 267
and migrants, measures concerning rights of 153, 156
violations of international humanitarian law 207–208
and war paradigm 28, 29
whether emerging international 'terrorism' paradigm 37, 38
Israel 126
Italy 46

judicial review, access to 116–17, 119
jus cogens rule 52

Kenya 272, 288, 293–4
Kerchove, Gilles de 268
Khadr Omar 310
Khan, Mohammed Siddique 263
Khobar Towers housing facility (Saudi Arabia), bombing (1996) 246
Klass v. Germany (1978) 237
Kraehenmann, Sandra 37, 138, 139, 201, 207–10, 214
Kwasniewski, Aleksander 252

La Rue, Frank 232–3
law-enforcement paradigm 34
lawfulness
of detention 63, 69, 115, 116
of drone strikes 129
of force 36, 38, 51
of intelligence services 111, 320, 329
of sanctions regime 105
of surveillance 120
life, right to 132
Lockerbie bombing (1988) 254–5
'lone wolf' terrorists 278
Luban, David 251
'Lucifer Effect' 250

McDonald, Michael 244
Macedonia 37, 46, 309, 331
McGuinness, Martin 242
McNulty, Paul 268
macro-legal perspective, immigration law 69
Manningham-Buller, Dame Eliza 253
Marighella, Carlos 240
masculinity
  conditions-conducive analysis 185–93
  defining 188
  hegemonic 189
  'hyper' masculinity 188–9, 190
  and patriarchy 188
  studies 188, 191
Memoranda of Understanding 56, 90
mens rea 59, 121, 277, 278, 279
metadata, intrusion into 137
MI5 (UK Security Service) 244, 263
micro-legal perspective, immigration law 69
Microsoft 233
migrants, measures concerning rights of 152–60
  see also immigration law
  border governance measures 157–8
  counter-terrorism and international refugee law 158–9
  illegal migrants 157
al Mihdhar, Khalid 263
Military Commissions 35
military courts, use of to try civilians 29, 35–6
MNA (*Mouvement National Algérien*) 248
Mohamed, Binyam 333
Mohamud, Mohamed Osman 244–5
Mubarak, Hosni 21
al-Muhajir, Abu Abdullah 242
Munich Olympic Games (1972), 'Black September' incident 13
Murphy, Cian 231

Nasr, Imam Hassan Mustafa Osama (Abu Omar) 252, 331–2
National Consultative Commission on Human Rights (CNCDH) 279
National Intelligence Priorities Framework 256
national responses to terrorism
  Authorization for the Use of Military Force, US (September, 2001) 26, 258–9
  externalization of measures to limit applicability of IHRL 40–51
  by France 25
  immediate aftermath of attacks 25
  key trends 25–76
  legal framework 29–35
  military courts, use of to try civilians 29, 35–6
  'war against terror' (US) 12, 26–7
  war paradigm, uses in counter-terrorism context 26–40
  whether emerging international 'terrorism' paradigm 36–40
national security
  administrative detention on grounds of 64, 112–17
  considerations in criminal justice processes 328–35
  State secrecy provisions 65–6
National Security Act 2011, Hungary 237–8
National Security Agency, US 48, 86, 137, 322
  technical intelligence services 260, 261
NGOs *see* non-governmental organizations
  financial services restrictions on 151–2
  and financing of terrorism 147, 148–52
  humanitarian assistance, impact of legislation on 74, 75–6
  and violent extremism 224
NIACs (non-international armed conflicts) 27, 28, 30–32
  and applicability of international humanitarian law 129, 130

degree of organization of the non-State armed group 130
intensity of hostilities 130
whether emerging international 'terrorism' paradigm 37, 38, 39
Niger 288
Nigeria
Boko Haram 29, 156
and preventive criminal justice strategy 272, 288, 293, 294
Special Investigation Techniques (SITs) 288
Terrorism Prevention Act 2013 272
'no-fly/selectee' lists 118
non-governmental organizations (NGOs) *see* NGOs (non-governmental organizations)
non-international armed conflicts *see* NIACs (non-international armed conflicts)
non-profit organization (NPO) 70, 142, 144
non-refoulement principle
see also refoulement; torture
attempts to circumvent absolute nature of prohibition of refoulement 44–5, 51–8
diplomatic assurances 56–8
legal framework 52–3
legal interpretations, disingenuous 53–6
codification 53
defining 52–3
exception to 215
obligations, and detentions abroad 43–4
risk of violation 68
scope of prohibition of refoulement 43–4
non-retroactivity principle, compliance with 82
non-State armed groups, as 'terrorists' 29
NPO *see* non-profit organization
nullum crimen sine lege principle 274
Nureddin, Muayyed 310

OAS (*Organisation de l'Armée Secrète*) 249
Obama, Barack 55, 195, 253
O'Farrell, Fintan 244
Office of the High Commissioner for Human Rights (OHCHR) *see* High Commissioner for Human Rights, UN
Office of the High Commissioner for Refugees 155
Office of the Ombudsman 103, 105
Organization of Islamic Conference (OIC) 207
Othman (Abu Qatada) *v. the UK* (2012) 57, 89

Pakistan 126, 259
Palestinian Liberation Front (PLO) 14
Panel of Eminent Jurists 314–15
Panel on Threats, Challenges and Changes (2004) 22
Paris terrorist attacks (2015) 25
Parker, Andrew 264
Parliamentary Joint Committee on Human Rights, UK 324–5
Patriot Act (Uniting and Strengthening America by Providing Appropriate Tools Required to Intercept and Obstruct Terrorism (Patriot Act), US (2001) 19, 65, 86
peer-to-peer encryption 261
Petraeus, David 251
PIAs (preliminary implementation assessments) 98
Pillay, Navi 262
Plan of Action to Prevent Violent Extremism (Secretary-General) 76, 78, 161, 217, 223, 227
conditions-conducive analysis 175, 182, 183, 187
Poland 46, 252–3

preliminary implementation assessments (PIAs) 98
preparatory acts or offences
French legislation criminalizing 'individual terrorist enterprises' 278–80
German case-law 275–8
increased criminalization of 59, 121–2
preventive criminal justice strategy 273–80
presumption of innocence 278
preventive criminal justice strategy 265–99
see also Special Investigation Techniques (SITs)
criminalization requirements 269–73
FTF-related offences
Australian Foreign Fighter Bill 283–6
Council of Europe Convention on the Prevention of Terrorism (2005), Additional Protocol 280–83
investigative powers and criminal procedure rules required 287–97
agent provocateur cases 289–92
protection of evidence from intelligence sources/covert investigation methods 292–7
national security considerations in criminal justice processes 328–35
offences relating to terrorism 269–86
preparatory acts 273–80
French legislation criminalizing 'individual terrorist enterprises' 278–80
German case-law 275–8
response to terrorism 265–9
rule of law 267, 273
witnesses, anonymous 294–5
privacy, online right to 135–8
Prophet Mohammed 243
proportionality principle 94
Provisional IRA 242
proxy detentions 44–7
'push' and 'pull' factors 182–3, 187
push back operations 67

R. v. Nuttall (2016) 290–91, 292, 295
'Rabat Memorandum,' GCTF 271, 292
radicalization
terminology concerns 163–4
Working Group on Radicalization and Extremism that Lead to Terrorism 180–81, 187
Rafferty, Declan 244
Rasul v Bush (2004) 27
refoulement
see also non-refoulement principle
absolute prohibition of 113, 159
attempts to circumvent absolute nature of prohibition of 44–5, 51–8
diplomatic assurances 56–8
legal framework 52–3
legal interpretations, disingenuous 53–6
indirect (chain-refoulement) 53
Rejali, Darius 247, 253
remedy, right of victims of violations to 308–11
resolution 1373 (Security Council) 18, 67, 93–100, 106, 122, 125, 153, 176
see also resolution 2178 (Security Council); United Nations Security Council (UNSC)
and accountability for counter-terrorism 313
adoption of 95
assessment of implementation 18–19
compared to resolution 2178 95–6
Counter-Terrorism Committee (CTC) set up by 93, 97

criminalization of material support for terrorism 146
criticism of 18, 22, 97, 197
evaluation of Security Council following 196
and financing of terrorism 271
impact of counter-terrorism measures on humanitarian action 73
measures 17–18, 93, 94
negative impact on human rights 18, 22
new binding rules of international law established by 93–4, 96
as reaction to 9/11 17, 93, 197
scope of 93–4
resolution 2178 (Security Council) 93–100, 103, 195–202, 224
see also foreign terrorist fighters (FTFs); resolution 1373 (Security Council); United Nations Security Council (UNSC)
adoption of 94, 204, 317
compared to resolution 1373 95–6
countering violent extremism (CVE) 161, 164, 235
online activities 228–9
as counter-terrorism binding resolution 202
driving forces behind 94–5
effects 196–7
expansion of legal obligations of Member States in relation to terrorism 93
foreign terrorist fighters (FTFs) 138, 140, 195, 200–202, 280
The Hague-Marrakesh Memorandum on Good Practices (2014) 201–202, 216, 222
human rights emerging from 211–15
obligations of States to comply with IHL 318
preamble 95–6
privacy rights, lack of mention 215
provisions relating to FTFs 200–202
and rule of law 95, 206
terrorism, failure to define in a 'legislative' Chapter VII resolution 202–206
responses to terrorism 78, 93–106
national level
Authorization for the Use of Military Force, US (September, 2001) 26, 258–9
externalization of measures to limit applicability of IHRL 40–51
key trends 25–76
legal framework 29–35
military courts, use of to try civilians 29, 35–6
US 'war against terror' 12, 26–7
uses of war paradigm in counter-terrorism context 26–40
whether emerging international 'terrorism' paradigm 36–40
outside international legal framework 90
post-2001 2, 17–22, 92–124
preventive criminal justice 265–9
rule of law 51, 61, 64, 76, 77, 79
by United Nations
before 2001 13–17
General Assembly 22–4
nuanced approach 24–5
post-2001 17–22
Revised EU Strategy for Combating Radicalization and Recruitment to Terrorism 184
Ricardo, Christine 192
rights-limiting measures 112–18
attempts to justify 19–20
detention 61–4, 112–17
intelligence information as a basis for 58–61
national security, administrative detention on grounds of 112–17
and resolution 1373 19

restrictions to rights permitted and conditions imposed 81–2
'terrorist listings and sanctions 112
rule of law 10
accountability 302, 303, 305–308, 312, 313, 316, 322, 325, 326, 331, 332, 334, 336, 337
conditions-conducive analysis 178, 184
foreign terrorist fighters (FTFs) 195, 196, 205, 206, 212, 219, 222, 228
impact of post-9/11 counter-terrorism measures on all human rights 95, 96, 99, 102, 107, 109, 138, 161, 169
intelligence services 263
preventive criminal justice strategy 267, 270, 273, 279
responses to terrorism 51, 61, 64, 76, 77, 79
UN responses to terrorism 22–5
Russian Federation 37, 39–40, 232

Saadi v. Italy (2008) 55
Sanctions List 100, 103, 104, 122, 209
and violent extremism 233, 234
Satray v. Malaysia (2008) 115
Saul, Ben 284
Scheinin, Martin (former UN Special Rapporteur) 18, 21, 92, 99, 102, 108, 117, 120, 204–205, 206, 210, 226
secrecy requirement, mass digital surveillance 134–5
Secret Intelligence Service (SIS) 243
Security Council *see* United Nations Security Council (UNSC)
Senate Select Committee on Intelligence 300, 301
Services Spéciaux 248, 249
Siemiatkowski, Zbigniew 252
Singapore 62
SISMI (*Servizio per le Informazioni e la Sicurezza Militare*) 252
SITs *see* Special Investigation Techniques (SITs)
Snowden, Edward 120–21, 260, 322
social media platforms 134
Somalia 126, 259
Soufan, Ali 252
Special Investigation Techniques (SITs) 237, 263, 287, 288, 289, 297
Committee of Experts on Special Investigation Techniques 262
Special Rapporteur on human rights and counter-terrorism, UN 48, 56, 61, 62
Emmerson as Special Rapporteur 6, 71, 211, 273
Scheinin as Special Rapporteur 18, 21, 92, 99, 102, 108, 117, 120, 204–205, 206, 210, 226
state security provisions 65–6
State terrorism 14
Storm, Morten 243–4
suicide bombers, female 185
Sulick, Michael 253–4
Suresh (Manickavasagam) v. Canada (2002) 55
surveillance
see also intelligence services; undercover activities
as anti-terrorism measures 119
biometrics, collection of 118, 119
body scanners 118, 119
bulk 47, 85–6, 133–5
extending powers beyond terrorism 119–20
extraterritorial programmes 47–8, 49
and freedom of expression 119
'function creep' 119
increased measures 118–21
international law, externalization of measures to limit applicability 47–9
mass digital 47, 121
examples 133
extent of operations 134

new counter-terrorism measures 133–8
privacy, online right to 135–8
required level of intrusion 135
secrecy requirement 134–5
state justification 133–5
'no-fly/selectee' lists 118
outlawing of bulk access to contents data 85
practices violating States' obligations under ECHR 322–3
'reasonable suspicion' concept, bulk interception 85–6
required level of intrusion 120
from target to bulk interception 133–5
SURVEILLE (EU-funded research project) 121
Sustainable Development Goals (SDGs) 178
Syria
draft revolution put forward by (1987) 14–15
drone strikes in 126
ISIL in 29, 95
Security Council rhetoric on armed conflict in 39
Szabó and Vissy v. Hungary (2016) 237–8, 323

Taliban, Afghanistan 26, 29, 30, 128, 209
see also Al-Qaida; Islamic State in Iraq and the Levant (ISIL)
and sanctions regime 100, 101
Tanweer, Shazad 263
technical operations 260–62
Teixeira de Castro v. Portugal (1998) 245–6
terrorism
acts of *see* acts of terrorism
causes 177–8
complexity of 79
criminalization of material support for, impact of laws 146–52
defining 14, 106–108, 167–77
categories of Inter-American Commission on Human Rights 171–2
lack of universal, comprehensive and precise definition 96–7, 166–7, 168, 170–73, 195, 281
model definition 108–109
failure to define in a 'legislative' Chapter VII resolution 202–206
financing of, addressing 69–72
or human rights, versus terrorism and human rights 77–9
individual terrorist enterprises, French legislation criminalizing 278–80
material support for, criminalization 146–52
national responses
Authorization for the Use of Military Force, US (September, 2001) 26, 258–9
externalization of measures to limit applicability of IHRL 40–51
key trends 25–76
legal framework 29–35
military courts, use of to try civilians 35–6
US 'war against terror' 12, 26–7
uses of war paradigm in counter-terrorism context 26–40
whether emerging international 'terrorism' paradigm 36–40
offences for a preventive criminal justice response to 269–86
preventive criminal justice response to 265–9
recruiting grounds for terrorist groups 154
related offences, defining 106–108
'terrorist listings and sanctions 112
'terrorists' 28

UN response
before 2001 13–17
General Assembly 22–4
nuanced approach 24–5
post-2001 17–22
upholding human rights while countering 84–90
as a violation of human rights 16
whether emerging international 'terrorism' campaign 36–40
Working Group on Radicalization and Extremism that Lead to Terrorism 180–81, 187
Terrorism Prevention Act 2013, Nigeria 272
Thailand 37
Theidon, Kimberly 190
'ticking bomb scenarios' 51, 249
Toonen v. Australia (1992) 237
torture
attempts to circumvent absolute nature of prohibition of 44–5, 51–8
diplomatic assurances 56–8
legal framework 52–3
legal interpretations, disingenuous 53–6
extraordinary renditions for purpose of 45, 252
and intelligence agencies 247–52
proponents of 247
'torture memos,' in US 54
Torture and the Ticking Bomb (Brecher) 250
transparency 131–2
Tunisia 275, 288

UN Counter-Terrorism Implementation Task Force (CTITF) 23–4, 143, 180
UN Global Counter-Terrorism Strategy and Plan of Action (UN GCTS), 2006 23, 79, 99
and accountability for counter-terrorism 305, 335
conditions-conducive analysis 174, 178, 180
new counter-terrorism measures 139, 141
pillar I 24, 76, 125, 139, 180, 196
pillar IV 196, 335
and UN Office on Drugs and Crime 266–7
UN Office on Drugs and Crime (UNODC) 283, 288
Terrorism Prevention Branch 266–7
undercover activities 244–5, 269
see also intelligence services; surveillance
agents/informers 269, 287–9, 291–2, 295, 297
officers 240, 241, 290
operations 237, 244, 288
United Kingdom (UK)
see also A. and Others v. the United Kingdom (2009)
Antiterrorism, Crime and Security Act 2001 87–8
control orders 88, 89
declaration of incompatibility by House of Lords 88
drones used by 126
and financing of terrorism 143
Government Communications Headquarters (GCHQ) 322
Independent Review of Terrorism Legislation in 315
Intelligence and Security Committee of Parliament (ISC) 253, 284
Intelligence Services Committee, Houses of Parliament 259
Investigatory Powers Tribunal 86
Joint Committee on the Draft Protection of Charities Bill 143
MI5 (Security Service) 244, 263
Parliamentary Joint Committee on Human Rights 324–5
and right to liberty 88–9
United Nations (UN)
see also UN Global Counter-Terrorism Strategy and Plan of Action (UN GCTS), 2006

Commission on Crime Prevention and Criminal Justice 283
Convention against Corruption 288
Convention against Transnational Organized Crime (UNTOC) 240, 241, 288
Counter-Terrorism Implementation Task Force Working Group on Tackling the Financing of Terrorism 23–4, 143, 180
draft Comprehensive Convention on International Terrorism 28
General Assembly *see* United Nations General Assembly (UNGA)
High Commissioner for Human Rights 3, 48–9, 56, 66, 98, 136, 213, 218
Human Rights Committee *see* Human Rights Committee, UN
mass digital surveillance by 121
nuanced approach 24–5
Office of the High Commissioner for Refugees 155
response to terrorism
before 2001 13–17
post-2001 17–22
Security Council *see* United Nations Security Council (UNSC)
Special Procedures mandate holders 35–6, 45
Special Rapporteur on human rights and counter-terrorism *see* Special Rapporteur on human rights and counter-terrorism, UN
UN Office on Drugs and Crime (UNODC) 266–7, 283, 288
Working Group on Arbitrary Detention 115

United Nations General Assembly (UNGA)
Ad Hoc Committee set up by (1996) 15, 171
and 'Black September' incident (1972) 13
definition of terrorism 172
powers, in relation to Security Council 94
resolution 3034 (1972) 13–14
resolution 40/61 (1985) 14
resolution 48/122 (1994) 16
resolution 49/60 (1994) 15
resolution 51/210 (1996) 15
resolution 52/164 (1997) 15
resolution 54/109 (1999) 15
resolution 59/290 (2005) 15
response to terrorism 22–4
and surveillance 47

United Nations Security Council (UNSC)
Al-Qaida sanctions regime 100–106
committees 199–200, 225
counter-terrorism framework 93–106
definition of terrorism 208
evaluation of role following resolution 1373 196
foreign terrorist fighters (FTFs), legal problems resulting from approach to 202–206
powers, in relation to General Assembly 94
resolution 1267 (1999) 93, 100, 101, 104, 105, 146
resolution 1368 (2001) 17
resolution 1373 (2001) *see* resolution 1373 (Security Council)
resolution 1390 (2002) 101
resolution 1535 (2004) 98
resolution 1566 (2004) 107–108, 173, 208
resolution 1624 (2005) 122
resolution 1963 (2010) 216
resolution 1989 (2011) 103
resolution 2178 (2014) *see* resolution 2178 (Security Council)
resolution 2242 (2015) 186
resolution 2253 (2015) 259

resolution 2354 (2017) 233
response to terrorism, post-2001 17–22, 93–106
Sanctions Committee 103, 105
United States (US) 87
Authorization for the Use of Military Force (September, 2001) 26, 258–9
Central Intelligence Agency (CIA) *see* Central Intelligence Agency (CIA)
Constitution 238
Detainee Treatment Act 2005 41, 55
detention of suspects in locations outside territory of 40–41, 43, 44
drones used by 126
enhanced interrogation techniques by 251–2
Executive Order 13491 on Ensuring Lawful Interrogations 55, 253
extraordinary renditions by 252
extraterritorial mass surveillance programmes 47–8
Federal Bureau of Investigation (FBI) 289, 290
Foreign Intelligence Surveillance Amendments Act 2017 47
Inter-American Commission on Human Rights (IACHR) 42, 171–2, 173
Inter-American Court of Human Rights 334
Internal Security Act (ISA) 19
Military Commissions 35
National Security Agency 48, 86, 137, 260, 261, 322
Patriot Act 2001 19, 65, 86
Recommendations and Report of the Stimson Task Force on US Drone Policy (2015) 128
Senate Select Committee on Intelligence 300, 301
torture, use of 251–2
'torture memos' 54
US Army Field Manual on Human Intelligence Collector Operations 253
'war against terror' 12, 26–7, 28, 30
'Uniting Against Terrorism' (UN Secretary-General report) (2006) 22
Universal Declaration of Human Rights 77, 135
UNODC (UN Office on Drugs and Crime) *see* UN Office on Drugs and Crime (UNODC)

Vienna Declaration and Plan of Action (1993) 16
violations of human rights/IHRL 76, 209
see also human rights; international human rights law (IHRL)
gross violations committed by terrorist groups 16
intelligence cooperation 110–11
serious 110, 308–11
State responsibility 309–10
violent extremism
complexity of 79
countering to prevent terrorism 216–22
measures to counter and prevent *see* countering violent extremism (CVE)
negative impact on human rights 162
terminology 162

Walker, Clive 228–9
'war against terror' 12, 26–7, 28, 30, 85
global 30, 52
past abuses 46–7
war crimes 38, 39, 40
war paradigm, uses in counter-terrorism context
general uses 28–9
legal framework 29–35

military courts, use of to try civilians 35–6
US 'war against terror' 26–40
whether emerging international 'terrorism' paradigm 36–40
websites, banning of 50
White House Summit on Countering Violent Extremism (2015) 217
witnesses, anonymous 294–5
Working Group on Arbitrary Detention 115
Working Group on Radicalization and Extremism that Lead to Terrorism 180–81, 187
World Summit Outcome Document (2005) 22, 101–102
World War II 254

Yemen 126, 259

Zimbardo, Philip 250